TOKYO

TOKYO

THE SHOGUN'S CITY AT THE TWENTY-FIRST CENTURY

by

Roman Cybriwsky

JOHN WILEY & SONS

Chichester • New York • Weinheim • Brisbane • Singapore • Toronto

OTHER WILEY EDITORIAL OFFICES

John Wiley & Sons, Inc., 605 Third Avenue, New York, NY 10158-0012, USA

WILEY-VCH Verlags GmbH, Pappelallee 3, D-69469 Weinheim, Germany

Jacaranda Wiley Ltd, 33 Park Road, Milton, Queensland 4064, Australia

John Wiley & Sons (Asia) Pte Ltd, 2 Clementi Loop #02-01, Jin Xing Distripark, Singapore 129809

John Wiley & Sons (Canada) Ltd, 22 Worcester Road, Rexdale, Ontario M9W 1L1, Canada

BRITISH LIBRARY CATALOGUING IN PUBLICATION DATA

A catalogue record for this book is available from the British Library

ISBN 0-471-97869 8 (hardback)
ISBN 0-471-97187 1 (paperback)

Typeset in 9/12pt Caslon 224 from author's disks by Mayhew Typesetting, Rhayader, Powys
Printed and bound in Great Britain by Bookcraft (Bath) Ltd, Midsomer Norton

This book is printed on acid-free paper responsibly manufactured from sustainable forestry, for which at
least two trees are planted for each one used for paper production.

In loving memory of my father,

Alex Cybriwsky
(1914–1996)

He taught me to travel

CONTENTS

PREFACE

This is an updated and substantially revised version of my earlier book published in 1991, *Tokyo: The Changing Profile of an Urban Giant*. Although only a few years have passed, a new profile of Tokyo is necessary because of the great changes that have taken place recently in this great city. Perhaps the most important development is that the bubble economy which sustained a heady period of growth and construction in the 1980s has been deflated if not burst, bringing depression to the city's real estate market, unexpectedly high levels of unemployment, and a shattering of confidence among many citizens in Japan's economy and their own futures. The depression is most evident in the hundreds of homeless people one finds now along Tokyo's streets and in makeshift tents in parks and along riverbanks. It is also seen in the growing alienation that is evident among many of the city's youth, and rising social problems ranging from increased shoplifting, teenage prostitution and other crime to new levels of public rudeness. The city was also affected by the 17 January 1995 earthquake that shook Kobe. In taking some 5000 lives and toppling thousands of homes, highways, bridges and other structures, the temblor was a wake-up to Tokyoites that their own city is at risk, even more so than Kobe because of weaker geology, higher densities, and similar, inadequate construction techniques. Then, just over two months later, Tokyo was traumatized by what is arguably the worst crime in its history – the rush-hour subway gassing on 20 March by terrorists that killed 10 commuters and injured thousands more. As a result, the city has been confronted with the fact that it is no longer the safe and secure place it used to be, and that bad things could happen to anyone and any time.

I have tried to capture the changing mood of Tokyo by rewriting much of what I had written before and by adding entirely new sections to this edition. The most prominent additions are about crime in Tokyo (part of Chapter 2), the rise of consumer culture (in Chapter 4), alienation among young people (Chapters 4 and 5), the problem of homelessness (Chapter 5), and Tokyo's growing population of foreigners (Chapter 2). I have also added to my earlier discussion about city planning (Chapter 6), with updates about new developments at Tokyo's waterfront, planning for increasing parks and greenery in the city, and various high-profile, new redevelopment projects such as Yebisu Garden Place (Chapter 5) and Makuhari New Town (Chapter 6). Chapter 6 also has a new section about the status of plans and discussions to move Japan's national capital functions from Tokyo. Because of Tokyo's increasing metropolitanization, I have also added attention to adjoining prefectures, particularly to the neighboring city of Yokohama, including its history (Chapter 3) and major planning projects such as Minato Mirai 21 at the waterfront (Chapter 6). About two-thirds of the illustrations are new.

I now turn to the pleasurable task of thanking the many people who were kind enough to help me with this book, saying first that all of its errors and other shortcomings, wherever they may find themselves, are my fault and my fault alone.

I begin with thanks to the reviewers of the first edition, especially Professors Gary Allinson, Theodore C. Bestor, Carolyn Cartier, Mikiso Hane, Richard T. A. Irving, the late David H. Kornhauser, Yasuo Masai, and Jack Williams. Their kindly worded criticisms and encouraging comments helped me correct mistakes and make other improvements. Professor Masai was especially generous with his time and personal library during my visits to his Risshō University office. I also want to thank the following individuals and organizations for permissions to use their tables and illustrations: Akio Tanaka for Table 5.1; G. R. Hovinen for Table 6.2; the Smithsonian Institution's Freer Gallery of Art for Figure 3.5; the Kanagawa Prefecture Museum for Figure 3.6; the Seiko Corporation for Figure 3.8; the Asahi Newspaper Company for Figures 3.9–3.12; the Mori Building Company for Figure 4.11; the Information Office of Ōsaki New City for Figure 6.5; and The Editorial and Distribution Office, Liaison and Protocol Section, Tokyo Metropolitan Government for Figures 2.12, 3.7, 5.13 and 6.1–6.4. Kaori Friess, Ayumi Nishikawa, Aoi Shimizu and Mikiko Togo drew the four sketch maps in Figure 2.15. Peter Lamb drafted other maps and graphics.

I also thank my employer, Temple University, for giving me the opportunity to live in Tokyo for the several years during which the research for this book was done, and for continuing to let me float back and forth between home base in Philadelphia, PA and the Temple University-Japan (TUJ) branch campus where I am often assigned classes and go to stay in touch with Tokyo. I am especially thankful in this regard to the various administrators who have supported this arrangement and made it possible, especially Dean Richard Joslyn of TUJ, Associate Dean Jeff Kingston, the previous dean John LeBourgeois, the previous associate dean, Bill Young, and my dean in Philadelphia, Carolyn Adams. I have also received excellent support from the fine library at TUJ, especially library director Tom Boardman. Temple University also contributed to my work by providing grants that supported travel to Tokyo for short visits and other research expenses. One grant was from the Center for East Asian Studies and the other was awarded by the Faculty Senate.

Many of my faculty colleagues at Temple University-Japan, Temple University, or both have also been helpful. In particular, I want to single out Sheri Blake, Dick Chalfen, Tom Dean, Bob Kidder, Jeff Kingston, Rob Mason, and Bill Nathan for providing me at various times and in various combinations with helpful bibliographic references about Tokyo, mailed 'care packages' of newspaper clippings and magazine articles while I was away from the city, and various leads about places to see and people to meet. Sheri Blake, now with the University of Manitoba, deserves additional thanks for treating me to marvelous home-cooked meals whenever I came to Tokyo, while Rob Mason was kind enough to put me up from time to time. Barbara Thornbury and Rei Okamoto (now at Oberlin College), exceptional professors of Japanese, helped often with advice and explanations about things Japanese and occasional short translations. Elizabeth Gutierrez and Lillian Jeng helped keep me on an even keel, as much as this is possible. So did long runs. From the world of colleagues outside Temple I thank the University of British Columbia's David Edgington, my co-author on the book I turn to next, for help with bibliographic sources and other leads; Tom Waldichuk of the University-College of the Fraser Valley for his helpful comments and suggestions for a part of Chapter 6; and John Western of Syracuse University for occasional editorial help and necessary moral support.

I have been especially lucky to have had the assistance of excellent students. I continue to owe a debt to the many former students who helped me with the first edition of this book. I remember them fondly as I go through the long list that was printed in the first edition, regretting that I have lost touch with many of them. They were exceptionally kind to me. Not only did they assist with translations, but some of them also wrote extremely interesting term papers about Tokyo neighborhoods that yielded new insights to the city, or conducted informative field trips to various parts of Tokyo as one of the assignments in my 'Metropolitan Tokyo' course. I will never forget the extra assistance that four of these students, now named Mami Nakamura, Ayumi Nishikawa, Aoi Shimizu, and Mikiko Togo, gave with last-minute errands for data, illustrations and permissions as I was preparing to leave Japan with everything I needed to submit the manuscript. Since the first edition was published, quite a few other students have been helpful with this edition, most especially Kaori Asano, Nobuko Ikue, Momoko Ōtani, Itsuko Nakamura, Yoshimi Tamai and Kazuhiro Uchida. Nobuko Ikue deserves special mention because she worked with me in both Philadelphia and Tokyo, helping with materials about Tokyo's waterfront and field research in the Daiba area. Special thanks are also reserved for Ayumi Nishikawa and Aoi Shimizu who helped with the second edition as well as the first. Both have remained great friends to whom I have turned often over the years, in Tokyo and in the United States, with requests related to this book and other projects. Aoi Shimizu's terrific MA thesis, which is cited in the Bibliography, provided some of the new information for this edition.

Finally, I want to thank those who gave the most to this project, my wonderful family – my wife Olga, our sons Adrian and Alex, and our daughter Mary. They are the ones who had to endure my many shifts of mood during writing periods, and who had their lives disrupted, first with a move to Tokyo from Philadelphia, and then with a move back to the Philadelphia area after they had begun to think of Tokyo as home. After then, they were patient with me every time I returned to Japan for one of my short visits, and every time I insisted on being left alone in my study to work. My two sons, both of whom are computer geniuses, were extremely helpful in putting up with my frustrations while solving the many computer problems that seem to single me out. Mary is a genius too, beautiful and cheery, and always puts me in a good mood. I am also thankful to Tania, our family's newest addition since Adrian introduced us. She, too, has put up with my ways and was helpful by being so nice. Most of all, I am thankful to Olga, whose love and support, and amazing strength and courage at a difficult time, has sustained all of us.

CHAPTER 1

INTRODUCTION

It has been a privilege to get to know Tokyo, especially at this time in its history. The city now sits at the top of the world as one of its largest and most influential urban areas, and looks forward with confidence to an even greater role as a leading global metropolis in the twenty-first century. Its base of influence is the Pacific Rim, of which it is, arguably, the economic capital, and its time in history is the so-called Pacific Century, which is either already in full swing or just about to begin, depending on how you define the term. Just as London was on the rise as the world's dominant city in 1800, and New York was ascendant in 1900, it is Tokyo that strives for primacy at the millennium marker.

In addition to being enormously important, Tokyo is also incredibly interesting. To be there is to experience one of the most dynamic and changeable cities of all time. It is also to experience a city that is uncommonly rich in traditions. This is a duality that, I think, represents the essence of Tokyo, and makes it so challenging to understand and fun to get to know. At one instant, one thinks of Tokyo as a thoroughly modern, international place that belongs very clearly at the forefront among the greatest cities of the world. It is superbly style conscious, is perfectly attuned to the latest trends in fashion and technology from around the globe and it is an unsurpassed mecca for culture. It is thoroughly delightful for its many spectacular examples of the most contemporary architecture, its wonderful department stores and shopping centers and its many other attractions. But in the next instant, there is a change of scene and something happens to present Tokyo as a small town rather than a giant city, and as a place that is forever tied to the past rather than at the cutting edge of the future. So too, one is reminded again and again that the city has been shaped very much by forces that are distinctively Japanese and very alien to the habits of other realms, especially those of the West. Yet, in these instances too, Tokyo displays uncommon greatness. As a result it is hard not to love the city and harder still to avoid becoming immersed in its myriad details.

SHIBUYA-HONCHŌ: A NEIGHBORHOOD NEXT TO THE HIGH-RISES

There are more than a thousand ways to show Tokyo's complex nature. A modest example begins just outside the window of the house in the Honchō section of Shibuya Ward where I lived with my family for two years while writing the first edition of this book (Figure 1.1). There is a big Denny's restaurant there, the same US franchise establishment with mostly the same foods that one finds all over America, especially at exits of interstate highways and next to suburban shopping malls. Its large red and yellow sign dominated the view from the room where I worked and used to light up my daughter's bedroom above. There is also a private

2
–

Figure 1.1   *The house in Shibuya Ward and its crowded setting*

tennis club on the same parcel. The eight courts are almost constantly in use whenever weather permits, as tennis is an extremely popular, albeit costly, sport in Japan. Many of the players arrive in BMWs and other expensive cars. Next door to the restaurant and club, and also visible from the house, is a twelve-story office building. This is the headquarters of one of the divisions of the Lotte Company, a giant, multinational corporation famous for candy and chocolates, other foods, and ownership of a baseball team in Japan's major league. Often in the mornings I could see the company's executives, uniformed female workers (the so-called *OL* – 'office ladies') and other employees lined up outside for group exercise and a pep talk from the boss.

A little further down the street, about five minutes' walk from the house, begins Shinjuku, one of the busiest commercial centers in Tokyo. During business hours it is one of the most crowded places on earth. The part of Shinjuku that was closest to us is a prominent cluster of ultra-modern skyscrapers – the most famous skyline view in Japan. It is the site of some of Tokyo's best international hotels and offices for the biggest corporations, as well as where the monumental new headquarters of Tokyo government was opened in 1991 shortly after we moved from the neighborhood. Designed by Tange Kenzō,[1] Tokyo's most prominent architect, 'City Hall' is a striking complex of three interconnected buildings, two of them super-high-rises, that is meant to be the city's leading symbol at the turn of the twenty-first century. One of the towers rises to 243 meters, just high enough to be the tallest building in Tokyo. I used to walk past the construction site nearly every day and keep watch on the progress. As I did so, I was always reminded of how dramatically Tokyo was changing, even within the short span that I had lived in the city, and felt particularly lucky to be a witness (Figure 1.2).

Tokyo looked a bit different when viewed from other windows in the house. I can't pretend that it is old Tokyo that is there, because the neighborhood itself is

Figure 1.2 *City Hall under construction. Workers are gathered for early morning instructions and a pep talk*

not very old, and because most of its oldest features, such as the first generation of houses and shops, had long since disappeared. The area's hot real estate market and the cataclysmic destruction that visited the city during the bombing raids of 1945 had seen to that. Nevertheless, there is much remaining that is a reminder of an earlier time, when Tokyo was a smaller city and there were no high-rises, and when internationalization (*kokusaika*) was not such a common buzzword. The house next door, so close that we could almost reach from a window and touch it, is an older building belonging to our neighbors the Tamura family. Tamura-*san* is a *tatami* maker. This is the thick straw mat that is used as the floor covering in traditional Japanese rooms. His workshop occupied the front of the house, in a room that opened directly onto the street and was fully exposed to all passers-by. He performed his craft by hand, in pretty much the same way that his father had worked in the same room before him. There never seemed to be a shortage of orders, as he stayed busy at work every day until well into the evening.

The neighborhood shopping street, *Fudōtsū shotengai*, is at the end of the block. It is a narrow lane, barely wide enough for one car to pass, and is lined on both sides with small shops whose fronts open widely to the street like the Tamura's, and invite customers in (Figure 1.3). I remember that more and more boutiques and other new arrivals had opened on the street, including an extremely busy supermarket, but that there were still quite a few of the older establishments left as well: fishmongers, rice sellers, a noodle maker, a cracker bakery, a medicines shop, a cubbyhole that sold only buttons, a glazier's shop, and countless other, small places for the local market. Tucked away to the side is the neighborhood's Buddhist temple. It is a new building but was designed in a traditional style. The temple has a welcome open space for community fairs and other gatherings in front, and a lovely Japanese garden in back. The garden offers such a contrast to the harsh lines and

4
—

Figure 1.3 *The neighborhood shopping street,* Fudōtsū shotengai. *The street is closed to cars during peak shopping times and becomes a place for neighbors to meet. The decorations are a project by the shopkeepers' association*

bustling activity of the city that surrounded it, that at times it seemed to me to be the most secluded and contemplative place in the world. The sound of traffic, the background hum of the neighborhood, was muffled by walls and greenery, and was replaced by the cawing of crows and rustling of leaves. It was also several degrees cooler on a steamy summer day – a place of deep shade instead of overheated concrete. Around the corner from the stores was the local public bath, where neighbors from some of the older houses and tiniest apartments, as well as many other people who simply preferred the facilities and neighborliness of the *sentō*, went regularly to wash.

There is a strong feeling of community. The street is a friendly place where hundreds of conversations take place each day among neighbors out shopping, and a play street for the many children who zip around on their bicycles or run around underfoot amid all the other activity. During the daily shopping rush just before suppertime the street is always closed to vehicles and becomes a pedestrian mall. A merchants' association (*chōkai*) makes sure that it is always decorated for the appropriate season, and that loudspeakers on the utility poles sound out popular tunes when pedestrians are out in force. Once in the first week of spring I watched as *chōkai* members took down the plastic snowflakes that had hung overhead for the past few weeks and replaced them with plastic cherry blossoms.

In the fall, in conjunction with a popular Shinto religious festival, the shopping street becomes the scene of a noisy procession that is known simply as *aki-matsuri* or the autumn festival. The highlight is the carrying of a heavy *mikoshi*, or portable religious shrine in which the spirit of a special deity is said to reside during festival days. It is toted on long poles held above the shoulders by neighborhood men, and moves along slowly for well over an hour down this street and into some of the side

Figure 1.4 *Carrying the* mikoshi *on busy Yamate-dōri at the neighborhood festival*

lanes. Shouts of *Washoi! Washoi!* call out a cadence that keeps the mob moving. Women, children, and other men press in on this procession, and sing and dance alongside in colorful costumes. Neighbors have considerable pride in the *mikoshi* itself, which is the property of the local shrine, because it is highly ornate, beautifully crafted, and expensive, as well as distinctive in design detail. Sometimes outsiders from other neighborhoods come to see these festivities and to admire the *mikoshi*, as there are many '*matsuri* aficionados' in the city who travel from neighborhood to neighborhood according to a publicized schedule of festivals (Bestor, 1989a, p. 252), but they were very clearly just bystanders. In this neighborhood, as well as in every other local area, *aki-matsuri* belongs to insiders (Figure 1.4).

Foreigners have been especially few and far between in this and almost any other neighborhood in Tokyo. The friendliness of the community is extended to them (or should I say 'to us') too, often to degrees that are quite excessive. For example, from time to time one is showered with gifts and offers of free meals and drinks from Japanese as a reward for just being in Japan, or for taking the time to engage in a few minutes of English conversation. In addition, there are many opportunities to form wonderful, lasting friendships. However, with most individuals there are also clear limits for foreigners and frequent reminders that in Japan any non-Japanese is forever an outsider. I remember a similar shopping street near my first address in the city, a more suburban-like setting in Setagaya Ward on the west side of Tokyo, where the dry cleaner returned a suit that I had taken in for pressing with a tag that identified me as *gaijin #2*, or 'foreigner #2'.

My first introduction to the dual nature of Tokyo came on my first morning in the city. My family and I had arrived in the city late the previous night and had been escorted to that new apartment in Setagaya Ward by my employer, who had already taken care of housing arrangements. Having heard so much about the cramped 'rabbit hutches' that Tokyoites are said to live in, we were very pleasantly surprised to see on arrival that our assigned quarters were, in fact, reasonably roomy and comfortable, and that they had all the necessary appliances for easy living, lots of big windows (but no drapes yet), and an attractive combination of Japanese and Western interior design. The neighborhood, we were assured, was an up-scale district in one of the city's 'better' wards, popular among aspiring professional people, and close to the international schools that my children were set to attend. In addition, we were informed that many of the neighbors had traveled abroad and spoke English, so it would be easy to make friends and get oriented. We were also told about the playground just outside the building where our children could play as my wife and I supervised them through the windows. Thus assured, we crashed into a deep sleep, our first ever on *tatami*, that lasted until mid-morning. What woke us was the commotion at our windows: a dozen or so of the neighborhood's school-age children had gathered outside our ground-floor apartment, faces pressed against the windows, looking to see the strange new creatures who had moved in to Apartment 110!

More than a dozen years have passed since that first night in the city. I now return to Tokyo at least once each year for two months or so to teach a course about the city and do research, still with thanks to my employer. I continue to be amazed that a place so big and crowded can work so well and be so friendly. Yet, at the same time there are new problems in the city that are getting worse and threaten to undermine its success. Most particularly, I worry along with a growing number of other Tokyo lovers that overdevelopment is destroying the city, and that those quiet and intimate neighborhoods that it harbors will some day disappear forever. Almost everywhere, it seems, there are look-alike new high-rises that intrude on views and crowd out older homes, as well as chain stores and restaurants like 7-Eleven's, McDonald's, and Kentucky Fried Chicken that outnumber 'ma-and-pa' establishments and transform distinctive urban districts into 'no place' and 'every place'.

I regularly visit my old neighborhood and always come away with mixed feelings. On the one hand, I am reassured that all is well when I see that the old house still stands, that our narrow lane is pretty much just like it always was, and that the shopping street continues to be a friendly place. Despite the opening each year of unfamiliar stores and nice-looking restaurants that advertise to a metropolitan market, a few people on this street still know me and say hello. On the other hand, right next to the tennis courts and the twelve-story Lotte building that had signaled the big city to me a few years ago are incursions that can only be described as enormous: the new main headquarters of NTT (the Nippon Telegraph and Telephone Corporation), one of the biggest and most influential corporations in the world, occupy a sleek, post-modern tower of 30 stories that opened on one side of a street in 1996; while the other side of the street is the site of 'Tokyo Opera City', a huge performance hall that promises to be among the best in the world plus a 54-story office tower! How can my old neighborhood survive in such shadows?

Even though I am no longer around Shibuya-Honchō enough to know many new details, I notice that my neighbors have adjusted, and am impressed. Mr Tamura still makes *tatami*, but now in a new building that stands where his previous house had been. They tore down the old one because it wasn't so good any more and replaced it with, what else, something taller. The workshop is still on the first floor and the family's now modern living quarters are on the second. But there is a third floor too, now rented to pay for the construction, but intended in the future for one of the Tamura children. And another part of this little empire, a street-level room that was formerly part of the *tatami* business, has just opened as the 'Cat Club', a hair-dressing salon operated by a daughter whom I remember as a young girl crazy about cats. You see, the Tamuras are not moving out; they're digging in.

And so it is that in Tokyo one experiences simultaneously the exciting dynamism of a major global metropolis and the intimate world of an unchanging small town that is always rooted in the past. The two are side by side always, or are intermixed in interesting ways, and give the city much of its distinctive personality. Moreover, occasional annoyances aside, it is almost always a very pleasing mix. This is one of the things that makes Tokyo exceedingly livable even though it has such exacting problems as extreme crowding, high living costs, and dangerous air pollution, not the least of which is the problem of second-hand cigarette smoke. Jonathan Rauch, like myself a big-city American and an admirer of Tokyo, summarized his thoughts on the city as follows: 'Until I came to Tokyo, I had never known the joys of small-town life' (Rauch, 1992, p. 81). Perhaps the city could be described, as still other authors have done, as an overgrown village, but that sounds like a pejorative and is not what I intend. There is nothing out of whack about these combinations of contrasting images. To me, Tokyo's duality is a positive attribute that enhances the urban experience in every way, and provides a continual source of enjoyment and stimulation. It has also convinced me that the city is well worth writing about.

'TOKYO WALKING'

This is a book about contemporary Tokyo, what it is like, how it got there and where it seems to be headed. The book also addresses suburban Tokyo and Tokyo's satellite cities, most notably Yokohama. These are ambitious considerations that began to attract me not long after I first arrived in the city in summer 1984, and that became increasingly irresistible the longer I stayed. From the very beginning, perhaps from the moment of that awkward first encounter with the children of Setagaya Ward, almost everything I saw in the Tokyo metropolis interested me. It was all so different from anything I had experienced before! I had always enjoyed exploring cities and getting to know their layouts and details about various nooks and crannies. However, in Tokyo the urge to get to know the city was stronger than ever before, because no matter where I went a special kind of urban differentness would reveal itself and draw me closer. Paul Waley, Tokyo expert, one of the first people I met in the city, and author of several enviable history books and guides, started his first book with similar thoughts: 'Tokyo is different with a difference. The ways in which it is different from other big cities are such interesting ways. One wants to think about them and speculate upon them' (Waley, 1984, p. ix).

In order to learn my way around the city, I took the early advice of Sugiura Noriyuki, a social geographer then at Keiō University, and walked through Tokyo again and again. I got to know not just the big streets, but also many of the little ones behind, and learned to pay close attention to details such as older buildings, the meanings of place names, historical markers, and other landscape cues. As befits a geographer, I usually walked with maps, especially old ones that record the past, and with the kind of detailed atlases of the city that are sold in all the larger bookshops. The city reveals itself during such walks, albeit sometimes grudgingly it seems, by releasing random bits and pieces of information about itself. The revelations are usually sudden and unexpected, and often result in moments of private embarrassment: 'Why didn't I know this before?' is a reaction that I had often after having pieced together something that came to make sense from the scraps of field notes. At the same time, even now when I think that I know Tokyo well, the city remains a challenge. Again, just when I least expect it – for example, when on a walk looking for one thing something else hits you in the face – a major piece of the urban puzzle reveals itself and shatters some understanding that had been stored away as secure. As a result, instead of being knowledgeable, I feel like a newcomer all over again.

Thus, the approach that I have chosen for these topics is to concentrate on the look of the city – on landscape or cityscape. This emphasis stems from broader interests I have in the relationships between built environment and society, and reflects a belief that thoughtful examination of the former can lead to insights about the other. Urban landscapes are especially interesting in this regard, because they reveal much about the people, including both present and past generations, who shaped them. That is, the many layers of development and redevelopment that one typically finds in a city tell of that city's history, and of the various influences from economics, politics, religion, culture, and other realms that have combined to give that place its particular character. Thus, the cityscape is a usable record of urban society, and can be read to introduce themes from any of a number of academic fields or topics of concern. For us, cityscape in Tokyo provides a convenient organizing theme that runs through all the chapters and makes the broad scope of this book manageable. This is an approach that academic geographers in particular employ often in analyzing a city and relating an interpretation (Lewis, 1976; Relph, 1987).

However, as interesting as it is to walk the city, Tokyo poses special problems in this regard. First, the city's repeated history of tragic disasters – huge fires that swept across entire sections of the city in the seventeenth, eighteenth and nineteenth centuries, earthquakes (especially in 1923), and wartime devastation (1945) – has destroyed most of the historic urban fabric that would otherwise be a material record of the city's past. Thus, there really is no 'Old Town' neighborhood as such to wander around in and get a feel for the conditions of earlier times. In most areas of the city, almost everything is new, having been built in the past generation or so, and there is comparatively little of the kind of mix of buildings from different periods, especially from earlier centuries, that one finds in most other great cities. However, this in itself is part of the record of Tokyo and a clue to its personality. Moreover, as we shall see, there is considerable history left in the landscape even though most buildings are quite new, and it is indeed possible to imagine the past while exploring the city today.

Second, we need to understand that there is much in the landscape of Tokyo that is designed primarily for show and that does not necessarily represent the true nature or innermost characteristics of the city. This is a difficult topic that I can only begin to address, but that catches an observer's attention almost immediately when visiting Tokyo. Consider, for example, the rather striking but curious situation that exists with respect to many of the city's most important public landmarks. In other great urban centers, such as New York with its Statue of Liberty and Empire State Building and London with Big Ben and the Houses of Parliament, public landmarks help to define the city and identify some its key characteristics or economic roles. In Tokyo, however, this function is confused because most of its big landmarks are actually imitations of other cities. Tokyo Tower, for example, which I had calculated to be the most common postcard symbol of the city until the new City Hall opened, looks too much like the Eiffel Tower to truly represent Tokyo; Tokyo Station, the city's central rail commuter interchange and one of its most distinctive buildings, is a copy of the main station in Amsterdam; Akasaka Detached Palace, the former residence of Japan's Crown Prince and now the official state guest house, is patterned after Buckingham Palace on the outside and Versailles on the inside (Conner and Yoshida, 1984, p. 214); and the massive domed sports stadium popularly called Big Egg is clearly an offspring of similar shapes in Houston, New Orleans and especially Pontiac, Michigan. Even the sleek, modern skyline of Shinjuku, the giant commercial center near where I lived, is often thought of as the city's answer to the glamor of New York. And then, of course, there is Tokyo Disneyland – a fantasyland designed to reproduce a fantasyland in, ahem, Southern California (Figure 1.5).

The point of this is to caution that the true essence of Tokyo is rather deeply held in the landscape, and that what is on the surface, while also a valid insight to the city, is just that – the surface image only. Thus, many first impressions of Tokyo, I think, can be misleading. For example, one might conclude from the city's famous landmarks, and from the hundreds and hundreds of business enterprises (e.g. restaurants and coffee shops) that use American and European themes in decor, that the city is truly international. However, as experience shows, it is much, much less this than it presents itself to be. I was dismayed when I learned on my first full day in Tokyo that no one at the Café Colorado, which I happened upon near my new home and hoped would be a place where I could effortlessly order a meal, spoke English (or Spanish). Despite the name and an architectural style that was straight from the shopping malls of America, this was Japan. So too, all the other restaurants named Colorado (it's a chain), the countless Kentucky Fried Chicken outlets, the coffee shops called Miami, and the billiards bars named Chicago (in Kichijōji), Los Angeles (in Harajuku), or New York (in Shibuya) that I would encounter later, would make Tokyo look international (or American), but on the surface only (Figure 1.6).[2]

Peter Popham, author of one of my favorite books about Tokyo, has thought about these subjects as well, and has written about how they apply to the famous high-rise skyline of Shinjuku. Here is a place that is 'very eagerly modern' and that represents 'the embodiment of the city's Manhattan fantasies', but that on closer inspection (Popham, 1985, pp. 101–2):

> . . . it's not like Manhattan at all; it's just like Japan, only fifty stories high. That most venerable Japanese magic trick, in frequent use since at least the eighth century, by which they solemnly and meticulously copy some product of another culture and wind up with something that is unmistakably Japanese is at work again.

Figure 1.5 *Tokyo Disneyland*

Perhaps the best way to express this characteristic of Tokyo is to introduce the distinction between what is said to be *omote* and what is *ura*. The literal meanings of these words are 'front' and 'back', respectively, or that which is 'outside' versus what is 'inside'. The two apply to many varied situations, are always an inseparable pair, and are mutually dependent and supportive of each other: *omote*, for example, is the 'official, public aspect of a person, place or institution' while *ura* is unofficial and private; *omote-ji* is the outer cloth of a kimono and *ura-ji* is the layer closest to the skin; and *Omote-Nippon* is Japan's urban–industrial eastern side that trades

Figure 1.6 *An example of cultural confusion: Fried chicken king Colonel Sanders dressed as Santa Claus*

with the world, while *Ura-Nippon* is the more traditional and secluded western side of the country. With respect to cityscape, we see that *omote-dōri* is a wide, public thoroughfare with important offices in tall buildings and fashionable shops, while *ura-dōri* are the private residential back streets that are hidden behind the big streets (Tasker, 1987, p. 78). Thus, in my former neighborhood, we saw the great contrasts that exist between the big streets with exotic businesses and huge public commercial center, on the one hand, and the intimate back streets that are the domain of neighbors only, on the other. The former represents the easily evident surface of Tokyo that makes the city look thoroughly modern and even Western, while the latter shows that Tokyo remains profoundly traditional. The city is actually composed of both facets, but the surface is nothing more than the skin, while the real heart of Tokyo, *ura*, is nestled in the interior, shielded from attention by the glitter of *omote* and more difficult to get to know. Our job in this book will be to consider both.

However, *omote* and *ura* are just part of the picture, and Tokyo is even more complicated than that. What is more profound about the city, and even more complex about understanding its landscape, is the contrast of images that one typically sees at any one place. This is true even deep in the heart of Tokyo, far off the beaten path in neighborhoods of *ura-dori* where outsiders almost never go, and where one feels convinced that here, at last, is the real Tokyo. I will never forget one such contrast that I saw during one of my first visits to *shitamachi*, the low-lying rivermouth area on the east side of the city that is one of its major plebian quarters. One of the first photographs that I took there was of a small clothing shop on a side street of Kuramae, a small neighborhood with a concentration of toy and doll wholesalers. Out front on hangers over the sliding door was a selection of *happi* coats[3] and one bright-red, slim-size Santa Claus outfit! Likewise, I remember my first visit to Sensōji, the very old and very important temple to Kannon, the goddess of mercy, in the Asakusa area of *shitamachi*.[4] On its Nakamise-dōri, the 'street of the inside shops,' which is a long lane of retail stalls that leads to the foot of the temple, I was amazed to see a selection of posters for sale of the 1950s American pop idol, James Dean. A more recent visit to Nakamise-dōri, nearly five years after the first, showed James Dean to be there still, but also that one shop had added 'Gorby Dolls', after Soviet Premier Gorbachev, to its inventory of things for sale. The Gorby Dolls are gone now, with thanks maybe to the goddess of mercy, but James Dean is still around. On Shin-Nakamise-dōri, the 'new' street of the inside shops that was added some time ago to handle the overflow crowds from the original street, there is a fast-food restaurant that recently opened: Hippo Inn, serving 'dogs and hamburgers'.

The crazy aspects of Tokyo's modern vernacular represent but a small fraction of the total scene. However, it is an important and telling fraction nonetheless, and to my mind, the most compelling evidence of an exceedingly engaging personality for Tokyo. Here is a city – clearly one of the most important in the world – in which major landmarks, much less many hundreds of smaller establishments such as restaurants and other businesses, take on the physical form of structures that represent places elsewhere! Everywhere I went in the city there would be some surprise – some example of cultural confusion – to greet me. If it wasn't James Dean at a major temple, then it would be one of a hundred or more other startling juxtapositions or bizarre landmarks: Japan's 700th (considered to be a lucky number) McDonald's restaurant, located in Shinjuku, with life-sized sculptures of the four Beatles near the entry and Superman crashing through a window on the second floor; the headquarters building of Fuji Latex Company, manufacturer of condoms, that is shaped like its main product (unrolled); or the pawn shop in Takadanobaba, an area of universities and special 'cram schools' (*juku*) close to where my university's campus once was, that until recently had a huge neon-lit, revolving fountain on its roof showing a much-bigger-than-life-sized, naked Marilyn Monroe squared off for combat against a hulking Japanese *sumō* wrestler.[5] Even my American home town, Philadelphia, is represented: in Shinjuku one finds a replica of the Liberty Bell (look high for it, recessed in an alcove near the top of an otherwise indistinguishable office tower), as well as a copy of the famous 'LOVE' sculpture by Robert Indiana that stands at a square near the Benjamin Franklin Parkway. Indeed, it seems that Tokyo must be, as Donald Richie has so cleverly characterized it, 'the *real* Disneyland' (Richie, 1991, pp. 41–5). It is more entertaining than the franchised theme park in Urayasu, a suburb near Tokyo Bay, and, of course, it has no admission fee.

What kind of city is Tokyo really, and why does it behave in these ways? It might be that not all these aspects of the city are meant to be understood, but I was hooked on these questions nevertheless and decided to get to know the place as best as I could.

CHAPTER 2

ORIENTATION

Perhaps the best place to begin is to address some of the most common questions that people abroad ask about Tokyo. Topics that get the most attention include the city's enormous size, crowding on trains and subways, the cost of living, crime (or lack thereof), and the city's vulnerability to earthquake catastrophe. In this chapter I continue the orientation to Tokyo by looking more closely at these topics, as well as some related ones. We begin by clearing up some confusion about the formal definition of the city and its boundaries, and some ambiguities regarding usage of the word 'Tokyo'.

DEFINING TOKYO

We begin with definitions because Tokyo has a unique administrative structure and rather unusual borders that often create confusion. Some of the details are not generally well known, even in Japan, and therefore need to be spelled out. The first point to make is that, technically, there is no such thing as the city of Tokyo. The legal entity was abolished in 1943, and was replaced with a larger unit that combined the city with Tokyo Prefecture to make a new and unique unit of government called *Tōkyō-to* or Tokyo Metropolis (Figure 2.1). We can think of this area as the old city plus many of its suburbs to the west, plus much other territory, most of which is further west than the suburbs and is not urbanized. This change was instituted by the national government during the height of the Second World War to facilitate defense of the national capital by streamlining local administrative structure; it has been retained ever since under kind of a 'regional government' model in which the central city and many of its suburbs function together as a unit.

One result of this is confusion about terminology regarding the word 'Tokyo'. There are at least three different definitions for places that are called Tokyo in casual usage, depending on whether one is referring to what is generally thought of as the central city only, to *Tōkyō-to*, or to the whole metropolitan area. The smallest of these areas is the central city. This is what used to be the City of Tokyo before the change in 1943. It is often called 'the 23 wards' or, simply, 'the ward area', after the neighborhood-scale administrative units that are left over from before the change, and that now provide various services of local government. This definition of Tokyo is a densely built-up, compact area of 598 square kilometers at the head of Tokyo Bay that focuses on the Imperial Palace and the Tokyo downtown (e.g. the famous Ginza district). The total population is 8 019 634 (official estimate, 1 February 1994). Table 2.1, which is keyed to the map called Figure 2.2, lists the 23 wards of Tokyo, and gives the population and the geographical extent of each.

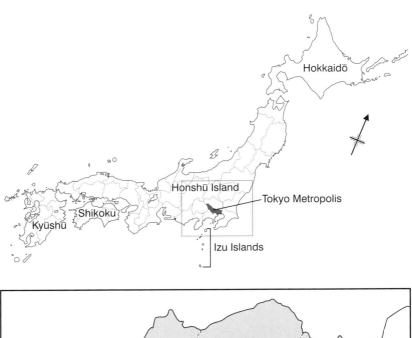

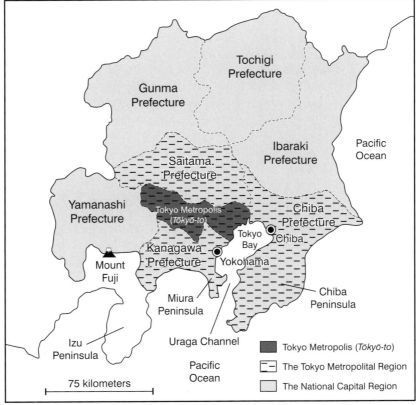

Figure 2.1 *Tokyo's location in Japan and its relationship to surrounding prefectures*

Table 2.1 Area and population of Tokyo's Wards and Municipalities, 1 January
1995

23 wards

Map number	Name of ward	Area $(km^2)^a$	Population	Number of households
1	Chiyoda	11.64	41 118	18 474
2	Chūō	10.15	72 794	34 040
3	Minato	20.31	150 341	74 623
4	Shinjuku	18.23	266 622	137 334
5	Bunkyō	11.31	168 050	79 211
6	Taitō	10.08	156 512	71 515
7	Sumida	13.75	217 311	93 029
8	Kōtō	39.10	366 056	155 579
9	Shinagawa	22.69	319 355	150 950
10	Meguro	14.70	235 668	116 692
11	Ōta	59.46	636 374	286 477
12	Setagaya	58.08	762 007	364 208
13	Shibuya	15.11	184 880	96 515
14	Nakano	15.59	296 713	150 941
15	Suginami	34.02	503 892	249 176
16	Toshima	13.01	236 009	121 304
17	Kita	20.59	331 613	147 754
18	Arakawa	10.20	172 923	74 463
19	Itabashi	32.17	497 671	223 191
20	Nerima	48.16	624 754	264 547
21	Adachi	53.15	624 178	250 151
22	Katsushika	34.84	422 571	172 421
23	Edogawa	49.86	583 747	240 607
	23 ward totals:	621.00	7 871 159	3 573 202

Tama District: cities, towns and villages

Map number	Name of municipality	Area $(km^2)^a$	Population	Number of households
24	Hachiōji	186.31	484 070	185 515
25	Tachikawa	24.38	155 832	62 988
26	Musashino	10.73	131 310	60 921
27	Mitaka	16.50	160 535	72 666
28	Ōme	103.26	133 854	47 954
29	Fuchū	29.34	210 791	88 489
30	Akishima	17.33	106 792	41 069
31	Chōfu	21.53	191 900	85 368
32	Machida	71.64	357 303	129 944
33	Koganei	11.33	104 870	46 008
34	Kodaira	20.46	165 177	67 475
35	Hino	27.53	163 061	66 002
36	Higashimurayama	17.16	134 992	52 854
37	Kokubunji	11.48	102 758	44 187
38	Kunitachi	8.15	65 719	27 942
39	Tanashi	6.80	73 325	27 725
40	Hōya	9.05	97 515	40 021

continues overleaf

Table 2.1 *continued*

Map number	Name of municipality	Area (km²)ᵃ	Population	Number of households
41	Fussa	10.24	60 207	24 095
42	Komae	6.39	72 868	32 229
43	Higashiyamato	13.54	76 494	27 246
44	Kiyose	10.19	67 273	25 673
45	Higashikurume	12.92	113 172	42 192
46	Musashimurayama	15.37	67 406	23 746
47	Tama	21.08	145 184	54 362
48	Inagi	17.97	61 465	23 070
49	Akigawa	22.44	53 853	17 935
50	Hamura	9.91	54 188	19 942
51	Mizuho	16.83	32 593	10 712
52	Hinode	28.08	16 486	5108
53	Itsukaichi	50.90	22 126	7144
54	Hinohara	105.42	3695	1249
55	Okutama	225.63	8447	2973
	Tama District totals:	1 199.89	3 695 261	1 466 804

Islands: towns and villages

Map number	Name of municipality	Area (km²)ᵃ	Population	Number of households
56	Ōshima	91.06	9950	4648
57	Toshima	4.12	303	148
58	Niijima	27.77	3309	1203
59	Kozushima	18.87	2394	737
60	Miyake	55.50	4054	1932
61	Mikurajima	20.58	251	127
62	Hachijō	72.62	9446	4315
63	Aogashima	5.98	203	114
64	Ogasawara	104.41	2304	1243
	Totals for islands:	405.724	32 214	14 467

	Totals for *Tōkyō-to*:	Area:	2186.61 km²	
		Population:	11 598 634	
		Number of households:	5 054 473	

ᵃ Land area as of 1994.

Source: Tokyo Statistical Yearbook, 1994, pp. 1 and 33.

The second meaning of 'Tokyo' is *Tōkyō-to*, the consolidated territory that is under the administration of Tokyo government. In addition to the 23 wards, *Tōkyō-to* consists of a large suburban and mountain area known as the Tama District and two groups of small islands far out in the Pacific Ocean. It is this geopolitical arrangement that has resulted in odd boundaries for Tokyo. The Tama District has a total area of 1200 square kilometers and approximately 3.8 million inhabitants. It extends west like a finger pointed from the ward area for some 60 kilometers, well into a mountainous district known as the Kantō Mountains or Oku-Tama ('Deep Tama'). Most of the population is in the lower-lying eastern end of the area,

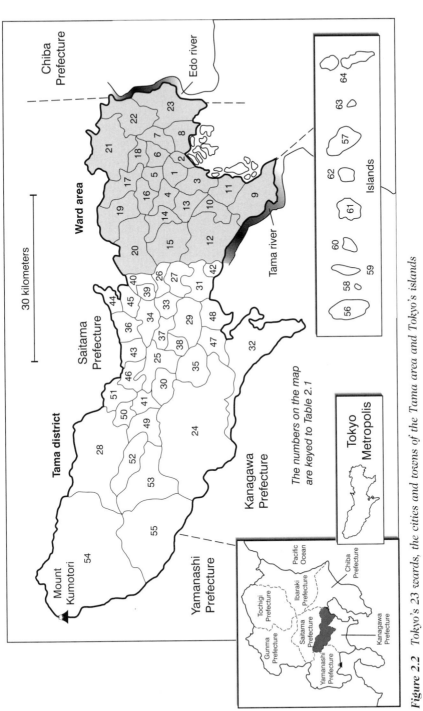

Figure 2.2 Tokyo's 23 wards, the cities and towns of the Tama area and Tokyo's islands

adjacent to the ward area, and in a rapidly urbanizing central zone of hills and tablelands. The furthest point is Mount Kumotori, some 75 kilometers from the Imperial Palace (Tokyo's symbolic center), at the boundary between *Tōkyō-to* and Yamanashi Prefecture. It rises 2018 meters above sea level and is the highest point in the metropolis. Its area is fairly rugged terrain that is hardly built up at all, but it is still 'Tokyo' nevertheless. Administratively, the Tama District comprises 26 cities, five towns and one village. These are also listed in Table 2.1.

The islands of *Tōkyō-to* lie far south of the city, and are a world apart in terms of climate, physical appearance, and the routines of life. They are joined administratively to Tokyo for convenience to provide their populations with services of local government. The nearer group of islands, called the Izu Islands, is a chain of volcanic islands stretching north–south from about 100 to 350 kilometers from the main part of the city. The other islands are the Ogasawara (or Bonin) Islands. They are situated some 1000 to 1300 kilometers south of the 23 wards, and are tropical in character. There are more than thirty islands in this group, including Iwo Jima, the famous Second World War battle site. Both groups add up to a little more than 400 square kilometers (a little less than one-fifth of the total area of *Tōkyō-to*), but number only 31 921 inhabitants.[1]

The third usage of the word 'Tokyo' refers to the metropolitan area over and above that included within the *Tōkyō-to* administrative unit. This is the least precise of the three Tokyos, because several definitions of the metropolitan area (the city plus its surrounding built-up area) are possible. Moreover, because of the proximity of the huge central city of Yokohama (nearly 3.2 million in 1995; 25–30 kilometers from city center to city center), the Tokyo metropolitan area more properly belongs to both cities. Therefore, one often hears terms such as the 'Tokyo–Yokohama conurbation' in connection with this area. However, because of Tokyo's far greater size and influence, the metropolitan area is most commonly labeled as if it were Tokyo's alone.

Some definitions of the Tokyo metropolitan area are quite technical. One delineation, by the census office of Japan, employs 'densely-populated enumeration districts' (over 4000 persons per square kilometer) as the basis for delimitation. The result is an irregularly shaped area of over 3100 square kilometers that stretches out radially for distances of up to 50 kilometers from the city center (Tokyo Metropolitan Government, 1990a, p. 6). Another delineation, developed by the Japanese geographers Ishimizu Teruo and Ishihara Hiroshi, employed commuting patterns to define limits for the Tokyo metropolitan area. In the mid-1970s, when their research was done, the Tokyo area extended as far as 55–65 kilometers from the center (Hall, 1984, pp. 179–80). Other definitions employed most commonly by national and local planning authorities employ prefectural boundaries to set limits for the metropolitan area. One such area, generally called the Greater Tokyo Metropolitan Area, is described as *Tōkyō-to* plus the three adjacent prefectures of Kanagawa (which includes Yokohama), Saitama, and Chiba. This is a territory of 13 553 square kilometers and approximately 32 420 000 inhabitants. Because they are not extensively urbanized, the distant islands of *Tōkyō-to* are sometimes excluded from this definition. The largest definition of the metropolitan area is the National Capital Region. This entity includes *Tōkyō-to* (less the islands in some sources), the three prefectures just named, and four other prefectures in a

Table 2.2 *Three Definitions of Tokyo*

Definition and common terms	Area (km²)	Population (1980) (×1000)	Population (1994) (×1000)	% change 1980–94
'The ward area' '23 wards' 'The central city'	598	8 352	8 020	−4.0
'Tokyo Metropolis' 'Tokyo Prefecture' 'Tōkyō-to'	2 162	11 618	11 790	+1.5
'Metropolitan Tokyo': 'Greater Tokyo Metropolitan Area'ᵃ	13 553	28 697	32 420	+13.0
'National Capital Region'ᵇ	36 883	35 700	40 190	+12.6

ᵃ Greater Tokyo Metropolitan Area includes *Tōkyō-to* (including the islands) and Chiba, Kanagawa and Saitama prefectures.
ᵇ The National Capital Region is all the Greater Tokyo Metropolitan Area plus Yamanashi, Gumma, Tochigi and Ibaraki prefectures.

surrounding 'outer ring' around the capital city. This territory dates back to 1956, when it was defined formally by national planners in an effort to regulate the expansion of urbanization. The population is now approximately 40.2 million. Table 2.2 summarizes the three definitions of 'Tokyo'.

ADMINISTRATIVE STRUCTURE

Because of the confusion that comes with having three meanings for the word 'Tokyo', it is especially important to clarify the administrative structure that governs the city. The designation *to* that is given to Tokyo is the only designation of this type in Japan, and is quite complicated. In some respects it is equivalent to that of *ken* or prefecture; in others it has similarities to municipal government in Japan; and in others still it is totally unique. Most often, *Tōkyō-to* (or Tokyo Metropolis) is grouped with the 43 prefectures of Japan and three other special designations (one *dō* and two *fu*), to make a total of 47 prefecture-type entities that are collectively called *to-dō-fu-ken*. While there are some differences in detail between them, each of these units, including Tokyo Metropolis, has a governor elected by popular vote for a four-year term, and a legislative assembly, members of which are also elected for terms of four years. The Tokyo assembly has 127 seats. The assembly and the office of the governor comprise what in English is called Tokyo Metropolitan Government (TMG). Another way that *Tōkyō-to* is like a prefecture is that it contains many units of local government within it. This includes the various cities, towns, and villages, as well as vestiges of an older system of counties (*gun*) and the governments of the 23 wards.

The establishment of *Tōkyō-to* as a self-governing entity similar to prefectural governments dates to 1947 when the Local Autonomy Act was put into effect after the adoption of the post-war Constitution. This ended the period since 1943 during which the *to* was little more than an agency of national government. About the same time, the wards that had comprised the pre-1943 city were reorganized. There had been 35 of them (since 1932), but they were consolidated first into 22 wards and then 23 when Nerima Ward was carved out of part of an oversized Itabashi Ward. These wards have a designation as *tokubetsu ku* or 'special wards'. In theory this means that they have responsibilities and powers equivalent to those of cities in other prefectures, as well as a structure of government that is like that of cities. For example, each ward has a popularly elected ward head (the *ku-chō*) with powers similar to that of a city mayor and an elected ward assembly. In this way, we can think of *Tōkyō-to* as a prefecture that is made up of 23 'cities' from the old urban definition, plus the 26 cities, five towns, one village and some leftover counties in the Tama district.

However, *Tōkyō-to* is also a municipality. Because of a complex division of responsibilities between Tokyo Metropolitan Government and the local government bodies, TMG administers many 'big-city' services in addition to having functions equivalent to those of a prefectural government. This includes such services as fire-fighting, police, public education, garbage collection and disposal, waterworks and sewerage, port and harbor administration, streets, many public transportation services (e.g. subways), and a large fraction of all public housing, parks, large urban renewal projects, and other works. Consequently, each of the 23 wards has fewer responsibilities in practice than one would normally expect from a city. What is left for them includes responsibility for local parks, smaller public improvement pro-jects, some public housing, many health centers and other social services, building certification, vital statistics and record-keeping, and other local or specialized functions. The purpose of this division is to strive to have both the advantages of a large centralized government that can efficiently coordinate major tasks over a wide area, on the one hand, and the advantages of a more intimate-scale local government, on the other.

Finally, we should note that in addition to being a prefectural government and a municipal government, Tokyo Metropolitan Government also has numerous unique responsibilities that come with being the national capital. These include the guarding of the National Diet and other government offices, protection services for foreign diplomatic establishments and official guests, protection of the Imperial Household, and 'the maintenance of Tokyo's cityscape befitting its status as the nation's metropolis' (Tokyo Metropolitan Government, 1984, p. 37).

JAPAN'S PRIMATE CITY

Tokyo is clearly the dominant city of Japan and one of the most important in the world. If we look first at the international picture and at population totals, the most common measure for urban importance, we see that here is truly one of the World Cities. According to the commonly cited list in the *World Almanac*, which bases its data on population estimates and projections produced by the United Nations, Tokyo is far and away the world's largest urban agglomeration. Its population in 1994 was estimated to be some 26 518 000, more than 10 million persons more than the second-place agglomeration, New York (Table 2.3(a)). Furthermore, according to this source, the city is projected to retain its top rank in 2015 even though many

Table 2.3 *Tokyo's Rank among the World's Largest Urban Agglomerations*

(a) *World Almanac* ranking. 'Urban agglomerations' are contiguous densely populated urban areas, without regard to administrative boundaries

Rank	City	Population (×1000), 1994	Population (×1000), proj. 2015	Annual growth rate 1990–95 (%)
1	TOKYO	26 518	28 700	1.4
2	New York City	16 271	17 600	0.3
3	São Paulo	16 110	20 800	2.0
4	Mexico City	15 525	18 800	0.7
5	Shanghai	14 709	23 400	2.3
6	Mumbai (Bombay)	14 496	27 400	4.2
7	Los Angeles	12 232	14 300	1.6
8	Beijing	12 030	19 400	2.6
9	Calcutta	11 485	17 600	1.7
10	Seoul	11 451	13 100	1.9
11	Jakarta	11 017	21 200	4.4
12	Buenos Aires	10 914	12 400	0.7
13	Osaka	10 585	10 600	0.2
14	Tianjin	10 378	17 000	2.0
15	Rio de Janeiro	9 817	11 600	0.8

(b) Rankings by Chen and Heligman (1994). 'Urban agglomerations' adhere to formal administrative boundaries. Populations in millions

Rank	1980 Agglomeration	Pop.	1990 Agglomeration	Pop.	2000 (projected) Agglomeration	Pop.
1	TOKYO	16.9	Mexico City	20.2	Mexico City	25.6
2	New York	15.6	TOKYO	18.1	São Paulo	22.1
3	Mexico City	14.5	São Paulo	17.4	TOKYO	19.0
4	Šao Paulo	12.1	New York	16.2	Shanghai	17.0
5	Shanghai	11.7	Shanghai	13.4	New York	16.8
6	Buenos Aires	9.9	Los Angeles	11.9	Calcutta	15.7
7	Los Angeles	9.5	Calcutta	11.8	Mumbai	15.4
8	Calcutta	9.0	Buenos Aires	11.5	Beijing	14.0
9	Beijing	9.0	Mumbai	11.2	Los Angeles	13.9
10	Rio de Janeiro	8.8	Seoul	11.0	Jakarta	13.7

Source: (a) *The World Almanac and Book of Facts 1996*, p. 838.

other cities, particularly Third World metropolises, are growing at faster rates. On the other hand, other sources also rank Tokyo at the top of the world hierarchy, but not necessarily number one. The difference is because of problems in defining the geographic limits of cities and their urbanized surroundings, use of different time periods for census counts and other factors. For example, a study by Chen and Heligman (1994), leading United Nations authorities on urban population totals, says that the Tokyo agglomeration was number one in the world in 1980, but number two in 1990 behind Mexico City. It is projected to be third in rank in the year 2000 (Table 2.3(b)).

Even more to the point about Tokyo's global importance than its population size is its huge role in the world economy. This, of course, is widely reported, as year

Table 2.4 *Value and Capitalization, Major Stock Exchanges, 1992 (SUS billion)*

	Tokyo	New York	London	Frankfurt	Paris
Value of stocks traded	476	1745	674	300	121
Value of bonds traded	117	12	1171	700	817
Total market value of stocks	2321	3878	933	321	328
Total market value of bonds	1278	2044	608	993	578

Source: Tokyo Stock Exchange, after Drennan (1996, p. 359).

Table 2.5 *Concentrated Command Points in the Global Economy: Tokyo, New York and London, 1989*

	Top 500 transnational firms (1984)		World's 100 largest firms		World's 25 largest securities firms	
	Number	Rank	Number	Rank	Number	Rank
Tokyo	34	3	30	1	8	2
New York	59	1	12	2	12	1
London	37	2	5	3	4	3
Total	130	–	47	–	24	–
Rest of world	370	–	53	–	1	–

Source: Sassen (1991, pp. 170 and 178–9).

after year Japan registers its famous trade surpluses with the rest of the world and garners for itself more and more wealth. The city is now the world's principal lender and biggest creditor, as well as a top-ranking city in numbers of large corporate headquarters, total bank deposits, and numerous other economic measures (Marlin *et al.*, 1986, pp. 549–50).[2] The Tokyo Stock Exchange, once only of interest within Japan, is now monitored worldwide, and ranks alongside the stock exchanges of New York and London in size and global influence (Table 2.4). In her widely cited book *The Global City*, Saskia Sassen identifies Tokyo, along with New York and London, as one of the three most powerful 'concentrated command points' in the global economy. Her data, compiled from a variety of sources, show that Tokyo ranks third in the world in number of headquarters of the 500 largest transnational firms; first in both income and assets of top 50 commercial banks and top 25 securities firms; first in the number of headquarters of the world's 100 largest banks; and second, after New York, in the number of the world's 25 largest securities firms (Sassen, 1991, pp. 3–4 and 168–82). Table 2.5 summarizes these data.

One way to visualize the practical implications of just how important Tokyo has become on the world scene is to consider what would happen if, suddenly, the city were gone (Hadfield, 1992). This is not just a fanciful exercise to think about: such a fate is a distinct possibility with Tokyo, if not a likelihood or certitude, because of extreme risk from earthquakes. On 1 September 1923, the city was almost totally destroyed by the Great Kantō Earthquake and the fires that raged for 40 hours thereafter. It could be leveled again, with even more damage, at any moment. The city's vulnerability to earthquake destruction is something for much of the world outside of Tokyo to be concerned about, not just out of humanitarian concern for

Table 2.6 *Populations of Japan's Largest Cities, 1994*

Rank	City	Population
1	*Tōkyō-to*	11 771 000
	Tokyo (23 wards)	7 874 000
2	Yokohama	3 265 000
3	Osaka	2 481 000
4	Nagoya	2 091 000
5	Sapporo	1 719 000
6	Kobe	1 479 000
7	Kyoto	1 391 000
8	Fukuoka	1 221 000
9	Kawasaki	1 171 000
10	Hiroshima	1 077 000

Source: *Japan Almanac 1996*, pp. 52 and 272.

the hundreds of thousands of lives that are known to be at risk but also because of the global economic repercussions that would follow a devastating quake. In 1923, the disaster cost over 100 000 lives and property damage that painfully taxed the entire Japanese nation. However, because the city had but a tiny role in the world at large, there was little impact abroad. Now, by contrast, because Tokyo has risen to such gargantuan economic heights, the impact of a giant shake will be felt immediately around the globe.

Given the importance of the topic, it not surprising that there are quite a few predictions about this. One scenario, put together by Oda Kaoru, an economist at the Tokai Bank in Nagoya, and retold in a most engaging manner by Michael Lewis (1989), is especially sobering.[3] It foresees a series of economic shock waves from the Tokyo quake that begin with the very instant that the city, including its stock exchange and all records of transactions, which in Japan are primitively kept, are destroyed. The value of the yen nosedives as investors scramble to unload Japanese stocks, except for the stocks of the giant construction companies, which increase in value just as the dust settles around the collapsed buildings that they had erected. Then, because of immediate plans to rebuild the city (estimated cost, $1.3 trillion!), Japan begins to liquidate its foreign assets: stocks, bonds, currencies and commodities, including real estate. These, it turns out, represent the 'national nest egg' to be used in the event of just such an emergency, even as the rest of the world has come to depend on them (Lewis, 1989, p. 76). The result is a disaster on Wall Street, in London, and other financial centers, high interest rates and economic depression in the United States and other 'dependencies', and a long period of declining growth in those countries. In the meantime, Tokyo, which has a history of fast reincarnations, reopens for business and its new stock exchange begins to record immediate gains.

Tokyo is even more dominant within the scope of Japan (Table 2.6). It is far and away the nation's largest urban center and vastly disproportionate in its influence on almost all aspects of daily life in the country. The nearly 11.8 million population total for *Tōkyō-to* represents nearly 10 percent of the whole country, and over-shadows not just the provinces but also all the other giant urban centers such as Yokohama (3.3 million), Osaka (2.5 million), and Nagoya (2.1 million). The

Table 2.7 Tokyo as Japan's Primate City

Category	Total number in Japan	Year	Percent of total in Tōkyō-to	Percent of total in Metro. Region
Area	377 801 km²	1994	0.6	3.6
Resident population	125 034 000	1994	9.6	25.7
Value of manufacturing production (yen)	3 406 087 billion	1991	6.5	24.2
Wholesale trade sales (yen)	5 729 816 billion	1991	34.7	41.2
Number of large corporations[a]	1 175	1989	55.2	61.4
Bill exchange (yen)	4 797 291 billion	1991	84.1	84.5
Number of foreign companies	1 208	1989	84.0	89.0
Number of foreign bank offices	127	1986	63.8	64.6
Persons engaged in computer service	14 613	1986	23.7	50.0
Number of college students	2 389 000	1993	26.0	42.6
Value of product of printing and publishing industries (yen)	132 739 billion	1991	43.3	54.1

[a] Capitalized at more than 5 billion yen.

Source: Tokyo Metropolitan Government (1994a, p. 87).

32.4-million Tokyo metropolitan area (*Tōkyō-to* plus Chiba and Saitama Prefectures, and Yokohama's prefecture, Kanagawa) is even more dominant. It represents about 26 percent of the national total. This is a remarkable concentration, given the fact that the city and the metropolitan area comprise only 0.6 and 3.6 percent of Japan's total land surface, respectively. What is more, the degree of concentration has been increasing in recent years.

The statistics cited here are from 1994, but as recently as 1970 the urbanized area's share of Japan's total population was only 23 percent, and in 1960 it was only 19 percent. This reflects the fact that the Tokyo area continues to be a magnet for migrants, as it has been for nearly all of its history, albeit at a decreased rate recently because of overcrowding and high costs. Geographers have long referred to such cities that are overly large in comparison to others in their country, and that therefore take huge shares of a nation's resources and investments and exert exceptionally great domestic influence, as primate cities (Jefferson, 1939).[4]

The disproportionate influence of Tokyo within the nation applies to nearly all important economic and cultural functions. Among other distinctions, the city is the political capital of Japan, the headquarters of its largest economic enterprises, its main contact with the world abroad, the leading center of higher education, its largest manufacturer, the dominant media center, the locus of the largest number of cultural events ranging from concerts to art exhibits, sports matches, and others. Several of these points are illustrated in Table 2.7. The historian Henry D. Smith II has gone so far as to describe Tokyo's relationship to the rest of Japan as 'urban tyranny'. He has pointed out, as an example, that because of the education and business contacts that are concentrated there in disproportionate amounts, the city is for all practical purposes 'the only road to success in modern Japanese culture' (Smith, H.D., 1973, p. 369). Consequently, anyone with ambitions has to spend

Table 2.8 *Comparison of Retail Prices: Tokyo, New York and London, 1993 (prices converted to yen)*

Item	Unit	Tokyo	New York	London
Rice	10 kg	3 837	1 845	1 812
Bread	1 kg	413	301	107
Milk	1 liter	210	85	91
Oranges	1 kg	419	201	154
Bananas	1 kg	208	143	128
Cola	1 can	99	52	42
Men's winter suit	1 suit	53 600	40 175	32 432
Skirt	1 piece	4 409	3 527	2 508
Tissue paper	5 boxes	519	765	776
Dry cleaning	2-piece suit	1 071	806	1 126
VCR/VTR	1 set	59 700	40 379	78 512
Compact disc	1 disc	2 895	1 750	2 176
Photo print fee	1 print	32	61	45
Movie ticket	1 show	1 808	834	1 140
Haircut	1 time	3 352	3 648	2 129
Permanent wave	1 time	6 732	6 922	10 356

Source: Japan Almanac 1996, p. 199.

time in Tokyo, if not actually to live there. Although most people in Japan think fondly of the city, there are many others in the rural areas and in some of the would-be rival cities who resent it for its primacy. For example, proud residents of Kansai, the Osaka–Kobe–Kyoto region, sometimes enjoy describing Tokyo as a young upstart without a deep history and lacking in style and grace.

Because so much that is vital to the economic and political life of Japan is concentrated in just one city, there are many appeals heard, both from inside Tokyo as well as outside, for decentralization. As we will see, for Tokyo itself the problem is one of excessive crowding, chronic traffic congestion, high land costs, and special difficulties in providing adequate supplies of water and energy for such a large population and removing wastes. The extraordinarily expensive cost of living and doing business in Tokyo, ranging from monthly rent for an apartment or a night's stay at a hotel,[5] to the price of a cup of coffee or taxi ride (Table 2.8; Figure 2.3), can also be attributed, at least in part, to the city's primacy. One of the problems that has resulted is a demonstrated loss of business in Tokyo to competitor cities in Asia such as Seoul, Hong Kong or Singapore where most costs are lower. The international conventions trade and regional offices of multinational firms have been most strongly affected.

For Japan as a whole, the problem of overconcentration in Tokyo is, in part, one of being 'more fair' to other regions. As in other countries, there is competition in Japan among local government units for the kind of investment that provides jobs and builds economic growth, and considerable unhappiness in many parts of the country that one region (and to a lesser extent the Kansai area and the urbanized area around Nagoya) has taken the lion's share of this. Demands for 'spreading the wealth' are especially vociferous in the case of economically depressed regions such as Tohoku (northeast Honshū, Japan's biggest island) and various remote islands and mountain districts that suffer constant outflow of population, especially of

26
—

Figure 2.3 *The melons on the top shelf are 4000 yen each. They are individually wrapped and boxed. The lower shelf is a little less expensive*

young people, to urban magnets. Consequently, almost all prefecture governments and numerous municipalities (over 50 cities by a count in 1988) operate offices in Tokyo to lobby in the Diet and among national ministries for deconcentration of the capital, as well as to entice private industry with offers of land and favorable tax advantages to relocate from Tokyo (Imaoka, 1988).

The other part of the problem for Japan as a whole of overconcentration in Tokyo is the considerable security risk that is involved. That is, having the vast majority of the nation's highest-placed politicians and top business and industrial leaders, as well as many of its most influential journalists, writers, educators, researchers, and other professionals, all gathered for most of the day within a few square kilometers of one another on a highly earthquake-prone site (see below) invites a national disaster of unthinkable proportions. This is not to mention the huge workforce that is concentrated each day in this same area as well, and the presence there of most national records and the records of hundreds of private companies. Thus, prudence itself calls for making Tokyo smaller and less of a primate city.

It is largely because of these and similar reasons that for over the last forty years there have been official policies in Japan, at least on paper, to contain the growth of Tokyo and spread economic development nation-wide (Tamura, 1987). The first formal step in this direction was in 1950, when the first Comprehensive National Land Development Act was passed. It came at a time when Japan was rebuilding from the war and migrants were flooding Tokyo for work opportunities, and was intended to assure a more equitable distribution of industry and other economic activity across the nation.

There have been four other National Land Development Plans since then (1962, 1969, 1977, and 1987), as well as a highly publicized 'last word' on the subject in 1971–2 by prime minister Tanaka Kakuei. This was his ambitious plan called

'Nihon-Rettō Kaizō-Ron' and published in English as *Building a New Japan: Remodeling the Japanese Archipelago*. However, as we will see, Tokyo kept growing through all of this, and, despite considerable earnest investment that went elsewhere, has strengthened its primacy over the rest of the country. Instead of deconcentration at a national scale, what took place was an unprecedented sprawl of the built-up area onto surrounding terrain, and incorporation of almost all of the nearby cities, small towns, and farmlands, as well as substantial portions of Tokyo Bay, into its urban–industrial orbit.

Plans and discussions about how to limit the size and influence of Tokyo are still active. There is special urgency to this now because of extremely steep increases in land prices that took place in the mid- to late-1980s. Indeed, as we will see near the end of this book, much of the attention about what is called 'the Tokyo problem' focuses these days on moving the capital of Japan, in whole or in part, out of the city to a new site or sites (Ito, 1988; Yawata, 1988). At the same time, we will also see that Tokyo continues to expand, and that the actions of private developers as well as government and official plans for the city push growth in all directions: outward to previously undeveloped terrain and new sections of Tokyo Bay, upward to new heights of skyscrapers, and downward to ever deeper subterranean levels. That is, we conclude that Tokyo is a giant city that everyone knows is far too big already, but that simply won't stop growing.

PHYSICAL GEOGRAPHY

The physical geography of Tokyo has had substantial impact on the development of the city and its distinctive character. This is seen first of all in the location of Tokyo with respect to the rest of Japan. The fact that the city is near the center of the country, approximately midway along the Pacific coast of Honshū, the country's largest island, has helped it evolve into a giant national metropolis and to consolidate its influence as the national capital. So too, Tokyo's growth has been enhanced by its setting in the Kantō Plain, the country's largest flatland. This area is a strategic hinge between the historic centers of Japanese culture to the west and southwest, and more recently integrated territories to the east and northeast. This aspect of geographic location accounts for the word 'Tokyo' itself, as well as for meanings implied in 'Kantō'. The former is translated as 'eastern capital', and contrasts with 'Kyoto', the city nearly 400 kilometers to the west, closer to the traditional Japanese heartland, that was the ancient capital. The word 'Kantō', on the other hand, means 'east of the barrier'. It is an older word than 'Tokyo', dating back to the Kamakura period of Japanese history (1185–1333), and reflects the fact that this large plain was once a frontier area located on the far side of a barrier station (*sekisho*) that separated the established provinces from new lands.

TOPOGRAPHY

The Kantō Plain covers parts of seven of Japan's four prefectures, and measures approximately 13 000 square kilometers (Trewartha, 1965, p. 438). It extends from the coasts of Ibaraki and Chiba prefectures in the east for well over 100 kilometers to mountains in the west; and from Tokyo Bay in the south for 100 or so kilometers again to mountains in the north. The 23-ward portion of Tokyo occupies the southern part of this area, at the head of Tokyo Bay. The city's suburbs sprawl in all landward directions, but especially to the west, in the direction of the Tama area and adjacent parts of Kanagawa prefecture, where urban development abuts the Kantō Mountains and other highlands. The northern part of the Kantō Plain, above its longest river, the Tone, is heavily agricultural. However, urban growth is making rapid advances there as well.

The historic core of Tokyo is in that part of the Kantō Plain where three rivers, the Edogawa, the Arakawa, and the Sumidagawa,[6] make their last meanders before emptying into Tokyo Bay. The land there is an extremely flat alluvial lowland that is barely above sea level. It is highly susceptible to flooding and other hazards, and has been the site of numerous disasters during the city's history. The original shoreline was marshy, but ambitious reclamation projects that began as far back as the late sixteenth century, when Tokyo was still a small settlement called Edo, changed all of this and added considerable land to the city total. Other parts of the Kantō Plain in Tokyo are not so low-lying. Much of the territory is in the form of upland plains formed by changes in sea level over geological history and by shifts in the courses of rivers. The largest and most important such place is called the Musashino Tableland, an expansive diluvial plain that extends for some 60 kilometers west from the center of Tokyo to the mountainous rim of the Kantō region. Elevations range from approximately 30 to 250 meters above sea level. Its eastern reaches, set apart from the lower elevations by sharp escarpments, extend into the heart of the city. The result is a clear distinction between low-lying, flat sections of the city close to the bay and the river mouths, *shitamachi*, and higher land inland, *yamanote*. We will see that this is an extremely important distinction in the life of the city.

The Musashino Tableland covers the western side of Tokyo's 23 wards, as well as many of the towns and suburban developments in the central part of *Tōkyō-to*, west of the ward area. Other more or less flat uplands are the Ōmiya Plain to the north, the Shimosa Upland in the outer suburbs in Chiba prefecture to the east, and the Sagamihara Upland in Kanagawa prefecture to the southwest. Each of these areas is covered with a thick stratum of volcanic ash (the 'Kantō loam') that is firm, dry, and otherwise well suited physically for the urban development that is taking place there. In the past, however, settlement there was retarded because the land was poorly watered for irrigated rice. Other prominent features of the Tokyo portion of the Kantō Plain are heavily dissected hills in the south-central area and in the west before mountainous terrain begins. The former zone is especially important. This is the Tama Hills area across the Tama River floodplain from the Musashino Tableland. Today it is being very extensively developed for housing and other urban uses because of its relative nearness to central Tokyo and Yokohama.

The mountains that define the inland limits of the Kantō Plain form an irregular semi-circle around the built-up area. The individual chains that make up the enclosure are the Tanzawa Mountains in the southwest, the Kantō Mountains in the west, the Mikuni Mountains northwest of the city, the Ashio Mountains to the north, and the Yamizo Mountains furthest of all in the northeast. Some of these groups include prominent volcanic peaks. Mount Asama, at 2542 meters in the

Figure 2.4 *A scene in Chichibu-Tama National Park in Tokyo's mountainous west*

Mikuni chain, is the highest. There are also several national parks and other attractive recreation areas (Figure 2.4). Mount Fuji, the graceful volcanic peak that is a symbol of Japan and the subject of so many paintings, photographs and post-cards, is beyond this mountain ring to the southwest. It is almost exactly 100 kilometers from the center of Tokyo, but is visible from the city because its height (3776 meters) rises above the intervening highlands. However, visibility is impaired by pollution. The best views are on crisp winter mornings and at dusk under clear conditions. In the latter case, the setting sun behind Mount Fuji presents Tokyo with a dramatic mountain silhouette.

CLIMATE

Tokyo's climate is influenced by the mountains and the sea. It is a type of climate that is described in geography texts as humid subtropical; in many respects it resembles that of coastal locations in the southeastern United States. There is a clear distinction between the seasons. Summers are hot, humid, and generally uncomfortable. Each year there is a month-long rainy season called *baiu* or *tsuyu* ('plum rain') from the middle of June into July. It is a most unpleasant time when the air is still and sticky, and when the city suffers an annual invasion of ticks, mosquitoes, and other tiny insects, as well as countless varieties of hardy and sometimes gigantic roaches. It is also a time when mold multiplies just about everywhere. On 20 July, a day called *doyo no hi*, the Japanese celebrate the end of this season by eating broiled eel to ward off mold-born diseases. Winters are cool, although only a few days have temperatures below freezing. Clear, sunny weather prevails, and there is little rain or snow. However, there is often a cold, dry wind that comes down from high elevations and puts a deep chill into the air. In the fall,

Figure 2.5 *Partying under the cherry blossoms in a Tokyo park. The annual ritual is a group activity involving lots of beer and* sake *and boisterous singing*

there are occasional typhoons that come from over open water and bring heavy rains and widespread flooding. For many people, the favorite season is spring when the weather is generally good and the city seems especially pleasant. The few days in spring when cherry blossoms are in bloom are particularly festive (Figure 2.5).

EARTHQUAKE HAZARDS

Perhaps no aspect of the natural environment of Tokyo is as momentous as the seismic characteristics of the site (Tokyo Metropolitan Government, 1995). As almost anyone who has spent more than a few days in the city learns by unnerving experience, Tokyo is at an extremely active earthquake zone and often undergoes subterranean tremors. This is true for Japan as a whole, because the country is where three tectonic plates (the edge of the Eurasian continental plate and the Philippine and Pacific plates) come into contact and create frequent spasmodic earth movements; but Tokyo is an especially dangerous site because of its nearness to the most violent lines of contact. In the summer of 1989, in an unusually active seismic experience, the Izu Peninsula, a weekend getaway area with mountain hot springs and rugged seacoast just south of Tokyo, was rocked with tens or hundreds of discrete shocks *each* day, reminding Tokyoites, at least for a while, of the danger to their city and the need for earthquake preparedness. An even greater reminder occurred on the morning of 17 January 1995, when the city woke to breaking news reports about a disaster taking place in Kobe, a major port city of about 1.5 million inhabitants to the west of Tokyo. The death toll from the Great Hanshin Earthquake, as the event came to be known, would reach 5000, with more than ten times that number of injuries, and widespread devastation, graphically documented in the media, to the principal business center, the harbor, major roadways, and many residential neighborhoods.

A second factor that makes Tokyo particularly vulnerable to major earthquake damage, in addition to the presence of the notably unstable fault zone, is that much of the city is built on loosely consolidated landfill. This applies to most of the downtown, all waterfront industrial districts, and many crowded residential areas. When shaken by a quake, this material could mix with underground water and become a liquid goo, causing the buildings that are built on it to collapse. This is a lesson that Japan learned from a deadly earthquake in Niigata Prefecture in 1964, when steel-reinforced buildings that were supposedly earthquake-proof collapsed (Ueda, 1990, p. 26). The city's low elevation (sea level and below in some sections) poses still another threat: the possibility of tidal waves (*tsunami*) that would be triggered by a sea-floor quake in Tokyo Bay or elsewhere offshore. To protect against this, there is an extensive pattern of breakwaters in the bay, sea walls and river walls at the waterfront, and massive gates that can close off river mouths to prevent a flood tide from surging in.

There are approximately thirty to fifty perceptible shakes in Tokyo each year, about two or three of which are strong enough to wake people from their sleep, rattle dishes, and do some minor damage. There is also a strong possibility that an even more substantial jolt could strike, causing widespread destruction and loss of life. This has occurred from time to time in the history of the city. The last such incident was in 1923, when the so-called Great Kantō Earthquake killed over 100 000 people in Tokyo and environs, leaving much of the low-lying wards of Tokyo and Yokohama in ruins. It registered 7.9 on the Richter scale and was centered in Sagami Bay close to the Izu Peninsula.

Experts agree that a major quake will strike Tokyo again. What is not known is when this will happen and how extensive the damage and loss of life will be. There seems to be a pattern of the biggest earthquakes, such as the one of 1923, occurring just about every 70 years (1923, 1853, 1771, 1703, 1633), so it is possible that the next giant shake will come soon. Such a possibility is very much a part of the background of living in Tokyo, and a major shaper of the urban personality. On the one hand, one sees that considerable energy is expended to prevent disaster and to be prepared in case the worst happens (Figure 2.6). On the other, one also discerns an air of fatalism in the city. Because of the earthquakes, as well as because of the devastating experience of wartime bombing raids in 1945 and a long history of destructive fires in the city, there is an attitude in Tokyo that time between disasters is limited, and that the city should therefore hurry forward at full steam with its business, now, while it still can. Perhaps no other major city in the world defines itself as being so transitory as Tokyo; no other city views its own history so much as a series of urgent rebuildings between disasters. We will discuss these aspects of Tokyo more fully in the chapters that follow.

THE VIEW FROM TOKYO TOWER

One of the best places for an orientation to Tokyo is to take in the view from Tokyo Tower. This is the famous broadcasting and reception facility-cum-tourist attraction

Figure 2.6 *Members of the neighborhood fire company at their morning inspection. The sign warns residents to be wary of fires after earthquakes*

that looms over the center of the city, and provides from its two observatories (150 meters and 250 meters) some of Tokyo's most sweeping panoramas. Even though there is a fairly stiff admission fee which other observation facilities in the city do not have, more than 120 million visitors had gone atop Tokyo Tower since the facility opened in 1958.[7] I have gone there from time to time to introduce the city to friends who come to visit me in Japan, to teach some urban geography to my students, and for a dose of inspiration when the writing of this book got slow. We will go there now for (1) an orientation to the geographical layout of Tokyo; and (2) insights to the kind of city that Tokyo has become after 400 years of development and to see the way that it continues to change today.[8]

The first thing to learn about the layout of Tokyo is that the center of the city is the Imperial Palace (Figure 2.7). Its grounds appear from Tokyo Tower as a huge void in the midst of a gigantic urban expanse; they are the place from which compass directions and distances from the city are described. The site is less than 3 kilometers from the tower, and stands out as a massive island of green (even in winter) that contrasts with the densely built-up surroundings. The whole city seems to huddle around this space, as indeed was the intention of the shogun (Japanese *shōgun*) Ieyasu who created this unique arrangement four centuries ago. The boundary between the city and the palace compound is quite rigid, as one sees lengths of stone walls and moats that are still in place from when Tokyo was a castle town called Edo. With a little imagination, one can even see that today's road network, including the traffic-choked elevated expressways that snake through the crowded neighborhoods of the inner-city, comes together at the foot of the palace, at the business district that first formed just outside one of the main gates.

The area that adjoins the Imperial Palace to the south and east is the Tokyo Central Business District (CBD). This is an immensely crowded and internally

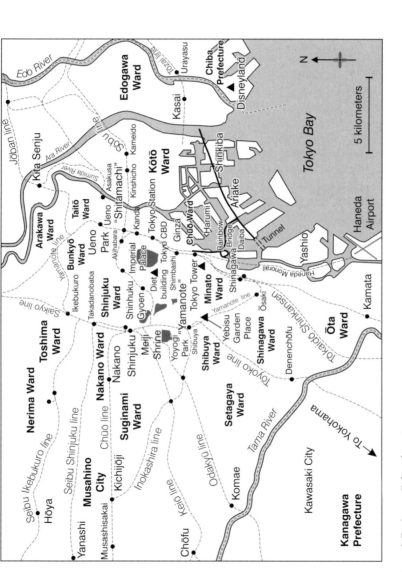

Figure 2.7 Inner Tokyo location map

complex area with numerous distinctive sub-sections defined by the specific economic activities that they conduct. Our high vantage point allows us to pick out some of these. The area that is closest to us (i.e. between Tokyo Tower and the Imperial Palace) is the national government center of Japan. It covers two neighborhood-scale sections of Tokyo called Nagatachō and Kasumigaseki, and has as its principal landmark the gray granite National Diet Building. The commercial focus of the CBD is to the east, on the other side of a sizable Western-style park called Hibiya Park. The principal office district, a place called Marunouchi, is just across a moat from the Imperial Palace, and is distinguished by a grid street plan and block-like office buildings of almost equal height. Tokyo Station, the hub of the rail network, is just beyond. Other office and retailing sections such as Ōtemachi, Nihombashi, and the famous Ginza are arranged in kind of a semicircle around Tokyo Station in the direction opposite from the Imperial Palace. As we will see in later chapters, these were once parts of *shitamachi*, the low-lying river delta area at the head of Tokyo Bay that was the domain of commoner classes, and that evolved during the nineteenth century into the business hub of the modern city.

What is left of *shitamachi* is on the other side of the CBD, to the east and north of the Imperial Palace. The main geographical features are the Sumida River and the dozen or more bridges that span it. This is the area of the so-called river wards (Sumida, Arakawa, Taitō, and Kōtō) and is thought of as Tokyo's historic district of old houses and old neighborhoods. We can't see the details from Tokyo Tower, but it is a highly mixed district of housing, warehouses and small factories, old commercial streets, and famous shrines and temples. Some of the greenery of Ueno Park, an important recreation facility and major concentration of religious architecture and public museums in Taitō Ward, is visible near the horizon 3 or 4 kilometers north of the Imperial Palace. On the horizon itself are the eastern wards of Tokyo (e.g. Katsushika and Edogawa), or on a clear day, the suburban towns of Chiba Prefecture. In general, this is the blue-collar side of Tokyo and many of the towns and neighborhoods there are known for industry and lower residential rents.

The Tokyo waterfront is visible from observation windows that face east and south. The area closest to the CBD, where the Sumida empties into the bay, is extensively built up with tall buildings and is ever more an extension of the business core. Further south the bayfront is called the Jōnan District, and is mostly industrial. We can see factory buildings, warehouses, gas tanks, and port facilities all along the rail corridor that stretches near the center of Tokyo to Haneda Airport and beyond. This is all reclaimed land, and on a clear day we can make out the geometric lines of ship channels that separate tightly packed industrial islands. Tokyo Bay itself is also a cluster of straight-line islands made of landfill. They are big in size, geometric in shape, and for the most part are also given to industrial land uses. However, impressive residential developments and commercial centers are also being built in the bay. We can see Rainbow Bridge, one of Tokyo's newest landmarks, connecting the 'mainland' with the new islands, as well as the Yurikamome Line, a glitzy, computer-driven monorail that takes passengers to the freshly laid beach at Daiba and the California-like shopping malls and condominiums nearby.

The view to the west from Tokyo Tower (and a little to the north) looks out over many of the city's better neighborhoods and its sector of greatest spatial expansion (Figure 2.8). The area closest to the tower is especially nice, albeit crowded by

Figure 2.8 *A view across western Tokyo from Tokyo Tower. Mount Fuji is seen in the distance on this clear winter day*

most cities' standards, and includes such prestigious residential districts as Azabu and Hiroo, and the famous nightclub district named Roppongi. A little further away are the high-rises that mark Tokyo's fashionable new commercial subcenters: Shinjuku, Shibuya, and Ikebukuro. Beyond them are miles and miles of city and suburb, as far as the eye can see. On a clear day, such as when I took the picture for Figure 2.8, one can see some of the residential areas of the Tama District of *Tōkyō-to* and of Kanagawa Prefecture, as well as the distinctive profile of Mount Fuji nearly 100 kilometers away.

Perhaps the most striking impression of the view from Tokyo Tower is of the immense size of the city. This is no surprise, of course, because hugeness is a fundamental characteristic of Tokyo and probably the single most important fact about it. Yet, the view is so impressive that I am still amazed with every approach to the observation windows, no matter how many times I go there. In every direction as far across the city's plain as the eye can see, as well as on new land reclaimed from Tokyo Bay, there is nothing but city! The built-up area extends for well over 50 kilometers in some directions, much further than one can pick out in detail, and seems almost limitless. Only on those days when Mount Fuji and the other mountains are visible does one actually see beyond the metropolis. Measurement is difficult because of problems with definitions, but it is safe to say that the total built-up area exceeds 3000 square kilometers (Tokyo Metropolitan Government, 1990a, p. 6).

What is more, almost all of this enormous territory is extremely densely built up. A great many of the buildings seen are high- or mid-rise structures, at least five or six stories tall, and there is almost no empty space between them. Where there are single homes, they are packed so close together that one sees only an unbroken surface of contiguous roofs. To be sure, there are also some parks and other open

Table 2.9 *Building Density in Tokyo, 1991–2*

	Number of buildings	Buildings per hectare	Land coverage ratio (%)	Capacity ratio (%)[a]	Height ratio (%)[b]	Average number of stories
Chiyoda Ward	15 268	13.8	30.2	207.8	74.8	6.9
Chūō Ward	19 123	22.6	34.3	210.0	65.7	5.9
Minato Ward	33 075	16.4	27.4	128.9	48.7	4.7
23 wards total	1 719 702	29.1	27.8	80.6	19.9	2.9
Urban areas in Tama Area	889 849	10.9	10.6	22.6	9.9	2.1

[a] Total floor space in buildings as a percentage of land area.
[b] Percent ratio of buildings with four or more stories to all buildings.

Source: Tokyo Statistical Yearbook, 1994, pp. 10–11.

spaces, including some large ones, such as that for the Imperial Palace; but they stand out as dramatic exceptions to an otherwise oppressive mass of urban material. The buildings push right up against the edges of the open spaces, and form high, thick walls that define their boundaries precisely and enclose them almost completely. This accentuates the great volume of Tokyo, and adds to the impression, which is probably correct, that one can see from Tokyo Tower (or other high observation point in Tokyo) more city, as defined by a combination of spatial extent and building density, than from any other spot on earth. Table 2.9 illustrates the impressive physical dimensions of Tokyo's built environment.

A third thing one notices almost immediately is that this gigantic mass of urban material is growing even bigger. Even now during a time of business slowdown, there is construction to be seen virtually everywhere! It seems that the whole city is pushing upward to new heights and outward in all directions, and that what was already enormous is becoming bigger still. Even Tokyo Bay is becoming urbanized, as large new islands are being fashioned in the distance beyond other new islands. Everywhere else one looks, there are new buildings that are measurably taller than those of their surroundings, and many, many construction sites where steel frames are pushing skyward announcing buildings that are yet to be. One can easily spot more than 100 separate such projects from the Tokyo Tower observation windows alone. They are identified by the presence of large, bright orange cranes and other construction machinery, and by the huge cloths, usually colored green or blue, that are widely used in Japan to shelter unfinished structures from the elements and shield passers-by from falling objects.

One is also somewhat taken aback by the incredible profusion of geometric shapes and building sizes that constitutes the rising mass of the new Tokyo. Some of the new developments are quite large and stand out as megastructures that tower over their respective neighborhoods and impose on them a new authority. The Manhattan-like skyline of Shinjuku, seen in the middle distance to the northwest, is one example. A little nearer is Yebisu Garden Place, a fresh cluster of office and hotel towers, giant condominium buildings, and a shopping mall that stands apart from the surrounding neighborhood on a site that was once a large brewery. Another example, a decade older than the Yebisu development, is Ark Hills. It too is a distinctive cluster of high-rise office and hotel buildings that dominate the surrounding area. The promotional literature for Ark Hills proclaims the project to redefine architecture for the twenty-first century and represent 'Where Tokyo is Headed'. Like so many of the other prominent new buildings in the city, the tallest towers in Ark Hills look a little like shoe boxes standing on end.

On the other hand, many of the other new buildings are so slim that they remind me of credit cards standing on end, or perhaps even pencils on end. Many are just barely wide enough to have elevators or stairways, and in quite a few structures the elevators are tiny and the stairways are affixed to the outside. Tokyo is so crowded and the cost of land so ridiculously high,[9] that one builds tall, even on the smallest of plots or the narrowest of land slivers, and does not worry so much about how the finished structure will be shaped or how furniture might be moved to the top floors. Nevertheless, one has to marvel at the skills of the city's builders as they maneuver cranes and other heavy equipment onto the most improbable sites, and create ways to squeeze in yet another high-rise where one would think that such a building could never fit. Often, the odd shapes that begin with a ground plan become even more convoluted at the upper stories, because of complex building regulations that control distribution of sunlight for street level and neighboring structures. The view across much of the city, therefore, is one of sloped, stepped, and otherwise contorted upper levels on high- and mid-rise buildings. We can refer to this as Tokyo's 'angular vernacular' (Jinnai, 1988, p. 116). This is particularly so for the new multi-story condominium structures that abound in central Tokyo that are called *manshon* (mansions) (Figure 2.9).

I should make it clear that building height is a relative concept, and that Tokyo, despite its impressive number of new, taller buildings, is not a high-rise city on the same scale as, say, Manhattan, Hong Kong, or the fashionable stretches of Rio de Janeiro. Most new buildings are in the 6–15 stories range, and only a small number are significantly taller. There are several limiting factors, not the least of which are extremely poor ground conditions and the ever-present danger of earthquakes. To a lesser extent, the lack of sizable development sites has also held back construction of super-tall structures. Consequently, the tallest buildings are not in the core of the city at all, but in outlying commercial centers, most especially Shinjuku, where bigger parcels were available for construction. Even then they fall short of the biggest structures in other leading cities. The tallest structure is the so-called Number 1 building of Tokyo Metropolitan Government headquarters, the new 'city hall' mentioned in Chapter 1. It has 48 stories and measures 243 meters (Table 2.10). In the downtown of Tokyo, the tallest building is only 152 meters (40 stories) high – only 5 meters higher than the first modern high-rise that was ever built in Tokyo, the Kasumigaseki Building completed in 1968 (147 meters; 36 floors).[10] However, developers are always on the lookout for engineering advances that promise to make tall buildings earthquake-safe, and many of them would hope to have super-tall high-rises in place in central Tokyo as soon as possible.

There are several other impressions that come to mind after these initial thoughts. One that follows directly from seeing the seemingly ubiquitous construction activity is that Tokyo is being given a whole new surface. As we survey the scene, we realize that there are very few older buildings (say, older than 20 or so years) to be seen anywhere within a broad circumference around the tower, and conclude that yet another defining characteristic of the city, in addition to

Figure 2.9 *A view across Tokyo's residential landscape in Shinjuku Ward showing mid-rise* manshon *buildings*

enormous size and density, is newness of the physical plant. The low-slung city of the past is almost completely gone: various parts of it were eradicated first by the earthquake and fire of 1923, then the 1945 disaster, and more recently by a super-active real estate market. Even buildings that themselves are still fairly new and clearly serviceable, such as some of those built in the 1950s and 1960s, are being replaced by structures that are newer and bigger. The few historic buildings (i.e. from the early part of this century or older) that are visible are exceptions that have to be picked out from the scene after some study of the surroundings. Many of them, it seems, will soon be gone as well. This is particularly true for the general area where Tokyo Tower is situated. It happens to be an extremely expensive and popular section of the city, directly in the path of expansion of Tokyo's Central Business District (CBD) and growing especially quickly in numbers of tall office buildings, large international hotels, stores and other commerce, and *manshon*. There is a certain irony, I think, that Tokyo is a rather new city even though it has recently celebrated its 400th anniversary.

Still another impression is that the overall form of Tokyo seems incredibly chaotic. This too is a fundamental characteristic that is part of Tokyo's general reputation. Not only is it a jumble of building shapes and sizes, it is also a maze of streets with no apparent plan and no relationship whatsoever to modern traffic needs. Most streets are small and narrow, and wind every which way in such fits and starts that no one even tries to give them names. The wider thoroughfares are different, because they have names and follow courses that seem normal by the standards of modern cities. However, they are surprisingly few in number given the vastness of the built-up area and the demands of traffic; they stand out as somewhat ill-fitting additions that slice awkwardly through older neighborhoods. So it is not surprising that every one of these roads is exceedingly crowded. There are also

Table 2.10 *Tokyo's Tallest Buildings, 1994*

Rank	Name of building	Ward	Number of floors	Height (meters)
1	Tokyo Metropolitan Government Building Number 1	Shinjuku	48	243.0
2	Sunshine 60 Building	Toshima	60	226.2
3	Shinjuku Center Building	Shinjuku	54	223.0
4	Shinjuku Sumitomo Building	Shinjuku	52	212.0
5	Shinjuku Nomura Building	Shinjuku	52	209.9
6	Shinjuku Mitsui Building	Shinjuku	55	209.4
7	Yasuda Fire & Marine Insurance Building	Shinjuku	43	200.0
8	NEC Headquarters Building	Minato	43	180.0
9	Keiō Plaza Hotel	Shinjuku	47	169.3
10	Toshiba Building	Minato	40	165.1
11	KDD Building	Shinjuku	32	164.4
12	Tokyo Metropolitan Government Building Number 2	Shinjuku	34	163.0
13	Tōhō Life Insurance Building	Shibuya	31	156.5
14	ARK Mori Building	Minato	37	153.3
15	World Trade Center	Minato	40	152.0
16	Mitsui Kasumigaseki Building	Chiyoda	36	147.0
17	Kōgakuin University	Shinjuku	29	143.0
18	Daiichi Kangyo Building	Chiyoda	35	142.5
19	Green Park Akasaka	Chiyoda	30	141.0
20	Hotel New Ōtani, New Building	Chiyoda	39	139.1
21	Akasaka Prince Hotel	Chiyoda	39	138.9
22	Keiō Plaza Hotel (South Bldg)	Shinjuku	35	138.7
23	Shinjuku NS Building	Shinjuku	30	133.7
24	Tokyo Hilton Hotel	Shinjuku	38	130.2
25	Sunshine City Prince Hotel	Toshima	38	130.0

several expressways that are visible from Tokyo Tower. They too are always jammed with slow-moving traffic, and follow narrow courses that are squeezed between tall buildings, meandering in great bends around prominent buildings as they pass through the center of the city. Perhaps it is the juxtaposition of so much that is new atop an old ground plan that reminds us of the city's past, and that convinces us (especially when we sit trapped in a traffic-stalled taxi with a meter running) that Tokyo is, in fact, a 400-year-old city that has been dressed up for new.

Finally, we observe that there seems to be little pattern to what has been built next to what. In kind of a land-use free-for-all that is also a fundamental characteristic of much of Tokyo, we see tiny single houses wedged amid tall hotels or modern offices, or in the shadows of busy elevated highways; shops and other businesses scattered all over what would seem to be housing areas; and factories and warehouses sitting amidst private residences or apartments, or next to the newest gleaming office towers. There is little evidence of coordinated land-use planning or the kinds of zoning restrictions that separate incompatible uses in most other cities – and even less evidence of attention to aesthetics in urban design. While some buildings stand out for their appealing architecture, the scene from

Tokyo Tower is for the most part a hard-featured and unattractive one. The high-rises are mostly blockish and uninspired, and most of the rest of the buildings, the mid-rises, are cluttered with water tanks, television antennas, advertising bill-boards, and neon signs on their roofs. Utility poles and wires are everywhere. Almost everything, it seems, is meant to be purely functional, but little is built with the kind of architectural elegance that is normally accorded to structures that are meant to last. The whole scene is a careless jumble, because Tokyo itself is not meant to last, perched as it is between disasters, and built for the moment (Popham, 1985, p. 34).

The area in the immediate vicinity of Tokyo Tower is a good example of the frequently bewildering mix of land uses that distinguishes Tokyo. We can look especially at Shiba Kōen, the large and now grossly disfigured park in which the Tower is situated. Although details are best studied on foot at street level, we can look directly down from windows in the lower observation level and see some of the odd juxtapositions that seem to be an essential feature of the city, and that make Tokyo such an incredibly interesting, albeit not necessarily attractive, place. The centerpiece is Zōjōji, one of the most important of Tokyo's many historic temples. It is famous for its old role as protector of Edo, as Tokyo was called in history, against evil spirits who might bring harm to the city from the southwest. It is distinguished visually by a great carved wooden gate that opens to the inner compound and a massive sloped tile roof on the main structure. Because of damage from the 1923 earthquake and fire and the bombing during the Second World War, Zōzōji is a historic site that was actually constructed in 1974. Next door, behind another historic temple gate, is a gigantic golf driving range. It has three decks of more than 50 drivers each, a bright green carpet covered with thousands of little white balls, a huge green net enclosing all the action, and the word *Maxfli* in oversized red letters facing both the tower and the golfers. This, in turn, is next to a large bowling alley with a huge tenpin on its roof. Next to that we see a wooded area in which some of the city's homeless men have built a small cardboard and plank shantytown. This and other sections of Shiba Kōen are bounded by wide and incredibly busy highways, including an elevated expressway that winds around the southern edge of the park. There is still another big bowling alley almost straight down from the observation window with 'Tower Bowl' written in Japanese on the roof, and a television studio next door. A small pocket of tiny, single homes that somehow survived all the changes is just beyond. Off to the side is a luxury hotel (the Tokyo Prince) with a big, inviting swimming pool and a wonderful, quiet Japanese garden that remains from a feudal-era estate.

There is, of course, nothing particularly unusual about seeing a district of a city that is mixed, even with incongruities as striking as these. Cities, after all, are always giant repositories of complex history and multiple cultural influences. What makes this case special, however, is the contrast between the site as it is now and the role that it played in history. In addition to Zōjōji, there were once *hundreds* of temple buildings there, as well as refectories and boarding houses for thousands of priests and novices. Moreover, the grounds held the mausoleums of most of Japan's shoguns. In Waley's words, this was 'the citadel of Tokugawa Buddhism' (Waley, 1984, p. 361). In just about any other culture, such a place would be considered a highly valued historic site, if not sacred ground, and would be preserved and protected forever. It would certainly not be an appropriate place for a tall steel tower, nor for bowling alleys and golf. But in the Shiba Kōen area too, just as we saw at the very start of this book with the example of my old neighborhood and will see again and again in a number of other places to be visited, Tokyo is different, very different. It has its own sense of history and its own priorities for land use; it has developed its own distinctive urban form.

Social Geography of the Rails

In some ways the most important topic for orientation to Tokyo is the city's train and subway network. This is how the vast majority of Tokyoites travel from place to place, and the circulation system that is the city's lifeblood. A map of the maze of subway lines that criss-cross under the inner part of the 23 wards is indispensable for getting around in Tokyo, as is a plan of the many train lines that radiate in all directions outside the city and connect with the subway network. At first sight, the system appears complicated, but it is actually easy to use and extremely convenient. It is also meticulously clean, safe, and on schedule. These aspects reflect an image of Tokyo as a perfectly tuned, smooth-running machine, a marvel of transportation planning, technology and social organization. However, the train and subway network is also hopelessly congested on most lines, particularly at peak times. Thus, the network also reflects an image of Tokyo as an overgrown giant.

It is not my intention to provide a detailed description of Tokyo's rail network. Visitors to the city have ample advice about this in guidebooks and maps, and from bilingual signs (Japanese and English) at all the stations. However, there is one train line that I do want to mention. It is more important than the others not just because of the great number of passengers that it carries but also because it is something of a Tokyo landmark and performs a critical role in the geographical organization of the city. This is the Yamanote Line, a line that is distinguished by its green-striped cars and the broad loop it forms around much of the center of the city (Figure 2.10). It is operated by Japan Railways (JR), the recently privatized rail system binding the nation. On a map the Yamanote Line looks a little like a fastened necklace with 29 beads corresponding to the 29 stations along the route. It takes 63 minutes to go around it completely, and during most times of the day, trains stop at the stations about every 3 minutes. Some of the stations, perhaps the bigger beads on the chain, are the most important stations in the metropolitan area. They are where the city's subways (most of them operated by Tokyo government) and train lines (most of them private enterprises) from the suburbs come together, and where hundreds of thousands of passengers transfer between them each day. Examples include Shinjuku, Shibuya, and Ikebukuro on the west side of the loop, Shinagawa on the southwest and Ueno on the north-northeast. Tokyo Station, generally thought of as the city's central station, is also on the loop. It is on the east side where the Yamanote Line cuts through the city's Central Business District.

One of the most important parts of geographical terminology in Tokyo concerns the distinction between areas within the Yamanote loop from those outside it. The

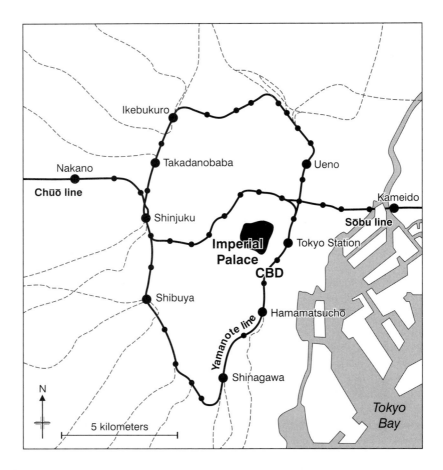

Figure 2.10 *The Yamanote rail loop around the center of Tokyo and feeder commuter lines from the suburbs*

inside is a commonly accepted definition of the inner city; includes all the Imperial Palace compound, much of the Central Business District, the national government center, and many historic sites and famous neighborhoods. The outside, particularly on the west side where the loop is stretched away from the center, marks the start of residential Tokyo and the direction to the suburbs. It is there that numerous rail lines come together from the elongated Tama area of *Tōkyō-to* and from the expansive sector of suburban growth in neighboring prefectures. On the other hand, parts of the eastern side of the Yamanote Line (and a little to the north) mark the boundary between the commercial core of the city on the inside and the historic neighborhoods of *shitamachi* on the outside. It is not the exact boundary, but it is close enough and is sometimes described as if it were.

The shape of the Yamanote loop is widely recognized in Tokyo, especially when combined on an illustration with the corridor of the Chūō and Sōbu Lines (also JR). This slices east–west through the center of the loop and, as Figure 2.10

shows, has a distinctive crook that is easily identified. These are features that residents look for when orienting themselves to almost any map of the city, be it of the street plan, the transit network, or some other pattern. Therefore, advertisers often draw sketch maps of the loop on their copy so that they can clearly explain the location of a place of business. In fact, Tokyoites know the loop so well that a great many of them, perhaps a majority, can recite the 29 stations in order without consulting a list and can name the other lines, both public and private, above and below ground, that intersect at all the transfer stations. So knowing the Yamanote Line is a matter of fundamental literacy about Tokyo. In the following pages of this book there will be numerous references to places as being 'inside' or 'outside' the loop, and to various stations and station-front commercial centers along its course.

In addition to this geographical orientation to the rail system, I want to introduce some sociological observations. For one thing, we see from the train and subway network another example, as with earthquakes, of the precarious nature of Tokyo. That is, the city is constantly at the edge of one type of disaster or another; with transportation the problem is that the system that works beautifully, like a flawless machine for 99-plus percent of the time, can fall apart completely almost at any moment. For example, on the rare occasion that there is a mechanical failure or an accident, a fast-moving ripple effect takes place across a wide area. Trains back up all up and down the affected line and sometimes on other lines too. As this happens, boarding platforms become dangerously crowded because prospective riders continue to arrive, as always, every minute, and access has to be closed. In the worst case, virtually the entire circulation system of a wide area would come to a complete halt. Fortunately, the employees of train and subway companies are well trained for such emergencies, and it never takes long before the problem is corrected and a reverse ripple brings everything to normal. It takes incredible planning to keep the transportation system in tune, including strict maintenance schedules for the trains that probably rival those for jumbo passenger jets, and minute safety regulations that govern every motion, it seems, of the conductors on the trains and the railway personnel on the platforms.[11]

There are also certain expectations that are put on passengers to keep the Tokyo machine moving. For example, we see the reasonable requirements that passengers board smoothly during the few seconds that trains doors are opened at a station, and that they adhere to a certain level of quiet and other decorum (Figure 2.11). Violations are infrequent, and are generally dealt with immediately and harshly. Not long ago I was fascinated by a story in the newspapers about two high-school boys who were exceptionally boisterous and rude on a train, and pushed aside an older man to grab a seat. By the standards of most cities, where much worse violations are common, this incident would hardly attract attention. But in this case, the police were called in. After a few days of investigation, they found the boys and made a lesson of them by publicizing their apologies to their victim and to the other passengers. (It was possible to trace the culprits because, like most Japanese youngsters, they wore uniforms that were particular to their school.) The purpose of calling the police and pressing the case was, of course, to make sure that problems of this type would remain minimal. Likewise, people who are caught at

Figure 2.11 *A crowded subway car during the morning rush. The attendant wearing gloves pushes in the last boarders as train doors slide closed*

fare cheating, particularly involving misuse of expensive monthly passes, are sometimes prosecuted and have their names printed in the press.

People who violate the system's rules in a more serious way, such as to actually delay trains, are dealt with even more harshly. Thus, in another incident an American schoolboy caused a panic among riders by releasing a garden snake on a crowded Chūō commuter train. This stopped the train and required its removal from the line until workmen could locate and dispose of the reptile. Newspapers the next day were filled with outrage at the incident, and with wise editorial observations about how foreigners don't understand Japanese rules and have to be taught to fit in. One writer opined that while such 'a deliberate prank . . . may be rather common in American society . . . the humor was lost on most adults here' (*The Japan Times*, 12 June, 1988). To make sure that there would be no imitations of the incident in the future, the boy's family was made to pay a heavy and well-publicized fine. In the same vein, when a person commits suicide by jumping in front of a train, which is apparently something that happens more often than officials care to admit, the family of the deceased is made to pay expensive penalties because of the disruption to train schedules.[12]

What such examples show is one of the most fundamental lessons about Japanese society. We see that Japan, or Tokyo in particular, tolerates few deviations from a norm and expects faithful adherence to established routines. That is, there is little tolerance for individuals who, for whatever reason, do not act like the others and would impede the general flow. People with serious injuries or with physical handicaps such as those that require a wheelchair do not fit into the transit system, and are excluded from it by design. Without exception, every station has multiple stairways that have to be negotiated to reach the trains; none has an elevator to the platform. So too, slow-moving people, such as some elderly folk, or

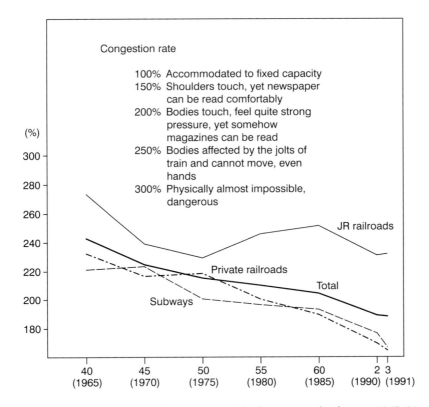

Congestion rate

100% Accommodated to fixed capacity
150% Shoulders touch, yet newspaper
can be read comfortably
200% Bodies touch, feel quite strong
pressure, yet somehow
magazines can be read
250% Bodies affected by the jolts of
train and cannot move, even
hands
300% Physically almost impossible,
dangerous

Figure 2.12 Changing crowding levels on Tokyo's trains and subways, 1965–91.
(*Source*: Tokyo Metropolitan Government, 1994a, p. 71.) © Tokyo Metropolitan
Government 1994

people with bulky luggage are discouraged from using the system. The only notable
exception to such inaccessibility concerns people who are visually impaired. In
their case, the system is at least partly accessible because trains and stations are
announced via loudspeakers, and stairways and boarding platforms have raised
warning markings that can be felt with a cane. Overall, however, we observe that
despite the great wealth of Japan, and despite the considerable kindness that most
Japanese reveal in person-to-person situations, there is comparatively little effort
made in the country to make public facilities accessible to movement-impaired
individuals.

At the same time, some behavior that is not tolerated at all in other societies is,
curiously, accepted as normal in Japan or, at worst, considered to be nothing more
than 'small problems' to be overlooked. It is well known, for example, that there is
considerable sexual abuse of women that takes place on crowded trains by indecent
touching. However, unlike the prompt action by police that follows other forms of
misbehavior, this problem has been pretty much ignored by law-enforcement
officials, and most unfortunately, by other passengers as well. One of my female
students, who like so many other young women has been a frequent victim of this,
once explained that if she were to complain on a train about a wayward hand, she

would become the center of attention among the passengers rather than the offender; that her requests for help from the people around her would be coldly ignored. In one experience, some fellow-passengers insisted that she should stop bothering the man who was feeling her because he is 'obviously tired from a long day of work'. There are, as one can imagine, frequent complaints about this problem from women's groups and others, occasional sympathetic editorials in the media, and even some promises by police to act. Nevertheless, there seems to be little or no improvement in the situation, and the norm that it is better to not rock the boat (or moving train) continues to dominate.

CRIME IN TOKYO

This brings us to the subject of crime. The topic is another of the most often asked about aspects of Tokyo, largely because of the city's reputation for low crime rates, and follows easily from our discussion of predatory behavior on trains. It is particularly timely, because one of the worst crimes in Tokyo's history has occurred recently, making public safety a crucial new concern. The crime in question is the 20 March 1995 nerve gas attack on the city's subway system that killed at least 10 commuters and injured thousands more. The incident made bold headlines around the world, not just because of the magnitude of the tragedy and the unusual way it came about but also because it was a terrorist strike. It could easily have killed thousands. In attacking the subway network during the height of the morning rush hour it was a strike against everyone in Tokyo, shattering their comfortable sense of security and changing perhaps forever how they feel about their own city. Intense news coverage continues even now, more than two years after the incident, as police investigations turn up new details about that day, and trials proceed of leaders and members of Aum Shinrikyō, the bizarre religious cult said to be responsible. The relentless search for suspects still at large is also a daily reminder that life in Tokyo has been changed (Figure 2.13).

The gassing incident also stands out simply because it was a major crime in a city where any crime, major or minor, is infrequent. Streets in Tokyo are so safe that anyone can walk almost anywhere, day or night, without fear of harm, and young children are commonly allowed to ride alone on trains and subways, sometimes cross-town, to attend school, visit relatives or for other purposes. The city's crime rates are most often compared with those for New York City, partly to point to the problem of violence in American society and partly to laud Tokyo's success. For example, despite the fact that both cities have approximately equal populations, in 1987 (the latest year for which authoritative comparative data are available) Tokyo had only 133 murders while New York had 1627. Similarly, there were only 412 robberies (defined as taking property with force or threat of force) in Tokyo that year in comparison to 78 890 that occurred in New York. Similar differences exist in the occurrence of other crimes such as rape, auto theft and burglary, although not necessarily at the mind-boggling ratio for robbery between New York and Tokyo of 191:1 (Bayley, 1991, pp. 5–6).

Explanations for Tokyo's low crime rates (as well as for low crime rates in other Japanese cities) inevitably focus on Japan's social characteristics. The most

Figure 2.13 *Tokyo-style 'wanted' poster. These are plaster models of religious cult Aum Shinrikyō members wanted by police in connection with the 20 March 1995 poison gas attack that killed subway commuters. The display is at a busy train station; passersby with information or possible leads are asked to call the hot-line telephone number that is given*

commonly cited reasons are informal social control by institutions such as family, schools, employers and the local community; the general absence of internal social conflicts that characterize other societies; and the strong sense of group identity and common loyalty that most Japanese feel with respect to their fellow-citizens. Low crime rates are also attributed to effective policing and criminal justice admin- istration.[13] Low rates of violent crime, particularly in comparison to American cities, are also said to result from the fact that guns and other lethal weapons are effectively controlled in Tokyo. Of the 7778 violent crimes committed in Tokyo in 1987, only 14 involved the use of handguns (Bayley, 1991, p. 9). Other factors that have been cited include less drug abuse in Japan than in many other countries, high rates of employment, and the presence of more pedestrians and bicyclists on the streets in Japanese neighborhoods, acting as a crime deterrent, than in other urban settings where people tend to be in cars (Bayley, 1991; Miyazawa, 1992; *The Economist*, 16 April 1994, pp. 90–96).

A special aspect of crime control is community policing from neighborhood- based 'police boxes' called *kōban* (Figure 2.14). In comparison to the 99 larger police stations in Tokyo in March 1994, there were 1232 of these tiny substations in the city, many of then outside train and subway stations through which people enter various neighborhoods. Most of them are staffed around the clock by police officers who alternate duty behind a desk in the *kōban* itself with daily patrols of the neighborhood. In this way, police are in daily contact with residents and shopkeepers in the local area, and are able to distinguish strangers from those who 'belong' in the neighborhood. They also know all the potential local sources of

48
——

Figure 2.14 *A typical neighborhood kōban (police box). The scene here is of the police box at the train station of a neighborhood in western Tokyo on a day when actors and a film crew were using the site to shoot a television program*

trouble – disreputable individuals, rowdy teenagers, or any questionable local bars – and are able to keep a close eye on them. Whenever there is an emergency call, police are able to respond immediately and apply their intimate knowledge of the area to solving the problem.

There are countless specific examples of effective policing, even for problems much smaller than the subway gassing. We have already seen two: swift action by authorities to identify the rude teenagers on the subway, and swift action to deal with the unfortunate youngster who had released a snake on a crowded train. Another example from the realm of public transportation is an impressive, wide-spread investigation by police to find the culprit or culprits responsible for placing rocks and other objects on rail tracks, endangering the riders. There has been a rash of such incidents recently in various parts of the metropolitan area – 71 in a recent six-month period in suburban Kanagawa Prefecture alone. Quite a few of the incidents have already been solved. Some of them are now known to have been the work of little children at misguided play, while others, documented on police surveillance video, turned out to be the commissions of large crows that apparently 'enjoy the cracking sound of rocks crashing onto the tracks' (Naitō, 1996, p. 3). But other incidents, including the placing of a washing machine on Jōban Line tracks in the outer suburbs, are feared to be the work of organized saboteurs who want to cause a disaster, and are still being actively investigated.

Despite the general effectiveness of police in Tokyo and sociological controls against crime, crime rates are rising in the city and are a source of increasing concern. As a result, there has been a remarkable profusion in recent years of private security forces hired by retailers and other businesses, and of video surveillance systems installed in stores and shopping centers, entryways to large buildings, public plazas, train and subway stations, and many other places where large numbers of people come together. So, too, rising concern about crime is seen in the fact that the Guardian Angels, the red-beret civilian crime fighters once identified exclusively with New York City, have founded a chapter in Tokyo and now patrol select streets and subways. However, most of their attention has been focused on helping inebriated salarymen find their way home and ripping down porno-graphic posters from utility poles and telephone booths (Stroh, 1996). According to Kunimatsu Takaji, commissioner-general of the National Police Agency, one crime in particular, over and above the subway gassing, is responsible for altering the public's sense of security – a brutal triple murder on 30 July 1995 at a supermarket in Hachiōji, a western Tokyo suburb (*Daily Yomiuri*, 30 July 1996). A 47-year-old female employee and two high-school girls who worked part-time were found shot in the head execution-style in the store's second-floor office in what might have been a robbery attempt. The public was shocked by the unusually ghastly nature of the crime, and is mystified, along with the police, as to who could have done such a thing. Despite an extraordinarily intensive police investigation and a team of 60 detectives working full-time more than one year later, there are essentially no clues or solid leads to follow.

In 1993 the number of criminal offenses reported in Tokyo rose by some 16 000 over the previous year to a total of approximately 257 000. This number translates to about 702 crimes each day, or about one every 123 seconds. Many of the most serious crimes are blamed on gangsters (*yakuza*) and crime syndicates. Many others are attributed to foreigners.[14] In 1993 foreigners are said to have committed approximately 4800 of the city's 257 000 reported crimes, an increase of approxi-mately 1100 over the previous year. Many Japanese consider such an increase to be the inevitable consequence of their country's internationalization and the growing numbers of foreign workers, students and visitors, particularly in Tokyo. A spon-taneous shoplifting spree on 7 December 1992 in Akihabara, Tokyo's consumer electronics district, by at least 28 members of a marching band on a short visit to Japan from an American college was reported widely in the media and talked about disapprovingly by the general public as a case in point. Similarly, the summer 1995 rape of a young Japanese girl by three United States servicemen on the island of Okinawa where they were based also called outraged public attention to crimes by foreigners.

Tokyo's Address System

There is one last item left in this orientation to Tokyo: the city's address system. This is not a guidebook, so the purpose is not necessarily to help a person get around the city or to locate some significant attraction. Instead, it is to describe more fully the way the city is organized internally. This is necessary because the Tokyo address system is fundamentally different from what is employed in most other countries, as well as different in detail from the norm for other Japanese cities. This creates problems for many newcomers to Tokyo, and adds to the reputation that the city is chaotic in street plan and impossible to negotiate.

What is perhaps most disconcerting to people who are unfamiliar with Tokyo is that except for a comparatively small number of wide, modern thoroughfares and a few other busy lanes, the city's streets have no names. We saw, for example, from Tokyo Tower that the streets below wind in such fits and starts that naming them and keeping track of which fork was a continuation of which street would be unworkable. Visitors to the city are also sometimes surprised to learn that it is their responsibility, instead of the driver's, to tell a taxi driver exactly where the desired destination is to be found. Well-known places such as major hotels or busy train stations pose no problems, but for small establishments such as a particular shop or a recommended pub (or heaven forbid, a private residence) the job of location is actually the passenger's. All that the driver is expected to do is to get to the right neighborhood fairly directly. Barrie B. Greenbie, author of an interesting recent book about Japanese space, has likened the experience of finding one's way around Tokyo outside the main commercial centers to being lost in the woods, even if one is with an experienced taxi driver (Greenbie, 1988, p. 55).

However, none of this is to suggest that addresses in Tokyo are all chaos and that people are always getting lost. In fact, quite the contrary is true. There is, in fact, an address system for the city; it works extremely well for people who understand its basic rules. The expectation that taxi passengers should know how to find the precise location of their destination once the driver has got close is not so onerous if one is prepared for this. There are two underlying principles. One is that addresses in Tokyo are based on a hierarchy of named areas rather than streets; the second is that points (or individual buildings) within the smallest (or lowest-ranking) of these areas are generally numbered according to the sequence in which they were built or some other criterion, instead of according to location. We can illustrate this by going over how an address is written, say, on an envelope to be mailed.

The top of the address hierarchy is Tokyo or *Tōkyō-to* itself, and this is written first. Then comes the name of the ward or the city, town, or village within the Tokyo metropolis. The level below that is the district of the ward or town. This is called *machi*, and also has a name. For example, the address from which I wrote the introduction to this book begins *Tōkyō, Shibuya-ku* (Shibuya Ward), *Honmachi*, with Honmachi (or *Honchō* as the combination of Chinese characters is also pronounced) being one of 29 *machi* within Shibuya ward. Below the level of *machi* is a hierarchy of numbered areas that continues the address. The largest of these is called *chōme*. Honmachi has six *chōme*, each about one-fifth of one square kilometer in size and with several thousand residents. Mine was number 2 *chōme*. Each *chōme*, in turn, is subdivided into numerous smaller numbered areas that are called *banchi*. We could think of these units as being roughly equivalent to street blocks, except that most of Tokyo has nothing so geometric that the word 'block' could apply. Finally, there is the actual building. This is a point that is identified by the last number of the address, the *gō*. I had number 14. My full address, therefore, was written *Tōkyō, Shibuya-ku, Honmachi 2-2-14*.[15] However, this was also the address of my neighbor, so it was required, as it is everywhere in Tokyo, to post the *banchi* and *gō* numbers and the family name at the front of the house. When I procrastinated in posting my name at an address to which I moved later (you are expected to have a special name plate made that costs much more than the material and labor are worth), one of my neighbors with the same address came by with a polite but insistent reminder that mail, various other deliveries, and visitors would be confused as to which house was whose.

This explains how a letter finds its way to the right destination, but how does a person who is travelling from one part of the city to another find the right place? Even though it sounds facetious to say so, the answer is by consulting a map, or even a series of maps at ever-larger scales. More than in any place I have ever seen, people in Tokyo depend on maps to get around or to give directions. Every book store has a special section devoted exclusively to maps, including many competing editions of rather thick map books that show considerable detail in color for every ward in the 23-ward area as well as for neighboring cities and towns. This is the kind of book that people keep in their cars, and that every taxi driver has on the seat beside him (always *him*, almost never *her*). Passengers on trains often have photocopies of needed pages from these atlases as they travel to their destinations. There are also folded maps sold at newsstands, and inset maps printed on matchbooks, on people's business cards, and on advertisements in newspapers and magazines, on advertisement posters that hang in subways and trains, and on the small tissue packets that one is always being handed on crowded sidewalks to promote some special sale or new business. There are even maps printed onto handkerchiefs.

So a person who needs to get to some unfamiliar place in Tokyo often consults one or more maps as a guide. The closer one approaches the destination, the more detailed is the map employed. Once in the right neighborhood, there will be large-scale maps that are posted on all-weather signboards showing locations for all the neighboring *banchi* and *gō*. These maps are located at subway and train station exits and at many prominent street intersections, and are usually maintained by the ward or municipality. In addition, there are often extremely detailed maps that are posted in individual neighborhoods that show all the buildings and property lines and that identify local businesses and residents. These maps are often the responsibilities of neighborhood associations such as associations of local shop-keepers. They are especially helpful because *gō* numbers are often not arranged in logical spatial order, but are scattered over a small area in unpredictable ways. And finally, if one still cannot find the right place, one can always ask for help at the local *kōban* or police box. There is one in every neighborhood; a major function, in addition to crime prevention and other police duties, is to maintain detailed maps of the surroundings and to give directions.

What makes this system work so well is that Tokyoites (or maybe Japanese more generally) have exceptionally good map skills. I see this in my students, who are far better at map reading than any group of geography students I have taught in North America, and from the many examples of outstanding informal sketch maps that I have seen people in Tokyo make on little scraps of paper when giving directions. These impromptu drawings are always prepared so quickly and so effortlessly, and they are almost always completely accurate! Usually, streets are drawn with double lines and intersections are made neatly so that no line goes across them. There are always just enough landmarks to guide the way perfectly from the train station exit or some other well-known starting place, but not so many that the map becomes cluttered (Figure 2.15). A taxi driver who has brought his fare to the correct

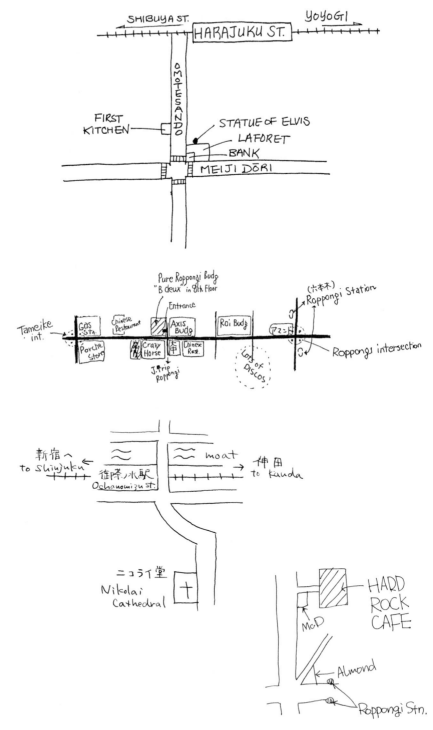

Figure 2.15 *Four examples of informal sketch maps used to give directions.*
(Thanks to Kaori Friess, Ayumi Nishikawa, Aoi Shimizu and Mikiko Togo)

neighborhood would typically expect to be shown such a map (or at least have it described in words) so that he could drive the last distance to the desired residence or place of business. Such cartography is a remarkable ability that comes from constant use of maps (and maybe also because of practice at calligraphy and other arts), and that the anthropologist Roland Barthes has discussed as being one of the distinguishing cultural characteristics of Tokyo's inhabitants (Barthes, 1982, pp. 33–7).

CHAPTER 3

HISTORICAL DEVELOPMENT

Tokyo is neither an especially old nor a new city, but instead has a history that is somewhere in between. It is older, for example, than all the cities of North America, but much newer than hundreds of other places, including such great capitals as Cairo, Beijing, Istanbul, Rome, London, and in Japan, Kyoto. However, the details of its history are as rich and interesting as those of any place in the world. They go on for page after page with captivating stories of political intrigue, powerful personalities and other exceptional characters, landmark events, great construction projects, and other details, all of them set in a context of a national culture that is unique and endlessly fascinating. Moreover, the Tokyo story stands out because it is the story of more millions of people than most other cities. In addition, it is a story of more frequent urban destructions and rebuildings than any other place in the world. And finally, it is a story of unusually rapid and profound social change and modernization. As any proud Tokyoite will gladly point out, in just over four centuries, the city was transformed from an insignificant castle town that had only local impact to the huge and powerful capital of a populous nation and then to one of the most important capitals in the world as a whole.

This chapter is a summary of those parts of Tokyo history that deal most directly with the physical development of the city. The goal is to understand the changing look of Tokyo over the four centuries of its existence, and to keep track of the sequential rings and layers of construction that constitute today's city. I have had considerable help with this from some excellent literature about the history of Tokyo that exists in English. Four writers have been especially important, and are cited often: Paul Waley, whom I have introduced before for his outstanding book *Tokyo Now and Then: An Explorer's Guide*, a book that is organized by district in Tokyo (1984); Noel Nouët, whose 1961 book *The Shogun's City* has recently been translated from French to English and is a superb account of the city from its founding through the fall of the shogunate in 1868 (1990); Edward Seidensticker, author of two richly entertaining and fact-packed volumes about Tokyo's modern development (*Low City, High City* (1983) and the more recent (1990) *Tokyo Rising*); and Henry D. Smith II, who has written numerous scholarly articles and book chapters about a variety of topics dealing with Tokyo history (e.g. 1973; 1978; 1979; 1986a, b).

EDO: FOUNDING AND EARLY GROWTH

Archaeological evidence indicates that human settlement in the Kantō Plain dates far back into prehistory. However, the origin of Tokyo is quite recent. It is generally accepted that the start of the city dates to 1457, when a feudal lord named Ōta Dōkan chose the site for his castle (Figure 3.1). There had been a small fishing

Figure 3.1 *Statue of Ōta Dōkan, Tokyo's founder. Shown here, the statue is outside Tokyo's old City Hall in the Marunouchi district. The statue has now been moved indoors to the atrium of Tokyo International Forum, a public hall on the site of the old government headquarters*

village there before that was called both Hirakawa, after the local river, and Edo. The latter word means 'estuary' or 'mouth of the river', and was also the family name adopted by members of the Taira clan who settled there in the twelfth century. The name Edo stayed with the settlement after Dōkan's arrival, and continued to be used for the place until 1868, when 'Tokyo' was adopted.

Figure 3.2 *Some of the remains of Edo Castle. The grounds are now the Imperial Palace grounds. The Marunouchi and Kasumigaseki areas are in the distance*

According to legend, Ōta Dōkan was led to Edo by the goddess Benten. She signaled him through the medium of a fish that jumped out of the water that he should erect his castle on a specific low hill that jutted close to the shore of Tokyo Bay (formerly Edo Bay). The hill was probably a wise choice, because even though it was low it commanded the head of the bay, the mouths of the local rivers, and access to the broad Kantō Plain. Moreover, there were certain political advantages to the location as well, as it strengthened the defenses between rival feudal domains in different parts of Honshū, the large Japanese island of which the Kantō area is a part.

Relatively few details are known about Edo of Dōkan's time. There is nothing tangible that remains, and what little record there is about the castle comes mostly from descriptions by poets who visited there (Waley, 1984, p. xx) (Figure 3.2). Even the river Hirakawa is something of a mystery. Its course was altered by Dōkan to improve navigation, and then changed again (along with that of Tokyo's other rivers) so many times in so many ways over the centuries that the original channel is now lost. However, as Waley advises in his history of the city, the pattern of river engineering is so confusing in Tokyo that these are 'waters we would be wise not to try to chart' (p. 24).

The Edo of Ōta Dōkan and his immediate successors never developed into anything more than a castle town (*jōka machi*) of moderate importance. The city's rise to prominence did not begin until 1590, a little more than 100 years after Dōkan's death, when the next great figure of Tokyo history appeared on the scene. This was the warrior chieftain Tokugawa Ieyasu, who would soon become absolute ruler of the whole of Japan and make Edo its undisputed capital and greatest city. The dynasty he founded, the Tokugawa shogunate, would rule the nation for almost three centuries. All of this would take place after 21 October 1600, following Ieyasu's victory over the armies of Ishida Mitsunari at the Battle of Sekigahara, an epic struggle for control of the country in a narrow valley in what is now Gifu Prefecture.

What had brought Ieyasu to Edo in 1590 was his service in another battle to Toyotomi Hideyoshi, before Ieyasu's ascendancy the most powerful warlord in Japan. In particular, the city and the eight surrounding provinces of Kantō were Ieyasu's reward for having masterminded the successful military campaign against Hideyoshi's principal rivals, the Hōjō clan who had controlled all this land from its stronghold in Odawara. As the Hōjō castle was about to fall, the *taikō*, as Hideyoshi was called, announced personally the offer of this spoils of war to Ieyasu, who in turn suggested that the bargain be finalized by the two of them urinating together in the direction of Odawara (Nouët, 1990, p. 25). Thus, as far as is known, Tokyo is the only one of the world's most important cities to have embarked on its course of modern urban development after a deal sealed with a piss.

As soon as he came to Edo, Ieyasu undertook to remodel the city. In doing so, he laid foundations for the urban form that would endure to the present day. Some of the best examples that are still seen are the altered courses of several rivers, the pattern of radial highways that lead from the center to outlying prefectures, the reclaimed marshlands near Tokyo Bay that are some of today's major office and retailing districts, and the flat topography of the vitally important Kanda district. In the last of these cases, a low mountain (Mount Kanda, actually a finger-like protrusion of the upland behind Tokyo) was cut down to obtain fill for reclamation in the bay, as well as to make room for expansion of the city inland. The most important legacy left by Ieyasu is the vast open area in the center of Tokyo that was the site of his castle. It is now the Imperial Palace of Japan and its grounds. Most of the original buildings put up by Ieyasu and successor shoguns were destroyed by the fires that periodically visited the city all during the Edo era, but significant sections of wall and moat still remain. The whole area measures substantially over 100 hectares, and stands out as one of the most highly revered places in Japan. It is also a striking void in the core of an enormously crowded city.

Construction of the castle was one of Ieyasu's first objectives.[1] He did away with the rudimentary structure that was left by Dōkan, and commenced work on the same site on a very elaborate fortification. A large labor force was recruited from several areas of western Japan to do the construction work, and many thousands of stone blocks were quarried in the Izu region and sent by ship to Edo. When the work was finished some 50 years later (during the tenure of the third Tokugawa shogun), Edo Castle measured 16 kilometers around the outside defensive perimeter and 6.4 kilometers around the inner perimeter. It was the largest castle in the world. It was also noted for an ingenious defensive plan. Its distinctive quality was a maze of moats arranged in a spiral that unwound outward in a clockwise direction from the heart of the complex. There was also a supporting pattern of strategically placed bridges, gates, high stone walls, and 36 lookout towers. In this way the center of the whole compound, where the shogun kept his primary residence, was most intimately protected.

The construction of such a gigantic complex was a massive undertaking that, by design, taxed the nation. Ieyasu used the project as a means to test the loyalty of supporters and to weaken the finances of political adversaries by demanding that they make huge outlays in material resources and corvée labor for the building effort. For example, he ordered each of the major *daimyō* (feudal lords) in western Japan to prepare a burdensome quota of thousands of large stone sections for the construction, and to provide all the required workers and means of transportation. The amount of the quota was pegged to the rice harvest in each domain. At one point in the construction, there were 3000 vessels gathered in the various ports of the Izu Peninsula alone to deliver shipments of stone blocks to Edo (Yazaki, 1968, p. 176). There was also considerable loss of life during the construction: ships loaded with stone sank at sea and took entire crews to the bottom, and stones fell as they were hoisted to the top of walls and crushed workers below. After the earthquake of 1923 loosened some sections of stone, skeletons of workmen were discovered behind walls. It may be that the victims had been sealed alive behind the foundations deliberately so that their strength would pass on to the building. As Nouët reported, this was a common practice at the time. Interestingly, pillar men (*hito bashira*), as such workers were called, were sometimes volunteers (Nouët, 1990, p. 49).

Another calculated repression was a policy called *sankin kōtai*. Begun by Ieyasu but then formalized during the rule of the third shogun, Iemitsu (1622–51), this was a practice that required all *daimyō* to spend alternate years in Edo, away from their own fiefs, in a specially designated section of the city. For *daimyō* from the nearby Kantō provinces, the change of residence occurred every six months. Even when they returned to their lands, they were required to leave behind their wives and children and their *samurai* retainers as hostages. Moreover, *daimyō* and other high officials were expected to maintain an expensive lifestyle in Edo, complete with multiple mansions (*yashiki*) near the castle and in the suburban hills, casts of servants, and many other luxuries. This stimulated demand for many types of goods and services in the city, and attracted thousands of craftsmen, merchants, and other 'townspeople' to Edo to make a living. One particularly famous element in this population was business-minded people from Ise province (near Nagoya) and Omi province (on Lake Biwa near Kyoto). Described as 'Omi thieves and Ise beggars' by the citizenry of Edo, they opened shops, banking houses, and other commercial enterprises, especially in the Nihombashi area between the castle and the bay, that would provide the foundation for the city's rapid ascendancy to top rank as a commercial center.

Thus, not only did *sankin kōtai* help to consolidate the power of the shogunate, it also provided the basis for the spectacular population growth that characterized Edo starting with the seventeenth century. The settlement exploded in size from only a few thousand inhabitants in 1600 to nearly half a million by the 1650s. By that time it had surpassed both Kyoto and the merchants' city Osaka as the largest in Japan. The population rose still more to over one million inhabitants by the end of the century and then to 1.3 million by 1720. By then Edo was far and away the largest city in the world. Other leading cities at the time were London with about 600 000 inhabitants and Beijing with just under one million. For the next nearly 150 years the population of Edo was remarkably stable, and did not begin to change measurably again until the *sankin kōtai* requirements were relaxed in 1862 and the number of residents dropped sharply. In the meantime, London surpassed Edo in population totals early in the nineteenth century to become the new largest city (Smith, 1979, p. 51).

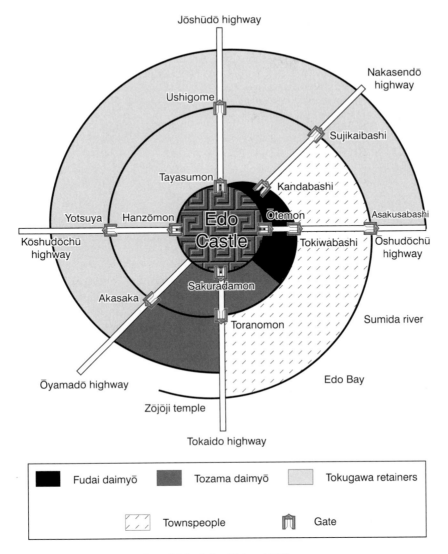

Figure 3.3 Schematic plan of Edo (after Naitō, 1987)

The spatial–ecological structure of Edo was a mirror of feudal society. This could be seen at the scale of the castle complex alone, as well as at the scale of all Edo. In the former case, the hierarchy of status within the top echelon of feudal Japan was reflected faithfully by the location of residence with respect to that of the shōgun. This was one of the intended functions of the swirl pattern of moats that defined the core of the settlement. The shōgun and his family occupied the innermost compound (*honmaru*), while favored *daimyō* and other highest-ranking officials were just outside the main gate to this enclosure. Lesser lords were located further out along the spiral. Servants and others without status (e.g. common soldiers) were outside this complex, where the swirl opened up to the rest of the city. The basic outline of this arrangement is illustrated in Figure 3.3, a spatial model of early Edo

Table 3.1 Land-use distribution in Edo (after 1818)

	Hectares	Percent
Edo Palace	131	1.7
Upper *daimyō* residences	796	10.2
Middle *daimyō* residences	340	4.4
Lower *daimyō* residences	1630	20.9
Samurai residences	1878	24.1
Townspeople's residences	1626	20.9
Government use	199	2.6
Additional *diamyō* use	5	0.1
Buddhist temples	1112	14.3
Shinto shrines	70	0.9
Confucian temples	5	0.1
TOTAL	7792	100.0

Source: Tokyo Metropolitan Government (1989b, p. 4).

that was developed by architectural historian, Naitō Akira (1987, p. 35). The distinction between *fudai daimyō* and *tozama daimyō* that is shown is one of closeness to the shogun; the former, who resided closest to the inner keep, had joined the shogun's forces before the Battle of Sekigahara, while the latter, the 'outside lords', had joined up after the victory and were kept at a little distance.

There was still another spatial arrangement to Edo, one that existed as a superimposed pattern on the spiral pattern. In addition to the castle, which was more or less in the center, the city consisted of two broadly defined and vastly different districts, *shitamachi* and *yamanote*. The former word means 'low city', and applies to the area of flatlands reclaimed from the bay and river deltas where the common people or townsfolk (*chōnin*) lived. *Yamanote*, on the other hand, is the 'high city' (literally, 'in the direction of the mountains'), and was the higher ground inhabited by the *samurai* class. It was also where many shrines and temples were located. Other castle cities (e.g. Osaka and Kyoto) had similar arrangements. In Edo, *shitamachi* and *yamanote* had roughly equal population numbers. In the 1720s, this was about 600 000 inhabitants each. The difference was in population density. *Shitamachi* comprised only 16 percent of Edo's surface and had a residential density of some 69 000 people per square kilometer, while *yamanote* was 69 percent of the city and had a density of 14 000 persons per square kilometer (Waley, 1984, p. xxvii). The rest of the city was the castle complex and water. Table 3.1 gives a breakdown of land use in Tokyo according to social class.

The social hierarchy of Edo is seen in some interesting conventions regarding maps of the old city (Figure 3.4). To begin with, Edo Castle was, as one might expect, always shown at the center to emphasize its paramount importance. Then there were patterns to the way place-names were fixed on the maps. The ideographs, which are usually arranged vertically in Japanese writing, were made to point in different directions depending on the status of what was being shown. Thus, the names of Shinto shrines and Buddhist temples all point toward the castle because of their higher prestige, while those names that identified ordinary shops and residences were drawn to point away. According to the interpretation by Isoda (1987, p. 60), this was to show that the shogunate was 'sustained by divine

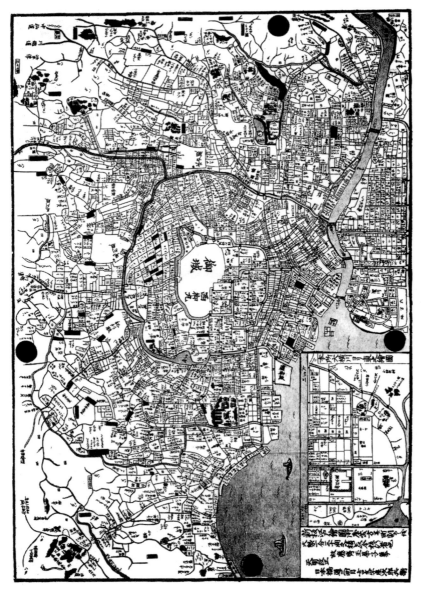

Figure 3.4 Edo in the early nineteenth century. Edo Castle is in the center, written with the name pointing west (toward the top of the map) in the direction of Kyoto. The orientations of other place names and the names of landholders are also strategically arranged. (From a map in the author's personal collection)

protection' by shrines and temples, and that commoners' establishments were required to show their respect by 'bow[ing] their heads' toward the castle rather than pointing their 'feet' (i.e. the last characters of their names) in that direction. Moreover, these maps are always oriented with west at the top and with the characters for 'Edo Castle' written upside down. In this way, the name pointed west toward Kyoto, the imperial capital, 'trampling [it] underfoot . . . as a graphic expression of the tension between the mythic authority and actual power'.

SHITAMACHI

The low city was a world unto itself. Isolated as it was by the strict social and occupational segregation of feudal Japan, it charted an independent course of cultural development. Much has been written about this, a lot of which Waley correctly characterizes as too weighty academically or overly long on sentimentality (1984, p. xxvii). Suffice it to say here that distinctive cultural characteristics were created among the *chōnin* of Edo, Kyoto, and Osaka, and that these varied from city to city as well as between *shitamachi* and the high-crust districts within cities. The differences included manners of speech, styles of dress, forms of entertainment, traditions of cuisine, and if one is to pay attention to the substantial literature that debates details about the subject, even the physical attributes of young women (Takeuchi, M., 1987, p. 51). Moreover, ways of preparing *sushi* varied geographically. The *nigiri-zushi* style, in which the vinegary rice is formed by fingers (as opposed to a press) and the topping (*tane*), usually raw fish, is placed on top, was first developed in Edo in the early nineteenth century and came to be strongly identified with its *shitamachi* area.[2] So too, such popular arts as *kabuki* (theater), *bunraku* (puppet theater), and *rakugo* (storytelling) were also distinctive creations of *shitamachi* that varied in detail from one city to another (Figure 3.5).

The heart of *shitamachi* was an area of reclaimed land known as Nihombashi, or 'Japan bridge'. This was the city's most prosperous merchants' quarter. It stood at the entrance to Ōtemon, the front gate of the castle, and was bisected by the Nihombashi River, an extremely busy canal that linked the city proper with the bay. The bridge that is referred to crossed the canal and became the first focus of commerce in the area. It is most closely tied to a fish market (*uogashi*) that was begun there early in the city's history by Ieyasu to supply the castle's food needs, and that is considered to be the start of commercial enterprise in Edo. The excess catch was sold at the foot of the bridge to the public, initially by a group of 36 fishermen (all from one family named Mori) who had been given license by the shogunate. As the population of Edo expanded, the fish market grew to encompass an ever wider area and more and more stalls, and then to more and more food and non-food products. The rice market (*komegashi*) and lumber market (*mokuzaigashi*) were especially prominent. The bridge, however, was always thought of as the center. In this way, the Nihombashi bridge, which was actually a rather modest wooden span, came to be identified as the *symbolic* starting point for the radial roads that lead out of Edo (i.e. these roads did not actually begin there), and the point from which all distances from the city to other provinces were measured. So

Figure 3.5 *A woodblock print by Utagawa Toyoharu (1735–1814) showing the life of Edo in the vicinity of Ryōgoku Bridge across the Sumida River. (Courtesy of the Freer Gallery of Art, Smithsonian Institution, accession number 03-217-1)*

powerful was the centrality that was attached to this point that even today, a twentieth-century descendant of that first bridge has the same symbolic meanings, while the Nihombashi district in general is still a main commercial area in the heart of the modern CBD.

Other sections of *shitamachi* were craftsmen's quarters. The earliest were at Kyōbashi, also on reclaimed land, to the south of Nihombashi, and Kanda, still further to the north. Each occupational group had its own quarter (*chō*) with its own gate and small guard house, and its own pattern of lanes and alleys, often an idiosyncratic maze. Many of these quarters were set apart by the canals that criss-crossed the city and served as its principal lanes of traffic. It is reported that there were some 1700 such *chō* in early Edo, each with some 300 to 350 residents (Rozman, 1973, p. 169; Yazaki, 1968, pp. 185–6). Many of the place names in central Tokyo today derive from the early occupational *chō*. Ginza (silver guild), Kon'yachō (dyers' quarter) and Kajichō (smiths' quarter) are but three examples.

As Edo grew and prospered, the original townfolks' areas spread out in various directions from the nucleus at Nihombashi. One form of growth was along the highways that led out of the city. Because of the *sankin kōtai* system, the number of travelers was always quite large, and post-stations at the approaches to Edo grew quickly into specialized towns of inns and various other businesses. This accounts for the start of such famous Tokyo districts as Shinjuku on the Kōshūkaidō highway to the west, Shinagawa on the Tōkaidō to the south, and Senju on the Nikko-kaidō to the north. Each of these places also thrived as edge-of-the-city entertainment districts for Edo residents. Other notable expansion of *chōnin* districts took place along the bayfront, where reclamation was continually providing new space for city growth, and in Honjo and Fukagawa across the Sumida River. Trans-Sumida urbanization was accelerated with construction of three bridges, Ryōgoku, Eitaibashi, and Shinohashi, that were completed after a great fire in 1657 to reduce central city residential density and to give Edo residents a route for escape from fires in the future. Fukagawa was to become especially important after 1780 for its lively pleasure quarter. In addition to these areas, there was expansion of *chōnin* wards north of the core along the Sumida. The main center there, a temple district named Asakusa that originated hundreds of years before Edo, developed especially quickly and by the end of the eighteenth century came to rival Nihombashi as the focus of *shitamachi* cultural life and innovation.

The fires of *shitamachi* deserve special mention. They were a chronic problem, as well as a defining characteristic of the city's life and culture. According to American anthropologist William W. Kelly (1994, p. 311), fires were such a common sight in Edo that a distinctive vocabulary developed to refer to them. One of the most common terms for the fires was *Edo no hana*, the 'flowers of Edo'. The word *hanabi*, meaning 'flower-fires', was also used. It is the modern Japanese word for fireworks. The city's fires were also referred to with the word *momiji*, comparing them to the bright colors of autumn maple leaves.

There were approximately 1800 fires in the city during the time of the Tokugawa shoguns (1603–1867), as well as many more that occurred later. By another measure, there were approximately 100 *major* conflagrations in the city during the Tokugawa period, and inhabitants of any one of the crowded towns-people's quarters would consider it unusual if they were not chased by fire from their homes at least once in any two-year period. The hazard was especially great because houses were made of wood and, at least in the early years, their roofs were of straw. Even Edo Castle was not immune from the destruction; it suffered at least eight large fires during the Tokugawa period. The largest of Edo's fires was the Great Meireki Fire, the 1657 fire referred to above. It started at one of the city's many temples, consumed completely nearly all the neighborhoods of *shitamachi*, most of Edo Castle, including its innermost keep, and took 100 000 lives, fully one-quarter of the city's population. The bridge at Nihombashi, at the very heart of the commercial downtown, was also consumed in the 1657 blaze – the first of ten times it burned during the Tokugawa period (Kelly, 1994, p. 313).

YAMANOTE

In contrast to the crowded plebian flatlands of *shitamachi*, members of the military classes kept their mansions on the higher ground of *yamanote*. In the case of *daimyō*, these were second or third mansions, to complement primary Edo residences close to the castle. Other mansions belonged to the thousands of *samurai* retainers of the shogun. Many of the properties were quite large, reflecting the wealth and prestige of the owners, and the whole area was generally thinly settled. The land was hilly and green most of the year with vegetation, and many of the slopes facing the west offered spectacular views of distant mountains and the peak of *Fuji-san*. In the early Tokugawa period (before 1657), the mansions of the wealthiest families were extraordinarily luxurious. But even here there was periodic devastation by fire, and practices were adopted after the Meireki conflagration to build less sumptuous dwellings to reduce losses after they burned down.

The *yamanote* district was also the location of many of Edo's shrines and temples. This was especially so after 1657, when many of these institutions were relocated there, to the outer reaches of the built-up area, as a safety measure because of their deserved reputation as fire hazards. The Meireki Fire, for example, was also known as the *Furisode* (long sleeves) Fire, because it is believed to have been caused by the accidental igniting of a flowing *kimono* during a religious ceremony.[3] The removal of shrines and temples was a great stimulus for development in *yamanote*, both because their numbers totaled in the hundreds and because of the many thousands of people who were attached to them. Moreover, all the largest temples created important commercial districts at their approaches. It was in this way that such famous sections of Tokyo as Shiba, Azabu, Yotsuya, Hongō, Ueno, and Asakusa, mentioned above, came to be part of Edo's urban sprawl.

YOSHIWARA

One other section of Edo should be mentioned at this point because of its tremendously important role in the social life of the old city. This is the famous pleasure quarter called Yoshiwara. It was established in the early years of the Tokugawa shogunate (1617) as a specially zoned district for prostitution and other entertainment, in part to keep an eye on the men of the city who might have in mind some plot against the shogun (Nouët, 1990, p. 90). The place prospered immediately, and during the eighteenth century became a city apart. It survived for well over 300 years. For most of this time, the number of prostitutes was between 2000 and 3000 and the number of brothels approximately 200. Then, as the merchant class of Edo prospered with the city's growth and found more time and money for diversions, Yoshiwara expanded and the number of prostitutes grew to approximately 4000 in 1790, 5000 in 1800 and 7000 by 1868, the end of the Edo period (Kojiro, 1986, p. 47). The place was finally closed in 1957–8, after falling victim to modern-day legislation that outlaws brothels. By then, however, it had declined greatly from the heyday during Edo.

The original location of Yoshiwara was a marshy area close to Nihombashi.[4] This accounts for the name meaning 'reed plain'. However, since this site was one of the casualties of the conflagration of 1657, a New Yoshiwara ('Shin Yoshiwara') was established shortly thereafter at the city's outskirts. The second site was a paddy field north of Asakusa, in a relatively out-of-the-way place that Edo officials favored because it effectively removed a nuisance from the heart of the city. Brothel owners were happy with the site because they were now allowed to stay open all night. This gave the place the nickname fuyajō, 'place without night'. A small moat was dug around the site to prevent customers from leaving without paying, and to keep the prostitutes from escaping. The latter was not an inconceivable possibility, because most prostitutes were young girls from the countryside who were working involuntarily. In most cases, their services had been sold without consent to brothel owners by impoverished parents (Hane, 1982, pp. 207–17; Longstreet and Longstreet, 1988; Seigle-Segawa, 1993).

Despite the prominence of prostitution in Yoshiwara, it would be wrong to think of the place as simply a large collection of brothels. During Edo, Yoshiwara offered many other diversions as well, and is more correctly remembered for having a broad range of entertainment in a setting of great splendor. Thus, in addition to its leading profession, Yoshiwara was also the refined world of the geisha and the teahouse, and of various new genres of Japanese music, art, and literature. Its cultural role expanded after 1841, when kabuki theater was banished to a nearby section of Asakusa (Surawakachō). As a result, the two areas fed off each other as complementary entertainment centers. That is, great crowds trekked regularly from the city to Asakusa for a performance and then a bit further to Yoshiwara for different types of fun. What is most significant about this is that clients were drawn equally from the samurai classes of yamanote and the merchants of shitamachi. The only requirement for participation was to have enough money to pay the night's tab. Thus, the social mixing that took place at Yoshiwara and Asakusa (as well as at some other pleasure districts) helped to blur the rigid social distinctions of the feudal order. This became one of the key preconditions for the making of modern society.

THE MAKING OF MODERN TOKYO

The modernization of Japan is dated formally to 1868. This is the year that the shogunate fell and feudalism ended officially, and when a new era under restored imperial rule was begun. The main catalyst for change was the unexpected arrival in 1853 in Tokyo Bay near Yokohama of a small fleet of four ships from America under the command of Commodore Matthew Calbraith Perry. This show of force, which represented a sizable fraction of the small US navy, made Japan end its self-imposed, 250-year long isolation from other nations and open its ports to foreign trade and ideas. It also showed to Japanese that their country lagged badly in military and technological development. The shogunate was beginning to weaken by this time anyway, because of internal problems that ranged from a series of famines in 1833–6 to ever greater economic hardship among *daimyō*. The latter problem had been brought on largely by the extravagant financial requirements of the *sankin kōtai* system such as keeping multiple mansions in Edo and at home, and costly processions with large retinues between the capital and the home province. Perry's ships added dramatic evidence from abroad that Japan's feudal order was flawed, and hastened the call for reform.

The new era that began in 1868 is called Meiji. The word means 'enlightened rule', a name that was given posthumously to the Emperor Matsuhito who, at the age of 14, then assumed the throne. He had a long reign until his death in 1912. The revolutionary changes that were in store for Japan under his rule were heralded in the Charter Oath he pledged to his ancestors on 6 April 1868, shortly after becoming emperor. Among other points, the Emperor promised to abolish feudalism and end social distinctions between 'high and low persons', to have a more open government based on public participation, and to advance Japan in all ways by seeking practical knowledge from every part of the world. He was directed to these objectives by powerful reformer-activists, most notably Saigō Takamori, Ōkubo Toshimichi, Itō Hirobumi and others, who set policy in his name and ran the affairs of government all through his era. The specific measures that were instituted included land and tax reform across the country (1873–81), establishment of prefectures with appointed governors in place of *daimyō* domains (1871), the start of universal schooling (1872), replacement of the hereditary *samurai* army with commoner conscripts (1873), and the promulgation of constitutional government (1879).

The impact of the Meiji Era on Tokyo was especially profound. First and foremost, the city was made the imperial capital. This took place in 1868, when the young emperor was carried by palanquin from the traditional palace in Kyoto to the vacated shoguns' castle in Edo. Second, the name Edo was dropped in favor of Tokyo, which means 'eastern capital'. Third, the new government set out to modernize the city physically according to Western lines, and to reshape lifestyles and customs according to ideas borrowed from Western cultures. We shall see that one of the things that emerged from this was a modern downtown or Central Business District (CBD) in the city. Thus, in these ways and many others, the Meiji Era was a period of unprecedented change in Japan. Nowadays it is often romanticized in films and on television, and is generally presented fondly as an extremely exciting time.

The changes in Tokyo were intended to draw attention to the city to make it an especially strong capital. This was to reunify Japan in the wake of fragmentation that had taken place during the dissolution of the Tokugawa Era. Moreover, a certain amount of rebuilding was necessary in the city anyway, because of declines that it had suffered during the tumult of the shogun's undoing. One symptom was a sharp drop in population that took place as soon as the *sankin kōtai* sytem ended in 1862. There had been some 1.3 million residents in the city just before the change, but in the next years as many as 300 000 people left, as *daimyō* returned gladly to their home provinces with their entourages. In doing so, they left behind extensive tracts of vacant land. The city had also suffered considerable damage during the last years of the old order from an unfortunate series of disasters, both natural and cultural. The troubles began with a pair of powerful earthquakes in 1854 and 1855, and were followed by incessant downpours and flooding, and by a deadly epidemic of cholera. Many residents blamed the problems on bad luck from Perry's ships.

The changing face of Tokyo during the Meiji Era is perhaps most clearly recorded in the famous woodblock prints called *ukiyo-e*. These 'pictures of the floating world', which are so popular nowadays both among serious collectors and as reproduction-souvenirs of Japan, often depicted landscapes and showed how people lived and worked (Meech-Pekarik, 1986). Prints of Edo, such as those by the great masters Hokusai and Hiroshige, illustrate a city that is unambiguously pre-modern. The people illustrated in townscapes walk rather than ride, wear traditional clothing, and work at their crafts in time-honored ways. Moreover, the city is seen to be a place of water, especially in *shitamachi*. Everywhere there are rivers and canals. In many prints these are shown to carry the city's commerce. In addition, the people are often shown to be either in boats or clustered at riverbanks or on bridges. We saw this in Figure 3.5. The buildings of the city are almost always small, low-slung, made of wood, and generally unimpressive (Lane, 1978).

All this changed during Meiji. We see this in prints such as those of the 1870s–1880s by Hiroshige III (a student of Hiroshige), Yoshitora, and Kiyochika. They show a city based on streets and wheeled traffic, and with such evidences of modern life as pedestrians in Western dress, multi-story banks and hotels, brick-faced shopping streets, gas illumination, and steam trains loading up in crowded stations. In some prints there are factories run by powerful machines. While these prints also showed that important bits and pieces of Edo still remained, for the most part they exhibited a new-style downtown in the place of old *shitamachi*, and a cosmopolitan air where the constricted world of the shoguns once dominated. Edward Seidensticker, who is without question the leading chronicler of Tokyo in English, has pointed out an interesting convention in many Meiji woodcuts regarding the changeover from a city of rivers and canals to one of streets on *terra firma*: 'When bridges are shown, as they frequently are, the roadway is generally an exuberant mixture of the new and the traditional, the imported and the domestic; on the waters below there is seldom a trace of the new and imported' (1983, p. 53).

A favorite example of a Meiji woodcut of Tokyo is a triptych of the main street in Ginza in December 1874 by Utagawa Hiroshige III (Figure 3.6). It is called 'A Scenic View of Tokyo Enlightenment' (*Tōkyō kaika meisho*), and emphasizes in all of its aspects the great changes that had recently come to the city. The focus is the crowds on the street and on the Kyōbashi Bridge over one of the remaining waterways. Little is seen of the river, and there is certainly no important activity

Figure 3.6 'A Scenic View of Tokyo Enlightenment'. This is a woodcut by Utagawa Hiroshige III from 1874, showing the bridge at Kyōbashi and the new brick and stone shops along the main street of Ginza. (Courtesy of the Kanagawa Prefecture Museum)

there. But on the bridge above, one sees a big omnibus filled with passengers and pulled by horses, rickshaws pulled by clothed men (pullers were mostly naked before 'enlightenment'), and numerous stylish pedestrians, some in Western and some in Japanese garb. Moreover, there are gas lamps on the bridge to illuminate the scene. The street itself, which is lined with cherry trees in bloom, is paved and has sidewalks. On both sides there are newfangled buildings made of brick and appointed with columns. There are also verandas, sash windows, and other imported touches. As opposed to the mixed land-use patterns of the past, this is clearly a new type of urban district. It is commercial-only in use, and the people there have evidently come, as commuters, from neighborhoods elsewhere. The only thing that is not new and unfamiliar is Mount Fuji, placed in the background by the printmaker to give orientation and stability to the scene (Meech-Pekarik, 1986, pp. 92–4).

The Making of a CBD

The street depicted in 'A Scenic View of Tokyo Enlightenment' was but one part of a major restructuring of the old city during the Meiji period. Many other changes were seen nearby, in a broad area of *shitamachi* extending from the foot of the castle down to the waterfront at Tokyo Bay, and that had at its center this Ginza street, the merchants' quarters at Nihombashi, the craftsmens' neighborhood at Kyōbashi, and other plebian areas of Edo's core. This is the area that, in general, became the modern downtown or CBD of the city during Meiji, and that is still the city's principal business district. The transition was effected in pieces during different years and at various specific sites, and is attributed to a combination of planning or direction from central government, numerous independent actions by private entrepreneurs who saw new opportunities in the center of the city to make a fortune, and significant advice and architectural assistance from the growing numbers of Europeans and Americans who had arrived in Tokyo to teach just about everything.

Many of the first changes were seen in the area around the castle. This was where the reorganization of government took place and where the new government center of Japan evolved. The first step was the emperor's takeover of the shogun's castle as the new Imperial Palace. Because it was said that the emperor did not require such elaborate defenses, some parts of the castle fortifications were dismantled and the stones were used to build bridges (Seidensticker, 1983, p. 25). Second, the *daimyō* tracts immediately to the south of the castle that had been vacated with the abolition of *sankin kōtai* were claimed by the military for barracks and parade grounds, and then by various agencies of government as sites for offices. The first were the Foreign Ministry (*Gaimushō*) and Finance Ministry (*Ōkurashō*) in 1869. Others, such as the Education Ministry (*Mombushō*), followed soon thereafter when the cabinet system of government was adopted. Eventually, almost all of Nagatachō and Kasumigaseki were given to government functions. This role was cemented in 1890 when the first Diet Building was erected there on a low hill. The only tract that was used differently was a *daimyō* estate turned parade ground in Kasumigaseki that was opened in 1903 as Japan's first Western-style park. This is Hibiya Park, which has formal gardens, a large fountain, indoor and outdoor concert facilities, and some sports facilities and playgrounds, and that serves still as a buffer between the government section and areas of the downtown that are given to commercial offices and shops.

A second focus of change was a district on Tokyo Bay east of the Palace known as Tsukiji. This is an area of reclaimed land that, like areas adjacent to the castle, also had been private residences of feudal lords. It was rebuilt after the city's opening to be a protected settlement for foreigners. The start of construction dates back to the last years of the shogunate and was a response by the old order to demands by foreign powers for extraterritoriality, but its inhabitation by foreigners actually coincided with the first year of Meiji. One of the principal landmarks was the Tsukiji Hoterukan. This was a large hotel completed in 1868 just across a canal from the main part of the foreigners' quarter. It stood out because of design. It was a striking brick building that combined curious Western accretions on a traditional Japanese timber-frame base. In doing so, it reflected the nation's awkward first encounters with the world beyond Japan. Even the word *hoterukan* was a strange new blend: the first syllables correspond to the Japanese pronunciation of 'hotel', while *kan* is based on the Japanese for 'inn'.

Another important landmark in the Tsukiji area was a place called New Shimabara. This was a pleasure quarter named after a district of the same type in Kyoto. It was staffed with close to 2000 prostitutes (including 21 males), and was intended in large part to entertain foreign diplomats who would negotiate political issues with Japan. However, it was not a particularly successful place, as the foreigners were said to come in considerable numbers to look but not to play (Seidensticker, 1983, pp. 38–9). Nevertheless, Tsukiji remained the principal residential district for foreigners until 1900, when the Unequal Treaties that so rankled the Japanese were revised and restrictions on foreigners' movements were relaxed.

Very little remains of the old foreigners' settlement. The Hoterukan had an especially short history, because it was destroyed by fire in 1872, while New Shimabara was closed a short time later because it was a financial disaster. In fact, the only surviving institutions from when Tsukiji was a foreigners' enclave are places started by missionaries: a hospital (St Luke's) which is still at its original site (now in a stunning, post-modernist high-rise), and a university (Rikkyō or St Paul's) which has since moved to a new location (Seidensticker, 1983, pp. 36–42). Nowadays, Tsukiji is most famous for the huge wholesale fish market that occupies a large corner of the area (but not the precise spot of the historic settlement), and for a mixture of edge-of-the-CBD land uses such as other wholesaling, various company offices, miscellaneous institutions and residences.

A tremendous fire swept through much of *shitamachi* in late February 1872. It broke out within the old castle compound at the headquarters of the Army Department, and was fanned eastward to the bay by high winds, consuming nearly 100 hectares of the heart of the city. The Hoterukan was among the several thousands of buildings destroyed. Because one of the worst-hit areas was a modest commercial quarter called Ginza (after a silver mint established there as far back as 1612), this fire is generally referred to as the Ginza Fire, or the Great Ginza Fire. Like the Meireki Fire, this was one of a long string of conflagrations that had plagued the city throughout its history, and would not be particularly well remembered today except for what followed. As Waley has pointed out, many of the new leaders of Japan during early Meiji had recently come to Tokyo from distant provinces, and were shocked to see the waste and destruction that the city's frequent fires engendered (Waley, 1988b, p. 5). Therefore, they were determined to make the city safer, and used the opportunity of this disaster to begin. They were eager to modernize Ginza in particular, because this area had recently gained in strategic importance. It was between Tokyo's fast-developing central business district at Nihombashi on the one side, and its brand new central railway station, completed just prior to the fire, at Shimbashi on the other. This made Ginza a gateway to Tokyo and made a grand project there a logical choice.

What resulted from these efforts is known as the Ginza Brick Quarter (*Gina renga gai*). A part of this area was described earlier as the scene of 'Tokyo Enlightenment' illustrated in the woodcut by Hiroshige III. The Brick Quarter was designed by the English architect Thomas Waters. He was retained by the governor of Tokyo to fireproof the district and make it a showpiece that would impress foreigners (Smith, 1978, p. 54). Construction took nearly a decade and was extravagantly expensive. However, when it was finished, there were over a thousand brick buildings there and in adjoining sections of Kyōbashi Ward. This compared to fewer than twenty in the rest of the city (Seidensticker, 1983, p. 59). As the Hiroshige III print shows, many structures were two-story brick buildings with colonnades and balconies. The gaslights were the country's first. Furthermore, the streets were lined with maples and willows in addition to the cherry trees, and pine trees were planted at the corners.

It should have been very beautiful. Hiroshige III showed it to be so, but this is, in part, because he chose to omit the many problems that characterized this development in its early years. The other side of the story is described in a captivating paragraph by Waley about the Ginza Brick Quarter's growing pains. He relates that all the trees except the willows withered and died, homes were badly built and became damp and dangerous, lizards and centipedes multiplied and infested everything, and human residents became ill with dropsy. As a result, many houses were soon abandoned, only to be invaded later by 'acrobats, jugglers and other itinerant entertainers – including dancing dogs and wrestling bears' (Waley, 1984, p. 89). Even worse, according to eyewitness recollections recorded by Shibusawa, 'second and third-rate houses were turned into private schools by English teacher(s)' (Shibusawa, 1958, pp. 110–11). All of this prompted authorities to introduce special subsidies to attract residents back. Eventually, in the 1880s, Ginza got back on track, as businesses took advantage of inducements to open there, geisha houses returned from temporary exile after the fire, and its central location began to work more strongly in the district's favor.

But even as the Brick Quarter was experiencing its string of troubles, other parts of Ginza, as well as its northern neighbors Kyōbashi and Nihombashi, were recovering quickly from the fire (or had been spared the devastation altogether), and were paving the way for a massive expansion of Tokyo as a commercial center. The leaders in this were the great financial houses that had been built by lending money to *daimyō* and selling consumer goods. The richest of the entrepreneurs came from the Mitsui family. Their wealth came largely from a dry goods store called Echigoya that was opened in Edo in 1673, and from profits taken in the performance of banking services for the shogun between Kyoto, Osaka, and Edo. During Meiji, this family became a stalwart financial backer of the government. In the course of introducing Western banking to Japan, the Mitsuis erected a massive, exotic-looking bank building in Nihombashi in 1872–3. This was soon appropriated by government as the First National Bank and became the nucleus of a financial district that developed soon thereafter in western Nihombashi and then spread to Marunouchi, an adjacent area closer to the Palace. This district's distinction as financial nucleus was cemented in 1882 with the opening there of the huge Bank of Japan, the nation's central bank and highest-order lending institution.

Echigoya, meanwhile, continued to prosper and evolved by the early twentieth century into Mitsukoshi, the first of Japan's great department stores. In many ways, it was an imitation of the American store Wanamaker's, and drew crowds by presenting culture and entertainment as well as merchandise (Seidensticker, 1983, p. 111). Other department stores appeared nearby soon thereafter. The second was Shirokiya, located just across a short bridge from Mitsukoshi, in the direction of Ginza. It too evolved on the foundations of an old Edo shop, this one dating back to 1663. Afterwards, other department stores opened, also in the direction of Ginza. These included Maruzen, Takashimaya and Ginza Mitsukoshi. The result is that a big part of the Nihombashi-Kyōbashi-Ginza area, including the territory of the Ginza Brick Quarter, became a large-scale retailing district.

There were many other examples in Meiji Tokyo of Western influence in the landscape. Another of the most memorable was the Rokumeikan, an elaborate hotel and gathering place completed in 1883 in the Hibiya section close to the government center. It was the work of another English architect, Josiah Conder, who was brought to Japan in 1877 at the request of the Ministry of Technology. He contributed immensely to the shaping of modern Tokyo by designing numerous striking buildings, and by training a whole generation of Japanese architects. Like the Hoterukan, the Rokumeikan was an unusual structure. It was covered with stucco, and combined Moorish, Mediterranean, and other European styles. Conceived by foreign minister Inoue Kaoru, it was commissioned by the Japanese government to be a place where cosmopolitan citizens could mix with foreigners. During its heyday in the middle and late 1880s, the building hosted countless elegant balls, formal dinners, musical performances, charity bazaars, and other Western-style 'high society' events. It was in this context that Shirokiya, the department store, came to specialize in Western-fashion women's apparel, and imported 'a certain Miss Curtis from Great Britain' to supervise its displays (Yazaki, 1968, p. 341).

This short-lived period is called the Rokumeikan Era. It is remembered fondly for its great splendor, and is often illustrated in films and television dramas that romanticize Japan's first successful experiences with Western ways. For the Meiji government, the purpose of having all of this was to demonstrate to foreigners that the Japanese were civilized and enlightened, and to convince the foreign powers with whom Japan had been forced to sign unequal commercial treaties in the 1850s and 1860s (the United States, Britain, the Netherlands, France, and Russia) that they should renegotiate. When the government failed at this, the Rokumeikan lost its popularity and began a decline that culminated in the razing of the building in 1941 (Barr, 1968, pp. 12–13 and 179–80; Seidensticker, 1983, pp. 68–70 and 97–100).

Figure 3.7 *Mitsubishi Londontown (today's Marunouchi area) in the early twentieth century. (Source: Tokyo Metropolitan Government.)* © Tokyo Metropolitan Government

Another important example of how Japan's response to the West was seen in the built form of Tokyo was the development of a new district that came to be called Mitsubishi Londontown (Figure 3.7). As the name suggests, it was a Japanese imitation of the British capital. Josiah Conder had a large hand in this too, as did some of his students and other designers. Its main features were four-story, red-brick buildings that were vaguely reminiscent of Victorian Kensington. However, Waley's observations of photographs from the period conclude that the development lacked 'the architectural conviction and spontaneity that grows out of native soil', and that it revealed a 'pronounced sense of disconsonance'. Instead of trolleys and carriages, the streets were served by rickshaws, and passers-by must have been completely disoriented (Waley, 1984, p. 33).

In contrast to the Rokumeikan and the Ginza Brick Quarter, which were projects by the government, Londontown was a creation of a private, family-owned business called the Mitsubishi Company. It was controlled by the powerful Iwasaki family, who conceived this plan purely and simply as a way to reap huge profits at real estate development. The land was immediately south of the Imperial Palace, very close to the main gate, and for many years was the preserve of top *daimyō*. It was vacated with the fall of the shogunate and, except for use as a parade ground for the army and some barracks, stood empty for nearly a quarter-century after the start of Meiji. For reasons that make little sense now, when we have the advantage of hindsight, the government was unable to make good use of the land, and sold it in 1890 to the Iwasakis for little more than a pittance (1.25 million yen). Citizens referred to the purchase as the Mitsubishi Wasteland, and wondered what good could be put there. The Iwasakis joked that they might plant bamboo and introduce tigers (Waley, 1984, p. 32). Instead, they undertook to develop an office-commercial center that not only housed their headquarters (in a building by Conder) but also the offices of many other companies to whom the Iwasakis rented space in other structures. The project covered several streets and was the largest private development in Japan up to that time.

Even so, there were many vacant lots that remained in the 'wasteland' until after 1914, the year when Tokyo Railway Station was opened adjacent to this development. The Iwasakis had arranged for its principal entrance to face their way rather than toward Nihombashi, and thus assured for themselves and all the Mitsubishi business concerns a central place in the life of Tokyo ever after. There is nothing that is left of the original architecture of Londontown today. However, the area is still the principal office center of Tokyo, and the Mitsubishi Company, now a gigantic corporate concern that is famous world-round, is still a major landowner. The separate headquarters buildings for each of the several companies that make up its 'family of companies' are scattered across the district and are especially prominent. The present name for the district is Marunouchi, a name that means 'within the circle of moats', but that in practice suggests a secure position within the inner circle of power in both the city and the Japanese nation at large.

THE RISE OF YOKOHAMA

The Meiji period was also the time when Yokohama became an important city. All through the Tokugawa centuries, it was nothing more than a poor fishing village on a muddy salt-flat, and was hardly known outside the immediate area, even in Edo. Probably it was because the place was so inconspicuous that the shogunate selected it as the site for discreet negotiations with Commodore Perry, which in turn put the village on the map. The negotiations concluded with the signing of the 1854 Treaty of Kanagawa under a large camphor tree on a lonely beach, and opened three ports for foreign trade: Nagasaki on the northwestern coast of Kyūshū island; Shimoda in the central Honshū coast; and Hakodate on the coast of southwestern Hokkaidō. A fourth international port, Kanagawa, an old post-station town on Edo Bay south of the capital, was designated in a second unequal treaty negotiated in 1858 by US ambassador Townsend Harris. Its attraction for the American was its location at the doorstep to Edo. However, the shogunate worried that the foreigners might gain extra advantage from Kanagawa because it was on the Tōkaidō, the busy Edo-to-Kyoto highway, as well as Edo Bay, while foreign ship captains complained that the waters off Kanagawa were too shallow. Consequently, Yokohama, the quiet fishing village nearby, was named as a replacement. Its new status was proclaimed officially on 2 June 1859, when Ii Naosuke, a minister of the shogun's weakening government, opened the port and directed that streets be laid out to transform the village into a city.

Yokohama grew quickly from that beginning. It was Japan's first window to learning from other countries, and the scene of commercial and cultural exchanges for years to come. As with other Asian treaty ports, the city was divided into discrete parts, one for foreigners and the other for locals. 'Kannai', meaning 'within the barrier', was a rectangular area in which foreigners were confined, while 'Kangai' ('outside the barrier') was its mirror image and was assigned to Japanese.

The two were separated by a broad avenue, Nihonōdōri, but shared a common park graced with cherry trees. The British and American consulates stood on one side of Nihonōdōri, facing Japanese government buildings and the customs house on the other side. Canals were dug through both halves of the city to drain the marshes. In the early years, guards were stationed at bridges to keep watch over foreigners' movements.

We know a lot about the look of early Yokohama because of the work of *ukiyo-e* artists who mapped the city and illustrated its buildings and commerce. The artists also documented the arrival in Japan of Western ways, that ranged from fashions to foods, and from to machines to musical instruments. Possibly the most skilled of the artists was Sadahide (1807–ca1878). He is known for his panoramic portraits of Yokohama, showing minute details about spatial relationships in the city's layout and the appearance of individual buildings. For example, his 'Complete Picture of the Newly Opened Port of Yokohama', completed in the winter of 1859–60 before the city was barely a year old, shows a busy harbor with ocean-going ships of several flags, two substantial wharves near the foot of Nihinōdōri, and lines of trading firm offices and warehouses along and behind the Bund, the waterfront street. The early print also shows Miyozakichō, a pleasure quarter similar to Tokyo's Yoshiwara, that had been laid out across a canal in a vacant area beyond the city's edge. Later portraits, sometimes created after recarving or replacing certain portions of the original print-block, documented new details as they evolved. A high-crust foreigners' section developed along the waterfront where the Grand Hotel and the private Yokohama United Club (men only) were social anchors, while on blocks further from the shore there was a growing Chinatown and dubious areas called 'The Swamp' and 'Blood Town' that were crowded with sailors' bars. As the city outgrew its boundaries, the Japanese expanded to the north across Yoshidabashi, the first steel bridge in the country, to areas called Isezakichō and Nogeyama, while the growing number of foreign diplomats, traders, educators and missionaries developed a community of fine Western homes, churches, schools and other institutions, including 'a dozen tennis courts run with social felicity by the Ladies' Lawn Tennis Club' (Poole, 1968, p. 26), high on a bluff to the south called Yamate, a word essentially the same as Tokyo's Yamanote.

The economy of Yokohama was based on trade. Early imports included cotton and wool textiles, while exports emphasized tea and silk. The silk industry came to be especially prominent, as civil unrest in China and a silkworm blight in the 1870s in France devastated competing economies. Great fortunes were made by both Japanese and foreign entrepreneurs who had made timely investments in the industry. The leader among them was Hara Tomitarō, a Japanese businessman who gained control over much of the export activity and then used his wealth to secure a position for himself at the top of the city's money-minded hierarchy. Sankeien, the estate that he left the city in 1906, includes a marvelous garden that is now perhaps Yokohama's premier visitor attraction. Other marks of a boomtown economy are Japan's first railroad line (the one to downtown Tokyo mentioned earlier) and first gaslights (both in 1872), first modern waterworks (1887), and first electric lights (1890). It was not until the 1920s, when nylon began its ascendancy, and when a great earthquake occurred in the Kantō region, that Yokohama's silk-based fortunes would be shaken.

INDUSTRY AND NEIGHBORHOODS

The Meiji period is also the time when Tokyo began its modern industrial development. There had always been industry in the city before, if only because of the great demand for manufactured products its huge population continually generated, but it was small in scale and traditional in organization and level of technology. It is said that the only large industrial site during Edo was the Ishikawajima Shipbuilding Yard built in 1849 by the Mito family in the northern part of Tsukishima, an island of reclaimed land that is close to the city center. Consequently, as late as 1874 the city ranked no higher than ninth in Japan in industrial production, and had an output of manufactured products that was barely one-quarter that of the leading city, Kyoto (Itakura and Takeuchi, 1980, p. 51).

All this began to change with the onset of the Meiji reforms, as both the number of factories and the scale of operations, as well as the variety of products made in the city, were greatly increased. While the new government also invested heavily in the industrial development of other cities and numerous rural locations (e.g. the fishing village of Yahata, now part of the Kitakyūshū urban agglomeration, where a giant state-owned steel mill was built), there was considerable favoritism that was extended to the capital (Smith T.C., 1973; Allinson, 1975, 1978). This is seen in the examples of several model factories that were built by the government in various sections of Tokyo and that employed imported technical advisors and equipment: a paper processing plant in Ōji; a cement factory in Fukagawa; a glass plant in Shinagawa; a huge spinning mill in Senju; and the Government Printing Bureau in Takinogawa (Yazaki, 1968, p. 352). As a result of such construction, and because of investment in factory production that followed, Tokyo was transformed quickly into a paramount concentration of heavy industry. This was so much so that by the time of the pre-war industrial build-up of the 1930s, the city ranked as far and away the number-one manufacturing center in Japan.

We can identify several reasons why there was especially heavy investment in industry in Tokyo in particular. As was the case with the Rokumeikan and the Ginza Brick Quarter, new factory technology was, in part, another front along which the new government endeavored to make Tokyo into a showpiece city. The goal was to impress foreigners and Japanese alike with the city's modernity, and to demonstrate that Japan could keep pace with the fashions and useful technologies that were advancing in other countries. Second, as the headquarters of nearly all of the most powerful private financial enterprises in Japan such as the Mitsui and Mitsubishi *zaibatsu*,[5] the city had the largest concentration of investment capital in the country and was a natural location for spending. So, too, the city was made into the nation's leading center of higher education, with Japan's Imperial University (now named Tokyo University), founded in 1877, being given the lead in studying foreign technologies and advancing industrial know-how in Japan. Finally, we can point to some geographical advantages of the city: its good harbor, urban rivers and ample flat land, the undeveloped space in the surrounding Kantō Plain for urban expansion, and the intermediate situation of the city within Japan between the established population centers to the west and frontier lands in the northern Honshū and in Hokkaidō.

The first 'industrial revolution' neighborhood of Tokyo was the section of *shitamachi* that was at the lower reaches of the Sumida. Now part of an oversized

CBD, this area had previously been a concentration of traditional crafts such as carpenters, plasterers, barrel-makers, stonemasons, metalworkers, tailors, roofers, and others. In early Meiji, it changed to embrace various new industries such as the making of shoes and clogs, carts, rickshaws, bricks, roofing tiles, Western-style clothing, and, before long, electric motors (Yazaki, 1968, p. 353). Almost all these enterprises involved larger production facilities than the previously dominant 'home shops'. Many of their products were put on display at an Industrial Exhibition that opened under government sponsorship in 1878 in Ueno both to disseminate information about latest technologies and to enlarge the domestic market for new products. As industry expanded, more factories were built further upstream along the Sumida, in the deltaic flatland between the Sumida and Ara Rivers that is today's Sumida and Kōtō Wards, as well as along the banks of the Arakawa itself. The Senju district was especially important. It became a major industrial rail corridor, and included among other notable plants the Senju Spinning Mill (1879) with as many as 25 000 employees by the turn of the century (a record size for the city), the Tokyo Cardboard Company (1886), the Senju Mill of the Ōji Paper Company (1888), and a large facility of the Tokyo Gas Company (1893) (Yazaki, 1968, p. 351).

A second important industrial area developed in the 1890s to 1910 period along the Tokyo Bay waterfront. It is called Keihin, a word that can be translated as 'metropolitan harbor'; it is written in Chinese characters that combine pieces of the words 'Tokyo' and 'Yokohama'. The area stretches along a reclaimed shoreline between these two cities for approximately 40 kilometers. In contrast to eastern Tokyo (i.e. the Sumida River area), Keihin was (and still is) particularly oriented to heavy industries that require imported raw materials. The most notable examples include steel milling, machinery manufacture, and various kinds of chemical industries. The sizable heavy industrial city of Kawasaki (see Table 2.6), developed in the early part of the present century on the site of a highway station town between Shinagawa and Yokohama near the mouth of the Tama River in what is now Kanagawa Prefecture, is near the center of this belt and represents its industrial character. Some of the most important large industrial facilities there were the Kawasaki Salt Plant built in 1907, Tokyo Electric Company, Nihon Gramophone Company, Meiji Sugar Company, Nihon Steel Tube Company, and the Tokyo Wire Company (Yazaki, 1968, pp. 465–66).

One of the key factors in the rapid rise of Keihin as an industrial region is the excellent harbor at Yokohama. The port facilities for foreign trade that were opened there shortly after the 1858 Harris Treaty were enlarged and improved again and again during the Meiji period, with the result that Yokohama developed as the nation's preeminent deepwater port. The Keihin area also benefited from the opening of a shipping canal in 1910 between Tokyo and Yokohama, as well as from a dense network of rail connections between docking facilities and the industrial precincts of Tokyo's waterfront. So, too, rail lines were extended inland from Yokohama to new industrial centers in the Tama region of Tokyo such as Tachikawa, Fuchū, and Fussa. The growth of these centers was especially intense later, well after the Meiji period during the industrial build-up of the 1920s and 1930s. Because of outstanding infrastructure, and because it is part of such a huge concentration of population, Keihin continues to be one of the biggest centers of industrial production in Japan.

As in other cities, industrialization had profound impacts on urban population growth and on neighborhoods. Tokyo, always a crowded city, swelled like never before in the last decades of the nineteenth century and early twentieth, expanding rapidly in all directions. It more than recovered the population losses that had taken place earlier when *sankin kōtai* ended, and grew in numbers to record proportions by the early twentieth century. From an estimated less than 500 000 inhabitants in the 1860s–1870s, the city reached 1 million by the 1890s, a second million by 1907, and more than 3 million by 1920 (Ishizuka and Ishida, 1988, p. 14; Smith, 1979, pp. 50–51). The main reason was a massive influx of young migrants who poured in from a poor and overcrowded countryside to seek work. This was the case even though there was also considerable rural-based industrialization during this time in Japan, a fact that provided local factory employment opportunities in some regions and kept overall rates of urban growth slower than, say, in the United States (Allinson, 1978, p. 449). Thus, Tokyo (and, to a lesser extent, Osaka) was an unusually powerful magnet for migrants from the countryside. In 1907, for example, perhaps the height of the industrialization–urbanization process, fully one-half of the city's 2 million residents were arrivals from outside (Ishizuka and Ishida, 1988, p. 14).

The physical expression of this influx was new neighborhoods at the city's edge, radial expansion of the city along highways and rail corridors that extended beyond built-up limits, and enormous increases in density in existing districts. Some neighborhoods became especially overcrowded, degenerating into unsanitary slums. This was especially true for several of the neighborhoods that had sprung up amidst the factories along the east bank of the Sumida. However, the worst conditions were said to be in three neighborhoods that were famous during the Edo period as government dumping grounds for freed convicts, beggars, drifters and Japan's 'untouchable classes', the so-called *eta* and *hinin*: Yotsuya Samegabashi to the west of the city center; Shiba Shin'amichō to the south; and Shitaya Man'nenchō to the north (Taira, 1969, p. 157). During Meiji, these 'three great ghettoes' (*sandai hinminkutsu*) became refuges for the most destitute migrants to the city, and for thousands of city residents who were unemployed or seriously underemployed as 'trifling craftsmen', occasional construction workers, or street performers (Ishizuka and Ishida, 1988, p. 14).

The literary response to the living conditions of industrial era slums in Tokyo was not as strong it was in the West where, for example, Dickens, Engels, Booth, and Mayhew wrote passionately about the dark underside of English cities. There were, however, several notable journalistic exposés, including the books *Poverty: An Exploration of the Cave of Hunger and Cold* by Sakurada Bungo (1893) and *In Darkest Tokyo* by Matsubara Iwagoro (1893). The most important of these studies was by Yokoyama Gennosuke (1871–1915), published in 1899 with supporting statistics as *Nihon no kaso shakai* ('Japan's lower classes') and then reprinted in 1949 and 1958. It was a classic study of the three worst neighborhoods in Tokyo (Smith, 1979, pp. 85–6). The author is said to have been so shocked by what he encountered in each of these districts that he claimed to 'rub his eyes twice' to make sure that he wasn't seeing things (Taira, 1969, p. 157). Thousands of people were jammed into dilapidated tenements called *nagaya* that extended back in long rows from narrow, unpaved alleys. The rooms, allocated one per large family, were tiny and measured only four and a half or six *tatami* mats in total (approximately 9 × 9 or 9 × 12 feet, respectively) (Yazaki, 1968, p. 366). Toilets, actually privies, were shared, and there was no water except for polluted communal wells. What is more, all three areas were infested by flies, rats and other pests, and suffered deadly epidemics of cholera, tuberculosis and other diseases. In the fashion of the Meiji period, when things Western were so quickly adopted in Japan, these neighborhoods, previously referred to as *hinminkutsu* ('caves of the poor people'), came to be called *suramu*, a modern addition to the Japanese language that was derived from a pronunciation of the word 'slum' (Smith, 1979, p. 86).

BEFORE THE CATACLYSM

In addition to the slums, there were many other urban problems in Tokyo during the years immediately before and after the turn of the century. Some of the others included a great flood in 1910 that covered the whole northern part of *shitamachi*, angry riots in 1918 over the high price of rice, and severe overcrowding and environmental degradation in just about every section of the metropolitan area. There were especially urgent problems regarding waste disposal. As Seidensticker described it regarding the sewage problem, Tokyo had become so large by late Meiji that distances between the center of the city and farms on the urban periphery exceeded the daily ranges of the all-important night-soil carts that had always made their scheduled rounds. This meant that houses and businesses in the center found that they could no longer sell their excrement, even if it was the more highly prized product of wealthy individuals with nutritious diets, and instead had to pay to have it hauled away, often, it turned out, by contractors who would simply dump the loads somewhere else in the city. There were similar problems with garbage disposal. Because household waste material accumulated too quickly to be carted away, Tokyo developed a pervasive bad smell from the burning carried out within city limits (Seidensticker, 1983, pp. 282–3).

However, despite such drawbacks, the last decades of Meiji and all but the last years of the short reign (1912–26) of the next emperor, the Taishō Emperor, were generally a high period in the life of Tokyo. Until the crash that came suddenly on the first day of September in 1923, the city quickly grew in population, profited from two war booms during which industrial production was greatly expanded, and invested heavily in new urban infrastructure that ranged from a dense network of commuter train and electric trolley lines, to ambitious flood-control projects along the Sumida, to increasing numbers of large, Western-style office structures, called *biru* after 1917 because of pronunciation of the loan word 'building', in an ever more impressive downtown. A major symbol of the times was the opening in 1914 of Tokyo Station, the new central station for the city that replaced the one at Shimbashi. In keeping with the craze for things borrowed, it was patterned in design after the main station in Amsterdam. Other highlights of the period included numerous new opportunities for public entertainment, new technologies such as electric lights, elevators, and telephones, new fashions in dress and other endeavors, and a brief period of societal openness and political reform during the First World War that is called the 'Taishō Democracy'.

Table 3.2   Specialty Stores in Ginza, 1910

Name of store	Specialties
Aoki kutsu-kabanten	Shoes and briefcases
Itōya bunbōguten	Stationery and office supplies
Jūjiya gakkiten	Musical instruments
Tamaya tokeiten	Watches and clocks
Kinararō ganguten	Toys
Satō hōshokuten	Jewelry
Kondo shoten	Books
Panya Kimura sōhōnten	Bread and cakes
Kyōbunkan shoseikan	Books, including Christian books
Mikimoto shinjuten	Cultured pearls
Yamano gakkiten	Musical instruments
Kurimoto undōguten	Sporting goods
Café Lion	Coffee house and restaurant
Sekiguchi yōhinten	Haberdashery
Sano tabiten	Japanese socks
Daimaruya goofuukuten	Dry goods
Shogetsu yōshōkuten	Western-style restaurant
Café Tiger	Coffee house and restaurant
Mazuda Lamp Ginzaten	Electrical lighting equipment
Morinaga Candy Store	Confections
Kikusui nagai tabakoten	Pipe and tobacco supplies
Takahashi stekkiten	Walking sticks

Source: Yazaki (1968, p. 441).

Two districts in Tokyo were especially revealing of the times. One was Ginza, far and away the most modern and most Westernized section of the city. The other was Asakusa. The former was famous for its department stores and its many new shops selling all the latest in imported goods and new domestic products (Table 3.2), a majestic new *kabuki* theater, and great crowds of *mo-bo* and *mo-ga* ('modern boys' and 'modern girls'), many of them from affluent families in the hilly sections west of the city center, who gathered there. Theirs was the practice called *gim-bura*, 'killing time' or 'strolling in Ginza'. They were attracted equally by the glitter of the main streets and the romance of small side streets lined with sophisticated cafés and trendy shops. The main intersection, now called Ginza Crossing, was especially busy. Its dominant landmark was a big clock that was imported from Switzerland and displayed in a two-story tower atop the Hattori Watch Company building, the predecessor of today's Seiko Corporation (Figure 3.8).[6]

In contrast to Ginza, Asakusa was more of a stronghold of traditions and a gathering place for the ordinary people of the city. In Seidensticker's words, it 'is where the masses went to do what the masses of Edo had been wont to do, find performances to view and thereby ruin themselves' (1983, p. 267). The place continued as a center of *kabuki*, although this was somewhat less the attraction than it was before; it was also a mecca for the popular new motion picture theaters and music houses. There were also plenty of places for roistering and lechering (Seidensticker, 1983, p. 267). The main symbols of Asakusa were its great temple, which remains even today as an unbroken link to the past, and the *Ryōunkaku*, the 'twelve-story pavilion'.[7] Built in 1890, this was Tokyo's first skyscraper and the first

82

Figure 3.8 *The main intersection of Ginza in 1895. The building with the clock tower is the former headquarters of the Hattori Seiko Corporation, the watch company. The site is now the Wako Department Store. Note the congestion of trolley cars and the combination of Western and Japanese dress that pedestrians are wearing. (Courtesy of the Office of Corporate Communications, Seiko Corporation)*

building in Japan to have an elevator (to the eighth floor only). There were shops, theaters, bars and restaurants on every floor, and three observation levels at the top that afforded a splendid view of the city. A marvelous print by Ichiju Kunimasa, showing the full length of the building as well as some fanciful kites, parachutists and balloonists, reflects clearly that it was mainly a pavilion of pleasure (Collcutt, Jansen, and Kumakura, 1988, p. 197). Unfortunately, the good times there would be short-lived, and the tower would soon become identified as one of the most enduring images of a great disaster.

THE GREAT KANTŌ EARTHQUAKE

All the routines that had come to characterize the Tokyo area, as well as several tens of thousands of lives, came to a violent end with the disaster that began precisely 'one minute and fifteen and four-tenths seconds before noon' on the first day of September 1923 (Seidensticker, 1983, p. 3). This was the instant of the sudden mighty jolt of the earth beneath the Kantō Plain, measuring an astonishing 7.8 to 7.9 on the Japanese scale, that is referred as the Great Kantō Earthquake (*Kantō daishinsai*). There was another tremendous shock about 24 hours later and several hundred minor aftershocks in the following days. The epicenter was in

Sagami Bay, southwest of the city close to the opening of Tokyo Bay, and there was extensive damage over a wide area that covered parts of seven prefectures (Tokyo, Kanagawa, Chiba, Ibaraki, Saitama, Yamanashi, and Shizuoka). The Tokyo–Yokohama conurbation was especially badly shaken. The worst damage was in the Kōtō section of Tokyo, between the mouths of the Ara and Sumida rivers, where the soil is very soft alluvium. In this area, nearly 30 percent of all houses were knocked down by one of the two major tremors. Also lost to the quake was the Twelve Stories at Asakusa, which snapped in spectacular fashion just above the eighth floor and tumbled to the street below (Figures 3.9 and 3.10). Among the considerable losses in Yokohama were most of the Western buildings of brick and stone in historic Kannai, the foreigner's settlement (Poole, 1968).

There was even greater destruction from the fires that broke out right after the earthquakes. The noonhour timing was particularly unfortunate, because residents had been tending charcoal or wood fires for cooking; the extreme violence of the first shock scattered embers that ignited numerous houses. The official count has it that 134 separate blazes broke out in Tokyo and then raged out of control for up to three days. The reason that things were so bad was that much of Tokyo (and downtown Yokohama) was, as always in its history, a densely packed tinderbox of wooden buildings, and because flames could be easily fanned by the day's unusually heavy breezes. Fire-fighting and rescue were made especially difficult because many water mains and fire hydrants had been ruptured by the quake, and because communications of all kinds were seriously disrupted. With so much aflame, the air above the city became intensely heated and unstable, which then created firestorms swept by winds of 70 to 80 kilometers per hour. Even worse, several cyclones or tornadoes developed in downtown Tokyo. These were especially deadly, because they were drawn by the presence of oxygen to the same open spaces in the city where much of the populace had sought refuge from the flames. One cyclone passed over the unprotected grounds of the Military Clothing Depot in the Honjo area, across the Sumida River in heavily devastated Sumida Ward, and suffocated approximately 40 000 people. A series of large oil paintings in Cenotaph Hall, a memorial building on the precise site, and a haunting bronze sculpture of children in flight recall this tragedy in gory detail.

It is not possible to know the exact extent of all the damage or the total loss of life. The generally accepted estimates report that, all told, 104 619 people died or were missing as a result of this disaster, and an additional 52 074 were injured. Of the dead and missing, 91 995 were from the densely built-up areas of Tokyo and Yokohama. The statistics also show that 73 percent of the houses in Tokyo were damaged and 63 percent were destroyed completely. Less than one percent of the worst damage was from the tremor itself, as it was fire that brought the most ruin to both the cities. The value of property damage is estimated to have been in the range of several billion yen. Insurance policies generally excluded damage from earthquakes (and the fires they started), so it became the burden of individuals and the government to finance almost all rebuilding (Stanley, 1983, p. 66). However, insurance companies made 'sympathy payments' of some 10 percent of the value of policies to many businesses and households, because government had expressed that the companies had a 'moral obligation' to pay what they could (Busch, 1962, pp. 159–60.)

Figure 3.9 *Remains of the Twelve Stories building in Asakusa after the 1923 Great Kantō Earthquake. (Courtesy of the Asahi Newspaper Company)*

The suddenness of the disaster and its terrible magnitude resulted in considerable confusion among the population in the days that followed. There was some ill-timed disarray in government to begin with, because the prime minister had died unexpectedly just a week before the fateful day. Furthermore, some particularly foul rumors began to circulate among the citizenry. One was that some unnamed

Figure 3.10 *Devastation in central Tokyo after the earthquake and fires of 1 September 1923. (Courtesy of the Asahi Newspaper Company)*

country in the West had developed an earthquake machine and was experimenting on Japan. Fortunately, this idea was contained before any violence was taken against Westerners. However, Korean residents of the city were not so lucky. They were an especially despised minority, mostly because of the long history of conflict between the two nations, and suffered frequent displays of bigotry in Japan on this account (Lee and DeVos, 1981). Soon after the earthquake, completely unfounded reports began to multiply that it was actually Koreans, and not flying embers, who were setting fires throughout the city. Rumors also claimed that Koreans were poisoning water sources. Because police services were badly disrupted, it was difficult to counteract these stories; citizens formed vigilante groups for protection against the supposed malefactors. This led to numerous atrocities and a toll of several thousand Koreans murdered by angry mobs. One method that the mobs used to identify Koreans, who are generally indistinguishable physically from Japanese, was to have suspects pronounce the common Japanese syllabary, '*ba, bi, bu, be, bo*'. When the sounds of b's were given as p's, as Koreans commonly do, the person was marked as a foreigner and was often killed on the spot (Busch, 1962, p. 109). To protect the immigrants, police had to establish a special barracks outside the city to house approximately 10 000 individuals.

REBUILDING THE CITY

The task of rebuilding Tokyo was put in the charge of Gōtō Shimpei (1857–1929), a former mayor of the city and important national political figure. He had long advocated grand plans to redesign Tokyo to make it more modern and efficient; and as mayor had established the Tokyo Institute for Municipal Research to guide him. In keeping with the drive for enlightenment that characterized the times, he was especially interested in learning the latest 'scientific methods' relating to city planning and public administration. His principal advisor on this was an American scholar he had befriended, Charles Austin Beard (1874–1948), who had started a similar institute in New York City. In 1921, after some study and comparison with New York, Gōtō proposed a massive, 800 million yen project for Tokyo that came to be called 'the big kerchief' because it covered so many aspects of the city. Among other improvements, it would pave and widen streets, expand water supply as well as electric and gas services, improve the harbor and other waterways, build parks, schools, municipal buildings, public halls, and other public structures, and provide a wide range of new social services to the citizens. The cost, however, was seen by critics as prohibitive: it was equivalent to nearly one-half of the total *national* budget and more than six times the annual city budget. The plan was never adopted.

The aftermath of the earthquake was a second chance for this rebuilding. An imperial proclamation less than two weeks after the disaster put to rest any ideas that came up among numerous commentators that the capital should be moved to a safer site, and got reconstruction started (Hayase, 1974, p. 195):

> Tokyo is the capital of our imperial nation, and it is the axis for the political and economic life of the nation. It is also the source of the nation's culture, to which all Japanese citizens have to look. Despite the destruction of the city by the unexpected disaster, it has not lost its position as the capital of the nation. We must plan not only for the recovery of the old capital but also for future improvement.

Accordingly, Gōtō, now in command of the 'Board of Reconstruction of the Capital City', sent a telegram to Beard in New York:

> Earthquake fire destroyed greater part of Tokyo. Thoroughgoing reconstruction needed. Please come immediately, even for a short stay.

The response came right back:

> Lay out new streets, forbid building without street lines, unify railway stations. (Hayase, 1974, p. 196).

However, once again the matter of cost got in the way. Because it was estimated that rebuilding Tokyo according to the Gōtō-Beard plan would require a sum that was three times the national budget, politicians began to resist the idea and withheld funds. There was also opposition from some influential landowners, who feared correctly that they stood to lose some of their accumulated holdings for use by public projects. As a result, only a few elements of the total scheme were actually put in: some trunk roads such as Shōwa-dōri and Taishō-dōri; grid-pattern streets in the Kōtō area and in the downtown around Marunouchi; and some new parks (e.g. Hamachō Park on the Sumida River near the downtown business district, and Sumida Park on the riverbank not far from the temple center at Asakusa). Otherwise, Tokyo built itself back up pretty much as it was before. It still looked more like Edo than the attractive sections of New York that urban reformers preferred, and because of the haste of reconstruction, it 'remained outdated, with narrow streets, slum areas, open sewers, and many other urban maladies' (Hayase, 1974, p. 199).

There were, however, some other changes that came to Tokyo after the 1923 disaster that were not necessarily directly a part of the Gōtō-Beard plan. One was an increase in the amount of land given to heavy industry. This was especially the case in the Keihin area, which expanded along the shore of Tokyo Bay from Chiba Prefecture to far south of Yokohama, and in Tokyo's western (i.e. Tama) and northern (Saitama Prefecture) suburbs and outlying towns. A large part of this was related to the build-up of heavy industry in Japan that marked the pre-Second World War period. For example, the growth of armaments-related industries, especially aircraft, had much to do with the rapid growth during the 1930s of Musashino, Tanashi, and Mitaka in the Tama district.

A second change was geographical expansion of the urbanized area not related to industrial expansion. An important stimulus was the earthquake itself which drove survivors to safer ground away from the congested center of the city. So, too, Tokyoites were pushed from the center by reconstruction activity. For example, thousands of households were displaced from older neighborhoods by the straightening and widening of streets that took place in the city during the late 1920s. This was done amidst numerous angry protests and demonstrations by homeowners and businesses who considered themselves to be inadequately compensated for their land (Ishizuka and Ishida, 1988, p. 20). Still another factor behind suburbanization was growth in the city's transportation network. There were new rail lines and highways that made distant lands more accessible and, from 1927, with the opening of a 14-kilometer subway line under the heart of the city (the Ginza Line), unobstructed travel to and through the center of Tokyo itself became possible.

A major beneficiary of post-earthquake urban expansion was Shinjuku, a rail interchange on the west side of the city that exploded in growth to become a major urban nucleus. Some of the department stores from Ginza relocated there immediately after the disaster, as did various other shops and institutions. Furthermore, there was great growth in the after-dark entertainment industry. As a result, by 1930 Shinjuku rivaled Ginza with as many as 200 coffee shops employing some 2000 waitresses and such popular new theaters as Teito-za and the Moulin Rouge (Waley, 1988a, p. 14). The nearby business center of Shibuya was another place that grew quickly after the earthquake (Mitsuoka, 1989). Its advantages included a strategic station on the National Railways line, good connections by road and later by rail to western suburbs and to the center of Yokohama, and (after 1939) status as the western terminus of the Ginza Line.

One of the consequences of suburban growth after the earthquake was that the city's boundaries had to be redrawn. This was done in 1932. Instead of 15 wards covering a small area huddled around the Imperial Palace and the CBD, the limits of Tokyo were enlarged about fivefold when the city annexed 82 adjacent towns and villages in five nearby counties (*gun*). The new territory was reorganized into 20 new wards, bringing the total number of wards to 35. The limits of this area are fairly consistent with what is now thought of as the 'City of Tokyo' (as opposed to today's 'Tokyo Metropolis' or *Tōkyō-to*). However, there was yet another redrawing of boundaries within this zone in 1947, with the result that the 'city' part of Tokyo Metropolis has now only 23 wards.

THE AIR RAIDS OF 1945

No sooner had Tokyo begun to settle back into normal routines than the national leadership led the country to war. This brought on a second disaster, even more widespread and deadly than the first – the bombing of the city by US forces, Japan's main adversary in the Second World War. The first raid was in April 1942 by a squadron of 16 B25s from the carrier *USS Hornet*, and did comparatively little damage. However, the raids by B29s near the end of the war in winter of 1944–5 were extremely devastating. There were 102 attacks in all, mostly against military targets and strategic industrial facilities, but also doing grave damage to the residential neighborhoods that were nearby. The planes came so often to Tokyo during this period that residents began to refer to them as *okyakusama* ('honored guests'), 'regular mail', and 'Lord B' (Daniels, 1977, p. 121). By the time the raids ended in the spring, the death toll had reached more than 100 000, and almost the entire city was in ruins. The count of casualties would have been even worse had not much of the population evacuated the city as the tempo of bombings increased.

The worst attack took place the night of 9–10 March 1945. It reflected a change in military strategy by the Americans, and, like the bombing of Hiroshima and Nagasaki some months later, was intended to hasten Japan's surrender by creating mass carnage among the populace. Instead of the high-explosive bombs that were used before to demolish individual structures, this attack was designed to set fire to the city and to have the flames spread widely. It was carried out by 334 B29 Superfortress bombers loaded to the maximum of six tons each with napalm and a new incendiary device containing magnesium and jellied gasoline. The principal target was Asakusa Ward, an overcrowded *shitamachi* area of wooden houses, narrow streets, and a very high roof density, but many other areas (including the Imperial Palace compound that had supposedly been off limits) were also struck. In the three hours between midnight and approximately 3 a.m. 700 000 bombs fell on the city (Guillain, 1981, p. 188). The result was an 'almost surrealist masterpiece of flame and agony reminiscent of Bosch, Bacon or Goya in their most tormented works', and more than 77 000 civilian deaths on that single night (Daniels, 1977, p. 125). The number of buildings that were lost was over 276 000. This attack has the unhappy distinction of being the most destructive single bombing mission with non-atomic weapons in history (Figures 3.11 and 3.12).

POST-WAR RECONSTRUCTION

With the end of the war, Japan was thoroughly defeated both physically and psychologically, and faced an extremely difficult rebuilding challenge. All the largest cities except Kyoto were in ruins, there were severe shortages of food, housing and other necessities, the economy was devastated and at a standstill, and the spirit of the people was all but broken. In the words of the Japanese press of that time, it was a situation of 'one hundred million people in a state of trauma' (Morris-Suzuki, 1985, p. 196). The fact that the country was able to recover so completely and so quickly, and to become an exceedingly prosperous nation with a

Figure 3.11 *Central Tokyo after the air raids of 1945. The foreground centers on Nihombashi, while the background shows Kōtō Ward across the Sumida River. (Courtesy of the Asahi Newspaper Company)*

Figure 3.12 *Taking a bath near the ruins of Ōtsuka Station, Toshima Ward, after the March 1945 bombing of Tokyo. (Courtesy of the Asahi Newspaper Company)*

high standard of living so soon after its crushing collapse, is one of the great modern-day miracles. It is primarily a tribute to the energies and determination of its citizenry, and a happy outcome for Japan of American generosity and of various enlightened policies of the US Occupation that followed the hostilities.

The story of Japan's rebuilding is discussed in many excellent sources (e.g., Burks, 1984; Kawai, 1960; Kosai, 1986; Reischauer, 1981; Storry, 1960; Uchino, 1978), and need not be repeated here. However, we might observe that the changes that came to Japanese society during reconstruction were just as revolutionary, if not more so, as those of the Meiji Restoration. The centerpiece was a new constitution, drafted somewhat hurriedly by the Americans but still in force by popular will more than 40 years later, that transformed the nation into a parliamentary democracy. It entrusted sovereign power to the people, made the emperor, who earlier had renounced claims to divinity, a completely powerless symbol of Japanese unity, and provided for a 30-article Bill of Rights that guaranteed basic human freedoms and outlawed most forms of social discrimination. Moreover, the country was demilitarized; responsibilities for defense were taken on by the United States. Other changes included the weakening of the powerful *zaibatsu* economic concerns so that industry and other business activity could be decentralized; radical land reforms that allowed tenant farmers to become owners; the enhancement of powers for labor unions; and, for the first time in Japan, the enfranchisement of women and extension to them of basic legal rights. Japan also came to be very culturally influenced by Americans. As Reischauer described it: 'the disillusioned and demoralized Japanese, instead of reacting to the army of occupation and its leader with the normal sullen resentment of a defeated people, regarded the Americans as guides to a new and better day' (Reischauer, 1981, p. 105).

In the course of reconstruction, various cities in Japan built memorials to their victims from bombing. In some of these cities, the memorial includes a remnant or more of a bombed-out building or other structure as a permanent reminder of the destruction caused by war. The best and most moving example is Peace Memorial Park and the A-Bomb Dome in Hiroshima through which a thoughtful Japanese friend once gave me an unforgettable tour. Tokyo, however, has nothing of the sort. In still another way that the city reveals itself to be different, it built no special landmark to its terrible ordeal, nor did it retain anything from the ruins for the sake of history. This does not mean that the carnage has been forgotten, because it has not. Instead, it reflects the fact that Tokyo is single-minded at looking forward and not back. As soon as it could, the city returned to business as usual on fully 100 percent of its land. One of the few exceptions is a small museum with maps, photographs and various artifacts from the air raids that was put up in Yokoamichō Park, a small park in Sumida Ward on the site of the Military Clothing Depot where so many citizens perished in the 1923 earthquake firestorm. Significantly, instead of having a name that recalls the destruction, this museum is called 'Reconstruction Memorial Hall'. In addition, some modest exhibits about the bombing were appended to Cenotaph Hall, a neighboring building that was mentioned previously as the principal memorial building to the 1923 disaster. This building, as I have already described, is rather unassuming. Its outstanding feature, however, is that the curves of the roofline take on a form that suggests a large bird with spread wings about to take off in flight (Enbutsu, 1994, p. 185).[8]

And take off is exactly what Tokyo did, as for the second time in less than a quarter-century it embarked on a fast, thorough rebuilding. Immediately there was the Herculean task of clearing away the cinders and the broken concrete, and making room for the city to grow. Because of a shortage of trucks and fuel, only some of the rubble could be hauled to landfill in Tokyo Bay. Much of it was piled into the canals, most of which were soon covered over forever. In this way, a distinguishing aspect of old Edo was to all but disappear. Just as fast, rudimentary huts sprang up where they could; street stalls came into business to offer food and drink and other necessities. Because of the widespread shortages of almost every-thing, and because the rationing system rarely permitted adequate supplies of necessities, black markets sprung up at every gathering point in the city and at every station along commuter lines. They specialized in illegally acquired foreign products, most notably from the supply rooms of the Occupation, as well as in food products that were brought in from the countryside by 'runners' (*katsugiya*) who circumvented both rationing laws and the police. As reported by Seidensticker (1990, pp. 153–4), there were an estimated 60 000 black market stalls in Tokyo at the start of 1946. This is a number that testifies to the terrible misery of that time and the desperation of honest men and women to make a living.

Some of the post-war black markets merit special mention, either because of their unusually large size or because they have survived, albeit in altered form, to the present day. Perhaps the most famous is a place called Ameyayokochō, a narrow alley lined with vendors' stalls strung out beneath an elevated railroad right-of-way near Ueno Station. During the worst shortages, the market was a lifeline of food supplies from the farming hinterland reached by trains to Ueno, as well as a steady supply of products of various kinds from the United States, especially sweets. This explains the name *ameya*, which is a pun on both the word 'American' and the Japanese word for 'sweet'.[9] As rationing began to be abandoned in the 1950s, Ameyayokochō changed its functions and now sells a variety of products at discount, ranging from fresh seafood to golfing supplies (see Chapter 5 and Figure 3.13). However, there is still something of a black market there, as some shops are known to specialize in easily transported foreign goods that Japanese travelers bring from abroad without paying import fees (Seidensticker, 1990, pp. 152–3). Other famous black markets were at Shinjuku, Ginza, and Ikebukuro. Bits and pieces of the one near Shinjuku Station's West Exit survive as a cluster of tiny eating and drinking stalls that is widely called 'Piss Alley' (Shombenyokochō). Still another black market, the one at Akihabara between Ueno and the CBD, was based on the collection of scrap electrical equipment, and eventually evolved into the world-renowned electronics emporium specializing in the latest products by Japan's great manufacturers that it is today.

There was less chance after the war than there was after the earthquake to beautify the city in its reconstruction, or to introduce much-improved urban design. One element of this problem was unprecedented population pressure. The number of residents of Tokyo (i.e. the ward area), which had declined during the war years by some 4 million persons largely because of evacuations to protect against air raids, swelled from a low of 2.78 million in 1945 to 5.38 million in 1950 and then 6.96 million in 1955. By 1960 the population had grown to 8.31 million (Ishizuka and Ishida, 1988, pp. 26–7). The arrivals included returned evacuees, soldiers back

Figure 3.13 *Ameyayokochō in the rain. Today the street specializes in the sale of fresh fish and other food items, but during the years immediately after the Second World War it was one of the city's leading black markets*

from their duties, repatriated Japanese nationals from lost colonies, and thousands upon thousands of desperate job seekers from impoverished prefectures and devastated cities. There were also thousands of US personnel from the headquarters of the Occupation and their dependents, all of whom made disproportionate demands for housing, office space and other land (Wildes, 1954, pp. 260–68). Thus, when the first public housing units were constructed in 1948 on what was previously military land, there were some 300 applicants for every available opening (Seidensticker, 1990, p. 160). What is more, these and other housing units built after the war were small in size and poor in quality: both were problems that would persist in Tokyo for many years. In the same vein, the intense crowding in the city meant that there was little chance to improve its poor record for park space. Always too few in numbers, the park situation actually worsened in the immediate post-war years as some parks, most notably Asakusa Park, actually disappeared to make way for urbanization. In fact, because of unusually great demand for land in Tokyo, as well as the scarcity of food, there was a period of three years between 1946 and 1949 when Shinobazu Pond in Ueno Park, long one of the city's most picturesque settings, was drained to make ground for crop production.

Before long, however, economic conditions in Japan would improve, and Tokyo would recover more fully from the defeat. This was seen first at the bayfront, where revitalization was stirred simultaneously by the rise of export-oriented manufacturing and the re-establishment of much of the heavy industry that was lost to the bombing, and in the CBD, where company offices, financial institutions, newspapers and other media, as well as other commercial concerns, came to life by the early 1950s. This was especially the case in Marunouchi, the no-nonsense office district close to Tokyo Station that replaced Nihombashi after the war as the nation's principal management center. Ironically, it was another war, the Korean War (1950–53), that provided a key spark for this by opening opportunities for Japan to expand manufacturing and international trade by servicing military procurement contracts. Other ingredients for recovery, all of them more fundamental than the accident of a nearby war, and of much longer impact, included the dedicated work and sacrifices by the citizenry, substantial technological innovation in manufacturing, and high rates of investment and reinvestment by government and business alike in export-related industries.

As the recovery of Tokyo advanced, the city returned to an earlier trend that had been established in the wake of the 1923 disaster – a westward shift in its own development. This had begun as a movement to the higher ground of *yamanote* to escape the fires of the old city, and was regenerated in the post-war period as a dominant pattern of growth associated with suburbanization and with plans for the deconcentration of the metropolitan center. Instead of having uni-nodal urban form focusing exclusively on the CBD, Tokyo began to be more polycentric, and created new commercial districts at the urban periphery. These were particularly important on the fast-growing west side of the city, where crossroads at Shinjuku, Shibuya, and Ikebukuro were transformed from local centers into major regional subcenters that would compete with the CBD in offices, retailing, entertainment and other functions. The word that entered the vocabulary to describe them, *fukutoshin*, means 'secondary heart of the city' (Seidensticker, 1990, p. 212). Especially after the hurried reconstruction of Marunouchi and other central office districts, a new heart was seen as necessary because of thrombosis in the CBD brought on by too many commuters on too little ground. As a multi-nodal arrangement of commercial districts in and around Tokyo continues to be a major goal of metropolitan planning, the three subcenters named here (but most especially Shinjuku) are indeed vital new centers in the life of the city.

Of all the many structures that were built in Tokyo during the post-war years, one stood out specifically as a monument to the reconstruction itself. This was Tokyo Tower, the instantly famous landmark that was opened to considerable fanfare in late 1958 in the emerging west side to signal the city's successful rise from the ashes, as well as its new 'international' outlook. While the official purpose of the tower had to do with transmission and reception of communication waves, its greater role was simply to stand tall and be seen. The height, 333 meters, was a calculated 33 meters taller than the Eiffel Tower at that time,[10] and its form, although not exactly the same, was quite enough like that of the structure in Paris to be called a copy. For the designer, Dr Naitō Tachu, an emeritus professor at Waseda University who was lovingly called Dr Steel Tower, it was a crowning achievement; it was his thirtieth tower, the biggest by far, and a chance to apply his vocation to an important patriotic goal. With the opening of the tower, which took place on Christmas Eve exactly ten years and a day after the war crimes hanging in Tokyo of General Tōjō and other defeated military leaders, Japan could present itself around the globe as a repentant nation that was fast rebuilding and desirous of being in touch with other advanced nations during this electronic age, rather than isolated from them. As in the Meiji period, when copying of Western building styles was the vogue, this particular message abroad about the onset of a new era for Japan was delivered in the language of architecture. What is more, the Japanese public, starved by hard times since the war for fun and frivolity, as well as perhaps for assurances about their future, took to the tower immediately. Despite a rather steep admission charge of 120 yen per person, there were long lines from the start at the elevators and great throngs of elbow-wielding sightseers at observation windows and coin-operated telescopes.

Tokyo Tower was but one symbol of post-Occupation progress. The formal debut of the new Japan into the family of friendly nations, and the public introduction of its reborn capital city, is generally ascribed to a later event: Tokyo's hosting of the 1964 Summer Olympics. Obviously, this was something that required enormous preparations and for which many key parts of the city had to be specially dressed. The need for Japan to put on a good show was all the more important given that the 1964 games were, in a way, a substitute for the 1940 Olympics – games that had also been awarded to Tokyo but which, for obvious reasons, never took place. Thus, the international spectacle of 1964 was a special stimulus for Tokyo to get on with the job of reconstruction, as well as a marvelous opportunity for the city to attract national monies to fund municipal projects. The city's single-mindedness at preparing for the games is seen in the fact that the governor of *Tōkyō-to*, Azuma Ryūtarō, elected in 1959 at the start of the pre-Olympics rush and in office until after the games ended, was also chairman of the Japan Olympics Committee.

Perhaps to emphasize the demilitarization of Japan after the war and the resurgence of the country as a peaceful nation, most of the sporting events were concentrated on land that had been appropriated from the army. Specifically, the main site of the Olympics was originally the Yoyogi drilling ground of the Japanese army, and after that a main base of operations for the US Occupation. It was that part of the west side of the city that was between Shibuya and Shinjuku (but more closely identified with the former), and close to the sacred shrine to the Emperor Meiji, that the Americans had renamed Washington Heights. At the request of the Japanese government, the land was repatriated in time to construct several of the key Olympics facilities on the site. The biggest part of Washington Heights became an athletes' village. These were temporary quarters, but were generally thought of as more than adequate and well planned. After the games the land would become Yoyogi Park, a welcome addition to a city that sorely lacked public recreation space.

The most spectacular permanent structure from the Olympics, and still the principal landmark of the Olympic years, was a facility that stood across from the village and hosted swimming competitions, ice sports, and basketball (Figure 3.14). This is the National Gymnasium complex, which is actually two adjacent buildings, designed by Tange Kenzō, a man of many landmarks who would have inordinate influence on the form of Tokyo from reconstruction in the 1950s to current projects in the 1990s. What caused the greatest international notice for this particular facility was its amazing roofline. In the case of the larger building, it was a giant swirl, and more of a spiral for the other building, and it stood tall amidst the landscaping as, simultaneously, a great show of traditional Japanese design motifs (including a hint of Mount Fuji) and a triumph of modern architecture. The fact that the larger building leaked rain is beside the point!

In addition to the Games facilities themselves, several neighborhoods in the area where the Olympics were concentrated were dressed up especially for the event,

Figure 3.14 *The National Gymnasium by Tange Kenzō and Inokashira-dōri, one of the new buildings put in for the Olympics*

and were then transformed still more by the visitors, both foreign and Japanese, who traipsed through them. An important example is the area called Harajuku, just city-side of the Washington Heights Olympics sites. The main street, called Omote-sandō because of its role as an approach to the Meiji Shrine, was widened and made into an especially attractive, tree-lined boulevard. Tokyoites began referring to it as their Champs Élysées, even though there is no resemblance except perhaps in the look of the trees (Waley, 1984, p. 430). The businesses that set up along it sold souvenirs of Japan to tourists from abroad, and Western products to Japanese who came to the area to see the Westerners. It was not long before this street, and the Harajuku area more generally, replaced Ginza (and before then, Tsukiji) as Japan's principal reception center for foreigners and foreign fashions. Young Japanese have been especially attracted to this district, and continue to congregate there to show off their dress and Western affectations, and to browse stores for the latest foreign fashions (see Chapter 5). The fact that the Japanese television and movie industries established major studios on portions of the Olympics land after the Games departed added to the glamor of the area.

Many other parts of the city, and not necessarily only those at the Olympics doorstep, were also spruced up in time for the Games. One important project on the east side of the city was developed to improve water quality on the Sumida River. The river was so polluted with sewage and other wastes that it stank, until a special water channel was dug to flush it clean just in time for the arrival of Olympics visitors. Elsewhere, there were new, international hotels, particularly in the area of the CBD close to the Imperial Palace, some new parks and public gardens, an impressive National Museum in Ueno Park, and in several locations some hasty bulldozing of slums and the construction in their place of ferroconcrete apartment complexes. In a clean-up of a different kind, vagrants and beggars were removed from parts of the city where they were most likely to be noticed, and sent off to institutions or other exile (Seidensticker, 1990, p. 235).

Transportation projects of various kinds received extra attention. They included several other so-called 'Olympics thoroughfares' (greatly widened and straightened streets) in addition to Omote-sandō. Wherever they were built, their cost was tremendously high because of the large number of streetside homes and businesses that had to be relocated and compensated. Aoyama-dōri, a trendy commercial avenue between the vicinity of the Imperial Palace and the popular business center at Shibuya, is a prime example. So, too, Tokyo's first expressways were built during the pre-Olympics rush. The highways that cut through the heart of the city were put on pillars above ground level, and followed the snaking courses of old canals and moats for at least a part of their routes. The subway system was much enlarged during this time. The principal additions included the Marunouchi Subway Line that connected the Shinjuku and Ikebukuro subcenters with the CBD at Ginza, a new station at Ginza, and various other new lines north, west, and east of the center. All these improvements, but especially the subways that connected residential areas with the urban center, were intended to give lasting benefit to the city over and beyond service to Olympics crowds.

There were two other transportation projects that stood out from all the rest. One was the Haneda Monorail Line, which was seen as being 'state-of-the-art' in intra-urban transportation technology; the other was the Shinkansen, called the 'bullet train' in English because of the shape of the lead car, state-of-the-art in inter-urban rail travel. The former extended from the Hamamatsuchō Station on the Yamanote Loop Line near the CBD to what was then the city's principal airport, and provides still, as it did on opening day less than a month before the start of the Games, a quick, quiet, and fairly priced ride into the city. The first Shinkansen line, named the Tōkaidō Line, also dates to just before the visitors arrived; it connected Tokyo Station with Japan's second city, Osaka, over 500 kilometers away in about three hours. The train's high speed – in excess of 200 kilometers per hour – the remarkable frequency of its schedule – departures approximately every seven minutes – and incredible record of punctuality have become well known around the world, and have been cited often by international observers since the Olympics as evidence of Japanese efficiency and technological know-how.

URBAN PROBLEMS

Tokyo had achieved much in rebuilding itself in time for the Olympics. However, there was also another side to the reconstruction story, one that detracted from the city's overall record and emphasized the great many urban problems that also characterized the city. These included environmental problems such as poor air and water quality, housing problems, traffic congestion, poor land-use planning, inadequacy of social services and urban infrastructure, and many other concerns. It is now common to describe the time around the Olympics as one during which inordinate attention was given to two goals, rebuilding of the Japanese economy and fabricating a positive international image for Tokyo, but very little attention to the needs of citizens in their neighborhoods. There were many illustrations of this, one of the most poignant of which was that during the Olympic Games themselves, which happened to be held during an unusually dry summer, water was severely rationed in the city. Seventeen of the 23 wards had water for only nine hours a day, and water trucks had to ply many neighborhoods to supply residents' basic requirements. At the same time, nearly two-thirds of Tokyo's citizens were without sewers, and depended on *kumitoriya*, night-soil trucks, to haul away their wastes (Seidensticker, 1990, pp. 233–4).

There were many other prominent symbols of things gone wrong. What observers from abroad picked up on most, and what has since become perhaps everybody's leading example of the way in which Tokyo can be unpleasant, is the unbelievably high levels of crowding on the city's trains and subways. From the time of pre-Olympics publicity (and even continuing to some extent today), newsreels and magazine photographers from around the world showed the great crush of Tokyo commuters, jammed inside trains like canned sardines, and pushed in tighter and tighter by white-gloved platform attendants. It was a scene so alien to outsiders that they could not help but gasp when they saw it, and perhaps even be a little amused by the seeming impossibility of so many human numbers in such small spaces. The new train and subway lines, each opened with some fanfare and grand promises about commuter relief, couldn't keep up with the demand, and themselves were overcrowded from day one. Thus, for Tokyoites the rail system became, literally, a hell of a way to get to work; the faces of riders told this story in no uncertain terms.

So too, there was amazement from abroad and dissatisfaction from within about the sorry state of housing. As late as 1968, fully 834 000 households in the city (28.1 percent of the total) were living in substandard accommodations, and 1 017 000 households (34.2 percent) considered themselves to be badly housed. The most common complaint was lack of space. For example, 45 percent of all families, not just those who voiced complaints in the survey, were in tenements that typically had shared toilets and kitchens, and that left only 10 square meters of private living space. More specifically, 176 700 families (6 percent) had less than two *tatami* mats (3.3 square meters) per person, and 702 400 families (24 percent) had less than three mats (4.95 square meters) per capita (Tokyo Metropolitan Government, 1972a, p. 23). Moreover, because of the high cost of land and rapid population growth, the trend of housing construction offered little hope for improvement. Forty-seven percent of housing units built in Tokyo between 1961 and 1965 had less than 29 square meters. This compared to 42.0 percent of units built between 1955 and 1965, 32.7 percent of units built between 1945 and 1955, and 21.7 percent built in pre-war days (Tokyo Metropolitan Government, 1972a, p. 19). It is because of such extreme levels of overcrowding that, much to the dismay of proud Japanese, the term 'rabbit hutches' was applied by Western observers to Tokyo's housing – and then stuck. The facts that these houses were often made of cheap materials and were fire hazards added to the problems.

It is largely because of the existence of serious problems that Tokyo entered another phase of its development shortly after the Olympics were concluded. The patience of the populace about living conditions was wearing thin, and citizens were increasingly anxious to finish the time of post-war sacrifices and enjoy the fruits of their labors. Among other things, they demanded what was then called,

Figure 3.15 *Yasuda Hall of Tokyo University, scene of student riots in 1968–9*

tongue in cheek, *sansu no jingi*, the three divine symbols of the imperial throne: television, washing machines and refrigerators (Tokyo Metropolitan Government, 1972a, pp. 14–15). Their anger boiled over during the summer after the Olympics when a great plague of flies descended on the east side of the city from a poorly managed garbage dump, and gave 'last straw' proof that citizens and their neighborhoods were being ignored in plans for the city (see Chapter 6). There was also growing resentment about the continuing US military presence in the city, even after the official end of the Occupation, and popular demands that bases and other

American facilities (a total of 21.3 million square meters in *Tōkyō-to* in 1969) be released to ease the shortage of space for citizens. The unrest of the times is also seen in the riots by students at several university campuses in Tokyo and other cities. The violent struggles between students and police to control Yasuda Hall of Tokyo University in 1968 to early 1969 are especially noteworthy. Long a bastion of power and privilege, this particular university had become a symbol of inattentive authority in Japan, and was besieged by large numbers of increasingly radical students (see Figure 3.15).

Azuma Ryūtarō, the Olympics Governor, read the signs clearly and did not bother to stand for re-election after the Games. The 1967 balloting elected a 'people-first' coalition of socialists and communists headed by Minobe Ryōkichi, the university professor turned governor, and sent Tokyo off on a new course. We will pick this story up later, in Chapter 6, when discussing the history of city planning. For now, let us leave it that Tokyo, rebuilt after the war but badly flawed as an environment for living, embarks in 1967 on a continuing program of building and still more building, but with considerably more attention to the quality of the outcome. The socialists stayed in office to work on this until the election of 1979, when the next governor, Suzuki Shunichi, a Liberal Democratic Party member with an approach to government that was decidedly pro-business, was elected for the first of his four terms (until 1995). However, even though the change of regimes was itself the cause of many important shifts in the details of Tokyo development, attention to building a better city for living was never diminished.

CHAPTER 4

CONTEMPORARY TOKYO

In all of its history Tokyo has never stayed still for long, but has changed with every need and opportunity. The first shogun took one look at the city that Ōta Dōkan had built and immediately began to rearrange it from top to bottom. He put in a new castle, realigned the flow of rivers, cut down Kanda Mountain, and proceeded to fill in the marshes and parts of the bay. His successors continued the work, reclaimed still more land, expanded the city in new directions, and rebuilt its established districts time and again after every destructive fire or flood. Under the Meiji Emperor, there was a whole new face (and new name too) that was given to the city, as the nation's isolation ended and foreign fashions and building styles became the rage in the capital. The Taishō Emperor saw it all burn in 1923 in the Great Kantō Earthquake. Then, just as soon as the city had been substantially rebuilt, there was the disaster of war and the firebombing of 1945. Tokyo rose from those ashes too, and in 1964 showed itself off to the world as a place of remarkable resilience and energy, and as a city that wanted to be counted among the elite of global urban centers. It did not win many points for beauty as the world looked on during those Olympics, but it proved to everyone that it was workaholic and that it would build whatever was needed to advance its goals.

Now, a little more than 400 years after Ieyasu's arrival in the city, Tokyo has reached the top of the world economically and is changing again. This time the rebuilding is by choice rather than after some calamity, but is as complete and far-reaching as any undertaking that has ever been done in the city before. It involves a huge range of projects, both private and public, that in various ways are intended to improve the quality of living in Tokyo and/or facilitate the needs of its important businesses, lavishing upon the city a completely new look. While most of the publicity about the construction boom focuses on the Central Business District, which is being extensively redeveloped to enhance Tokyo's status as a world leader in finance and trade, the transformations extend as well in one form or another into every residential neighborhood, commercial center, and industrial zone in the rest of the city and all its suburbs. To emphasize the immense scale of what is going on, as well as to highlight the city's exceptionally transitory nature, the rebuilding can be described as a thorough reconstruction of Tokyo – the third reconstruction (after 1923 and 1945) in less than a century (Haberman, 1987).

With this chapter we turn our attention to the contemporary city and the enormous changes, both social and physical, that are taking place. We will begin with a look at the key social and economic trends that both characterize the city and underlie its physical transformation, trends that I have grouped under five headings: (1) population redistribution within the metropolis; (2) the aging of the population; (3) economic shifts; (4) the rise of consumer culture; and (5) the movement toward increased internationalization. We will then discuss the city's changing physical form. It will be convenient to generalize the city into two parts:

(1) the center, particularly the Central Business District where people work and also go shopping or for various forms of entertainment; and (2) the periphery, where increasing proportions of Tokyoites have their homes and community life. We will see that the center is huge, perhaps the most overgrown business district in the world, and that it is getting bigger by expanding into surrounding neighborhoods. The periphery grows too, in part with people displaced from the center. Thus, the presentation of Tokyo in this chapter will be of the classic 'hole' in the 'urban donut' and the mass that has grown around it.

SOCIAL AND ECONOMIC TRENDS

POPULATION REDISTRIBUTION

The time of population explosion that had characterized the post-Second World War period is over, and the rate of population growth in *Tōkyō-to* as a whole has stabilized. We see, for example, that in the 1950s the rate of population increase in *Tōkyō-to* was 54.3 percent, growing from a total of 6 278 000 inhabitants in 1950 to 9 684 000 in 1960, and that the rate slowed to 17.8 percent in the 1960s and 1.8 percent in the 1970s. During the 1980s the growth rate remained low – approximately 2.0 percent. According to the most recent count, that for 1995, there has now been a slight downturn in population: between 1990 and 1995 the total for *Tōkyō-to* declined by more than 2.0 percent, from 11 856 000 to 11 599 000.

However, while total population numbers in *Tōkyō-to* have changed little in recent years, the geographical distribution of population has changed greatly. The dominant trend has been a decline in the number of residents living near the center of the metropolis and extremely rapid growth at the edges – the 'urban donut' phenomenon. The largest declines have been in the three innermost wards of the metropolis, Chiyoda, Chūō and Minato Wards. This area contains the Tokyo CBD and has lost many residential neighborhoods over the years to the expansion of commercial land uses. The loss of population goes back at least as far as the early twentieth century. The present (1995) population total for these three wards is just over 264 000, less than one-third of the peak census count of 818 000 in 1920. So, too, the old *shitamachi* wards of the city (by this definition, Arakawa, Bunkyō, Kōtō, Sumida, and Taitō Wards) have dropped significantly. The peak census year for this inner-city district was 1940, when the total was 2 011 000, but there have been steady declines since then (except for the immediate post-war rush to the city) to a level of 1 081 000 in the census of 1995. Another inner ring of wards, the 'subcentral wards' that are just beyond the CBD and the *shitamachi* area, has lost numbers as well, in this case from a peak in 1965 of 3 824 000 to 2 930 000 in the latest census. Thus, the overall total for the 23 wards that comprise the historic boundary of Tokyo City has dropped as well. The peak was in 1965 when 8 894 000 people lived there, but by 1995 the total has fallen by more than 1 million to approximately 7 871 000 (Table 4.1).

These declines contrast with all the rest of the Tokyo metropolitan area: i.e. the Tama region of *Tōkyō-to* and all the neighboring prefectures. The Tama area has grown nearly elevenfold since 1920 (from 340 000 to 3 695 000 in 1995), and now

Table 4.1 Population Trends in the Tokyo Metropolitan Region, 1920–95 (*population totals in thousands*)

	1920	1940	1960	1980	1990	1995
23-ward area	3359	6777	8311	8350	8164	7871
Central Wards[a]	818	767	545	339	266	264
Shitamachi[a]	1418	2011	1546	1181	1137	1081
Subcentral Wards[a]	911	2831	3635	3314	3107	2930
Outer Wards[a]	212	1168	2585	3516	3653	3596
Rest of *Tōkyō-to*	340	570	1373	3268	3692	3727
TŌKYŌ-TO TOTAL	3699	7347	9684	11 618	11 856	11 599
Chiba Prefecture	1336	1588	2306	4735	5555	5754[b]
Kanagawa Prefecture	1323	2183	3443	6924	7980	8184[b]
Saitama Prefecture	1320	1608	2431	5420	6405	6692[b]
CAPITAL REGION TOTAL	7678	12 726	17 864	28 697	31 796	32 401[b]
23 wards as a % of Capital Region	43.7	53.2	46.5	29.1	25.7	24.3
Tōkyō-to as a % of Capital Region	48.1	57.7	54.2	40.5	37.3	36.3

[a] The Central Wards are Chiyoda, Chūō and Minato Wards.
Shitamachi is defined here as Arakawa, Bunkyō, Kōtō, Sumida and Taitō Wards.
The Subcentral Wards are Katsushika, Kita, Meguro, Nakano, Ōta, Shibuya, Shinagawa, Shinjuku and Toshima Wards.
The Outer Wards are Adachi, Edogawa, Itabashi, Nerima, Setagaya and Suginami Wards.
[b] Population counts for Chiba, Kanagawa and Saitama Prefectures are for 1994. The Capital Region total is for 1994 as well. The population of *Tōkyō-to* in 1994 was 11 771 000.

Sources: Fujii (1987, p. 13) and various census sources, primarily *Tokyo Statistical Yearbook, 1994*.

has nearly one-third of the total population of the Tokyo government unit. Kanagawa, Chiba, and Saitama Prefectures have grown in spectacular fashion as well, more than doubling in population in 35 years between 1960 and the census of 1995. The result is rapid overall growth for the Greater Tokyo Metropolitan Area as a whole. It now totals more than 32 million inhabitants. Ever-larger fractions of this total reside outside the *Tōkyō-to* unit. In the early part of the century what is now *Tōkyō-to* comprised about one-half of the population of the four-prefecture metropolitan area (e.g. 48.1 percent of the total in 1920; 57.7 percent in 1940), but this has dropped to 39.1 percent in the 1985 census, 38.5 percent in 1990 and 26.3 percent in 1995. What all of this means in the context of the 'third rebuilding of Tokyo', our principal topic in this chapter, is tremendous expansion of housing, commercial centers, and employment places at the edges of the metropolis, and the redevelopment of previously residential districts in the center.

AGING OF THE POPULATION

Because of declining birth rates, increased longevity, and, to a lesser extent, reduced numbers of young migrants to the city, the population of *Tōkyō-to* is older on average than ever before. This, of course, is related to the aging of Japan overall: a

Figure 4.1 *Tokyo's population is aging. The elderly residents are in a small park in Arakawa Ward*

trend that is evident in many other advanced societies as well. According to official statistics, *Tōkyō-to* now has more than three times the percentage of total population aged 65 years or older than it did just a quarter of a century ago (12.6 percent in 1995 versus 4.0 percent in 1962). The flip side of this is that younger age groups have declined in proportion: between 1962 and 1995 persons aged 0–14 decreased in *Tōkyō-to* from 23.5 percent of the total population to 12.9 percent. Such trends are expected to continue, with the result that by the year 2025 as many as one in four of all residents in Tokyo will be aged 65 or older (Figure 4.1).

There are distinct geographical patterns to the aging of the population within *Tōkyō-to*. This, too, is a familiar pattern in urban areas in advanced societies: the center, particularly the older neighborhoods with declining population totals, tend to have higher proportions of elderly residents; the periphery, especially those areas that have grown recently as bedroom suburbs of the central city, tends to have greater proportions of young families with children (Knox, 1982, pp. 74–100). Thus, the 23-ward area as a whole has 13.5 percent of its population aged 65 or older, as opposed to only 10.9 percent in the Tama District and the 12.6 percent for *Tōkyō-to* as a whole mentioned above. The CBD wards and historic *shitamachi* wards are older still, generally having between 15.0 and 21.0 percent of their populations aged 65 or more. Chiyoda Ward has the highest percentage of the elderly, 21.2 percent. In the Tama area, by contrast, the percentages of elderly residents are generally in the 9.0 to 12.0 percent range (Table 4.2).

Tokyo's aging population has indirect but important impact on development trends in the city and patterns of construction. For example, land developers wanting to assemble sites for larger projects are often on the lookout for properties owned by older people, calculating that land might become available after an owner's death. Sons and daughters who inherit such property are often forced to

Table 4.2 *Population Composition by Age Group, 23 Wards and the Tama Area, 1995*

	% of population aged 0–14	% of population aged 15–64	% of population aged 65+
23 wards	12.2	74.3	13.5
Tama District[a]	14.5	74.6	10.9
Tōkyō-to	12.9	74.5	12.6

[a] Includes the islands.

sell it to pay the city's extraordinarily high inheritance taxes. In this way sections of the city with concentrations of older housing inhabited primarily by aged residents become prime targets for speculators, and are often redeveloped in sizable chunks. An interesting hypothesis for some future doctoral dissertation would hold that the expansion of the Central Business District in Tokyo has been guided geographically, in measurable part, by the location of property left by departed landowners. We will return to this topic later when discussing development pressures on inner-city neighborhoods.

Equally important (and less morbid) as impacts on the city of aging population are changes to the design of newer housing. For example, multigenerational living arrangements, an established cultural tradition in Japan, are being adjusted to provide for greater separation under the one roof between elderly parents, on the one hand, and their adult children and growing families, on the other. Separate 'in-law suites' with their own kitchens, baths and private entrances are ever more common features of Tokyo's housing construction, both in the city and out in the suburbs. They stem from increased longevity on the part of the elderly,[1] and a desire, possibly by elderly parents and younger generations alike, for more privacy. Other impacts on the physical city of an aging population include growing numbers of seniors' centers that have opened in neighborhoods all through the metropolis; certain parks and other recreation areas constructed with what are believed to be interests of the elderly in mind (e.g. there are several new bird-watching facilities in Tokyo); and smaller changes such as preferred seats (often colored gray) for seniors on buses and trains. Not coincidentally, quite a few of the older schools in Tokyo have closed because of declining numbers of children. Some of them have been converted to neighborhood seniors' centers; others have been razed and their sites converted to commercial uses.

ECONOMIC SHIFTS

One of the most important aspects for understanding the current rebuilding of Tokyo is to think of it as investment in Japan's capital city by government and big business, in a remarkably smooth-working partnership, which makes sure that the economic successes of the country will continue in the future. There are no punches pulled about this at all. There are especially large ambitions for Tokyo in the area of international trade and finance, and the rebuilding of the city is part and parcel of a plan to assure that the city achieves as high a place as possible among

Table 4.3 *Comparative Office Rents,*
Tokyo and Other Cities, November
1989 (annual occupancy costs per
square foot; $US)

Tokyo	159
London (City)	139
London (West End)	116
Hong Kong	100
Paris	69
Sydney	56
Zurich	51
New York	51
Toronto	47
Madrid	47
Washington	47
Moscow	47
Singapore	45

Source: Colliers International/taken from Davies *et al.* (1990, p. 14).

the world leaders. One goal is to attract multinational companies to open in Tokyo and use the city as the main base for East Asia or Pacific Rim operations. This is to compete against Hong Kong, Singapore, and other fast-rising capitals in the region, and to take over some of the trade that Hong Kong would lose if its reunification with China were to fail to work out for business. Even more, it is hoped that Tokyo can surpass New York and London in international finance and stock dealings, and that the city will be the next century's undisputed number-one global financial center. Tange Kenzō, one of the leading architects for the city's rebuilding, was quoted in *The New York Times* not long ago as saying: 'Paris is a symbol of the 19th century . . . Manhattan may be the symbol of the 20th century. If we can succeed in our plans, Tokyo could become the model for the 21st century' (Haberman, 1987, p. 14).

A major objective of the rebuilding is to provide more space for offices for the growing number of companies, both Japanese and foreign, which concentrate in Tokyo. Because it is the overwhelming city of choice and business necessity for any firm that does business in Japan, vacancy rates for offices in Tokyo have been extremely low, typically 0.2–0.3 percent.[2] Moreover, rental prices have been exorbitantly high (Table 4.3). It has not been uncommon, for example, to pay as much as Y55 000–65 000 per tsubo (3.3 square meters) each month for office space in Ōtemachi, Marunouchi, and other desirable sections of the center (*Nihon Keizai Shimbun*, 21 February 1988). Furthermore, most offices are notoriously crowded and working conditions in them, as measured by space per employee, standards of office decor, personal privacy, and other amenity indicators, are almost always substantially inferior to those in rival cities abroad. Consequently, some of the most important and visible aspects of the Tokyo that are now emerging include the redevelopment of existing commercial districts, most notably the CBD, to make room for new office towers that are taller and more comfortably equipped than those they replace, as well as the redevelopment of non-commercial districts to permit expansion for offices and related uses.

Closely related to this is a structural shift taking place in Tokyo's economy: that of declining emphasis on manufacturing and increased attention on the services sector. This is part of a more general shift of the national economy to post-industrial economic foundations, as well as a shift within Tokyo specifically away from large factories. The latter has been a city objective since the late 1950s when regulations were put into effect restricting expansion of industrial sites within the 23 wards and encouraging the relocation of factories to the Tama area and neighboring prefectures. This was to reduce urban pollution levels, to cut down on traffic and to foster economic growth in outlying sections of the metropolis. In many cases it also paved the way for the redevelopment of industrial sites for new offices, hotels, commercial centers and in some cases, for large housing estates. Many of the most impressive of these changes have taken place in and near the CBD, at the innermost reaches of Tokyo Bay, the lower stretches of the Sumida River and in the newly fashionable neighborhoods of Tokyo's west side.

We can see the outlines of this economic shift by looking first at the three gross categories: primary, secondary and tertiary industries. The first two of these have declined markedly in recent decades, while the tertiary category has grown. In 1950 primary industries (e.g. farming, fishing, forestry) accounted for 6.4 percent of all employment in *Tōkyō-to*; secondary industries (mostly manufacturing and related employment) were 37.1 percent; and tertiary industries (e.g. offices, commercial establishments, education, government and other services) were 56.2 percent. By 1970, the primary category had dropped to only 0.9 percent of the total, the secondary category increased somewhat to 38.2 percent because of the post-war push for economic growth, while the third category grew to 60.7 percent. The census of 1985 showed even greater growth in tertiary industry – up to 69.8 percent of the total – and further declines in the other two categories. The decline in the secondary is especially notable: it dropped to 29.3 percent of the total after programs were started in Tokyo to relocate industry and redevelop key factory sites for other uses (Tokyo Metropolitan Government, 1987a, p. 24 and 1990a, p. 3). Finally, according to the most recent data available, those for 1991, the primary sector has dropped to a tiny percentage (0.1 percent), as most of the last farms and fishing vessels based in Tokyo have gone; the secondary sector declined even further, to about 24.4 percent of the total employees; while the tertiary category has grown to exceed three-quarters of total employment (75.5 percent; *Tokyo Statistical Yearbook, 1994*, Table 35, pp. 86–9).

Detailed patterns are shown in Table 4.4. This table breaks the economy into 11 major industrial groups, and uses both the number of employees in each group and the number of establishments as measures of economic activity. The total economy of *Tōkyō-to* is clearly growing. The total number of employees increased from 6.7 million in 1972 to almost 8.8 million in 1991, while the number of business establishments grew from 643 973 to 777 470. The fastest-growing sectors include services (e.g. education, medicine, various business services), finance and insurance, and wholesale and retail trade. The last category includes the great many shops of all kinds that are found in Tokyo, as well as the city's thousands of eating and drinking places, and accounts for 42.4 percent of all business establishments. It sometimes seems that at any given time during the day or evening, one-half of the city's population is out shopping or sitting in some restaurant or coffee shop, and

Figure 4.2 *The morning rush of office workers entering their building in Shinjuku on their way from the commuter rail station*

that the other half is serving them from across the counter. By contrast, declines are registered for the primary industries and manufacturing. In manufacturing this is especially evident in terms of numbers of employees. As Table 4.4 indicates, the number of factory workers in *Tōkyō-to* declined by more than 314 000 between 1972 and 1991 (from 1 849 743 employees to 1 535 509), and the percentage of the total workforce that is employed in this category has slipped from 27.5 percent to 17.5 percent. However, manufacturing is still extremely important in the Tokyo economy, and in terms of gross municipal product (a measure that is not illustrated in the table), ranks number one in the city at 12 825.2 billion yen (1986 figure; 21.9 percent of the total) (Tokyo Metropolitan Government, 1990b, p. 46).

Perhaps the most striking feature of Tokyo's manufacturing sector is that it is composed primarily of small factories (as defined by small numbers of employees). According to statistics for 1994, 64.0 percent of all manufacturing plants in the city with more than three workers employed only 4–9 workers and an additional 18.7 percent employed only 10–19 workers. The factories with only 4–9 employees accounted for 19.3 percent of all persons engaged in manufacturing and only 14.4 percent of the total cash earnings of Tokyo's factories, indicating that on the whole the city's small factories are not particularly profitable (*Tokyo Statistical Yearbook, 1994*, Table 53, p. 134). What is more, the proportion of small manufacturing companies is increasing rather than decreasing. This indicates that the erosion in manufacturing that is shown in gross statistics involves mainly large and medium-sized firms. Other statistics show that a great many of the larger companies have relocated to the seven prefectures of the Kantō region outside *Tōkyō-to*. Of the industries remaining in Tokyo, the most numerous category is printing and publishing. It is composed mainly of small firms, and accounts for 21.7 percent of all factories in *Tōkyō-to*, 22.1 percent of all workers in manufacturing, and

Table 4.4 *Economic Structure of Tokyo, 1972–91*

| | Number of employees | | | | | |
| | 1972 | | 1986 | | 1991 | |
Sector	Number	Percent	Number	Percent	Number	Percent
Agriculture, forestry and fisheries	10 501	0.2	10 609	0.1	4586	0.1
Mining	7682	0.1	6509	0.1	5273	0.1
Construction	487 358	7.3	561 516	7.1	605 460	6.9
Manufacturing	1 849 743	27.5	1 644 835	20.7	1 535 509	17.5
Utilities	34 494	0.5	39 522	0.5	34 347	0.4
Transport and Communication	482 892	7.2	538 521	6.9	573 281	6.5
Wholesale and retail trade[a]	2 028 915	30.2	2 608 705	32.8	2 671 269	30.4
Finance and insurance	319 342	4.8	407 307	5.1	511 878	5.8
Real estate	111 206	1.7	174 314	2.2	229 472	2.6
Services	1 177 305	17.5	1 901 783	23.9	2 373 176	27.0
Government (not elsewhere classified)	208 026	3.1	220 592	2.8	232 201	2.6
TOTAL	6 717 644	100.0	7 956 726	100.0	8 777 116	100.0

Number of establishments

Sector	1972		1986		1991	
	Number	Percent	Number	Percent	Number	Percent
Agriculture, forestry and fisheries	767	0.1	1029	0.1	252	0.0
Mining	203	0.0	185	0.0	128	0.0
Construction	37 493	5.8	49 111	6.2	49 466	6.3
Manufacturing	119 852	18.6	127 338	16.0	111 690	14.4
Utilities	692	0.1	612	0.1	526	0.1
Transport and Communication	14 341	2.2	27 508	3.4	28 212	3.6
Wholesale and retail trade[a]	301 119	46.8	361 416	45.3	329 763	42.4
Finance and insurance	7767	1.2	12 141	1.5	14 261	1.8
Real estate	32 686	5.1	44 264	5.6	48 487	6.2
Services	127 065	19.7	181 193	22.7	192 552	24.8
Government (not elsewhere classified)	1988	0.3	2121	0.2	2133	0.3
TOTAL	643 973	100.0	797 483	100.0	777 470	100.0

[a] Includes eating and drinking places.

Source: Tokyo Statistical Yearbook, 1987, pp. 98–101; 1994, pp. 86–9.

Table 4.5 *Traditional Crafts Industries in Tokyo (50 Companies or more)*

Craft	Companies	Employees	Production value (million yen)
Murayama Ōshima pongee	73	849	1091
Yellow hachijō silk	95	104	115
Tokyo-style silver utensils	200	252	3000
Tokyo-style hand-printed silk	280	760	2600
Edo lacquerware	90	615	8600
Edo tortoiseshell works	144	420	4500
Tokyo-style Buddhist altars	74	208	980
Tokyo-style picture frames	60	186	1080
Edo ivory carvings	65	377	8250
Edo cabinet work	50	110	630
Edo cut glass	104	514	1274
Edo embroidery	74	273	730
Edo wood carving	76	115	550
Edo metal carving	57	63	148

Source: Tokyo Metropolitan Government (1990b, p. 49).

23.9 percent of the value of finished product. Other important categories of manufacturing industries are fabricated metals (14.1 percent of all factories), general machinery and equipment, electrical machinery, apparel manufacturing, precision machinery (e.g. cameras and lenses), and leather and leather products.

There is also a strong traditional crafts industry in Tokyo. It is concentrated largely in the eastern part of the city, particularly in the *shitamachi* wards, as well as in some of the offshore islands of *Tōkyō-to* (e.g. Ōshima and Hachijōjima), and has suffered long-term declines in both numbers of employees and numbers of firms. However, recently it has been targeted by economic planners as an economic sector that should be preserved in the city and given what a government document refers to as 'a second chance in the limelight' (Tokyo Metropolitan Government, 1990b, p. 48). Table 4.5 lists the largest of Tokyo's traditional crafts industries.

CONSUMER CULTURE[3]

A popular guidebook about Tokyo begins its chapter about shopping with the observation that Japanese are people who 'love to spend and have the yen to do so' (Rivas-Micoud, Zanghi and Hirokawa, 1991, p. 107). In Tokyo, it is easy to see the basis for this perception, because the city often seems like an endless array of shopping centers and department stores, as well as restaurants of every imaginable cuisine and price range, and countless bars, coffee shops, video arcades, *pachinko* parlors, and every other kind of business establishment that you can think of. Another successful guidebook, assembled by architect Richard Saul Wurman, declared the following about Tokyo with its opening words (Wurman, 1984, p. 2):

> Tokyo is the world's largest department store. Its aisles are the subways and highways, filled with twice as many taxis and people as New York City. Its warehouse is the port and markets. Its business card is the multiple signature found in its neon skyline. Its jewelry department is the mechanical necklace created by the Yamanote line . . .

My point is that Tokyo is an enormous market, and that this attribute is one of the key factors underlying Tokyo's incessant building and rebuilding. In fact, it would be no exaggeration to state that shopping is one of the principal reasons for Tokyo's very existence: we saw, for example, that historic Edo was transformed into a great urban center only after Tokugawa Ieyasu had instituted policies to make his capital a city of consumption. Specifically, Edo grew because it was an unprecedentedly large market for everything from stone for construction of the castle, to building materials and art objects for the mansions of *daimyō*, to fresh fish brought by boat to Nihombashi for sale to the public. In this chapter and later we emphasize that, today, Tokyo's growth and development continues to be shaped, in significant part, by the city's role as Japan's capital of consumption, and that much of the building and rebuilding that now defines the city is done to stimulate consumption. A disproportionate amount of the construction in Tokyo is of commercial centers: expansion of the Central Business District, expansion of 'secondary' commercial centers such as Shinjuku, Shibuya and others; construction of department stores and shopping plazas at virtually every train and subway station of any consequence in the metropolis; and construction of brand-new commercial cores in each of the several sprawling 'new towns' that have been erected in recent years at the urban periphery.

One sees Tokyo's culture of consumption at seemingly every turn.[4] The most striking scenes take place on Sundays, Japan's principal shopping day, when literally millions of people in the metropolis take to the malls and department stores, as well as to movie theaters, concert halls, theaters, museums, games arcades, restaurants, coffee and dessert shops, and other places of consumer pleasure. Busy commercial streets are closed to vehicular traffic and become jammed with pedestrians moving in great throngs among the stores. During the mid-afternoon peak, some stores, as well as the lengths of certain popular shopping streets, become so crowded that one can hardly walk except to be carried by the wave of humanity and shopping bags. In the bookstores, of which there are many, the largest crowds elbow for space at magazine racks to read about which new fashions they should buy, or to learn about which ski resorts or golf courses they should try, the best package deals for travel abroad, the schedule of Tokyo's movies and concerts, and even the choice of foods being served at newly opened restaurants in the local area. Similarly, a ride on any commuter train or subway car reveals a consumer orientation. It seems that everywhere the eye turns to avoid eye contact with other riders, there are hanging banners and posters that tout all kinds of products: the latest issues of popular magazines (which themselves are filled with advertisements); upcoming TV programs (which will be interrupted again and again by still more commercial messages); schools that teach English; wedding chapels and reception halls; package tours to mountain spas and beach resorts; houses and condominium apartments for sale in distant suburbs; tickets for concerts and museum exhibitions; sales at department stores; and so on. Even cemetery plots are promoted on the trains, some of them promising perpetual views of Mount Fuji.

Young people – those of high school and college ages and 'young urban professionals' in their 20s and 30s – are especially visible as consumers. Especially on the fashionable west side of Tokyo, it seems that almost all of them are impeccably dressed in the latest, expensive fashions, and sport just the right

Figure 4.3 *Many young people in Tokyo are very conscious of fashion and take great care to look good*

accessories: designer handbags and backpacks, designer watches, designer sunglasses or eye glasses frames, etc. (Figure 4.3). Many of them also drive expensive luxury cars or top-of-the-line motorcycles, go on shopping trips on a whim to Hong Kong or Seoul, take mini-vacations to Hawaii, California Disneyland, or Australia's Great Barrier Reef, and at home have the best stereo sound equipment, personal computers, and other new 'toys'. Cellular telephones, called PHS ('Personal Handyphone System') in Japan, are also popular, having exploded in use since the mid-1990s (Figure 4.4.). Whether they are still in high school (or even younger) or ambitious company employees in the business world, young Tokyoites are now always getting or making phone calls, be they passengers in taxis or riders on crowded trains, customers at restaurant tables or noodle shop counters, or wading through crowds looking for their appointments. More than once I have witnessed couples find each other in dense crowds by communicating on the phone about their exact whereabouts as they walked.

One of the most popular fashions among teenagers is used clothing – principally American fashions once worn by strangers abroad. While most items are priced as bargains, saving youngsters money as they add to their wardrobes, other used items, referred to as 'vintage' clothing, sell for extraordinarily high prices for preferred labels and models. For example, a browse through a current issue of *Checkmate* (No. 208, February 1997), subtitled 'Magazine for Fashion Conscious Young Men', reveals a pair of 'vintage' Levi's 501XX jeans for sale for 'only' 168 000 yen (about $1500)! These particular pants are said to be desirable because the leather label over the back right pocket is warped just so, and because pockets have interior rivets. There are ads for quite a few other, similarly priced used jeans, used Levi's 507XX shirts that sell for as much as 198 000 yen (more than $1700!), and worn leather jackets that cost almost as much as new cars. In another popular fashion

Figure 4.4 *Cellular telephones are Tokyo's newest status symbol, especially among young people. The phones are called* PHS *in Japanese, standing for 'Personal Handyphone System'. This is a sales counter in Shinjuku*

magazine that I had been handed, the March 1997 issue of *Asayan* ('GET! Magazine for Street Boys'), there are used sneakers (classic Adidas!) advertised for the equivalent of hundreds of dollars. The price escalates to well over $1000 if the signs of wear are just right, or if the used shoes are a special model such as first-edition (1985) Nike Air Jordans.

Many young people feel an enormous pressure to be in step with such fashions and to have the money that is required to purchase them. In the words of singing idol Matsutoya Yumi, a person famous for a brand of 'new music' (*nyu-muzikku*) that reflects the culture of youth in suburban Tokyo (Tanaka, 1994, p. 1):

> When I run out of money that is when I die. There is no other way, really. If you take away the economic power from what I want to do, there's nothing left at all.

For many young Tokyoites, especially those from affluent families, the money comes from parents who themselves are spend-happy consumers. Many other young people work seemingly endless hours at *arubaito* (part-time jobs) to earn spending money. It seems that many of them toil for hours at one side of a counter selling hamburgers and shakes in a fast-food outlet or clothing and accessories in some shop, just for the chance to cross to the other side of the counter and buy something. There is also a growing problem of shoplifting by young people in Tokyo. It is mostly unreported as yet because shopkeepers do not want to lose face with customers (Woronoff, 1991, pp. 127–8), but evidence that theft is rising is seen in the recent proliferation of surveillance cameras in stores, anti-theft sensors on merchandise, and uniformed security guards roaming the aisles and posted at doors.

A particularly distressing development is an apparently enormous upsurge in recent years in prostitution by teenage girls for the specific purpose of getting money to buy consumer luxuries. Referred to as *enjo kōsai*, 'compensated dates', the problem has recently been the subject of literally hundreds of newspaper and magazine articles, both in Japan and abroad, as well as the focus of several television news exposés. The typical pattern is for high-school girls to make appointments with middle-aged salarymen through sex-oriented telephone clubs, charging them the equivalent of hundreds of dollars for a single liaison in a 'love-hotel'. As one such 16-year-old girl explained casually in a newspaper interview about her craving for Louis Vuitton bags, Chanel perfume, and other designer goods (Stroh, 1996, p. A8):

> Girls in my school tend to be split up into the girls who have such things and girls who don't. If you have the brand-name things, you're important.

Another young girl who has entered this economy, quoted by a student of mine who researched the problem, explained her situation very matter-of-factly:

> I prostitute to get tickets for concerts by famous musicians. I am not wrong. It's the price of tickets [that young people are expected to pay] that is wrong.

However, it is important to note that not all of Tokyo is so consumer oriented. Another aspect of the city is one of people who work incredibly hard, often for low wages at more than one job, simply to meet basic living expenses. For thousands of Tokyoites, it is a challenge to pay the rent on time and have enough left over for food and transportation around the city, and not even thinkable to have designer goods, expensive vacations, and other luxuries. Many young people, including students known to me, work at odd jobs principally to pay tuition and buy books, and keep any travel plans they might have or thoughts of fancy cars as dreams for the future. In fact, some sections of the city stand in direct contrast to the glitzy districts of Tokyo's west side, and can be seen principally as places of difficult work and unadorned living. These contrasts will be an important aspect of the next chapter of this book.

INTERNATIONALIZATION

We can also understand the current rebuilding of Tokyo as one facet of what is being called 'internationalization' or *kokusaika*. This is a common buzzword in Japan these days, and refers simultaneously to a number of different things: (1) the increasing influence that Japan has achieved among the nations of the world; (2) the increased facility that many Japanese have now with foreign ways and languages; and (3) the growing presence on Japanese soil of foreigners and foreign companies. In our context, the word refers especially to still another aspect of internationalization: (4) the rebuilding of Tokyo to make it more comfortable and more appealing to foreigners, particularly those with high-level business or diplomatic credentials. A key part of this is the construction of office buildings and other infrastructure to enhance Tokyo's standing as a leading international business center. We see these goals expressed explicitly in a recent influential official development plan for the city – *The 2nd Long-Term Plan for the Tokyo Metropolis*. Under a heading called 'Correct Approach to Internationalization' the document dictates, among other things, that 'Tokyo should be made a comfortable and friendly city for both foreign visitors and foreign residents', and that 'it is important to make Tokyo a safe, beautiful, comfortable and dignified city by increasing and improving parks, roads and other facilities, and shaping a tasteful cityscape'. All this, we are informed, is 'required in order to make Tokyo a truly international city that can lead the world in keeping up with the progress of internationalization' (Tokyo Metropolitan Government, 1987b, pp. 21–2).[5]

There is actually nothing particularly new in all this. Japanese have long been extremely sensitive to what foreigners say about their country, and have felt particularly aggrieved by any unfavorable comparisons of how they live and work. This has been true since that day in 1853 when Commodore Perry's 'black ships' anchored near Tokyo in Sagami Bay and began meddling in internal affairs; it continues to be true today. Time and again I am reminded by experience that even the smallest unfavorable comments about Japan or Tokyo from a foreigner can be irksome to Japanese, even when those comments are but a small part of a larger complimentary evaluation. During Meiji, the leaders of Japan responded to the foreign presence with an aggressive internationalization push that gave certain sections of Tokyo an exaggerated Western veneer. I think that today too, in response to the complaints that foreigners most often make about Tokyo (high prices for everything from rent to a cup of coffee, chronic traffic jams and non-stop crowds, and typically small, somewhat primitive housing units), there are calculated efforts to put on a different face. Developers have responded most energetically. Seeing an opportunity for profit, they have put up great numbers of Western-style houses and condominiums close to modern office districts and international embassies, several new Western hotels, and various other facilities (especially shopping) designed to cater to the foreigner market as well as to Japanese with 'international' tastes.

The push to be international can be applied to virtually every aspect of the urban scene, including the most mundane. If I may be a bit irreverent, I can tell about one example from a fringe area of city planning that I had never considered before, that of toilet planning. Alerted by an intriguing notice in a newspaper, I once attended a daylong conference in Tokyo (and a field trip the next day) called the International Toilet Forum. It was sponsored by the Japan Toilet Association, a group representing manufacturers of toilets and related equipment; it had as its purpose an evaluation of public toilet facilities in Tokyo and other Japanese urban areas from the standpoint of comfort of foreigners. There were sessions entitled 'Looking at Our International Cities – Tokyo, Yokohama, Nara, Kyoto, Kobe – from Toilets' and 'Future Toilet Policies from an International Viewpoint', as well as a featured address by an architectural critic, Kawazoe Noboru, called 'Urban Planning – From the Toilet'. There was an amazing late afternoon session: 12 foreigners representing 12 different countries (including every one of the world's inhabited continents, participants were reminded) giving testimonials called 'My Experiences with Toilets' in which they compared public facilities in Japan with those back

Figure 4.5 *Panelists at the 1988 International Toilet Forum discussing 'My Experiences with Toilets' from an international perspective. This is an example of Tokyo's internationalization efforts*

Table 4.6 *Foreign Residents in Tokyo, 1990*

	Total	Korea	China	Philippines	USA	Others
23 wards	133 203	57 209	34 428	5 498	9 282	26 786
Tama District[a]	25 870	12 497	4 525	1 421	2 607	4 820
Tōkyō-to	159 073	69 497	38 953	6 919	11 889	31 606

[a] Includes the islands.

Source: Tokyo Statistical Yearbook, 1994, Table 22, p. 54.

home (Figure 4.5). Everyone was perfectly serious, and I had the feeling that I was the only person among the 300–400 attendees who wanted to laugh. All the Japanese listeners, it seemed, were thoroughly professional and totally dedicated to the issue, behaving as if they were on some sort of sacred mission to contribute to the internationalization of their country's capital.

Despite the attention given to Tokyo's emerging international profile, it is important to point out that foreigners comprise only a small part of the city's total population. According to data for 1990, there were 159 073 foreign residents in *Tōkyō-to* as a whole, up from 121 663 in 1982 and 110 862 in 1978 (*Tokyo Statistical Yearbook*, 1994, p. 54; *Tokyo Statistical Yearbook*, 1982, p. 32). While such numbers are large enough to make up the population of a small city, they represent only slightly more than 1.0 percent of the total for *Tōkyō-to*. What is more, nearly one-half of the foreigners in Tokyo (i.e. most of those from Korea and many of those from China) were actually born in Japan; they are counted as foreigners because their parents were not Japanese. Table 4.6 gives a breakdown of Tokyo's foreigner population by nationality. In addition to the Koreans and Chinese,

Table 4.7 *Daytime/nighttime Population and Daily Inflow/outflow in Tokyo's Three Central Wards, 1 October 1990*

	Day population	Night population	Day index[a]	Daily incoming population	Daily outgoing population
Chiyoda Ward	1 036 609	39 305	2 637	1 007 494	10 190
Chūō Ward	748 288	67 621	1 107	697 604	16 937
Minato Ward	883 952	156 325	566	775 236	47 609
23 wards total	11 287 948	8 099 153	139	3 642 278	453 483
Tōkyō-to total	14 483 495	11 762 030	123	3 208 273	486 808

[a] Day population index = (day population/night population) × 100

Source: *Tokyo Statistical Yearbook*, 1994, pp. 66–7.

who comprise 43.8 and 24.5 percent of the foreigner population, respectively, there are also several thousands of foreigners from the Philippines and the United States, and from countries included in the 'others' category such as Thailand, Indonesia and Iran. Many of the city's laborers come from the latter group of countries, as well as from the Philippines, Pakistan and other Southeast and South Asian nations.

THE CENTRAL BUSINESS DISTRICT

Nearly 2.5 million commuters arrive each working day in the three central wards of Tokyo (Chūō, Chiyoda, and Minato) that correspond to the CBD and its fringes (Table 4.7). This is probably the largest daily flow of people in the world, and speaks to the immense importance of the Tokyo CBD as a place for employment, shopping, and many other activities, as well as to its considerable geographical extent and high levels of crowding during the day. According to data for 1990, the daytime population of these three wards was 2 668 849, contrasting with a nighttime total of only 263 251. The daytime population density was 89 056 persons per square kilometer in Chūō Ward, 73 723 in Chiyoda Ward, and 43 566 in Minato Ward. These numbers contrasted with a daytime population density of 'only' 18 271 persons per square kilometer for the 23-ward section of Tokyo and 6633 persons per square kilometer in Tōkyō-to.

Although the combination of Chūō Ward, Chiyoda Ward and Minato Ward is a convenient definition of the Tokyo CBD plus its fringes, there are no agreed-upon boundaries for the CBD itself because the limits would vary according to the definitions one would use. However, the core of the area is well known and easy to identify: it is the same district at the foot of the Imperial Palace where over 350 years ago, when Edo Castle was there, the city's first merchants set up a fish market near the boat landing at Nihombashi. For our purposes, we can say that the CBD extends in all directions from this core to cover the area between the Imperial Palace grounds to the west, the mixed residential, commercial, and light-industrial quarters of Kanda to the north, the banks of the Sumida River and its mouth at Tokyo Bay to the east and southeast, a zone of industry, warehouses and trans-portation facilities near Tokyo Bay a little further to the southeast, and the higher

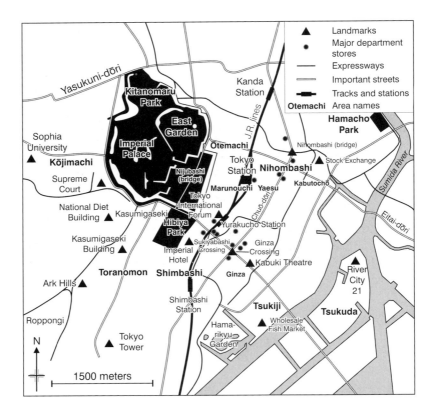

Figure 4.6 *Tokyo CBD location map*

grounds and loftier status neighborhoods of *yamanote* to the west, not far from Tokyo Tower. This is an area of some five or six square kilometers, and consists of several distinctive subdistricts, each with its own personality and physical appearance and special role in the overall CBD economy. We will first discuss those areas in the core of the CBD, and then the areas of CBD expansion (Figure 4.6).

THE CBD CORE

The center of the CBD, both geographically and symbolically, is Tokyo Station. This is the ornate, red-brick train facility that was built over eight years during late Meiji and early Taishō, and was completed in 1914 to be a landmark of the city's new modernity. It sits strategically between the Marunouchi office district that the Mitsubishi family developed 100 years ago on empty land next to the palace, and the retailing core of the city, where the great department stores were born, in Nihombashi, Kyōbashi, and Ginza. The station is far and away the busiest disgorger of commuters among the many other train and subway stations in the center, and is often shown by foreign (and domestic) news correspondents as the backdrop for reports about Japan's economy and its 'modern army of office samurai' on its way

Figure 4.7 *The Marunouchi office district as seen from the walls and moats of the Imperial Palace*

to work in surrounding office buildings. Some 2500 trains stop there each day, and nearly 700 000 passengers pass through its turnstiles. In fact, we can say that Tokyo Station is now the center of all Japan, because it is the hub of the *shinkansen* network, the high-speed bullet trains that connect the capital city with almost all the largest cities in the country. A substantial fraction of the early-morning activity comes from Tokyo-based company employees and government bureaucrats who pass through the station to board high-speed trains (one leaves every few minutes during peak times) for a day of meetings in Nagoya, Osaka, Kobe, or some other regional center.

Marunouchi is Tokyo's premier office district (Figure 4.7). It is right at the main exits of Tokyo Station, and stretches between the track corridor on the one side and the Imperial Palace grounds on the other. It derives much of its prestige, as well as its exceedingly high rents, from this centrality. The Mitsubishi Company (actually, *group* of companies) is still the prime landowner, and sets the tone for this district in terms of both physical design and rhythms of activity. The 'Londontown' plan of a century ago did not survive the 1923 earthquake-fire and the area has since been redeveloped. Much of the present landscape dates to the time of post-war reconstruction. The overall design is a no-nonsense setting where the important work of big companies can go on without needless distractions. The streets are laid out in an orderly grid, and the blocks are covered from end to end with big office buildings that are functional, but almost totally without adornment. There are not even many restaurants or drinking places – highly unusual for a crowded commercial area in restaurant-rich Tokyo – except for company cafeterias in some of the buildings, and numerous smaller establishments tucked away in the basement levels to serve 'set breakfasts' and daily 'set lunches' to workers on the run.

A walk through Marunouchi reveals its single-minded dedication to work. The day starts early, in part to overlap with the workday in New York and other overseas locations, and extends well into the evening. The first commuters begin to emerge from Tokyo Station and other nearby stations as early as 6 a.m. By 7 a.m., the pedestrian traffic has become a steady march. The subterranean passages connecting stations with workplaces fill with dress-alike men (dark suit, dark tie, white shirt, trench coat in bad weather) carrying briefcases and with smaller numbers of women, and resound with footsteps. Almost no one speaks. It is a fast and silent march, through the passageways, up the stairs to street level, down the block, and into the buildings. Once inside, most of the women, 'office ladies' or OL's as they are called, change into company uniforms. We see them on the sidewalks throughout the day, often in pairs, as they emerge from buildings to run errands. The buildings themselves – the Marunouchi Building, the New Marunouchi (*Shin Marunouchi*) Building, the Marunouchi Center Building, the Mitsubishi Building, the Mitsubishi Heavy Industries Building, the Mitsubishi Electric Building, the Mitsubishi Shōji ('commercial') Building, the Mitsubishi Bank Building, as well as numerous other banks, insurance companies, other corporate enterprises, and the Central Post Office – all reflect the sameness. Except for Mitsubishi Bank, which is a new tower twice as high as the rest (24 stories), they are trim and level, because of the restrictions on building height; most are made of similar materials arranged in similar ways on the facades. Perhaps it is in Marunouchi that the old Japanese maxim about human behavior, now a cliché among foreign observers of the country, that the nail that sticks out higher than the rest is the one that gets hammered down first, is most clearly reflected in the landscape.

The other side of Tokyo Station, called the Yaesu side, is somewhat different. There is still the silent, morning procession to work, the long working days, and a lot of rather drab architecture, but there is also more individuality in the design of buildings, considerable mixture of land uses, and plenty of distractions from neons, billboards, and other calls to attention. The non-office land uses include a multi-level department store, Daimaru, built into this remodeled side of the station, and a big underground shopping mall that sprawls in labyrinthine fashion between the station and its more distant exits some blocks away. However, Yaesu is still big business first. A large digital clock high up on a bank building across the street from the station heralds this. In addition to telling the time, it outlines a map of the world, and gives up-to-the-minute quotations for the price of the yen in the New York and London markets.

Just to the north of Tokyo Station is Ōtemachi. Named after the nearby Ōte Gate of the Imperial Palace-Edo Castle, the area is part spillover of offices from overcrowded Marunouchi and part an alternative to Marunouchi's conformism. It is generally newer than Marunouchi and a number of its office buildings are taller. This area, too, has an impressive list of tenants. Among others, there are the head offices of Fuji Bank and Sanwa Bank, the Yomiuri Newspaper publishers, Sankei Newspapers, Nihon Keizai Newspapers, the global communications giant NTT, Nippon Steel, and the Mitsui Mutual Life Insurance Company. There are also several large banks in the area. Government offices include the Immigration Bureau, the Publications Center, and Tokyo's International Post Office. Sometimes observers note physical similarities between Ōtemachi and the office tower sections of Midtown Manhattan, but with lower buildings. A statue of Shibusawa Ei'ichi (1840–1931), who founded more than 500 companies before retiring in 1916 and is acknowledged as Japan's guiding light in its transition to capitalist economics, stands in a small park near the Nippon Steel headquarters and reflects the area's orientation to business.

Still another major concentration of economic power is Nihombashi, just across an old, narrow canal, the Nihombashi River, from Ōtemachi and northeast of Tokyo Station. This was the heart of commerce in old Edo, and where the city's first financial houses and early department stores originated. The blocks closest to the canal, near a place where some of the stone wall of Edo Castle can still be seen, is given to some of the biggest banks. The Bank of Japan, the nation's central bank, is the most imposing structure. One part of it, on the site of Tokugawa Ieyasu's gold mint, is a massive stone building designed in neoclassical style that dates to the 1890s, while the other part is a modern high-rise faced with stone and built to look like a fortress. Across the street is the high-rise headquarters of the giant Bank of Tokyo. The Industrial Bank of Japan and the Yasuda Bank and Trust Company, also in impressive buildings, are across the canal where Nihombashi borders Yaesu. The center of Nihombashi is still the domain of the Mitsui financial empire, the old rival to the Mitsubishi interests. The headquarters of the Mitsui Bank (recently reorganized as the Taiyo Kobe Mitsui Bank) and the flagship store of the Mitsukoshi Department Store chain are there, side by side on the main street. Both are elegant structures in the classic European style that was popular in Tokyo during late Meiji, and are strong examples of the persistence of tradition in Tokyo's fast-changing CBD.

The Tokyo Stock Exchange, obviously another major center of economic influence, is a subsection of Nihombashi called Kabutochō. It is down-canal from the core of Nihombashi, and is somewhat removed from Tokyo Station (about 20 minutes' walk away) and its adjacent office districts. It developed there because the port was once nearby, and because it was closer to the city's Grain Exchange and warehouses with grain and other commodities. The Stock Exchange is surrounded by numerous securities companies and related establishments, many of which spill over into neighboring Kayabachō, and has emerged as the nucleus of still another important subdistrict of the CBD that is oriented to finance. The area has been an active zone for office building construction in recent years, partly because land costs have been a cut or two lower than closer in to the center, and partly because of an influx of new companies after the Tokyo Stock Exchange began accepting its first foreign members in early 1986.

The main street of Nihombashi is Chūō-dōri. Its length from the Mitsui buildings in Nihombashi to Shimbashi (about 2.5 kilometers) is the principal retailing spine of the CBD. It extends along a major trolley corridor that shaped the district nearly 100 years ago, and is anchored at either end by clusters of department stores at stations of the Ginza Subway Line, the city's first underground. The Nihombashi end (Mitsukoshimae and Nihombashi Stations) has, in addition to the main Mitsukoshi Store, the flagship stores for the Tōkyū and the Takashimaya chains, while the Ginza–Shimbashi end (Ginza Station) has, among others, Matsuya, Matsuzakaya, Wako, and a major branch of Mitsukoshi. In between and along side streets are many other stores, restaurants, and other business establishments. On

Figure 4.8 *Miyuki-dōri in Ginza, one of the district's fashionable shopping streets*

most Sundays, the principal shopping day in Japan, Chūō-dōri is closed to vehicles and becomes a huge pedestrian mall. A side street called Miyuki-dōri has several exclusive boutiques and galleries, and is especially fashionable (Figure 4.8). Other side streets specialize in the popular nightclubs for which inner Tokyo (e.g. Ginza) is well known. All of them are quite expensive.

The Ginza retailing district has expanded in recent times (since the 1960s) along Harumi-dōri, a busy street that is perpendicular to Chūō-dōri, in the direction of Hibiya and Yūrakuchō. The area near the track corridor that leads to Tokyo Station, long the city's leading center for movie going and theaters, has three huge, new department stores in gleaming high-rise towers. They face Sukiyabashi Crossing, one of the busiest street intersections in the city, and a busy public square where thousands wait each day to meet their social or business appointments. Along the rail tracks behind the high-rises is Tokyo International Forum, a brand new (1996), luxurious convention and exposition center. Designed by Uruguay-born American architect Rafael Vignoly and costing an astounding 165 billion yen ($1.5 billion) to build, the project sits on prime land that was once the site of Tokyo's City Hall, and is a specific example of urban development to promote internationalization.

Not far away, now on the south side of the Imperial Place grounds and about 20 minutes' walk southwest from Tokyo Station, is the national capital district. It covers most of Nagatachō and Kasumigaseki. Because it is an area of former *daimyō* estates, as well as because of the monumental nature of many of its buildings, it is much less crowded than the CBD and has some greenery and open spaces. The largest is Hibiya Park, downtown Tokyo's 'Central Park' or 'Hyde Park', and a pleasant buffer between the business core of the city and the government buildings. The National Diet Building (*Kokkai-Gijidō*) is the centerpiece of this district (Figure 4.9). It is an imposing gray granite structure built in a Prussian style and

Figure 4.9   *The National Diet Building*

embellished on top with a rather ill-proportioned ziggurat. The site is a low hill that overlooks the palace grounds and the other government buildings: the Prime Minister's Office, the headquarters of various ministries, court buildings, offices for members of the Diet, the National Diet Library, and many others. Because of the large numbers of government buildings, their substantial proportions, and the atmosphere of workaday hustle and bustle, it is all a rather impressive scene. In total, the message that Tokyo is a substantial center of power and a strong capital is well conveyed.

CBD EXPANSION

We can identify several specific areas within Tokyo's three central wards that are leading edges of CBD expansion. One is the city's waterfront, where Tokyo Bay reaches closest to the heart of the city and the Sumida River has its principal distributary. This is a rather large district of industries, warehouses and docking facilities on reclaimed land, and includes several close-in offshore islands, loosely connected peninsulas, and sections of 'mainland'. Various parts of it are now being transformed for expansion of offices, hotels, and other uses related to the CBD. Two of the best examples, seen clearly from Tokyo Tower, are the World Trade Center building, a tall office tower and trade show facility adjacent to an important rail corridor in a district called Hamamatsuchō; and the Tōshiba Building, world headquarters for the giant electronics firm that is on a former manufacturing site. Both buildings are 40 stories high. Right now they appear as somewhat lone towers in an area that is still primarily industrial. However, as we will see in a later chapter, there are grand schemes to transform the entire waterfront near them into an especially important part of an expanded CBD.

Similarly, the CBD bank of the lower reaches of the Sumida River is another zone of CBD expansion. A major target there is the Shinkawa area, long a district of *sake* wholesalers, other warehouses, small stores and old wooden houses. However, nearness to the Stock Exchange area of Kabutochō, combined with lower land costs and the presence of larger development sites (because of the warehouses), has caused an office building boom that promises to incorporate this neighborhood quickly into the main part of the CBD. Riverfront sites are most desirable and have been taken by the biggest companies for the tallest buildings. The Sumitomo Twin Building, a 24-story and a 21-story office complex constructed by the Sumitomo Warehouse Company, a member of the huge Sumitomo financial group, is the most imposing (Satō, 1988). The same pattern is true in the neighboring riverfront district called Hakozakichō. There, the biggest builder has been the IBM Corporation, which has its headquarters for Asian/Pacific operations on the river in a new (1989) 25-story tower. The IBM Building is also distinguished for having one of the best public promenades at the waterfront of central Tokyo. A newer (1994) showpiece along the lower Sumida is St Luke's Garden, a 51-story office tower and 38-story residential building joined at 110 meters by a soaring pedestrian bridge.

Similar land-use transition, in which warehousing, transportation facilities, and industry are replaced by CBD land uses, is also seen in other areas of central Tokyo. An area called Shiodome, for example, close to Ginza and Shimbashi, is slated for conversion to a sizable cluster of office towers, hotels, high-rise residences, and shopping centers – a 'new town in town'. The opportunity comes from a 26-hectare rail freight distribution center that is being displaced further out (Tange, 1987, pp. 28–31; Yada, 1989a, pp. 33–6). Similarly, parts of the Shiba area near the waterfront to the southwest of the center, long known as a center of manufacturing in Tokyo, especially of electronics products, are being converted to offices and related land uses. Just like the Tōshiba Corporation has done with its office tower near the waterfront, another electronics giant, NEC, has recently completed a landmark headquarters high-rise (43 stories; distinctive shape) on a formerly industrial site.

Another direction for CBD expansion is north into Kanda. This has been an area of small shops, artisans and craftsmen, and residences, as well as a district of colleges and a university campus put up during the enlightenment programs of the Meiji era. Its nearness to the center, convenience for train and subway lines, and higher prestige compared to changing industrial districts has drawn a flood of builders in recent years, and changed some sections into high- and mid-rise boomtowns seemingly overnight. This has been particularly the case along arterial streets (e.g. Yasukuni-dōri) and near important train stations (e.g. Ochanomizu). There are no showpiece high-rises that stand out alone as in the previous examples; instead, there are multi-story buildings just about everywhere, and the rooflines of the entire district seem to be rising from one and two stories to seven, eight, ten, twelve, or more, almost in unison. Many different kinds of businesses are involved, but printing and publishing, the number-one manufacturing industry in Tokyo, is a leading staple in Kanda.

However, the most spectacular growth is reserved for the west side of the CBD, south of the Imperial Palace. This includes several districts that are contiguous to

Figure 4.10 *A part of Tokyo's expanding CBD. This is in the Akasaka district of Minato Ward, looking at office buildings lining Aoyama-dōri near the Akasaka–Mitsuke subway station*

the CBD or the adjacent government center such as Akasaka, Toranomon, Uchisaiwaichō, Shimbashi and Nishi-Shimbashi, as well as some districts somewhat further afield from the CBD that are expanding rapidly with high-rise commerce and are likely to coalesce soon with the center. Examples from this category include Roppongi, Aoyama, Shibuya, Shinagawa, and Shinjuku. Already, the major roads such as Aoyama-dōri and Shinjuku-dōri that connect the CBD with what are supposed to be outlying commercial subcenters (e.g. Shibuya and Shinjuku, respectively) are lined along most of their courses with tall office buildings. Moreover, major intersections and subway stops such as Aoyama-Itchōme, which has the Aoyama Twin office towers and the high-rise headquarters of the Honda Corporation, one of the most attractive new buildings in the city, are mini-CBDs in themselves. Consequently, it is not difficult to imagine that in the not-too-distant future, the whole west side of Tokyo within the Yamanote Loop (and all areas within the loop north, south, and east of the center) will become part of one super-enormous business center. If this happens, it would be about as big as the entire city was during the height of the Tokugawa Era, when Edo was the most populous urban center in the world!

There are several reasons why CBD growth has been especially active toward the west. One is that the west is the principal direction of *yamanote*, the higher ground and higher-prestige zone that has been a feature of the city since early Edo times. As a result it has been the direction of quickest expansion of Tokyo as a whole. Most of its better suburbs are to the west, as are most of the giant new commercial subcenters, largest and busiest nightlife districts, and centers of fashion and many popular trends. Second, the west side of Tokyo is where most of the city's foreign embassies and consulates are located (often on grounds that were once feudal estates), and where the majority of foreign diplomats, foreign business executives, and other highly placed foreigners in Tokyo reside. Consequently, this is where Tokyo shows its international side most, and where many of the foreign firms doing business in Japan have been drawn. For the same reason, the west is where most of the city's large international hotels (as opposed to the smaller 'business hotels' that are more typical in Japanese city centers) have chosen to locate. Finally, I note a true down-to-earth advantage that the west has: it is more stable geologically than the delta lands and reclaimed flats east and south of the center, and therefore more desirable for the construction of tall buildings.

The Toranomon area, a fast-developing office district adjacent to Kasumigaseki, presents a fascinating, albeit somewhat idiosyncratic, case study of CBD expansion. Until recently, the area was a neighborhood of homes, shops, and small businesses, a great many of which were owned by the same families that had inhabited the land for generations. This was a typical pattern for inner-city Tokyo. However, in recent years Toranomon has undergone an almost total transformation, and it is now one of the hottest office rental markets in Tokyo. Peter Popham, whose book *Tokyo: The City at the End of the World* I introduced as being one of my favorites, describes this change as being largely the doing of one company, the Mori Building Company, the third largest landowner in Japan (after the Mitsubishi and the Mitsui interests), and one man, its founder and president until his death in 1993, Mori Taikichirō (Popham, 1985, pp. 73–84).

The son of a rice dealer, Mori was born in 1904 and raised in Toranomon. He began his career in academics, rising to the rank of professor and dean of the faculty of commerce at Yokohama City University. He turned to real estate in 1959, and took it upon himself as a personal mission to transform his old neighborhood into one of the hubs of Tokyo commerce. In an exceptional interview with Popham, he explained that he saw long ago that 'the ordinary old Japan could not survive, it would be defeated by the advanced nations, so we had to struggle to achieve rapid Westernization'. Therefore, he began acquiring property from his neighbors and 'Westernizing' it by converting it to offices. His first building, *Mori Biru 1* (Mori Building 1) was completed in 1955. Now there are approximately 80 'Mori Birus' in and near Toranomon, most of them identified by numbers in the sequence of construction. From our perch in Tokyo Tower, where we conducted an introductory reconnaissance of the city, we can see the words 'Mori Biru 40', 'Mori Biru 35' and 'Mori Biru 37' (in Japanese), among other Mori numbers, high up on the buildings in Toranomon that face us. This naming system was adopted because there is a custom among many Japanese families to give children names that indicate the order of birth (Ichirō, Jirō, Saburō, etc.), and because Mori looked upon his buildings as if they were his children (Popham, 1985, p. 74).

One of Mori's beloved recent offspring is the grand-scale project called Ark Hills. It is named this because it is where Akasaka, Roppongi and Kasumigaseki come together. It is different from most other Mori developments because it is a complex of several buildings rather than just one. It is Mori-san himself who proclaimed this place in advertising to be 'Where Tokyo is Headed' (Figure 4.11). What makes Ark Hills special is that it is a mixed-use development: in addition to the office towers and hotel, there are private residences in three of the high-rises and various 'community facilities'. According to the publicity, this is to stimulate a reversal of

Figure 4.11 An advertisement for the Ark Hills development of the Mori Building Company. It boasts that 'It's Where Tokyo is Headed', a reference to both the centrality of the complex and its design. Several other mixed-use developments similar to Ark Hills have been constructed in Tokyo since Ark Hills opened in 1986. (Courtesy of the Mori Building Company)

the depopulation of inner Tokyo – depopulation that Mori himself had much to do with. In Toranomon, for example, in the 1980s alone, the number of residents slipped from 4838 in 1980, to 4111 in 1985, and then to 3231 in 1989. By 1996 the population had dropped further – to only 1294. How this depopulation was accomplished and how it has affected established neighborhoods will be our topic soon. For now, we turn to the flip side of CBD growth in Tokyo – the expansion of residential areas well beyond the center.

THE RESIDENTIAL RING

AFFORDING A HOUSE

Scattered around the Tokyo Metropolis are quite a number of 'model home parks'. These are displays of new houses, complete with interior furnishings, that are put up by housing developers to give potential home-buyers a chance to comparison shop in one location. Almost always the displays are temporary, occupying a piece of land that is awaiting some larger development later, but the houses are spacious and beautifully appointed. The example I know best stood until recently alongside the commuter rail tracks near Shinjuku Station, the 3 million passengers a day commuter hub on the city's west side. The ground was once a rail freight yard that stretched for nearly 400 meters along the tracks and 50 to 100 meters deep.[6] Some of the nation's biggest housing developers, Misawa Home, Mitsui Home, Seibu House, and others, had put up a total of 27 quite beautiful and in some cases remarkably luxurious, suburban-style single houses, as well as some appropriate front-yard landscaping, along either side of a new street paralleling the tracks. Especially on weekends, when families have time to spend together, people come to such places to inspect the choices and perhaps place an order with one of the sales agents. No one actually buys exactly what is on display, because the models are too expensive for most budgets and most houses too big for typical lots in and around Tokyo. What is actually sold, then, are scaled-down versions of dream houses to some people, and dreams for a house in the future to others.

The market for new housing in and around Tokyo is huge. According to one source, a current (1994) official housing plan for the Tokyo Metropolis, the number of new and rebuilt residential units to be built during the period 1991–2000 could go as high as 1 750 000 (Tokyo Metropolitan Government, 1994a, p. 44). There are many reasons for this. A sizable fraction of the metropolitan population, especially in the 23-wards section of Tokyo, is generally poorly housed and anxious for improvement. Surveys show that about one-third of the 23-ward population is 'dissatisfied to some extent' with where they live, and that an additional 8.6 percent is 'very dissatisfied' (Tokyo Metropolitan Government, 1988, p. 48). Most complaints are about neighborhood crowding and cramped residential quarters (Tokyo Municipal News, Summer, 1988, p. 8). Furthermore, the fact that this is a time of considerable prosperity in Japan has raised people's expectations about housing and redefined standards. Moreover, demand for housing has been stimulated by the demographic structure of the population, which now has a disproportionate share of young households with dwelling needs that change with marriage, divorce, the birth of children, changes in employment, and many other factors.

The specific location of the Shinjuku Rail-City Housing Display Grounds, being at trackside at a busy mass transit interchange between the business-oriented heart of the city and its largest sector of residential suburbs, reflects good marketing strategy. Because this site and others like it are visible from the trains that pass, they remind commuters as they travel to and from work about a financial objective that many of them hold. This marketing message is reinforced by advertisements

Figure 4.12 *An advertisement for houses for sale near Minami Osawa in Tokyo's suburban Tama area. The houses have four rooms plus 'LDK' (living room–dining room–kitchen) and are 6 minutes from the local commuter rail station, 37 minutes to Shinjuku Station and 39 minutes to Shibuya Station. This is a reproduction of one of the hundreds of leaflets that have been put in my various apartment mailboxes over the years*

for real estate posted in the trains themselves, in ads in the newspapers and magazines that train riders always seem to be reading, and on the backs of the small tissue packets that one is always being handed near train station exits and in busy commercial centers. There are also plenty of leaflets about houses for sale that are stuffed each day in residential mail boxes, especially in apartment buildings and overcrowded condominiums (*manshon*) where young working people are known to live (Figure 4.12). Indeed, it is as if there was some sort of massive propaganda machine at work, repeatedly encouraging the metropolis's laborers to toil on and promising them the imminent reward of a dream house. In one specific ad, a train-car poster promoting a particular single-family housing development in suburban Saitama Prefecture, an adorable little girl, about four years old, in a very comfortable domestic setting and holding a kitten, says sweetly to her *sarariman* (salaryman) father, '*otōsan gambare*' – 'keep it up daddy, give it your best' (Nussbaum, 1985, p. 81).

For most *otōsan* (and, of course, as well as for home buyers who are not fathers) the greatest hurdle to homeownership is the price of land. This is a problem probably found in every country with private ownership of land, but in Tokyo it seems to be particularly severe. Prices are so high that most people who do not already own a piece of the city are priced out of the market, and have to resign themselves to continue to exist in tiny apartments or move to some inconveniently located place far from the city center. A 1993 survey by the Japan National Land Agency found that the average price of residential land in Tokyo Metropolis (*Tōkyō-*

Table 4.8 *Average Land Prices by Use, 1993 (1000 yen per square meter)*

	Residential	Commercial	Quasi-industrial	Industrial
Three central wards	3262.4	9620.3	2245.0	–
23 wards	763.9	4950.3	890.9	631.0
Tama Area	340.6	1440.8	348.4	240.0
Tōkyō-to	521.9	4189.3	759.1	591.9

Source: Tokyo Metropolitan Government (1994a, p. 85).

to) as a whole was 521 900 yen per square meter (approximately $4700). This was higher by far than any other prefecture in Japan, the next highest being Osaka (*Ōsaka-fu*) with an average cost of residential land of 303 700 yen per square meter (*Japan Almanac 1996*, p. 201). If land in Tokyo is affordable, it is likely to be at a distant (western) edge of the Metropolis, where land costs are below the *Tōkyō-to* average. The three central wards are prohibitively expensive – more than six times the average for residential land in Tokyo Metropolis as a whole (Table 4.8). Hence, we have still another reason for the decline of population in the central wards and conversion of residential land to commercial uses.

The geographical distribution of land values varies not just with distance from the center of the city but also with distance usually measured in terms of 'numbers of minutes' from train or subway stations. Convenient walking distance from a station is most expensive, even if it means being on a crowded and noisy street, followed in order by bicycle distance and feeder bus distance. The cheapest housing, then, is far from the city, at a local stop on a slow train line, and then some distance away from that stop requiring the commuter to spend time waiting for a bus. Even there, the cost of 'a nothing-special flat out among the power lines' can be prohibitive: say, ten or fifteen years of bread-winning (Kauffman, 1988, p. 78). So, if a piece of real estate is possible at all, or even a circumscribed volume of air in a multi-story condominium, it usually takes considerable savings, a long-term mortgage, and generous help from relatives or friends (Nussbaum, 1985).

It is because the cost of land is so high that the great majority of sales made at model home parks like the one that stood in Shinjuku are to people who already own property and who intend to replace older houses with new ones. This is another important dimension of 'the third rebuilding of Tokyo', and accounts for much of the construction that one sees around the city. One aspect of this is, very simply, people who want to improve their living conditions by having a house that is larger, more modern, or better tailored for changing household needs. Many others erect a structure that accommodates two generations of the same family. For example, it is rather common for parents to assist their adult children who are priced out of the land market by combining resources with them and replacing their old house with one that can be shared. This dovetails with traditional patterns of multi-generational living in Japan, so that there is nothing particularly new about this in concept. What changes is the increased extent to which multi-generation living is forced on Tokyo families by land costs. There are also novel architectural designs that blend the traditional house with layouts that increase privacy and appeal especially to modern tastes. We saw a specific example of this in Chapter 1, with my former neighbor the *tatami*-maker and his family. In the time since we moved from that neighborhood in Shibuya Ward, this particular family, like so many others in and around Tokyo in recent years, has knocked down its old house and replaced it on the same ground with a new structure that is taller, has more modern amenities, and includes space for two generations of the family, as well as rental space for additional income.

As expensive as land is in Tokyo, it was recently much more expensive. For example, in contrast to the figure of 521 900 yen per square meter for residential land in *Tōkyō-to* in 1993 that was cited above, the comparable figure for 1989 (cited in this book's first edition) was 853 500 yen per square meter. Likewise, in contrast to the figure of 1 880 000 yen per square meter for residential land near Roppongi Station, a prime inner-Tokyo location, that was cited above for 1995, the comparable 1989 figure was 6 790 000 yen per square meter. Clearly, what has happened is that the tremendous speculative bubble in the value of land that had developed during the heady economy of the 1980s has burst, suddenly dropping land values for all purposes – residential, commercial and industrial – to pre-1980s levels. Land values have continued to slip with the prolonged economic recession of the 1990s in Tokyo and Japan as a whole. For our purposes, the lower cost of land means that many more Tokyoites than had been imagined earlier are now able to buy housing or trade up to larger units. I know several such people personally; they thought that they would never be able to buy property in Tokyo, but were surprised to see that suddenly some bargains (by Tokyo standards) were available. Thus, demand for new construction has increased and Tokyo has kept building even though the economy has been slow (see Figures 4.13 and 4.14).

TYPES OF SUBURBAN DEVELOPMENT

It would be wrong to think of the residential ring around central Tokyo as being nothing more than bedroom communities, or to assume that all places there are the same. As in any other large metropolitan area, the broad zone that surrounds the main city is extremely diverse and contains many types of areas, both residential and other. Because the previous paragraphs concentrated exclusively on new single-family housing, it is necessary now to present a more balanced account of the urbanized ring around Tokyo and show a fuller range of the kinds of places found there and the various forces that shaped them.

Suburban expansion is not new: it has been going on in one form or another for more than a century. Even during Edo (before 1868), new districts were continually being added to the edge of the city, be it on reclaimed land close to the center near the bay or in the form of 'ribbon urbanization' along some of the highways leading from the city to the provinces. With the coming of railroads in the 1880s and 1890s suburban expansion increased. The first train line to be used by commuters was the Chūō Line (the 'central' or 'middle' line), due west of the city. It was developed by private interests in the 1880s primarily to link Tokyo with Yamanashi, a provincial city about 90 kilometers away. Starting in 1889 it stopped at four stations in the

Figure 4.13 *A view across Tokyo's crowded residential landscape in the western suburbs*

Figure 4.14 *The city and countryside come together here in Chōfu, a growing residential town on Tokyo's west side*

farmlands on the west side of Tokyo: Hachiōji, Tachikawa, Kokubunji, and Sakai. It eventually transformed small settlements there into populous commuter centers. Other early lines were the Ōme Line, built in 1894 to connect Tachikawa with Ōme in the western mountains; the Seibu Ikebukuro Line (1915), originally an industrial corridor for hauling limestone and silk, but now a key commuter link through western suburbs north of the Chūō Line; and the Keiō Line (mid-1910s) running from Shinjuku to Hachiōji, Fuchū, Chōfu and other settlements south of the Chūō corridor (Allinson, 1979, pp. 22–3).

However, because of poor scheduling and considerable distances between stops, service was slow in the first years and the pace of suburban growth was unimpressive, at least until 1923. The Great Kantō Earthquake began to change all this. Its disaster chased residents and businesses alike from the heart of the city and stimulated public demands for improved access to the periphery. As a result, other train lines were soon extended west, southwest, northwest, north and east of the city, and the number of stations and the frequency of trains increased. The urbanized area began to expand more quickly than ever before, especially to the west and southwest where the most ambitious transportation projects were located; what was once a tight urban cluster started to transform itself into a sprawling metropolis of sizable proportions.

Extending commuter rail lines to the suburbs was largely the initiative of private companies. The most successful of them saw opportunities for profit not only in train fares but also in land sales and housing development along the tracks that they extended, in retailing near busy train stations, as well as in various other related enterprises. In the manner of entrepreneurial land speculators at the edge of cities in numerous Western countries, company founders bought up farm land and forests beyond the urbanized area in advance of transportation, laid tracks and built stations, and developed housing subdivisions and entire new towns for a growing metropolitan population. The largest enterprises went so far as to build giant department stores at terminal stations close to the central wards of Tokyo (e.g. at Shinjuku, Shibuya, Ikebukuro and Ueno), branch stores at key commuter stations along their tracks, and chains of supermarkets that covered every point where there was growing settlement. Because of severe central-city housing shortages, their advertising messages to move to the suburbs were well received by Tokyoites, many of whom were eager to live in fresh surroundings where they could have ample room and cheaper accommodation. 'To the suburbs where cosmoses bloom' was one of the popular advertising phrases of the 1930s (Ishizuka and Ishida, 1988, p. 22).

Perhaps the most successful of the giant companies born in this way is the Seibu Group. Founded in the mid-1910s by Tsutsumi Yasujirō (1889–1964), a remarkably entrepreneurial migrant to Tokyo from a farm in Shiga Prefecture, the company grew quickly from a few small investments into a huge, highly diversified concern spanning real estate and railroad holdings, hotels, golf courses, ski resorts, the Seibu department stores and supermarkets empire, amusement parks, consumer credit and insurance firms, the championship Seibu Lions baseball team and stadium, and many other ventures. It is now divided among two feuding sons, the younger of whom, Yoshiaki, was once said by *Forbes* magazine (27 July 1987) to be the richest man in the world. His personal fortune, then estimated at over $21 billion, has included 220 000 square meters of land in Tokyo and 150 million square meters nationwide, the Seibu Railway system in Tokyo's western suburbs and elsewhere, 30 golf courses, 30 ski resorts, and almost 60 Prince hotels (Nagaharu, 1988, p. 193; Downer, 1994). The company has had an especially great impact on the development of the commercial subcenter at Ikebukuro, where it has one of the world's largest department stores, and on a broad sector of Tokyo's west side and western suburbs reached by the Seibu Ikebukuro Line, the Seibu Shinjuku, and other Seibu lines. A similar concern, although without a baseball team and some of the other kinds of Seibu holdings, is the Tōkyū Corporation. Its focus is Shibuya, a train-station commercial center in which the company owns several department stores, and from which it (or its predecessors) extended train lines to Yokohama and to western suburbs (the Den'en-Toshi Line and the Inokashira Line) and developed extensive residential areas where once there were just farms or hills.

Still another powerful force behind suburban growth, in addition to the transportation/land development firms, was industry. The plentiful undeveloped land that surrounded Tokyo was ideal for the demanding space requirements of large factories, particularly once a rail network was extended connecting likely factory sites with port facilities. An example from the west side of Tokyo, where we have been looking most closely, is an industrial corridor that grew up along the Nambu Line, a freight carrier that opened in 1929 between Tachikawa in Tokyo's Tama district and the port of Yokohama. Some of the important industries that developed there were electrical equipment in Koganei and Mitaka, aircraft manufacturing in Fussa and Tachikawa, and precision instruments, heavy machinery, photographic film and electrical equipment in Hino. The suburban area grew still more during the late 1930s, after the government declared that new factories producing war material should be situated away from the center of Tokyo but within a 20-mile radius. Thus, the town of Fuchū attracted Nihon Sūkō, a firm that would begin production of tanks in 1940; Musashino, a town on the Chūō Line, became the largest site for the Nakajima Aircraft Corporation's manufacture of military planes and plane engines (Allinson, 1979, pp. 55–7). In each of these cases, housing for workers was developed close to the factories, so that each of these towns (as well as several others north and east of the central city) is properly classified as a self-contained urban center, with its own employment base, in addition to being a bedroom appendage for commuters to central Tokyo.

Thus, there are quite a few different kinds of suburban communities surrounding Tokyo. Some resemble central cities and have busy commercial centers at the train stations that serve them, industrial districts stretched out along the tracks and local rivers, and large tracts of cheaper housing nearby called *danchi*. Employers provide some of these for their workers, while other *danchi* are built by government, including local government and the national Japan Housing Corporation (JHC). Typically, *danchi* are planned clusters of drab multi-story apartments, identical except for an identifying number painted in black high up on a gray concrete wall, and all with tiny units described as having 'privacy provided by lock, steel door, and private bath' (Honjō, 1975, p. 378). JHC's *danchi* are especially numerous, both inside the 23 wards and in Tama and the suburban prefectures. Their scale is often several thousand units at one site, which often happens to be a less accessible place where land is cheaper, and therefore generally includes some minimum of community facilities such as shopping, schools and recreation areas. While not attractive physically, such public housing units have been extremely important in providing secure shelter for hundreds of thousands of

Tokyoites in the face of an overall short supply of housing, rapid metropolitan population growth, and high prices on the open market.

Other suburbs are known for their institutions. There are several places where college and university campuses have been relocated from the 23 wards and where dormitory students make up sizable parts of the population. Hachiōji, a town in the western foothills nearly 30 kilometers from the center of Tokyo that was designated for this purpose by Tokyo Metropolitan Government, is a good example. Other college towns were developed by business as part of their real estate promotions, such as Kunitachi to the west of Tokyo. Developed originally by the Seibu empire as a planned community with spacious, regular-sized lots, it grew because of a focus on Hitosubashi University, one of the nation's largest (Allinson, 1979, p. 54). Still other towns are known as exclusive suburbs for the rich. Den'en-chōfu, a planned garden city associated with the Tōkyū Corporation, is a prime example. Sometimes called, 'Japan's Beverly Hills', it is an area of stately single houses, beautiful gardens and private clubs, and a fine commercial district with fashionable boutiques and expensive restaurants. It is arranged spatially in a distinctive pattern formed by ginkgo-shaded streets emanating like wheel spokes from a European-style central train station (Chapman, 1987).

Still another type of suburb is the planned new town. This has been important in Tokyo planning since the 1960s. It combines public and private investment to construct self-contained new cities that include commercial, educational, and other urban functions with a range of housing choices at designated sites outside of the central city. The largest of these is Tama New Town, a project started in 1965 in the Tama Hills area west of Tokyo's 23-ward zone by Tokyo Metropolitan Government and two public corporations, the Urban Development Public Corporation and the Tokyo Metropolitan Housing Supply Public Corporation. It covers over 2300 hectares and has over 160 000 residents. When finished in a few years' time, it is expected to house more than 300 000 individuals and to be one of the most important subcenters in the metropolitan area. A fuller discussion of Tama New Town and other planned centers in the suburban ring is given in Chapter 6.

EXURBAN SETTLEMENT

As in many large metropolitan districts, the greater Tokyo area has a zone of dispersed housing and other scattered urban land that lies well beyond the city and its ring of crowded suburbs. This area is sometimes called exurbia. Among other land uses, it consists of housing developments, second homes, small satellite towns built around particular local industries or resources, and isolated country houses owned by long-distance commuters who exchange travel time and convenience to the urban center for privacy and environmental amenities. This is a good place for me to say a few words about distant reaches of exurban Tokyo that are growing with urban commuters and functioning more and more like integral parts of the city.

Perhaps the most noticeable areas of exurban residences are in the foothills and mountainous areas that lie beyond the limits of the Kantō Plain. This includes the Oku-Tama ('deep' or 'distant' Tama) area beyond Hachiōji, Akigawa, and Ōme cities, where the Chūō and Keiō Lines, and the Seibu-Haijima and Ōme Lines, push deep into narrow valleys between steep wooded hills; as well as mountainous areas of the several prefectures that encircle Tokyo and its suburbs. The direction of Mount Fuji, the slopes of which are west of Kanagawa Prefecture's high ground at the boundary between Shizuoka and Yamanashi Prefectures and too far to commute from regularly, is especially popular. For many of the riders, the outer limits for commuting are marked by express station stops in the centers of such towns as Odawara, a historic castle town in Kanagawa Prefecture about 75 kilometers from central Tokyo that is both on the shore of Sagami Bay and at the entry to the mountainous Fuji–Hakone–Izu National Park complex, and Enzan, Yamanashi, and Kōfu, all of which are in Yamanashi Prefecture 90–100 kilometers from central Tokyo. Additionally, there are distant commuters to the center of the city from the hills and beautiful shorelines of the Chiba Peninsula and to both Tokyo and Yokohama from the scenic hills and shoreline towns on the Miura Peninsula between Tokyo and Sagami Bays. Picturesque tourist towns on the north shore of Sagami Bay such as Enoshima and Kamakura (both in Kanagawa Prefecture) also have special appeal. Kamakura, for example, is distinctive as an ancient capital city replete with famous temples and historic sites set amid green hills with spectacular views of the bay and its beaches.

The social context of such long-distance commuting begins, of course, with the gigantic extent of Tokyo itself, and its great crowding, high land costs, and other characteristics. For many households the economic calculation is quite simple: pay more in time and train fares to live far from Tokyo, but in return gain considerably in both the cost of housing and in the cost of time and travel to weekend amenities. Over the years that I lived in Tokyo, I have met quite a few people, both Japanese and foreigners, who reside in such places as Odawara or Atami (on Sagami Bay on the Izu Peninsula) and commute to Tokyo. They explain that the train ride of two hours or so is actually an advantage: they get a seat all the way in and can use the time spent riding to sleep or read. Some friends who are professors, journalists and artists, and whose schedules do not always require five or six days per week at an office, have been particularly enthusiastic about such arrangements. They gloat about their spacious studies or private gardens, stressing that these amenities would not have been attainable in the land market of Tokyo. Another variation on long-distance commuting is keeping two addresses: a main home at the distant outskirts of Tokyo for living and a room or cubbyhole apartment in the city for those days when being 'on the job' is most important.

I am certain that the attraction of distant edges of the Tokyo metropolis will increase in the future as the city continues to grow outward, and as the nature of work continues to evolve in Japan to emphasize white-collar occupations and new freedoms from the office. For many people this is a welcome development: it allows not only for an escape from urban ills but also for residence in settings that are especially highly prized in Japanese culture: mountainous backdrops, views of Mount Fuji, rocky shorelines, tall stands of cypress or other trees, and productive paddy fields, orchards, tea plantations and other rural scenes. On the other hand, this is also a case of a city that is already thought to be too big becoming even bigger, and yet another example of where urbanization paves over the countryside. In this regard, it is not surprising that there are often complaints from rural towns that the city is overtaking them, and that there is too much growth in their direction, too fast. A specific example that I was able to follow was the 'green revolt' against a 920-unit housing complex for US military personnel in the hills above Zushi, a 'surf-suburb' close to Kamakura (Tracey, 1985).

THE SQUEEZE ON INNER-CITY NEIGHBORHOODS

We can now return from the suburbs to the 23 wards of Tokyo to see a third major dimension of present-day urban development in the city. (The first two were redevelopment and expansion of the CBD and expansion of the residential ring around the city.) We can call this the intensification of land use in established neighborhoods close to the center of the city. Because of high land costs and expanding commercial functions, there is unprecedented pressure to put every available parcel to intensive use, no matter how small or awkwardly situated, and to build as many stories to a structure as regulations allow. Everywhere one looks in the neighborhoods surrounding the CBD, there is redevelopment: older houses are giving way to new; single-family structures are yielding to multi-family buildings and apartments; small 'ma-and-pa' stores are replaced by commercial chains and shopping centers; and busier streets are coming to be lined ever more with high-rises and non-stop ribbons of slow-moving traffic. Open space, always at a premium in Tokyo, is even more scarce. A view from any high place, be it Tokyo Tower, the Sunshine 60 observation level in Ikebukuro, or the private windows of a friend's company high up in the Aoyama Twin office complex in the super high-rent *yamanote* area west of the CBD, confirms this again and again (Figures 4.15 and 4.16).

For the residents of these neighborhoods this means a tremendous change in their surroundings and living patterns. In some sections of the city, particularly those places directly in the path of CBD expansion or the expansion of other business districts, residential displacement by commercial uses has been almost total. We saw this in Toranomon, for example, where only a few small pockets of single houses remain, and where population decline has been extremely steep since the 1970s and 1980s when the neighborhood became a prime target for office development. In other areas a little more distant from the CBD, residential land-uses remain in place, but under conditions of much higher density. Long-term residents of these neighborhoods often complain about too much crowding, too many new stranger-neighbors, the demise of old neighborhood shops and other businesses and their replacement by impersonal chain stores, increased traffic and noise, high rental prices, and about the many inconveniences that are brought on by non-stop construction activity in their midst. A recent poll conducted by Tokyo Metropolitan Government identified the ten most common complaints among residents in the central wards as follows, in descending order:[7]

- Too many people
- Too much traffic
- Small living quarters without private gardens
- High costs of housing and other necessities

Figure 4.15 *The inner-city housing squeeze in Tokyo. This is in Minami-Aoyama, Minato Ward. High-rises are invading older neighborhoods of single homes. The smokestack in the center is from one of the dwindling number of public baths that are still found in the city*

Figure 4.16 *Billboard advertising manshon units for sale in a building that represents Tokyo's new vernacular. The irregular ground-floor plan of the building corresponds to the odd shapes of many lots in the city, while the slope of the upper stories on the left side is to meet zoning requirements dealing with sunlight*

- Scarcity of greenery
- 'Clear blue or starry skies can't be seen'
- Noise and vibrations because of traffic and construction
- Rush-hour congestion
- Pollution of rivers, the sea and the atmosphere
- Lack of playgrounds for children

A good example of all of this is the neighborhood in a corner of Shibuya Ward where I used to live. It is a mix of old and new, and of residential and non-residential uses just down the street from the bustling high-rise center of Shinjuku. Our house there was illuminated by the neon from a Denny's restaurant across the street, was so close to the neighbors that we could just about touch their houses by reaching from windows, and shook whenever a truck or a bus passed on the nearby street. A visit a year later revealed some of the changes. The house was still there, but a six-car parking lot where our children used to play during the day had been developed into a six-story building under construction; a small vacant lot that was tucked without street frontage behind a neighbor's house now had an oversized house on it; several of the single houses on the street behind us and on a parallel street nearby were gone, replaced by condominium structures of the *manshon* type; and a little candy shop that my children liked was gone too, replaced ironically by the offices of a distributor of American chocolate bars. Everywhere, there is more of a feeling of being closed in – perceptibly more so than ever before. There is less sky to see, the last vacant lots are gone, and giant high-rises, those for the new City Hall completed in 1991 and for 'Tokyo Opera City' (1995), now loom over the neighborhood, reminding our former neighbors that big-city Tokyo is just down the street and getting closer.

There are many ways in which developers from outside a neighborhood acquire the parcels they need for construction of high-density buildings. They can offer homeowners high prices for their holdings, being fully confident that the money they spend will be returned with profit from high rents or sales of condominiums. They can also be assured that within certain guidelines set down in the building codes there will usually be little red tape to delay fast completion of a building project, and that once finished there will likely be plenty of takers in space-starved Tokyo for the residences, offices, or commercial units they construct. Second, developers can (and do) wait for owners of desirable parcels to die so that they can acquire the land from heirs. The key is a stiff inheritance tax, equal in many cases to more than 50 percent of the value of the land and due in cash within one year. Especially in an inflated land market such as that of the 1980s, this forces heirs to either part with land they inherit or develop it at higher density. The tax, which seems to exist primarily to stimulate land development, can be so onerous that from time to time it leads heirs to commit suicide. Some of the biggest developers in the city are said to keep an eye on the age and health of owners of the real estate they want, so that they can be ready to make an offer when the time comes. Still another mechanism, similar in its effect to the inheritance tax, is the *koteishisan*, the fixed property tax. Owners find that because of rising land values and encroachment by high-rent land uses, their tax assessments go up faster than their ability to pay; they are therefore sometimes forced to seek relief by selling their land to a builder.

There is at least one other force to be mentioned at this point as a major stimulus for the rampant land development that has been taking place in Tokyo's close-in neighborhoods: the activities of persons called *jiageya*. The word is translated literally as 'land raisers', and refers to a special category of real estate agents and land speculators who are especially adept at acquiring hard-to-get parcels for inner-city construction projects. Part businessman and part gangster, they number in the hundreds and comb the 'hot' neighborhoods of the city in search of older homes and small shops to buy, so that the land can be converted to *manshon* or office buildings. In doing so, they prey on the misfortunes of the landowners who are caught in a bind by inheritance and property taxes, and employ a variety of tactics, both legal and illegal, to convince owners to part with land that they would otherwise prefer to keep. This ranges from harassment such as repeated telephone calls and personal visits to various levels of threats and intimidation. In the worst cases, when an owner has been stubborn about keeping the land or holding out for an especially high price, *jiageya* have resorted to arson and violence. One occasionally reads stories in the press or sees 'human interest' pieces on the TV news about homeowners who fight back, either alone or in small organized groups of angry neighbors, and attempt to stem the tide of high-density development around them (Gill, 1990). A typical result of such confrontations is that the hold-out is surrounded sooner or later by incompatible new construction, and therefore becomes isolated both physically and socially in her or his own neighborhood.

However, one should not assume that the redevelopment of Tokyo's residential neighborhoods is the work of outsiders only. The inhabitants of the neighborhoods themselves are very much a part of this, and often make use of opportunities of their own to upgrade their properties and perhaps to derive some rental income. In fact, since the start of the 1990s there has been a rather substantial boom in Tokyo (and other Japanese cities) in construction of three-story houses on the sites of two-story ones, mostly by homeowners themselves working with contractors. A typical pattern is to replace a two-story '4LDK' dwelling (four bedrooms with a combined living and dining area and kitchen) with a three-story '5LDK+EV' structure: five bedrooms with a combined living and dining area and kitchen, plus elevator. According to a recent survey of 200 new triple-deckers in Tokyo, reasons for construction include: 'to secure a larger living space' (86.5 percent); 'to secure sunlight and ventilation' (54.0 percent); 'to make maximum use of space within the limits of building laws' (41.0 percent); 'for two-family living' (40.0 percent); 'to secure space for a carport' (31.0 percent); and 'to provide extra rooms for hobbies' (20.5 percent) (Saitō, 1996). For many people, the increased value of their land has provided a fund to borrow against to pay for the new building. At the same time, the unexpected large drop in land values in the 1990s created an economic crisis for such investors, making it difficult for them to repay their loans and plunging some of them into bankruptcy.

One example of 'indigenous redevelopment', thankfully one without bankruptcy, concerns my former neighbors, Tamura-san, the *tatami*-maker and his family. In the time since my family and I moved away, the Tamuras have torn down the old building that housed their workshop and residence, and have replaced it with a substantially bigger structure. Most of the street floor is still a workshop, but now with air-conditioning and a better parking space for the pickup truck. A tiny hairdressing salon operated by a now-grown daughter is also at street level. The family lives on the floor above. A rooftop deck provides still additional space, for laundry drying and children's play. To make it all affordable, they added a third floor. It is rented to friends, but after a few years might be where one of the Tamura children will live after marriage. Thus, the new house is a multi-generational building designed to solve the housing problems of young people in an expensive city. Moreover, it will help to keep a family in place on the same land it has occupied for more than a half-century.

The Tamura's new building typifies the new Tokyo in still other ways. One characteristic is a slanted roofline on the north side. This is common in most Tokyo neighborhoods for buildings three stories and taller, because of zoning regulations protecting neighbors' access to sunlight and ventilation. Second, the new building looks like so many other buildings in Tokyo because it comes almost entirely from the limited variety of standardized parts in builders' catalogues. It has the same doors, windows, balcony railing and rain gutters that are seen everywhere in Tokyo, and is covered with the same, easily washable white-brick tile that other buildings have. The overall impression is of a bright, clean and highly practical house that, for better or worse, is totally non-distinctive.

A second example of indigenous redevelopment, one with a different twist except for the white tiles and other standardized parts, is the story of a tiny neighborhood convenience shop and adjacent old house down the block from my university. Seeing an opportunity to profit from the growing campus, the aging owner demolished his old structure, replacing it with a six-story building tailor-made for the local situation: the street level is where he parks his car and maintains several vending machines for students to put money in; floors two through five were made into classrooms for rent to our overcrowded school (only two rooms per floor on this tiny parcel); the top floor is reserved for his own residence, now much better equipped and more comfortable than the drafty wooden house he had before. Some of the other neighbors were not particularly happy to see this, because they would have preferred to keep the area as a quiet district of single houses. However, they have had to accept the higher density as the ineluctable trend of Tokyo and an inevitable consequence of being in a close-in location, as people in all other close-in neighborhoods have learned to do.

Finally there are certain neighborhoods in the belt between the city's commercial core and the residential ring that are exceptions, at least in part, to the intensification of land uses that is being experienced almost everywhere else. These are the super-rich areas that have had the power to exclude, at least from some streets, encroachment by taller buildings, incompatible land uses, and hastily made *manshon*. There are no huge expanses of such territories, only bits and pieces among other nicer districts, especially in certain sections of Minato Ward, Shibuya Ward, and other areas of the old *yamanote* district. In some cases fine old houses remain, but more typically the landscape is of large modern houses along quiet, tree-lined streets, and private gardens that show just a little from behind the seclusion of walls and impressive gates. Some of the houses, for example some that have been pointed out to me in Jingūmae and Minami-Aoyama near the trendy Omote-sandō area, belong to movie stars and popular singers. Others are where rich industrialists, financiers, land developers, politicians, and others at the top of Japan's economic hierarchy live. One commonly sees black Nissan Presidents, Japan's limousine of choice, on these streets and on the streets of other nearby high-status districts, as well as the most expensive Japanese and foreign sports cars.

Certain sections of this 'rich side of town' are known for their concentrations of foreigners, especially highly placed business executives, ambassadors and other top diplomats, and other VIPs. This is particularly true for Hiroo and Minami Azabu in Minato Ward, both areas with numerous embassies and foreign diplomatic missions that are sometimes referred to as gilded ghettos for foreigners. In addition to the large single houses that one finds in these neighborhoods, there are also numerous fancy, Western-style apartments that are called *homat*. These are multi-story buildings that were developed especially to meet the residential needs of the city's growing number of foreigners with generous housing allowances from the embassies or corporations that employ them. They stand out for the comparatively large number and oversized proportions of their rooms, the attractive landscaping of their grounds, and monthly rents of several thousands of dollars per unit.

HISTORIC PRESERVATION

Because of the terrible destruction that Tokyo experienced twice this century and the thorough makeover by the real estate industry that the city is now undergoing, there is very little historic urban fabric immediately visible. Almost the entire city is comparatively new, having been built since the Second World War; the few districts that pre-date both present-day reconstruction and the bombing tend to be only a little older. Many of the oldest intact neighborhoods in Tokyo date back only to the rebuilding that took place after the 1923 earthquake. There are only bits and pieces of the city that pre-date that tragedy, and certainly no 'old town', such as many other cities have, that would give visitors and local residents alike a feel of the nineteenth century or earlier city (Barr, 1997b). The only place to see historic Edo is in museums: the Fukagawa Edo Museum in Kōtō Ward, where some old streets of *shitamachi* have been rebuilt for display; and the Edo–Tokyo Museum in the Ryōgoku section of Sumida Ward, an enormous showcase of history that Tokyo Metropolitan Government opened in 1993. The latter is a 'must-see' attraction for visitors, not just for its displays but also because of its distinctive architecture (Figure 4.17). Residents also see old Tokyo in stage sets at movie and TV studios where the ubiquitous *samurai* dramas are filmed. For an in-person look at old Japan, visitors are almost always steered to Kyoto, the historic capital that was purposefully spared the bombing, never to Tokyo. In fact, to many people Tokyo seems to be a city where history has been all but eradicated and that lives only in the present (Popham, 1985).

It is tempting to joke that any essay about historic preservation in Tokyo would be extremely short. However, the topic is much more complex than it seems at first, and deserves careful attention. For one thing, there are, in fact, a number of significant older structures that have somehow survived all the convulsions that have befallen the city. This includes small clusters of ordinary houses and 'ma-and-

Figure 4.17   *The Edo–Tokyo Museum*

pa' shops scattered among neighborhoods such as Tsukudajima in Chūō Ward, Mukōjima in Sumida Ward, and Nezu in Bunkyō Ward (Enbutsu, 1993); and various larger structures that are properly counted as important historic landmarks (Cybriwsky, 1997). The latter group includes sections of the fortifications (walls and moats) of Edo Castle, several prominent temples from the Edo Era (rebuilt with new materials since the Second World War, sometimes as a matter of course to keep them looking fresh and new), and various Meiji Era buildings related to government, commerce, higher education, and other uses. The red-brick Tokyo Station building, completed in 1914, is a prime example of a surviving landmark (Figure 4.18). Despite recurrent attempts by developers to put up high-rises on the site, the station building stands in the midst of the CBD's financial and corporate headquarters nucleus as a rare relic of the craze for West European architecture that gripped Japan during its time of modernization. However, because of damage from the war it is missing its upper two floors and its once-prominent cupolas. A grassroots group with the wonderfully descriptive name 'Group of Citizens Who Love the Red Brick Tokyo Station' is given much of the credit for staving off the most recent threat to the building's existence, expressed most forcefully during 1987–8 by high-risers representing, among others, the powerful Mitsubishi trust (Fujimoto, 1987).

There are also many other examples of historic preservation. In some of the older neighborhoods there is a small but discernible trend for citizens to restore old houses and shops, and to use them in preference to new construction. In some locations there is active support for this by the Tokyo government, which itself is becoming increasingly interested in promoting the historic ambience of specific districts. A recent publication from the Planning Office promises that 'efforts will be made to preserve at least the facades of historical and traditional buildings as they are remodeled', and that 'Historical and Cultural Promenades' will be built to link

144

Figure 4.18 *Tokyo Station. This is the historic west side of the station, facing the Imperial Palace*

moats, shrines and temples, gardens and slopes' (Tokyo Metropolitan Government, 1990a, p. 90). There are also more and more fights between citizens and developers in Tokyo about the latter's plans to demolish old structures. This is especially the case in certain sections of *shitamachi*, the old low city, which are close to an expanding CBD. For several years one of the most interesting conflicts has been about plans to put in a parking lot for as many as 2000 cars under a pond in a historic temple setting called Shinobazu Pond (Figure 4.19). The project is promoted by storeowners in the nearby commercial center of Ueno, as well as by officials of Taitō Ward, but opposed by a coalition of several citizens' groups. One of them, 'The Society of the Lovers of Shinobazu Pond', has argued convincingly that development would destroy the water table and do away with the pond's abundant plant and animal life (Ma, 1989; Symposium Executive Committee, 1990).

A second reason for having a look at historical preservation in Tokyo is that there is a rather unusual twist to it. Because the city has learned by experience that none of its buildings can have a long life expectancy, it has adopted a perspective on historic preservation that invests little emotional stock in what is built on the surface, and instead concentrates its genuflections to history on *sites*, even if those sites are empty or covered with something new. We saw an example of this in our orientation to Tokyo when we looked at Shiba Kōen, the park that contains Tokyo Tower. This is the place that, in addition to the tower, has two bowling alleys, a golf driving range, and various other uses with no relevance whatsoever to the past, even though the ground is best remembered as the burial place for shoguns and the site of historic temples. Even more to the point is the Imperial Palace compound. This is the symbolic center of the city and covers more than 100 hectares, but has no castle or old palace. The emperor lives in a new (1964) building, scaled-down in size to reflect the diminished status that was given to the position after the Second

Figure 4.19 *Shinobazu Pond in Ueno Park and one of the park's many historic temples. In the background is part of Ueno's busy commercial district*

World War, but the grounds around him are deeply revered for what they once represented. Not only is the area inviolate to developers, even though the world's most expensive real estate is right next door, it is extremely private and almost totally inaccessible to the public.[8]

There are many other aspects of central Tokyo that reflect the city's past even though the surface is all new buildings and other changes. Another example is the physical layout of the CBD and other older-developed districts. It is not just that the center is given to what little is left of the Edo Castle complex. We also see that the pattern of streets and major roads, as well as other infrastructure, has been carried over from Edo and is everywhere in evidence as the substratum for today's urban form (Jinnai, 1995). With a little imagination, from the high perspective of Tokyo Tower, we still make out the old clockwise spiral that characterized the shape of Edo amid today's tall buildings and car-choked streets. Most of the moats that formed the spiral have long since been paved over and the retaining walls dismantled, but there are just enough remnants in place to make it possible to extrapolate and to visualize the bigger complex that existed more than two centuries ago. Moreover, if we consult a plan of old Edo as we look at the modern city, we see that expressways in the CBD and other wide roads follow the courses of former moats and canals almost exactly (Jinnai, 1988, p. 13). We can also see that certain key intersections and important bridges near the approaches to the modern CBD correspond precisely to the distribution of old gates along the outer perimeter of Edo's defensive spiral.

It seems ironic that we should look for expressways and other busy roads to see the form of the old city amid central Tokyo's many thousands of new buildings. Yet that is just what we do, because the configuration of these thoroughfares follows the moats and canals that shaped Edo during the time of the shoguns. What is more, we can still see some of the old waterways of Edo hidden beneath today's modern highways. In some cases, the canals of *shitamachi* have been transformed into little more than storm sewers beneath pavements, but they are there nevertheless and follow ancient courses. Better-known examples are the several 'rivers' that flow through the central city below street level within concrete embankments, and that have along their lengths above them expressways or other roads supported on thick concrete pillars. These are waterways with little light and virtually no aesthetic appeal, but they do carry away rainwater and, in some cases, provide limited transportation functions. The scene of the underside of a modern highway covering over what could otherwise be a charming central city watercourse is one of the most frequently cited examples of environmental degradation in modern Tokyo (Jinnai, 1987, pp. 26–8) and unambiguous evidence of the city's pressing lack of space. However, it is also a reminder that 'the structure of old Edo survives as the substructure of modern Tokyo', and that modernization of the city has involved little more than substitution of one urban component for another within a stable configuration (Jinnai, 1987, p. 24).

Perhaps the most striking specific example of the survival of older aspects of Tokyo beneath the hubbub of the modern city is at Nihombashi, where the famous 'Japan Bridge' crosses an old watercourse that is now called the Nihombashi River. The original bridge, which was put up in 1603 under orders from Ieyasu, was the nucleus of Edo's first commerce and the symbolic starting point for journeys to all parts of Japan. It is, of course, long since gone. The present structure – a European Renaissance-style span erected in 1910–11 during the height of the Meiji period's fascination with Western architecture – is a beautiful structure that graced the CBD in the early part of this century and blended with stately buildings that lined the river and reflected in its waters. It was repaired after damage from the 1923 Great Kantō Earthquake and the 1945 bombing, and is one of the oldest structures still standing in the CBD. However, in the early 1960s, in the rush to prepare Tokyo for the 1964 Summer Olympic Games, the Number 4 Loop Line of the Shuto Expressway was put in over the Nihombashi River, and the bridge was all but obliterated. It still carries a lot of traffic, as it is part of the busy Chūō-dōri, an important thoroughfare crossing the heart of the CBD, but in terms of view it is clearly subservient to the newer road above.

Visitors have grumbled that the bridge at Nihombashi is almost impossible to photograph well because of obstructions and poor lighting; they express displeasure that authorities have allowed such desecration of a significant landmark. The response to such critics is that the landmark *is* there, intact, and a working part of Tokyo. Nowadays, instead of fishmongers and *samurai* processions, the bridge is crossed by salarymen in dark business suits and 'office ladies' in the required company uniforms, as well as by taxis and private cars. However, this in itself is a meaningful continuity: despite the time that has passed, and despite the fact that the present structure is not the original bridge, the traffic at Nihombashi still reflects the main business of the contemporaneous city. In this way, the bridge is another example of how, in central Tokyo, the present is played out on foundations that were laid down in the past.

Another way that the past survives in central Tokyo is through the proper names that have been given to various locations such as neighborhoods, important streets,

Table 4.9 *Selected Historic Place Names in Central Tokyo*

Chūō Ward	
Ginza	Place of the silver mint
Irifune	Ship's entrance
Horidorne	Place where the moat ends
Kayabachō	Place where miscanthus (used for roof thatch) grows
Koamichō	Place for drying fish nets
Kyōbashi	The capital bridge
Nihombashi	Japan bridge
Ningyochō	Place where there are doll shops
Tsukiji	Reclaimed land
Tsukudajima	Island with cultivated rice fields
Yaesu	A mutation of Yayosu, the Japanese name of the Dutch sailor Jan Joosten
Chiyoda Ward	
Daikanchō	Place where government officials live
Fujimichō	Place with a view of Mount Fuji
Kajichō	Place of ironsmiths
Kasumigaseki	Barrier of mist
Konyachō	Place where there are dyers
Hanaokachō	Place where there is a hill with flowers
Nagatachō	Place where the Nagata family resides
Ōtemachi	The place in front of Ōte Gate to Edo Castle
Minato Ward	
Akasaka-Mitsuke	'Red slope watchtower' or 'approach to the castle'
Aoyama	Taken from the family name of a *samurai* who lived there
Azabu	A combination of 'flax' (*asa*) and 'cloth' (*bu*)
Enokizakachō	Place with a slope planted with hackberry
Ipponmatsu	One big pine tree
Roppongi	Six trees
Toranomon	Tiger gate

and numerous train and subway stations. It might appear at first that this is a trivial detail, not substantially different from what happens in the many other cities that employ historic toponymy. However, place names take on special importance in Tokyo, first, because the city has an unusual lack of more tangible links to its past; and second, because place names in Japanese are typically highly descriptive and unusually effective in conveying messages such as lessons about the past. Thus, some names in central Tokyo remind citizens about the characteristics of the natural environment, others honor specific individuals who played significant roles in the city's early growth; while still other names recall the layout of the old city and the historic origins of particular subsections or their economic functions. Examples from each of these categories are listed in Table 4.9. We can imagine, therefore, that a worker in the Tokyo CBD might commute from home on the Marunouchi ('within the circle of moats') subway line, get off at Ōtemachi Station (named after a main gate to Edo Castle), and walk a short distance along Eitai-dōri (a less geographical word that means 'Eternal Ages Street' but that is also the name of an historic bridge) to an office tower on Sotobori-dōri ('Outer Moat Street') in an area called Yaesu, a subdistrict of the CBD that is named after a shipwrecked Dutch sailor, Jan Joosten (Japanese pronounced his name 'Yayosu'), who lived in Edo during the time of the first shogun.

The past is also visible in contemporary Tokyo in the design of many special touches that are added to new buildings and other redevelopment sites precisely to create historic ambiance. This is something that Sugiura, a Tokyo geographer, referred to as 'the urbanization of nostalgia'. As a specific example, he described a current trend to incorporate homey, country-style restaurants, often clearly associated with one of the mountain provinces in Japan and sometimes having thatched roofs and other 'authentic' decor, into the bowels of giant office towers and other megastructures. This is to create a 'world of make-believe . . . right underneath the concrete jungle', to remind today's Tokyoites of their rural or small-town origins and give them an escape from the fast-changing, giant metropolis where they work, albeit if only for an occasional meal like mother's. He counted 343 such restaurants listed in telephone directories, more than one-half of them in the CBD and most of the rest in other parts of inner Tokyo with extensive redevelopment (Sugiura, 1987, quotation from p. 14). I think that this pattern is a Tokyo variant of a wider trend in cities across the world in which design aspects of new development projects, particularly large mixed-use developments near centers of cities, often simulate exotic geographic locales or romanticize history (Sorkin, 1992).

Another example of new urban landscaping that recalls the past is the core of Ginza. An area of several blocks has recently been redecorated in a fashion that suggests themes from both the famous Ginza Brick Quarter and the high-life in the CBD during the Taishō era: simulated historic street lamps and signs, brick sidewalk pavements, and rows of willow trees along the side streets. In addition, some of the police boxes (kōban) in the area have been refurbished in historic-looking fashion. They are made of brick and have the same Victorian-style design that was popular along the main street of this business district during Meiji. In fact, there are at least two police boxes shaped like the cupolas that were lost in 1945 to Tokyo Station. The same is also true for public toilets in this neighborhood.

The police box at the busy Sukiyabashi Crossing between Ginza and Yurakuchō is a well-known and much-photographed example. While it is an extremely tiny building in comparison to the megastructures of steel, glass and neon that surround it – the huge Hankyū and Yurakuchō Seibu Department Stores, the Sony Building, and others – it occupies a prime site in this setting and is just as much a landmark as the other buildings. There is something extremely telling about its relative proportions and its spatial relationships: the historic building, such as it is, is small and clearly inferior to the main business of Ginza (which is selling). But it is in the middle, and all the other buildings, big and impressive as they are, have to gather around it to compete for the passing pedestrians. This is elemental Tokyo: huge, new, showy and rich, but underneath is a nucleus, however small, that in one way or another binds what is on the surface to the past.

CHAPTER 5
FACES OF THE METROPOLIS

The Tokyo metropolitan area is composed of so many different places, each with its own distinctive character, that it is not possible to cover all the areas within the scope of one book. The best one can do is to write at least something about the most important places, and to be representative in making choices about which of all the other landmarks, neighborhoods, commercial centers and other types of areas in the city and its environs to include. For this, I find the concept of 'epitome districts' to be extremely useful. These are parts of a city where 'one can see the bigger place in compression or in miniature', and can be used to represent other places. In the words of Grady Clay, whose writing introduced this concept to me, epitome districts are the 'special places in cities [that] carry huge layers of symbols [and] that have the capacity to pack up emotions, energy, or history into a small space' (Clay, 1973, p. 38).

This chapter introduces a succession of epitome districts of different kinds in the Tokyo Metropolis. They are the places I need to write about in order to be representative and reasonably complete about the city. Some of them have already been introduced in the earlier chapters, but now require more detail; others will be mentioned for the first time. We begin with (1) the Imperial Palace, the traditional center of Tokyo epitomizing traditional and unchanging aspects of the city; and then cover, in order: (2) Shinjuku center, the emerging new center of business and municipal government in Tokyo; (3) Shibuya and several nearby districts on the west side of Tokyo that represent the youth and vigor of the city, as well as its considerable material wealth and proclivity for fun; (4) selected parts of the Sumida River wards, where we can see Tokyo hard at work behind the scenes, and where play is much more in line with traditional Japanese cultural patterns than in the trendy west side; (5) Sanya, a slum neighborhood that is somewhat hidden away in Tokyo and that is something of a secret that many Japanese prefer not to mention; and (6) a selection of 'suburban' localities in the Tama district of Tokyo that collectively represent newer forms of living and working in the metropolis.

THE IMPERIAL PALACE

Perhaps the most important of all epitome districts in Tokyo is the very center of the city. This is the site where Edo Castle, the imposing fortress that accounted for the founding of the city more than 400 years ago, once stood, and that is now the location of Japan's Imperial Palace. It is where we are reminded of Tokyo's history, and reflect on the persistence of tradition in the heart of an otherwise dynamic, fast-changing city. It is also one of the clearest examples of Tokyo as a unique city – a city that follows its own rules for how it should look and how its part should be internally arranged (Figure 5.1).

Figure 5.1 *Student tour group at the Imperial Palace. This is a popular site for photographs, with the historic bridge Nijubashi and a watchtower in the background*

The grounds of the Imperial Palace cover 110 hectares; they are much larger than required for just the emperor's residence and the Imperial Household Agency offices. Consequently, most of the land is empty, and is given to forests, meadows and fields. There used to be a golf course there too, because the previous emperor, Hirohito, took a liking to the game when he visited England as a young man in 1921, but for more than a half-century it has reverted to nature and is habitat now for rabbits, pheasants, and other small creatures. Popham described this urban center as 'an enormous void . . . so vast [that] it seems to belong to a different city, perhaps a different civilization' (Popham, 1985, p. 93). The French anthropologist Roland Barthes was so astounded by this scene when he visited Tokyo more than a generation ago that he wrote it up in his now-famous book as an 'empty center' for Tokyo, a 'sacred nothing' around which this great and unusual city turns (Barthes, 1982, pp. 30–32).

Such a sizable undeveloped area would be remarkable in the center of any city, but there are a number of things that make this particular tract especially amazing. There is the incredible contrast between the emptiness of the palace grounds and the super-crowded Central Business District immediately next door. This contrast is more profound than in other cities, even the case of Manhattan and Central Park, because in Tokyo the emptiness of the core is emptier and the crowdedness of the CBD is more crowded. There is simply no other situation like this in the world. From Tokyo Tower or another high vantage point, it appears like a large, dark-green island of trees and other vegetation (and a little bit of roof belonging to the emperor's residence) that sits idly amidst a dense sea of high-rises and traffic that completely engulfs it. The two seem to have absolutely nothing to do with one another. There are no clear connections between them such as by road, and no evidence of any movement by people or traffic. In fact, we see that the palace grounds are surrounded by walls and moats that are just as effective as barriers today as they were in the age of the shōguns more than a century ago. There is also an additional barrier in the form of a wide (nearly 100 meters), desolate plain of coarse gravel between the palace area and the main part of the CBD. It is usually unbearably hot in summer and bitterly cold and unprotected from winds in winter, and is one of the most unpleasant places I have ever experienced. It is supposed to be a refuge from fire for CBD workers in the event of a disaster, but the more evident effect is to isolate the palace even more from the city, increasing the distance between the two environments.

The second characteristic that makes the Imperial Palace area highly unusual is that it is so intensely private. In most urban settings, the center is a highly public space where people gather for business or enjoyment or some other common function. In central Tokyo, however, the largest tract of land is reserved for the exclusive use of one man and his family; the public is almost totally excluded. The only exceptions are the East Garden, where since 1968 visitors have been allowed to stroll the grounds and stand at the remnant stub of Edo Castle's once-soaring central tower (see Figure 3.2); and Kitanomaru Park, where palace guards once lived, an area of museums and pleasant picnic grounds accessible since 1969. Otherwise, the compound is completely closed. However, on two days each year, the day after New Year's Day and the emperor's birthday, the public is permitted to enter a portion of the preserve for a few minutes at a time and under the tightest of security. My family and I went in 1985, along with tens of thousands of Japanese and a sprinkling of other foreigners, and received New Year's greetings from Emperor Hirohito (or the Shōwa Emperor as he was renamed after he passed away.)

Another detail about the unusually private nature of the site is that there are not even many available places at the top of tall buildings nearby for visitors to get a good peek behind the walls. The only place of this kind listed in the guidebooks is the Kasumigaseki Building a few blocks to the south. It has a low-key observation level on the thirty-sixth floor that gives a panorama of the city and a view of rooftops within the palace compound.[1] Office building workers in Marunouchi and other central districts can, of course, look out their windows to see the palace, but I am told it is considered extremely impolite to peer too intensely into this private compound, so people rarely do this. Moreover, out of respect for the privacy of the imperial family, the palace building is not shown often in photographs or on television, even when there is front-page news about the emperor. In fact, a sign (in Japanese only) hangs above the Kasumigaseki Building observation window requesting that visitors refrain from taking photographs.

Such deference is all the more remarkable given that Japan has changed so much in recent times, and that the role of the emperor has been significantly redefined since defeat of the country in the Second World War. The imperial system is now a glaring anachronism that makes little practical sense for a modern democracy. But it persists nevertheless, protected in the postwar constitution of 1947 as 'the symbol of the State and of the unity of the people'. While many citizens strongly object to having an emperor at all, many others are fiercely loyal to the idea, seeing it as an essential Japanese institution (Nishibe, 1989). The great outpouring of national grief that followed the 1989 death of the Shōwa Emperor was testament to the latter. The sadness was recorded by news media from around the world during the elaborate funeral ceremony that took place some six weeks later. However, even as the solemnities were under way, video rental shops across the country reported record levels of transactions, as hundreds of thousands (or perhaps millions) of Japanese had apparently had their fill of uninterrupted TV coverage of emperor-related events and sought something else to watch.

The Imperial Palace tract is also especially interesting because it is such an obvious impediment to what might be called 'normal' urban development. The presence of such a large empty area in the midst of a huge metropolis ignores powerful economic imperatives about land values and violates most accepted tenets of urban land-use planning. The land is simply too expensive and the CBD too starved of building sites to allow space to be given to the residence of a single family and its associated offices. Any sizable piece of the grounds that might be put up for sale would be worth untold *billions* to developers for offices, hotels, retailing, or any other spillover of downtown land use. Moreover, city planners might like the opportunity to put the tract to some more 'rational' uses that would ameliorate crowding in Tokyo and reduce the growing problems of long-distance commuting. It would also be good to improve the flow of downtown traffic. Even though the Shuto Expressway, one of Tokyo's most important highways, has a carefully measured right-of-way through the northern margin of the palace area, the imperial tract as a whole is a major obstacle for roads, rail and subway lines that focus on downtown, and the cause of considerable congestion where traffic is forced to skirt around the perimeter of old walls and moats.

Because of such problems, it must be tempting sometimes for city planners to mentally remap the center of Tokyo without including the Imperial Palace grounds, or at least to substantially reduce the size of the tract. Such a fantasy might come from the constant frustration of having so many problems to solve on so little land. But it would be a fantasy only, and a fleeting one at that. The imperial land is not for sale and it is unthinkable for most people in Japan that it ever would be. While the Tokyo that surrounds this core is as changeable as any urban scene can be, the core itself always stays intact. It has been nibbled away somewhat in modern times for a highway, a museum, and some other public uses, but as a whole the place never changes. In fact, in kind of a magical way, it is still the site of Edo Castle – even though Edo Castle has been gone for centuries. Now the tract is identified with the Imperial Palace, but there is really no 'palace' there either. The famous building that was erected during Meiji was destroyed in the 1945 hostilities; the present structure was completed in 1964. It is an ample house, but it is unspectacular and unassuming, not so important in itself as a building. It is the site that is sacred, even if there is not much that is built on it; it is the site that is protected as the center of Tokyo.

A Japanese friend explained some of these ideas to me with great determination and every expectation that I, like so many other foreigners, would misunderstand. In the West, we attach special reverence to important buildings and often go to great pains to preserve them through the ages and reconstruct them faithfully if they are damaged. But I am taught this isn't done so much in Tokyo, because Tokyo is so impermanent (Richie, 1991, pp. 33–40). Instead, there is an intangible substratum from history that is fixed forever, and that provides a base for all the changes that swirl around it. Consequently, a different conception of Tokyo begins to take shape. The city is not 'empty' at the center, but is instead focused on a deeply solemn place filled with history and cultural meaning. Moreover, instead of the formlessness apparent at a first look from Tokyo Tower (or from other observation facilities), one begins to see a city with a strong ground plan that focuses, in a unique way, on a highly prominent center. So, too, in complement to the view that Tokyo is constantly changing and redeveloping, and always building upward and outward, one sees that Tokyo is also a city that stays very much in place, confidently holding on to its past in some rather special ways.

Shinjuku: Tokyo's New Center

The Imperial Palace will probably always remain the spiritual center of Tokyo; adjacent business districts such as Marunouchi and Nihombashi will probably always be thought of as the city's traditional centers of economic power. However, Shinjuku, located five to six kilometers west of this center, has recently emerged (especially since the 1960s) as a formidable commercial nucleus in its own right, laying legitimate claims to being the new principal center of the Tokyo Metropolis. Already, Shinjuku's main train station, Shinjuku Station, is far and away the busiest station in the city (and for that matter in the world), handling more than 3 million passengers each day. This is in comparison to the 0.7 million who pass through Tokyo Station. Other distinctions include having most of Tokyo's tallest buildings (see Table 2.10), being the city's number-one retailing center (as measured by number of stores and value of sales), and having one of Tokyo's biggest and best-known nighttime entertainment districts. Furthermore, since 1991 Shinjuku has been the site of the government center of Tokyo Metropolis (Figure 5.2).

The new-found centrality of Shinjuku is part and parcel of a grand strategy in Tokyo, in effect now for nearly 30 years, to remake the city into what planners call a 'multi-nodal metropolis'. The idea is to relieve the CBD of some of its congestion and ease the burden of commuting for long-distance train riders by stimulating growth of commercial centers closer to where Tokyoites live. This has been particularly so at key mass transit interchanges between the residential periphery and the center.[2] Shinjuku has been a principal beneficiary of this planning because it lies at an especially important junction of passenger rail lines: it is where several crowded commuter lines, including the Chūō ('main' or 'central') Line of the Japan Railways system and the private Keiō and Odakyū Lines, come in from the fast-growing western suburbs and intersect with both the Yamanote Loop around the city center and the city's subway system. Other reasons for favoring Shinjuku include its reputation in the city as an alternative business center (e.g. it was where many of the downtown's businesses were re-established after the 1923 earthquake, as well as the site of the city's largest black market during the time of post-war shortages), and the fortuitous presence of a substantial redevelopment site close to the station (an outmoded water-filtration plant) that was available for new building projects (Sode, 1987, pp. 119–70).

The principal showpiece of the new Shinjuku is the prominent cluster of about fifteen high-rises, most of them around 50 stories, that is formally called the New

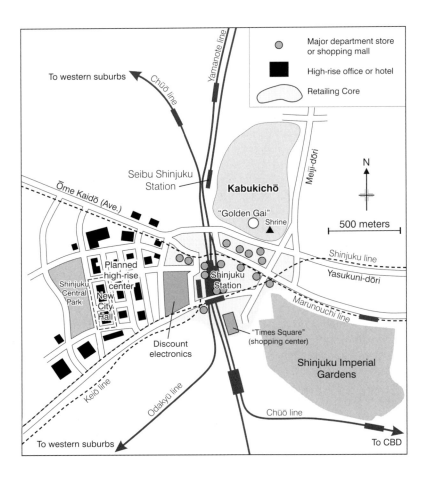

Figure 5.2 *Shinjuku location map*

Shinjuku City Center (*Shin Toshin Shinjuku*), or simply *Nishi Shinjuku*. As the name implies, it is on the west side of Shinjuku Station (*nishi* means 'west'). It is an on-going redevelopment project, announced publicly in June 1960, covering the 107 hectares of the old waterworks and several of the adjacent blocks. Its core is a carefully laid-out arrangement of office towers and international hotels interspersed with straight, wide streets, sheltered pedestrian concourses, and various combinations of public plazas, enclosed shopping malls, fountains and sculptures, and landscapers' greenery. There is also a sizable park called Shinjuku Chūō Kōen, Shinjuku Central Park. The first high-rise building was the Keiō Plaza Hotel, completed in 1971. Other important early structures include the Shinjuku Sumitomo Building, the Shinjuku Mitsui Building, the Yasuda Fire and Marine Insurance Company head office, the Shinjuku Nomura Building, the Shinjuku Center Building, and the Century-Hyatt, Hilton, and Washington Hotels, all opened in the 1970s and 1980s. Several other tall buildings were added in the 1990s, most prominently the new headquarters of Tokyo Metropolitan Government, often called

'City Hall' in English, and the Shinjuku Park Tower building, a 52-story mixed-use complex combining office uses, a major hotel, exhibition space, and retailing.

The new City Hall opened in March 1991. Relocation to this district had been a pet project of Suzuki Shunichi, Tokyo's enormously powerful governor between 1979 and 1995, and is in itself a telling indicator of the rising importance of Shinjuku. Its purpose is to bring the center of government closer to the geographical center of population, and to do away with the overcrowded and exceptionally unimpressive offices of city administration that had been in Marunouchi in the CBD. The design, by Tange Kenzō (1913–), the same architect who designed the outmoded City Hall (and who, therefore, has been given a rare chance to redeem himself), is intended to make the new City Hall not only the number-one landmark in Nishi Shinjuku but also a major symbol of Tokyo itself, both nationally and internationally, replacing Tokyo Tower in this role. In fact, according to promotional literature touting its state-of-the-art, high-technology construction, the new City Hall is intended to launch Tokyo 'toward the 21st century and beyond' (Tokyo Metropolitan Government, 1989b, p. 74). Governor Suzuki has described the complex as 'a gift for the metropolis' citizens of the 21st century' (*The Japan Times*, 10 April 1991, p. 18; also see Kenzo Tange Associates, 1991–3 and Tabata, 1991).

The specific site of City Hall overlooks Chūō Kōen and faces the city's sprawling western suburbs. It consists of three buildings: two massive skyscrapers with distinctive shape and texture, and a lower semi-circular assembly building that opens onto a public plaza. The taller tower, the so-called Number One Building, rises to 243 meters and is the tallest building in the city; the Number Two Building rises to 163 meters and also ranks among Tokyo's giants. The architectural details are fascinating, intended to convey images of Tokyo as both a traditional city (early Edo) and a city of 'international stature as a world leader' (Kanzo Tange Associates, 1991–3, p. 31). At street level and below, there are aspects of the project that recall Edo Castle: stone facing that resembles the castle's walls, a kind of moat, and traditional Japanese greenscaping. This contrasts with the public plaza, called *Tomin Hiroba* or Citizens' Plaza, that Tange has said was meant to evoke the Vatican's St Peter's Square. It also contrasts with the facades of the towers above; they are meant to suggest the circuitry of a modern computer and the shapes of specific international landmarks. The Number One Building, for example, has a twin towers configuration above the 150 meters level that Tange has explained as an echo of Notre Dame cathedral in Paris (Figure 5.3). Because of the project's great size and visibility, as well as a price tag reported to be as high as 157 billion yen, critics have said that City Hall is either Tange's monument to himself or a monument to Suzuki, or both, and that it is a symbolic return to Edo Castle, the imposing center of power around which the city once revolved. Unkind nicknames that have been applied to the complex are 'Tax Tower', referring to the high cost, and 'Tower of Bubble', a label applied by Kurokawa Kisho, a prominent architect who was once a student of Tange's, to refer to the extraordinarily buoyant economy that enabled construction (*The Japan Times*, 10 April 1991, p. 18).

City Hall and the other tall buildings that comprise the Nishi Shinjuku redevelopment are sometimes referred to as Tokyo's Manhattan, i.e. the city's answer to the skyline of its principal rival metropolis abroad. As Popham put it, Shinjuku is

156

Figure 5.3 *Tokyo Metropolitan Government Headquarters, Tokyo's new City Hall. The photo shows the twin towers of Building Number 1*

'the embodiment of [Tokyo's] Manhattan fantasies' (Popham, 1985, pp. 101–2). The skyline of this district is represented often in Japanese film and television as the setting for big-city detective adventures and other dramas, and the backdrop for commercial advertising for various 'urban-sophisticated' consumer products such as cigarettes, whiskey and luxury cars. This is similar to the way that the more famous profile of New York is often represented in America and other countries, and has resulted in Shinjuku's becoming what is certainly the most widely recognized urban scene in Japan. Emulation of New York is sometimes quite direct. I have a Christmas card illustrating the Shinjuku skyline on a quiet snowy night (both quiet and snow are rare), Santa and his reindeer in the sky above, and the unmistakable reflection of the *Statue of Liberty* on the glass skin of one of the high-rises! Statues of Liberty are also seen on billboard advertising (for example, for cigarettes) and atop some 'love hotels'. So, too, I have a key chain that says 'Tokyo Megalopolis' and shows a montage of Tokyo's landmarks and the profile of New York's Chrysler Building. What is more, there is a waterfalls-fountain in Shinjuku's 'Central Park' (*Chūō Kōen*) called Niagara Falls, and a new (1995) shopping plaza (on the site of the former Shinjuku Rail-City Housing Display Grounds; see Chapter 4) called Times Square.[3]

The physical appearance of the redevelopment area in Nishi Shinjuku contrasts sharply with other parts of the commercial center. This is particularly so for several of the blocks closest to the station on the west side and for just about all of Shinjuku's large east side. This is where Shinjuku displays the dazzling side of Tokyo capitalism: it is a world of lights and flashing neon of every shape and color; of giant billboards and multi-story advertising banners; of commercial jingles blaring non-stop from electronic loudspeakers; of hard-sell claims about 'low, low prices' from touts with megaphones; and of every type and size and fashion of store, restaurant or bar, and other commercial establishment imaginable. This is Tokyo's main shopping area, larger now than Ginza and the other commercial nodes of the CBD, larger than all the other giant shopping centers scattered in all directions around the metropolis. Comparative statistics are hard to come by, but it seems that the east side of Shinjuku Station alone does more retail trade than number-two ranking Ginza (41.5 billion yen versus 38.7 billion yen in 1985), that Shinjuku's west side is fourth in the metropolis (25.4 billion yen), and that the two 'halves' of Shinjuku combined are pulling away from the competition and becoming ever more dominant (Fukuda, 1990, p. 21).

One of the biggest concentrations of commercial activity in Shinjuku is right at the station itself. Such a location pattern is typical and stems from the tendency of huge department stores to build right into the station buildings themselves because they own the rail lines (Hattori, Sugimura and Higuchi, 1980). In Shinjuku, specific examples are the Keiō and Odakyū Department Stores on the west side of Shinjuku Station. They rise several stories above track and street levels, looming like the lords and masters they are over the entire west exit area. Their rail lines, the Keiō and Odakyū Lines, extend west to the suburbs and bring commuters and shoppers directly to the entrances of the stores. Because this has been such a cushy business arrangement for them, both stores have been able to expand to nearby parcels where they have built branch stores and other types of shopping centers.

A second major concentration of commerce is the massive east side of Shinjuku Station, especially along Shinjuku-dōri, a former streetcar corridor now the main avenue from Shinjuku to the center of the city. This is the historic core of the neighborhood, the place where its business began to expand when the train station opened in 1885, and the section of Shinjuku that prospered most greatly after the 1923 earthquake because of devastation to the CBD. Descendants of some of the earliest shops are still there: e.g. the famous Takano fruit parlor-cum-shopping center that grew from Takano Kichitarō's fruit stand of 1885; and the huge and equally well-known Kinokuniya book store that began about the same time as a roadside charcoal shop (Waley, 1988a, p. 14). There are also a great many newer businesses, including several of Tokyo's largest camera and electronics emporiums, and a seemingly endless array of clothing boutiques, accessory shops, and other fashion outlets. The famous Mitsukoshi department store, a branch of the one on Chūō-dōri in Ginza (see Chapter 4), is also here, having come in after the earth-quake. So, too, there is Isetan, a huge department store and major landowner in east Shinjuku that is across the street. Both of these establishments have art galleries and museums on their upper floors, and are considered to be centers of high culture in addition to major retailers. A large part of their routines includes cultural programming during the day, as well as opportunities for shopping for prosperous housewives from the residential neighborhoods served by Shinjuku's train lines. On most Sundays, traditionally the busiest shopping day in Japan, Shinjuku-dōri is closed to vehicular traffic and is given over to pedestrians.[4] From about noon until dinner time the street is jammed with families spending their one day of the week together among the shops, with young couples and older couples, and with hordes of fashion-minded teenagers and college students.

The area close to Shinjuku Station, both west and east of the tracks, is also the site of a great many restaurants, coffee shops, and other types of eating and drink-ing establishments. This is in response to the considerable pedestrian volume that the station generates. It also reflects a natural symbiosis between these establish-ments and the other business functions of Shinjuku. Many of the restaurants open early and serve breakfasts to the first arrivals in Shinjuku, the so-called *asagata ningen* or 'early-morning crowd'. These are people who prefer to get a jump on the day at work or who will soon be opening the stores in the surroundings, as well as those who prefer to finish their commuting before the trains overfill. It is not uncommon to see individuals in the latter group dozing behind a newspaper in a breakfast restaurant. For many other restaurants the main source of business is lunch, either to workers or those who have come to Shinjuku to shop or go to a movie in one of the local theaters. Still other places do a big business delivering meals to workers who are too busy to leave their offices.[5] All over Shinjuku and other commercial centers one sees small motorbikes specially equipped on the back with carrying devices for food, most notably for bowls of noodles. A special category of establishments, generally called *kissaten*, serves coffee or tea and snacks during the day to customers who use them as venues for business meetings or other appointments, or for a quiet rest. The popularity of *kissaten* is due to a variety of reasons, including overcrowding or lack of privacy in offices, and accessibility to the train stations that bring the different parties in for a business appointment or personal meeting together.

Still another category of restaurants is busiest at the end of the day when people go out for dinner and drinks. Many of them are especially set up for groups. This is because it is a common practice in Japan for co-workers to go out together *en masse* after the office closes (Forbis, 1975, p. 75), and because other kinds of groups such as reunions from schools and clubs often come together at convenient transit centers to eat and drink. There is a place in front of a major exit of Shinjuku Station, the entry to a multi-level shopping center called Studio Alta, that is especially well known as a staging area for groups (and couples too) who arrange to meet for a night out in Shinjuku. On any given evening there may be well over 100 000 individuals enjoying the bars and restaurants of this neighborhood. The reason that so many people can fit into Shinjuku (to answer what would be a perfectly reasonable question, given the numbers involved) is that much of the restaurant business, here and elsewhere in Tokyo, is arranged vertically, often in tall, slender buildings that contain nothing other than places for food and drink. Starting from two levels below ground, and then rising six, eight or even more levels above, a given building might have twenty or more eating places inside. Typically, there is a long neon sign that runs along the outside, top to bottom, that lists the establishments inside floor by floor. One place in Shinjuku, a building called Ichibankan, is described in Popham's book as being typical of this commercial architecture. It is all bars, 49 of them, on its eight floors (Popham, 1985, pp. 110–11).

KABUKICHŌ: SHINJUKU'S SIN CITY

There is one subdistrict of Shinjuku that is more popular than all the others for nightlife. This is Kabukichō, named after a *kabuki* theater that was once planned there but never built. Located a few minutes' walk north and east of the station, it is itself an 'epitome district' that speaks volumes about how Tokyo works and about the intricacies of certain aspects of Japanese society. To put it simply, here is a place that is much more than just the largest and bawdiest entertainment district in the city; it is a gigantic fantasyland for adults, a total escape, if only for a few minutes or a few hours, for the tens of thousands who enter on a given day from all of the ills and oppressions that surround them (Nakawa *et al.*, 1989, p. 26). It is most famous for its several hundred sex businesses: hostess clubs, strip shows, peepshow parlors, 'no-panties coffee shops', pornography emporiums, and massage parlors that Japanese now call 'soaplands'.[6] A lot of what goes on is just downright kinky (Van Hook, 1989). Prostitution has been illegal since 1957, but it thrives in this setting nonetheless. There are also a great many 'legitimate' diversions: restaurants and bars with every kind of cuisine and decor imaginable, movie houses, bowling alleys, video arcades, *pachinko* (a type of pinball) parlors, and *karaoke* clubs. They are no less important in the overall activity of the area and attract a varied clientele that includes women, students, and others, in addition to carousing salarymen. Nevertheless, for many Tokyoites, perhaps the uncounted thousands and thousands who wouldn't set foot there because of the first reputation of Kabukichō, the place is not an escape from problems at all; it is one of the problems. For them, as well as for some of the Westerners who have observed the scene (Levin, 1986; Pons, 1984), Kabukichō represents some of the worst of Japan: rampant exploitation of women, Japanese and foreign, as well as such widespread problems as excessive drunkenness, gambling, and gangsterism.

The busiest time in Kabukichō begins at dusk when the lights go on and the streets come aglow with neon (Figure 5.4). Huge crowds of customers, just released from work or from school, cross Yasukuni-dōri, the broad traffic-choked boulevard separating the district from the main part of Shinjuku, and descend on its more than one thousand places of pleasure. They are beckoned by flashing signs of every

Figure 5.4 Kabukichō, Shinjuku's 'Sin City'

shape and color, by tall columns of neon that run the length of tall buildings and list the names of pubs and eateries, by touts carrying signs and calling out invitations, by scantily clad bar girls who appear in the doorways and smile at likely prospects, and by fantasyland architecture that ranges from bar and restaurant buildings shaped like medieval castles from Europe to a giant mechanical crab affixed to a seafood restaurant that claws at the attentions of passersby. Even the Mister Donut shop, certainly one of the tamer establishments in the neighborhood, is inviting; it is a sleek post-modernist arrangement of glass and neon that is spacious and comfortable, and that fits through its decor all the glitter of the neighborhood. A special subsection of Kabukichō, a place called Golden-gai, is a maze of some 240 tiny establishments, some no bigger than three or four bar stools, packed together at street level in what is no more than a quarter of a city block. The buildings are seedy and falling apart, and it is something of a wonder that they have not been demolished in the face of the considerable rebuilding that has gone on in the surroundings. Perhaps it is because they appear to be in imminent danger of being urban-renewed away, and because they look dangerous, like the haunts of gangsters that TV is fond of portraying, that it has become a mark of prestige in the nightlife world of Tokyo to be welcome there and to have a seat among the regulars (Kennerdell, 1988).

Still another area, the secluded far side of Kabukichō, specializes in what are called love hotels. These are establishments that rent rooms by the hour. They cater to couples on dates and furtive office romances, and to married couples who might lack privacy in small houses or apartments. They are busy not just at night but during the day, too, especially it seems during the Sunday afternoon leisure time that is so much a part of the Japanese routine of life. The architectural design of love hotel buildings and individual guestrooms emphasizes fantasy. Themes from foreign lands and past eras (e.g. fairyland castles) are especially common (Pons,

Figure 5.5 *One of the many architecturally distinctive love hotels in Tokyo. The ape promotes a games arcade. This example is from the commercial center at Ikebukuro in 1990. Neither the hotel building nor the ape is there any longer, as both have fallen to redevelopment*

1988, pp. 404–9). Figure 5.5 shows a good example from a similar subdistrict in the Ikebukuro commercial center north of Shinjuku.

The history of Kabukichō is actually quite recent. It did not emerge as an entertainment area until after the Second World War, when a local residents' association proposed to make it this in its plan for rebuilding after the bombing. This was in keeping with a long-standing tradition in Tokyo for having specialized quarters for pleasure, such as Asakusa and Yoshiwara, at key locations in the city (see Chapter 3). It was supposed to have been high-class (*kaori takai*) entertainment, including the *kabuki* theater that was never built, but it soon turned to sex. This was, in part, to satisfy US Occupation forces encamped nearby, and was, also in part, the doing of gangsters (*yakuza*) who moved into the area and took over many of its establishments. At the same time, its cinemas showed the first European movies in Japan (the proverbial 'art film'), and helped to make Kabukichō a favorite haunt for students and intellectuals. This was especially so during the radical 1960s (Waley, 1988a, p. 15). Nowadays, the place fits a new social ecology. It sits just off the busiest commuter interchange in the metropolis, and is a perfect location for after-work or after-school gatherings on the way home from the city. There are other places like it in Shibuya, Ikebukuro, Ueno, and the other train-station commercial centers around the edges of the central city, but they are not nearly as big nor so raunchy. What makes Kabukichō unique is its special appeal to salarymen from nearby office districts and the commuter routes that focus on Shinjuku. The gangsters are in firm control of the sex trade, the pinball arcades, and many of the other businesses: they know exactly what thousands of routine-weary men are looking for.

Yamanote Playgrounds: The 'Good Life' in Tokyo

If Shinjuku represents the new center of Tokyo and the world of the salaryman, then several other places on the west side of Tokyo represent the high-living consumer culture that has recently overtaken Japan (Clammer, 1997; Tanaka, 1994). We see this especially among the city's younger population: its great many high school and college students, its students in special cram schools, its recent graduates and other school-leavers, and its growing numbers of *shinjinrui*, a commonly used word meaning 'new breed' that describes the city's highly conspicuous class of trend-loving 'young professionals'. Shibuya, Harajuku, and Roppongi, as well as some of their neighbors such as Daikanyama, Ebisu, Aoyama, Hiroo and Azabu, are especially popular haunts. These areas are located within a few minutes of each other by car or train, and comprise an extremely fashionable section of Tokyo. This is the core of the modern-day *yamanote*, the direct descendant of the privileged side of old Edo, and the spiritual capital for the many new high-status neighborhoods that have formed in the expanding west of the city. For us they give insights to some of the 'good life' that Japan, and especially its capital city, is blessed with during this time of prosperity, as well as to certain excesses of consumer culture.

Shibuya is the largest of these places. It is about 3 kilometers south of Shinjuku and is a similar gigantic commercial center focused on a huge, desperately over-crowded train station. Shibuya Station is one of the busiest stops along the Yamanote rail loop around the center of the city. Like Shinjuku Station, it is a major transfer point for commuters between the suburbs and the CBD, as well as a popular destination for thousands and thousands of workers, students, shoppers, and others who disembark there each day and enter the surrounding neighborhood. As is typical of large train station-centered commercial districts in Japan, including Shinjuku, the spatial structure of Shibuya includes various specialized subdistricts: e.g. an area of department stores and other retailing; an area of banks and office buildings; several specialized areas of restaurants, coffee shops, and other eating and drinking places; a large nighttime entertainment zone (and some smaller ones); and a quiet district of love hotels (Cybriwsky, 1988a). Figure 5.6 illustrates the typical layout for commuter-oriented commercial centers like Shibuya and Shinjuku.

The subdistrict of Shibuya given to retailing is especially large and, if the rate of expansion of its leading stores is any indicator, extremely profitable. Two major department store chains dominate the trade. One is the huge Tōkyū chain and the other is Seibu. In addition to the flagship stores, which themselves are opulent multi-level consumer showcases, they have, between them, at least 15 giant branch stores within a few blocks. During the construction boom of the 1980s, the two companies averaged two large new retailing buildings in Shibuya each year (Wade, 1988, p. 39). Some of the main Tōkyū holdings include fancy multi-level shopping malls (e.g. Tōkyū Plaza, 109, 109–2, One-oh-Nine, and One-oh-Nine-30s),[7] a large underground shopping concourse near the train station, and a huge 'do-it-yourself' and gadgets store called Tōkyū Hands (Figure 5.7). There is also a second gigantic department store, a branch, built directly into the train station. As in so many other big commercial centers in Japan, the rail lines that feed to its entrances are

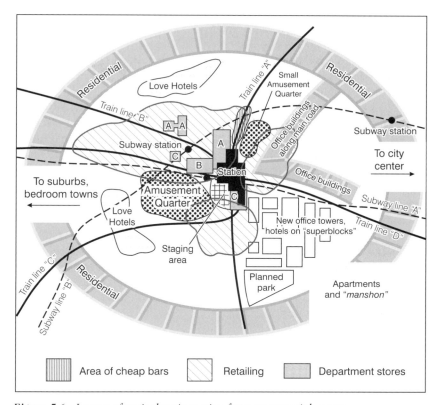

Legend:
- Area of cheap bars
- Retailing
- Department stores

Figure 5.6 *Layout of typical train-station-front commercial center*

Figure 5.7 *The main intersection in Shibuya, a popular commercial center that attracts hundreds of thousands of high-school and college-aged shoppers on a typical Sunday. The hub is the train and subway station in the background, built into the Tōkyū Department Store, although many visitors to Shibuya also arrive by car*

owned by the same parent company. These are the Tōkyū Shin-Tamagawa Line to the western suburbs and the Toyoko Line to Yokohama. Seibu, on the other hand, which owns no Shibuya train lines (but which does own several train lines in other areas), is concentrated a bit further from the station. One of its branches, called 'Loft', is a competitor to Tōkyō Hands. Another is 'Seibu Seed', a megastructure large enough to be a flagship department store just about anywhere else; its name makes me picture an analogy between farm crops in the field and sprouting department stores.

Two general characteristics distinguish Shibuya, one demographic and the other cultural. The key demographic point is that a disproportionate fraction of the district's users are young: according to one estimate nearly 60 percent of the district's visitors are under age 30, as compared to less than 50 percent in Shinjuku and about 40 percent in Ginza in the CBD (Tanaka, 1994, p. 86). They come after school or work and on their days off, in couples or in groups, and number as many as 100 000 on a typical evening, 250 000 on a busy Saturday night, and 250 000 again on Sunday afternoon. Such numbers make Shibuya probably the single greatest gathering spot for high-school and college-aged youth in the world. Some streets, for example the popular Spain Street with its many boutiques and accessory shops, get so crowded at times that they become, literally, wall-to-wall with people. So, too, Hachiko Square, the sizable public plaza in front of Shibuya Station where people commonly wait near a statue of a faithful dog to meet their dates or other appointments before venturing into Shibuya, fills regularly to overflowing with thousands of arrivals (Katō, 1979; Sode, 1987). A relatively new development, one that has come in since the mid-1980s and that itself reflects the increasing affluence enjoyed by younger generations, is enormous nighttime and Sunday afternoon traffic jams on the streets in the vicinity of Shibuya Station because thousands of junior and senior high-school and college students, collectively called *shibukaji-zoku*, cruise around the area showing off their shiny new cars.[8]

The second distinguishing point is that Shibuya is extraordinarily trendy. Its young shoppers come to see and be seen, being attentive to the minutest details of fashion and in step with whatever is hot, sometimes, it seems, no matter what the cost. They roam in and out of stores, studying the latest fashions and import items, trying on garment after garment, and often selecting purchases with friends to make sure they are getting exactly the right things and the same things. It is in this neighborhood where one sees the $1000 used jeans and $1000 used sneakers that the most extravagant spenders like to show off (Chapter 4). Shibuya's young people also hang around in the restaurants and coffee shops, and go for movies, bowling, pool, *karaoke* and other amusements. Visiting travel agencies is also popular. One of these businesses is seemingly at every turn, in every instance lined in front with tall racks of glossy brochures that promise fun in Orlando, Okinawa, Hawaii, Australia, Canada's Rocky Mountains, ski resorts in the Japanese Alps and other desirable destinations. Table 5.1, adapted from Tanaka's marvelous study of Tokyo as a city of consumption (Tanaka, 1994), compares Shibuya and Shinjuku according to Tokyoites' perceptions of them, highlighting key demographic and cultural differences.

If we go just a little distance from Shibuya, north to the next neighborhood, Harajuku, we see even more evidence of a comfortable material existence

Table 5.1 *Social Perceptions of Shinjuku and Shibuya*

Shinjuku	Shibuya
Old Mass	New Mass
Developed in 1950–70	Developed in 1980–90
Kantō, inland-oriented	Shōnan,[a] ocean-oriented
Regional culture	Urban culture
Earthly	Sophisticated
Entertainment district	Fashion district
Somewhat dark	Somewhat bright
Somewhat poor	Somewhat rich
Volume retailer, large stores	Specialty stores, boutiques
Price-conscious	Quality, design-conscious
Men in 30s–40s	Women in 10s–20s
Youth from the countryside	Youth from the city
Migrant mentality	Resident mentality
Blue-collar	White-collar
Tourist groups or single men	Nuclear family, single women, students

[a] Shōnan is the recreation beachfront of Kanagawa Prefecture.

Source: Tanaka (1994, p. 86), after research by Uemura.

(Watanabe, 1992). There, at the doorstep to the Meiji Shrine, the famous landmark memorial to the emperor whose reign is synonymous with Western influences and modernization in Japan, is yet another super-trendy area. Just like in Shibuya, some streets are as good as heaven for teenyboppers. Takeshita-dōri is store after store with young fashions, costume jewelry, and cute ('Hello Kitty!') accessories, as well as lots of hamburger and fries places and ice cream shops. On Sundays in good weather, a broad boulevard in nearby Yoyogi Park is closed to traffic and youngsters take over completely with end-to-end rock and roll bands and throngs of energetic dancers moving in unison (Figure 5.8). Other sections of this district, such as along Omotesandō-dōri, the landscaped boulevard that was put in to make Tokyo impressive for the 1964 Olympics, rank among the top centers of high fashion in the world. There are fabulous boutiques (typically with fabulously high prices) all over this area, some in tall shopping center buildings, others in cubbyhole shops on quiet side streets. There are also several of the most famous fashion designer studios and some outstanding art galleries. These are the places that you read about in shoppers' guides to Tokyo and in-flight magazines.

The nearby streets, once an unassuming residential area, are now highly desirable addresses, particularly for status-conscious young professionals. As in the other areas of Tokyo-style gentrification nearby, rents are astronomical and many of the living units are small, but the surroundings boast great shops and nightspots. Partly because of its proximity to television and recording studios, this is the area where many of Japan's best-known screen personalities and music stars have chosen to live. A popular pastime for some of the many visitors who descend on Harajuku, especially on Sundays and holidays, is to try to spot a favorite actor or actress in the crowds or in a passing Mercedes or, as many teenage girls are wont to do, keep vigil in front of the home of an idolized singer. The back-street areas around Harajuku, such as the Jingūmae neighborhood, are also fine places to explore new trends in residential architecture. Even from the outside, one sees

Figure 5.8 *Part of the mostly very poor music scene on warm-weather Sundays along Inokashira-dōri near Harajuku Station*

terrific examples of creative design and new ideas for efficient use of crowded space.

Both Shibuya and Harajuku are also known for nightlife. Shibuya is especially crowded and appeals mostly to students. Its main entertainment district begins directly across the street from the station, and is entered through a symbolic gate or arch marked *Senta-dōri*, or Center Street. This is a common architectural device in urban Japan that signals passage into a world of play.[9] The entertainment district is large, almost as big as Kabukichō, and emphasizes food and drink, clubs that play popular music, *karaoke*, concerts and movies, and the same video arcades and other amusements that stay busy during the day. As one might expect in a place where the numerical balance between students and salarymen is the reverse of that in Kabukichō, there is a lot less of the sex-for-money business in this area. However, there is just as much, if not more, public drunkenness. The going-home scene just in time for the departure of the day's last trains from the station (around midnight) is especially unrestrained.

An even more famous place for nightlife is Roppongi. Located in the direction of the CBD from Shibuya and Harajuku, and not far from Tokyo Tower, this is Tokyo's premier section of trendy bars and fast-paced discos, and its liveliest district during the small hours when every place else has gone to sleep. It is an exceptionally popular haunt for some of the high-living 'glitterati' of Tokyo who can afford expensive clubs and who follow a personal time clock that departs wildly from the mainstream of the city. It is also a popular hang-out for many of the foreigners in Tokyo: well-heeled business travelers and diplomatic emissaries; the many fashion models from the United States, Australia, and Europe who find good work in Tokyo; US military personnel from nearby bases; and the various rock stars and other entertainers who come to perform in Japan from abroad. As such, it is something of

Figure 5.9 *Yebisu Garden Place, showing the centerpiece French chateau and a hotel tower and condominium in the background*

a 'foreigners' ghetto', a sort of modern-day reincarnation of the old enclaves during Meiji where foreigners were kept and entertained. The Roppongi scene, both night and day, when the neighborhood is known for fashion boutiques, art galleries, and some exceptionally nice lunch restaurants and coffee shops, is often glamorized in movies and on television dramas. As a result, it enjoys a very fashionable image among many Japanese, and is often thought of as being synonymous with the good life of the international jet set.

The newest addition to the good-life scene in Tokyo is Yebisu Garden Place. Located at Ebisu, between Shibuya and Roppongi, it is Tokyo's best example of a planned, mixed-use redevelopment project promoting a fashionable urban lifestyle. Once the site of a track-side brewery, the place is now a self-contained island of consumer pleasures: a department store and shopping mall, an especially opulent Westin Hotel, many restaurants, museums (including one about beer!), movie theaters, and other amusements for the public. A centerpiece is an expensive French restaurant in a replica chateau. There is also an office tower and luxury high-rise residences. The complex is reached by people mover (a moving sidewalk) from Ebisu Station or by car, with parking provided underneath. Especially on Sundays Yebisu Garden Place is jammed with young couples and families on outings, enjoying the controlled new environment (Figure 5.9).

There is a mix of conclusions that one comes away with from Shibuya and its new *yamanote* neighbors, as well as an urge for some sermonizing. One conclusion is that Japan's youth are lucky indeed, and that older generations, particularly the so-called *yake-ato no ha* ('the after the fire people') who had worked so hard and lived austerely during the difficult postwar years, have handed over to their children and grandchildren quite a prize. Clearly, life has come to be comfortable in Japan's capital, and affluence is widespread. Unfortunately, a second conclusion is that perhaps too many young seem to have and want everything, and are badly spoiled. Thus, another impression of this part of Tokyo is one of shock and sadness at the excesses of materialism. While many of the big-spending youth are from wealthy families who can afford lavishness, many others have modest means and work many hours at part-time jobs striving to keep pace with the escalating consumer standards of their age group. In this context, it is not surprising that according to some young Tokyoites the point of life is to have money, as pop idol Matsutoya Yumi once revealingly proclaimed in an interview, or that distressing social problems such as shoplifting and teenage prostitution to obtain luxury goods are on the rise (Chapter 4).

THE OTHER SIDE OF TOKYO

There is also an entirely different side of Tokyo. If instead of going west from the center, where most of the city's fashionable residential districts and business centers cluster and where there is the most growth, we go a short distance east or north to the vicinity of the Sumida River and its mouth, we come to what is left of *shitamachi*, Tokyo's old plebian section. It is much more of a private and unassuming district than the flashy neighborhoods we have just left, but is very much alive nonetheless and fully an integral part of Tokyo. Because change has come there more slowly and has taken some different directions than in other parts of the city, *shitamachi* is sometimes nostalgically referred to as 'the real Tokyo' (Figure 5.10). It is where many of the most traditional aspects of the city are visible, where there are fewer trappings of imported Western culture, and where an outsider in Japan, such as myself, stands out most sharply. There are also distinct contrasts in economic base, social characteristics of the Japanese population, physical conditions of the living environment and other considerations. We shall go there now not just to balance our view of the city but also for fundamental lessons about what an important section of Tokyo is actually like. For our purposes, we can define the area to be visited as Arakawa, Taitō, Sumida, and Kōtō Wards, and those portions of Chūō Ward that have not been incorporated yet into the expanded CBD.

Perhaps the most striking impression is that here is truly a part of the city given over to work. Other places are busy too, in fact extremely so as we have seen in Marunouchi and other parts of the CBD and in the Shinjuku subcenter, but in this case much of the work is of a type that all those other centers depend on before they themselves can begin. I think of this area as the foundation for the rest of the Tokyo economy. It is home to thousands of small and generally unheralded companies that function at the broad base of the city's economic pyramid, supporting with their work the enterprises of big corporations above them and the routines of the city's more conspicuous districts. Among a hundred or more other distinctions, this is where many of the taxis and taxi drivers that serve the center of the city come from; the central place where fresh fish and other seafoods are sold and distributed; the district where many of the city's newspapers, magazines, business cards (*meishi*), and seemingly indispensable cheap comic books for commuters (*manga*) are printed; the factory zone where many of the cardboard boxes and wrapping papers are made that retailers, manufacturers, and others in the city

Figure 5.10 *A quiet scene in an old neighborhood in Taitō Ward*

require for their businesses; and the place where many of the tissue packets are put together that advertisers press into your hands as you pass busy train stations or shopping centers. There are also many warehouses and other storage facilities; wholesaling companies, transportation facilities such as bus and truck terminals, rail sidings, and piers; dispatching centers for package delivery services; and a great many factories of all sizes, but mostly small.

A good idea of the workaday rhythms of this area and the scale of its enterprises is seen at Tsukiji, a district in Chūō Ward at the mouth of the Sumida that is known for its huge fish market (Figure 5.11). Its name has been mentioned before as the site of a foreigners' compound in the nineteenth century. Now, however, it is *Tōkyō no daidokoro*, 'Tokyo's pantry'. This is where some 14 000 restaurateurs, *sushi* chefs, and retail fishmongers come each day to purchase their supplies of fish. They shop at one or other of 1677 stalls, most of them tiny, family-run operations, competing fiercely for business within the confines of a centralized market the Tokyo government set up in 1935 (Bestor, 1989b, pp. 17–18). All night long, trucks with fresh seafood arrive from fishing ports all over Japan and from Narita Airport, the biggest fishing port of all, and unload their wares. Auctions start at 5:30 a.m. and are finished a short while later. The careful inspection of rows after rows of huge tuna by buyers who peer with flashlights inside deep incisions is something to see. Purchases are then taken by barrow to be cut and resold at one of the stalls, or to one of hundreds of trucks and vans that are double and triple parked to make deliveries to supermarkets and other retail outlets. Many purchasers pedal away on bicycles, headed for the *sushi* shops of Ginza, Shimbashi, and other nearby districts with full polystyrene crates stacked one atop another and strapped precariously on the back. Much of the rest of the day is given to retailing. All told, some 65 000 people work in or visit the market each day (Bestor, 1989b, p. 18).

Figure 5.11   *The early-morning tuna auction at Tsukiji fish market. Here buyers are inspecting the catch before the bidding begins*

As we tour through the Sumida River wards, we see many other specialized districts that provide important services or materials to the rest of Tokyo. Some of the most prominent examples include Kiba and Shin ('New') Kiba, two areas, one older and the other its planned replacement, of sawyers and lumberyards in Kōtō Ward; Kuramae in Taitō Ward, an area with some 300 wholesalers of toys, dolls and fireworks stretched out along a street called *gangu tonya-gai* (toy wholesale street); Bakurochō-Yokoyama, also in Taitō, Tokyo's *sen'i tonya-gai*, the principal textile wholesale street; Kappabashi (Taitō, too), a street where kitchen and restaurant supplies are sold, including the fantastic plastic replicas of everything from *sushi* to spaghetti to sundaes that many restaurants in the city display in their windows as their menus; and Inarichō (Taitō Ward once again), a concentration of 50 or so shops that sell Buddhist and Shintō household shrines. Not far away from all these places, but actually just within the boundaries of Chiyoda Ward, is the famous electronics-wholesaling district called Akihabara. This is where tourists and natives alike descend on giant electronics emporiums for the best buys on cell phones, cameras, video equipment, stereos, and other products from Japan's well-known electronics and photo-equipment manufacturers. This area also has a dense maze of tight little alleyways in which electronics parts and equipment such as wiring, transistors and various knobs, dials, and circuit boards are sold. Nearby is what is left of the Kanda Market. This has been the largest wholesale produce market for the city, but it is now being relocated to modern facilities elsewhere. Its rhythms and traffic patterns have been similar to those I described for the Tsukiji Market.

The residential environment is also a sharp contrast with other parts of the city. It is hard to generalize, because there is a variety of neighborhoods, including several pleasant ones. However, on the whole, the housing stock of the Sumida River wards is older, lower in quality and more lacking in amenities than that of

Figure 5.12 *One of the thousands of small at-home workshops that comprise the broad base of Tokyo's manufacturing pyramid. This example from Shioiri in Arakawa Ward shows the proprietor tooling small metal pieces for automobile window assemblies*

higher standards elsewhere. Greenery, open space and quiet are particularly lacking. Many neighborhoods are a mix of residential and non-residential uses; a large fraction of the population lives among factories, warehouses, parking lots, shopping streets and other non-residential neighbors. There are also many examples where people work at home. Small-scale industries such as printing shops, carpentry, metal stamping, or the assembly of small parts in the front rooms of old houses that open right on to the street are conspicuous (Figure 5.12). Many of these are family-run operations that work under contract on a piecework basis for bigger companies. In some of the back streets of the Sumida area small clusters of *nagaya* still stand. These are wooden tenement structures of a type that were once the principal dwelling form for commoners in old Edo. The original structures are all long gone, so what remains are survivors of the newer generations of these buildings that were put up in the late nineteenth century and the early part of this century as workers' housing in factory zones. They were miserably crowded slums then, and now serve as reminders of the hard times that this part of the city has endured (Waley, 1989b).

Even some of the newer housing is not so attractive. I am thinking in particular about a type of multi-story apartment development that is called *danchi*. Some of these dwellings have been built by large employers to house their workers, but most of the newer projects are by Tokyo Metropolitan Government and the Housing and Urban Development Public Corporation as part of their overall program to relieve the housing shortage for low- and moderate-income families. They are found in virtually every ward and town in the metropolis, and should not be identified solely with the Sumida area. However, *danchi* are especially numerous and visible in Kōtō

Figure 5.13 *The Shirage–Higashi flood control project in Sumida Ward.* (Courtesy of Office of Information, Tokyo Metropolitan Government.) © Tokyo Metropolitan Government

Ward, particularly on newly reclaimed land close to Tokyo Bay where there are thousands of units. While some of the construction seems to be very well planned, many other examples stand out because of the ugliness of their design, their isolation from other neighborhoods and from basic facilities such as shopping and schools, and the small units inside. One public housing project in Sumida Ward is especially noteworthy. It is a part of a 'disaster prevention plan' for the Shirage Higashi neighborhood along the Sumida; it consists of a long row of 18 or 19 almost identical multi-story *danchi* arranged end to end and connected to each other to form an impregnable flood wall against the river (Figure 5.13).

The largest business center in the Sumida wards area is Ueno. In many ways it is the equivalent of Shinjuku or Shibuya on the other side of the city: it has an overcrowded commuter station where several train and subway lines intersect; a busy retailing center with major department stores and the usual mix of fast-food restaurants and chain boutiques stores; a growing subsection of banks and office buildings; a busy nighttime entertainment zone; an area of love hotels, and so on. However, economically the place is also evidently a cut or two below the other centers. Like nearby Asakusa, the second biggest commercial center in the Sumida area, there is an expansive discount shopping area that reflects both the lower income levels and higher proportions of older people among the clientele. At Ueno, this area stretches beneath an elevated rail corridor. Instead of the overpriced trendy stores on Tokyo's west side, there are stalls with cheap imported clothing, imitations of popular brand names, discount cosmetics and toiletries, and various kinds of seconds and remainders. Ueno is also the place where Tokyoites know they can obtain counterfeit telephone calling cards at a fraction of the price of real ones;

Figure 5.14 *A fruit stand on Ameyayokochō, a lively shopping street in Ueno*

they are sold at the station and along all major streets by shadowy young men from Iran. One Ueno street, Ameyayokochō, which runs along side the tracks, is always especially crowded (see Chapter 3). It was one of the leading black-market centers during the desperate shortages of food and other necessities that plagued Japan after the Second World War. Today it is a colorful and unusually noisy market in which sellers of fish, fruits, nuts and other foods, as well as products ranging from golf clubs to East German military insignia, shout out bargain prices and other sales pitches to passing customers (Figure 5.14).

One of the clearest reminders that this part of the city differs profoundly from the more affluent west side comes from watching the passenger traffic at Ueno Station. While there are the usual commuters to the city center from outlying wards and the suburbs, the station is also a major approach to Tokyo from farmlands and mountain provinces to the north and east; it counts among its many users disproportionate numbers of poor job seekers in the city, country folk on holiday, and farmers with produce to sell in city markets. In this way, Ueno Station resembles transportation centers in Third World capitals (Figure 5.15). In warm-weather months, for example, dozens of old women arrive to sell their fresh vegetables directly to restaurants and other pre-arranged buyers in the city or at rented stalls in neighborhood commercial centers. They come on early trains from Tochigi and Ibaraki prefectures and other rural locations, carrying huge baskets, bent over physically from a lifetime of hard work and dietary deficiencies. Some-times they are called *gyōshōnin*, a generic word translated as 'itinerant peddler'. In winter, many of the passengers arriving in Ueno are seasonal laborers (mostly males), displaced from the north by ice and snow, and coming to the capital to work in construction until it is time to prepare rice fields in the spring. Because of this, the Ueno area abounds with lower-cost hotels and rooming houses and cheap eateries. It is also one of the largest concentrations in Tokyo (and in Japan as

Figure 5.15   *Shoe-shiners in front of Ueno Station*

whole) of people who sleep in the streets. At all times of the year, there are hundreds of individuals who sleep in the corridors and stairways of the train station, in doorways, on benches in Ueno Park, and in a growing number of card-board and tent 'settlements' hidden in the park's bushes and stands of trees.[10]

That the Sumida River side of Tokyo is the lower-status side of the city is clearly explained in the detailed case study of Arakawa Ward by Wagatsuma and DeVos (1980). Although they are careful to point out the many charms and attractions of living in this district, as well they should, they emphasize that large parts of Arakawa Ward have negative connotations in Tokyo's public consciousness. This is particularly the case for some of the neighborhoods close to Minami Senju, an aging commercial center in eastern Arakawa on the city side of a key bridge across the Sumida. The reasons for this begin far back in the history of the district, when certain events took place that stained the reputation of the area in the thinking of pre-modern society, and that set in motion a succession of land-use decisions relating to Arakawa Ward that continue to taint the place today. As the authors refer to it, Arakawa's unkind fate has been to become 'a place of disposal'. This is particularly so in matters related to the disposal of corpses, an unavoidable task in any city and one that Arakawa has performed for Tokyo since early Edo times. There is a lot of superstition attached to this even today, so that for many Tokyoites the fact that Arakawa has the city's largest crematorium (at a site close to Machiya Station) is reason enough to be biased against the ward and its residents. It is particularly unfortunate for the ward's reputation that many people in the city, especially those from the west side, go there only for services after the death of a family member or friend, and that cremation is what they think about whenever Arakawa or the Machiya neighborhood are mentioned.

The background to all of this is fascinating. One of the first chapters concerns a temple that was near Minami Senju during the Tokugawa shogunate that came to be called *Nagekomi-dera* ('the throw-in temple') or *Muen-dera* ('the temple for the unrelated'). This is where the bodies of prostitutes from Yoshiwara (see Chapter 3) were brought for cremation and burial. Because of a belief that a deceased prostitute would come back to haunt a person who treated her corpse with respect, the bodies were typically wrapped in straw, as was the custom for dead animals, and thrown in the yard of the temple where an already-tainted caste of workers would take over. Some people remember that the ashes of 10 000 prostitutes were buried in this way at a site in Arakawa Ward near the boundary with Taitō Ward. In the same vein, the area near Minami Senju was the principal execution grounds during the shogunate of criminals and political opponents. This was done by beheading, crucifixion or burning. Many of the victims had their severed heads put on stakes for display. By 1868 more than 200 000 individuals had been disposed of in this way. At about the time that the execution site was established another highlight of Arakawa's history, if highlight is the right word, took place: the decision in 1669 by more than twenty temples from closer to the center of the city to put up consolidated cremating facilities at Minami Senju. It was a logical site because it was then outside the limits of urban development and near the shogun's killing fields. Other crematoria soon followed, as did settlements of employees, almost all of whom were members of a feudal-era outcaste group called *hinin*. It was *hinin*, for example, who assisted with executions and took the bodies away for disposal.

The topic of outcaste groups in Japan, especially in contemporary society, is an extremely delicate issue about which there are no official statistics and few people who are willing to talk. Yet it is well known that so-called 'status discrimination' is still practiced against the descendants of *hinin* and other outcaste groups, even though the individuals who were thus labeled were supposedly emancipated shortly after the modernization of Japan began in 1868 (Hane, 1982; Suginohara, 1982; Yoshino and Murakoshi, 1977). Although the problem is identified mostly with the Kansai region (Osaka and Kobe), it is also present in Arakawa, Taitō and other lower status places of Tokyo. It is whispered that employees of the big crematorium near Machiya include descendants of *hinin*, and that the residential population of Arakawa and Taitō Wards includes numerous descendants of *hinin* and another outcaste group, an untouchable caste once called *eta* ('filth') but now more commonly referred to (but still in hushed tones) as *burakumin* ('the hamlet people'). The presence of this population is said to explain the concentration of such industries in the Sumida wards, especially in the vicinity of Minami Senju and next to the crematorium, as leather-working and rag- and scrap-picking. These are occupations that were traditionally assigned to the outcastes (Wagatsuma and DeVos, 1980, p. 215).

Yet another significant characteristic of this 'other side of Tokyo' is a steady, long-term decline in population, much steeper than that for the 23-Ward section of Tokyo as a whole. This is in contrast to most other wards (except the CBD) which have gained in numbers over the long term, except perhaps in the most recent counts. The population of Arakawa Ward has declined from 247 013 in 1970, to 198 126 in 1980, 190 061 in 1985, and to 184 809 in 1990. An estimate for 1996 gives Arakawa's population as 171 469. Trends for Taitō Ward and Sumida Ward are similar (Figure 5.16). Related to this is a high rate (by Tokyo standards) of housing vacancy. For example, a 1993 housing survey showed that in Arakawa Ward the

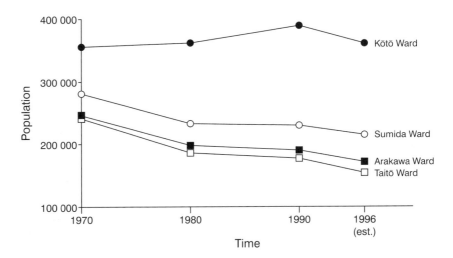

Figure 5.16 *Population trends, Sumida River wards, 1970–96 (est.)* (*Sources:* *Tokyo Statistical Yearbook* and Tokyo Metropolitan Government)

percent of all dwellings that were unoccupied was 9.5 and that in Taitō Ward it was 8.3 (*Tokyo Statistical Yearbook, 1994*, p. 162). This reflects the fact that many people move out of this part of the city if they can afford it, and comparatively few young people move in, despite all the housing pressures elsewhere. So the population is disproportionately aged, which is still another distinguishing characteristic of the Sumida Ward area (see Chapter 4). Such demographic trends have apparently so alarmed officials of Taitō Ward that they have instituted a possibly first-of-its-kind policy to pay young newly-weds to live there. The offer, which was initially limited to 200 couples, was for up to 50 000 yen per month in rent subsidies; it required that no partner in the marriage be over 40, the combined ages of the couple be under 70 and that the income level of the household be less than 8 million yen annually (*The Japan Times*, 17 June 1990, p. 20).

SHITAMACHI NOSTALGIA

I don't want to dwell on the negative. Still another distinguishing feature of the Sumida wards, one that deserves at least as much attention as the previous descriptions, is the area's rich cultural traditions. Indeed, this is the focus of the vast majority of literature about the area, be it in Japanese, English or other languages. There is presently a revival of interest in national history and traditional culture among the public in Japan, as well as renewed interest in seeing and experiencing some of the city's older neighborhoods and historic centers. One indicator of this is the commercial success of the several guidebooks that have been published recently about historic sites in *shitamachi*. One such book, by Enbutsu Sumiko, is in English and is especially good (Enbutsu, 1993). Another indicator is the immense recent popularity of a film series shown in movie houses, on television, and on rental video about 'Tora-san', a middle-aged itinerant peddler from Shibamata, an aging blue-

Figure 5.17 *The historic Tsukishima neighborhood as seen from a nearby office tower. The River City 21 complex (Chapter 6) is in the background*

collar neighborhood in Katsushika Ward at the eastern end of *shitamachi*. There are more than 40 episodes, a typical one showing Tora-san wandering the countryside in search of adventure and the quintessential warm spirit of Japan, and then tearfully returning home to family and neighbors and proclaiming that what he was looking for was there all along. So, too, we see new interest in urban nostalgia reflected in the popular series of pen-and-ink postcards called 'Old Tokyo Today' by artist Kiritani Itsuo. The simple, austere drawings of old houses and shops along the back streets of various *shitamachi* neighborhoods are haunting records of a fast-disappearing past and a special kind of urban beauty (Kingston, 1988).

Some parts of the *shitamachi* area are becoming increasingly popular as places for day trips and urban explorations. This is particularly true for small enclaves of well preserved old-style houses and traditional local shops that still exist within larger residential areas such as Kanda, Shiba, Tsukiji, Nezu, Tsukishima and Ryōgoku (Fujimori, 1987a, p. 417). In Tsukishima, for example, a reasonably intact Edo-era fishing village on a landfill island in Tokyo Bay close to the CBD (Figure 5.17), aficionados like to stroll the old streets and alleyways for a flavor of bygone days, to visit the strikingly beautiful Shintō shrine, Sumiyoshi Jinja, tucked away next to a tiny harbor of fishing boats, and to sample *tsukudani*, a popular local food made of small fish or seaweed boiled down over many hours in soy sauce. In mid-July, people from many parts of the city like to come here for *bon'odori*, a joyous religious festival celebrating the annual return of the souls of one's ancestors, observed during the summer months in cities and towns all over Japan. It always involves singing and dancing and colorful traditional costumes. The event in Tsukishima is said to be especially well staged, and has been designated an 'Intangible Cultural Asset' by Tokyo Metropolitan Government (Enbutsu, 1993, p. 124).

The attraction of the Ryōgoku area is *sumō*, Japan's own national sport. Located in Sumida Ward across the Sumida River from the CBD, this district houses Tokyo's main sumō arena, an impressive structure called the Kokugikan, and draws huge crowds whenever there are tournaments or exhibitions. Visitors go not just to the matches but also wander the neighborhood, looking in on various 'stables' where favorite wrestlers live and train, shop for *sumō* souvenirs and visit local eateries known for hearty meals. They also look for a taste of neighborhood history. Ekō-in, a temple dedicated in 1657 to the victims of an Edo-era fire but also known for *sumō* traditions, is a particularly popular attraction. One of its major features is a huge stone marked with the Chinese character for 'power', commemorating the extraordinary strength of *sumō* wrestlers (Enbutsu, 1993, p. 148). In 1993 the Edo–Tokyo Museum opened next to the *sumō* arena, adding to historic Ryōgoku's appeal for visitors (see Chapter 4).

For many Tokyoites the best place to go for a dose of traditional culture is Asakusa. This became the principal entertainment center of Edo, thriving during the Meiji Era and Taishō as a busy theater district before destruction in the 1923 earthquake. The numbers are enormous: 1.7 million visitors to its main temple at the New Year; 2 million visitors to a mid-May festival called the *sanja matsuri*; almost 1 million to see the fireworks along the Sumida River at the end of July. Even non-traditional events in this neighborhood are becoming popular: there is an annual samba festival in Asakusa now which was attended recently by an estimated half a million individuals (Simmons, 1988, p. 39). All of this represents a big turn-around in the fortunes of the district, which had declined markedly after the 1923 disaster, and then declined again in the 1950s and 1960s when new subway lines began to compete with Asakusa's Ginza Line and take passengers to other sections of the city. As Tokyo shifted westward to centers such as Shinjuku and Shibuya, Asakusa was left behind. Its revival is attributed to heightened public interest in investigating the old sections of the city, as well as to skillful promotion and dedicated work on the part of merchants, residents, and local public officials. There is a civic association composed of about 45 proprietresses of local shops called *Asakusa okamisan-kai* ('the Asakusa Women's Association') that has been instrumental in bringing about the beautification of Rokku, a century-old theater subdistrict of Asakusa, and the restoration of some of its historic buildings. An important achievement was the reopening in November 1988 of the Asakusa Tokiwaza, a once-prominent Meiji Era entertainment palace that closed down in 1984 after a long period of hard times.

Asakusa's major landmark is the famous temple called Asakusa Kannon, or Sensōji (Figure 5.18). It is actually a fairly new building, having been built of ferroconcrete in 1958 to replace the Edo Era structure destroyed in the air raids of 1945, but its history is much older than the city itself, going back perhaps to the year 628 when two fishermen brothers are said to have caught a small golden statue of the goddess Kannon in their nets in the Sumida. The temple was built to safeguard that image, which may or may not be buried somewhere beneath it. This is a detail that does not matter much in practice, because Kannon, the goddess of mercy, has a large public following, and believers continue to flock to her shrine as they have for centuries. Because of the traditional design of the temple building itself, the layout and design of other structures in the temple precincts, and the

Figure 5.18   *The faithful (and some tourists) gathering at Sensōji, the great temple in Asakusa*

evident devotion of the many believing visitors, Sensōji is a 'don't miss it' attraction for tourists.

The entry to Sensōji is through a huge decorative wooden gate called Kaminarimon. Translated as 'The Gate of the God of Thunder', the gate guards the temple complex, and is itself a significant Tokyo landmark. It is distinguished by the terrifying images of the gods of thunder and wind to either side of the opening, and by a giant red lantern that hangs overhead. Because it is the subject of an extremely well-known 1857 *ukiyo-e* print by Hiroshige, almost every Japanese recognizes the lantern and associates it and the famous gate with Edo's *shitamachi*. So, too, the long commercial street that leads from Kaminarimon almost to the steps of Sensōji itself is a part of the 'Edo experience' that visitors to Asakusa expect. Called Nakamise-dōri, 'the street of the inside shops', it is lined, just as it was two centuries ago, with small shops of every variety. Many of them are old and famous, and offer such fare as traditional foods or snacks, delicate ivory carvings (still being sold in Japan), Edo-period firemen's banners or beautiful *kimono*. Others have today's products (see Chapter 1). The street is gaily decorated, especially during festivals, conveying the same sense of pleasure that visitors must have experienced during earlier times when Asakusa was the most popular gathering place in the city.

GENTRIFICATION OF *SHITAMACHI*?

One other aspect of the growing interest among the public in the city's old neighborhoods, and perhaps an inevitable one at that, is a developing trend for a 'return to the city' migration. There are no statistics about this that I know of, and the movement still seems to be pretty small, but it is clear in some of the *shitamachi* neighborhoods that increasing numbers of young professional people are moving in from outside the area and settling in old houses by choice. From my own contacts, a disproportionate number seem to be artists, writers, educators, architects, and other professionals. They are attracted, it seems, by central location, the historic ambience of certain specific neighborhoods, a relatively sizable stock of old housing with interesting architecture and lower prices. I have also heard new arrivals talk excitedly about the 'wonderful social mix' that exists in *shitamachi*: young people and old, rich and poor, professional and blue-collar, lots of traditional craftsmen. This is in welcome contrast, I am told, to the social and architectural homogeneity of new housing developments in other parts of the metropolis, especially the aesthetically sterile and greatly overpriced apartments and *manshon* abounding in the fashionable west side. More than once I have heard it said that because of the squeaky-clean tiles that cover the surfaces of so many new buildings, the new Tokyo was coming to look like a public toilet rather than a city. Some of the preferred alternatives are Yanaka in Taitō Ward, Nezu at the border between Taitō and Bunkyō Ward, and the Minowabashi area, where Tokyo's last trolley line ends, in Arakawa Ward.

All this sounds very familiar to me, like the time when the so-called 'urban pioneers' reinvested in the inner cities of graying American urban centers because it was both what they could afford and preferred. Their arrival was a welcome infusion of new blood and physical improvements to neighborhoods that had previously lacked both, but that in most cases was followed by profit-seeking developers who changed old neighborhoods into hot property overnight, displacing long-term residents and routines. It would be terrible if the same happened in *shitamachi*. What distinguishes this area as 'the other side of Tokyo' is that, unlike most of the rest of the city, it has not been hot property, and is, therefore, in all its good and bad points, different. Unfortunately, in some of the preferred neighborhoods there are plenty of signs that it is going to be a hard fight to preserve the ambience of the past and the social mix. There are more and more squeaky-clean *manshon* popping up among the old houses, as well as more high-rises and other intrusive developments. Sometimes these are erected by the biggest of builders. So it is not inconceivable that, as old prejudices about 'good' versus 'bad' sides of the city die, and as the problem of housing supply and cost persists, this 'other side of Tokyo' will be swallowed up by overdevelopment in much the same way that happened in parts of the west side. The key that will determine which path endangered areas of *shitamachi* will take – traditional residential districts or fast-developing pieces of the new Tokyo – will depend on the outcome of struggles between citizens and developers such as the fight described earlier over Shinobazu Pond (Chapter 4).

THE UNDERSIDE OF TOKYO: SANYA

There is one neighborhood within this 'other side of Tokyo' that is so different from the rest that it needs to be considered separately. It is called Sanya, a name that is written with the Chinese characters for 'mountain' and 'valley', and Tokyo's closest equivalent to a slum. Located in Taitō Ward and overlapping the boundary with Arakawa, it is a place few people from other sections of the city know and that almost no one goes to except those who live there and the few who work there. It is the secret 'underside of Tokyo', a place inhabited in large fraction by the castoffs of society and ignored by almost everyone else. Even most maps of the city fail to identify it, and either use formal place names only for the *chōme* in the area or, more often, are designed to have boxed map titles or legends where Sanya would have been.

The approach to Sanya is through a place called Namidabashi, now a street intersection but originally the name of a bridge that crossed a small river. On one side of the river was the city; on the other was Kozukappara, the shogun's bloody execution grounds. Namidabashi thus separated the doomed from the rest of Edo; it was where families said their final farewells to relatives who were about to die. Hence the name for the bridge: Namidabashi, 'Bridge of Tears'. There is now a narrow pedestrian bridge in the vicinity leading from the closest train station across the tracks in the direction of Sanya. It is no exaggeration to say that in walking the few tens of meters in that direction, down to the main street of Sanya, a street that locals sometimes call the 'Street of Bones', one still leaves the familiar world of the city and enters a sad place where Tokyo seems to end.

I can think of several examples that show unequivocally that, for Japanese at least, the neighborhood is clearly beyond the limits of safe entry. On a number of occasions I have gone to Sanya with some of my students, all Japanese, to teach them about the place, and have noticed how nervous and apprehensive they get during the approach as they read the cues of an unknown landscape. I'll never forget one particular incident when one of the students, speaking for the small group as a whole, begged in a voice choked with fear that we did not cross the Namidabashi intersection, but that we look in on Sanya instead from across the street. In a similar vein, James Fallows, for several years the Tokyo correspondent for *The Atlantic* and one of the few people to write about this neighborhood, also described a Japanese friend who felt afraid to enter this realm (Fallows, 1988, p. 16). Finally, a friend of mine from Sanya, an American who was one of the subjects of an ABC News piece on the area in 1988, reported that the American journalists who interviewed him had to bring a camera crew from abroad, because the Japanese cameraman who usually worked with them (and who had previously covered combat in Southeast Asia) was afraid to enter.

There are about 45 000 people who live in Sanya, most of them in Fallows' words 'normal working-class Japanese', but about 7000 of whom are 'flophouse occupants' and homeless people living in the streets (Fallows, 1988, p. 16). This is Skid Row, a neighborhood of vagrants and alcoholics, of day laborers and nighttime drinkers. Most of the occupants are men, the majority of whom are middle-aged or older, and many of whom are in Sanya for a long time, perhaps the rest of their lives. Others are drifters. They come from elsewhere in Tokyo or to Tokyo from the hinterlands for a variety of reasons, most of them familiar stories in Skid Row areas in general: family problems, broken romances, lost jobs, failed businesses, trouble with the law, mental illness. Those who work do so on a temporary basis, usually lining up positions through one of the local employment agencies that takes a commission for providing the services of unskilled labor, or by standing early in the

182

Figure 5.19 *Homeless men trying to keep warm on the streets of Sanya*

morning on the main street and waiting to be selected for work at some construction site by employers who drive by in vans whenever they are short of labor.
Those who wait at the curbside to be selected for work are called *tachinbō*,
'standing pole' (Caldarola, 1968–9, p. 513). All the hiring is said to be controlled by
yakuza, Japan's gangsters. The work is sometimes dangerous, and workers' benefits
are nil. It is also seasonal. In recent years there has been increased competition for
the better jobs from younger men from Third World countries such as Bangladesh
and Pakistan, both legally in Japan and illegally, who also work for low wages and
minimal benefits.

Housing in Sanya reflects its poverty. For those who have some money, which is
generally the youngest and healthiest inhabitants of Sanya, there are dozens of
cheap hotels and rooming houses. The top end of the scale is a tiny, private room
with color televisions and shared toilets and baths that rent for about 4000 yen per
day. Prices for these units have been going up lately, because wages have risen due
to a labor shortage. At the bottom end of the scale, or about 2000 yen, one can go to
one of the several shelters that rents mats on the floor of large rooms shared by
twenty or more men. These are generally old buildings, crowded and dangerous.
Many other men of Sanya, especially the worst-case alcoholics, stay outdoors. They
are on the sidewalks, in doorways, on the side streets, and in a small local park. The
'Street of Bones' is lined with such men, often arranged in small clusters around a
fire. Others are found alone on the pavement (Figure 5.19). There is little help from
government and not nearly enough charity from the public at large; every winter
some people die from exposure after passing out drunk. Much of this is explained in
an excellent new book about the neighborhood, *San'ya Blues*, by Edward Fowler
(1996).

That there is also a Sanya in nearly every other great city in the world is beside
the point. I include this description not just to represent Tokyo more fully in its

various aspects but also to stress that even here, at the very bottom of the urban scale, the city is being shaped by powerful traditions and unchanging beliefs. The piece of real estate that is Sanya became tainted a long time ago when Tokugawa Ieyasu selected a site nearby for executions. It has never recovered. It was a place no one wanted, and inevitably became the place where, one after the other, successive waves of outcast groups would settle. Not just the *hinin* and *burakumin* from feudal times but in Meiji times there were the descendants of these groups, superannuated prostitutes from Yoshiwara, criminals and many of the city's poor, no matter what their background. The arrival of the last of these categories was increased after 1895, when a tough law was put into effect to chase cheap lodging houses from most parts of the city and confine them in designated districts such as Sanya. In this century, the population swelled at different times with Korean laborers and with soldiers returning to Japan after the Second World War. Many of the latter had lost their homes and families, or they felt shame about Japan's defeat and went into self-exile. It is said that much of the construction force that prepared Tokyo for the 1964 Olympics came from these ranks. A large part of Sanya's reputation for heavy drinking stems from the after-hours activities of returned veterans.

It is interesting that a vastly disproportionate amount of the charity that goes to this district comes from the small proportion of foreign residents in Tokyo. This is the case for operation of the largest 'soup kitchen' in Sanya, a free medical clinic, and for a large fraction of the donations of clothing, blankets and food. Some of the Western churches in the city and the well-heeled membership of the Tokyo American Club have been particularly generous. A number of the few social services volunteers who work in the neighborhood are foreigners too, particularly Christian missionaries (Betros, 1985b). There are, however, a small number of remarkable Japanese individuals who are exceptions, and who also work in Sanya and share with its poor their considerable talents in medicine and counseling, often as volunteers without pay. The article by Fallows includes an interview with one such individual. Most other Japanese have chosen to ignore this problem, as indeed do most other societies in their own backyards. However, in Japan, Sanya has the added stigma of being 'poisoned ground' and a concentration of social castes that, despite the advent of modern times, are still discriminated against and generally avoided. Sanya is now, as it always has been, 'a safe distance away'.

OTHER FACES OF HOMELESSNESS

Not all of Tokyo's homeless live in Sanya, and not all of them are day laborers or people addicted to alcohol. Homelessness is now a much larger problem in the city, affecting thousands of other people, including both men and women, many other neighborhoods, and having many causes. What is more, it seems to be getting worse – at least since the start of the 1990s when the so-called 'bubble economy' that had earlier sustained the country burst. Like Sanya itself, homelessness is another of those uncomfortable topics that official statistics fail to acknowledge and few Japanese want to discuss – a 'hidden' problem that is plainly evident to even the most casual visitor because many of the homeless are, almost literally, underfoot in several of the city's busiest districts.

It is not known exactly how many homeless people there are in Tokyo. The official estimate by Tokyo government is approximately 3000, but that total seems low given the number of homeless people one routinely sees in going around the city during the course of a week. A more realistic estimate, offered by a Tokyo Salvation Army official who works with the homeless, is between 5000 and 10 000 (Guzewicz, 1996a, p. 43). However, even those numbers might be low, given the rapid growth of the problem in Tokyo and the fact that many of the homeless who are not 'underfoot' in well-traveled districts where they can be counted, hide themselves in out-of-the-way places. The lack of an accurate count also has to do with the fact that the number of homeless people changes from year to year, apparently in response to turns in the economy. It also changes with the seasons, being related to seasonal needs in Tokyo and other cities for construction workers and seasonal cycles in agricultural labor. It is also a fact that Tokyo government has not conducted a full census of homelessness, relying instead for information on 'surveys'. Perhaps the Japanese adage '*kusai mono ni wa futa wo shiro*', 'unpleasant things are best kept hidden', accounts for the lack of accurate data.

Whatever the total number of homeless, it seems clear that the large majority of them are males, the largest group being in their 40s and 50s. However, women are becoming more common, both alone and with male spouses. Newspaper and magazine accounts based on interviews with homeless people make it clear that the poor state of Japan's economy is a major factor behind the 1990s increase in homelessness, sending people to the streets after they can no longer afford to pay rent (Alford, 1996; Nakazawa, 1993). Unemployment, once almost unheard of in this country famous for its lifetime employment practices, has been on the rise, as financially strapped companies of all types have had to trim workforces. Additionally, many companies have closed altogether because of business failure. Older workers who have been laid off find it especially hard to obtain new jobs. This is partly because many employers prefer to hire younger applicants and partly because many of them assume that a jobless person has probably done something wrong to deserve unemployment. Quite a few of the homeless in Tokyo are migrants to the city, having come to it in search of employment from rural areas and small towns where economic conditions are especially poor. However, instead of quickly finding work, as migrants to the nation's capital have done with success over the years, they encounter a weak economy in Tokyo, high rents, age and gender discrimination, and even some regional prejudices. They live off whatever savings they brought with them, occasional small earnings, and make do on the streets when the money is depleted.

The geography of the homeless is interesting. The largest concentration, estimated by the Salvation Army to number 1000 individuals (Nakazawa, 1993, p. 36), is at Ueno, the major commercial center of the Sumida River wards we have just discussed as being 'the other side of Tokyo'. Many of the homeless there are in Ueno Station, a principal entry to Tokyo from rural provinces to the north and east. Many others are in Ueno Park nearby. Other large homeless concentrations are in Asakusa, the historic temple area and commercial center near Ueno; Tokyo Station, perhaps the largest entry point for migrants to the city; and in Shinjuku,

Ginza-Yurakuchō, Ikebukuro, Shibuya, and many other busy commercial centers around the Yamanote loop (see Chapter 2). They find shelter in train stations and their networks of underground corridors, the grounds of temples and shrines, small parks and playgrounds, and on promenades along rivers and other waterways. They are also encamped under bridges and beneath the stairways of pedestrian overpasses. In most cases, the homeless stay in cardboard boxes or customized cardboard cubicles. However, in some areas of the city, such as forested sections of Ueno Park and the riverfront promenades at Asakusa, many of the homeless live in makeshift tents of plastic sheets folded over ropes.

The situation in Shinjuku deserves special mention. After Ueno, this is the largest concentration of homeless people in Tokyo, having a total estimated to be in the range of several hundred individuals, perhaps 500 (Nakazawa, 1993, p. 36; Wilkinson, 1996, p. 1). It is also the city's most visible concentration of homeless, as most of its denizens are clustered in Shinjuku Station and the labyrinthine underground corridors that lead to it, in plain view of the hundreds of thousands of commuters who pass by each day. The underground provides protection from bad weather, access to public lavatories, and resources ranging from leftover food discarded by nearby restaurants to a plentiful supply of current newspapers and magazines left behind each day by train and subway riders. About 200 of the homeless reside on Shinjuku Station's west side, amid heavy pedestrian traffic, in a tidy settlement made of cardboard boxes. Some of the dwellings have two or more rooms made by connecting cardboard sheets, and are equipped with futons, a few basic kitchen items, and ropes for drying laundry. In some cases calendars hang from cardboard walls, giving an added sense of permanence and domesticity. A few of the residents earn small incomes reselling magazines that have been salvaged from trains and recycling bins, or by collecting used telephone cards to sell to flea marketeers. Others are sometimes paid by ticket scalpers to stand in lines to purchase tickets for concerts or popular sporting events, or find other odd jobs (Nakazawa, 1993, p. 38). As with the homeless elsewhere in Tokyo, almost no one begs, even though there are plenty of passersby who could be approached. In fact, there is little contact of any kind, including eye contact, between Shinjuku's shantytown dwellers and the throngs of shoppers, commuters and evening revelers who pass each day (Figure 5.20).

In January 1995 Shinjuku was the scene of a dramatic confrontation between homeless people and police. Approximately 200 homeless people who had been living in cardboard boxes aligned along an underground passageway leading from the train station were forcibly removed and had their boxes confiscated by as many as 820 police, security guards and metropolitan government officials. The 6 a.m. raid, timed to be concluded before the crush of commuters arrived, followed earlier warnings that the homeless should vacate the area because of plans to construct a moving walkway connecting Shinjuku Station with the new City Hall. The raid took place two days before the scheduled start of the project. Many of the evictees and their supporters responded by throwing bottles, eggs and flour, setting off fire extinguishers, and locking arms in resistance. At least one homeless person chained himself to a pillar in protest against the police action. Four people were arrested in the melee and two, including a guard, required hospitalization (*The Japan Times*, 25 January 1996, pp. 1–2).

186

Figure 5.20 *A protest by homeless people in Shinjuku Station. The sign says that the Tokyo government should negotiate about jobs*

The incident was front-page news across the nation and was reported widely abroad. Not only was there the element of irony that people were being moved for a people mover, but the incident made public some topics about which Japan had been quiet: that homelessness is a growing problem; that it is not simply the result of alcohol addiction or mental illness, but increasingly is tied to unemployment and other economic problems; and that the country has little idea what to do about it. The situation is so bad that in Shinjuku Ward, where the evictions took place, the office responsible for looking after the homeless is the Department of Environment and Pollution – the same department that deals with street cleaning, trash pickup, vermin, insects and loud noises (Nakazawa, 1993, p. 36). Sometimes shelters are provided by local governments, but there are few of them and they are always temporary and isolated. The shelter that was offered to those evicted from their shantytown in Shinjuku was several kilometers away in another ward, in a building that was to be dismantled two months later (Guzewicz, 1996a, p. 51). One critic described the facility as a concentration camp surrounded by canals and barbed wire, with doors that are shuttered between 5 p.m. and 9 a.m. (Wilkinson, 1996, p. 1).

Providing financial assistance to the homeless is also problematic. In part this is because of requirements that recipients need to have an address and be registered as residents of the local government jurisdiction to receive welfare. Cardboard boxes, bridges and corridors do not qualify as addresses. Furthermore, when a homeless person applies for aid, his (or her) family members are often contacted to see if they can provide the financial assistance themselves, even if those relatives live in another part of Japan. People who prefer not to let their problems be known back home know how to avoid speaking to authorities. As a result, the only source of help for most homeless people in Tokyo comes from charities such as the Salvation Army and churches and schools for foreigners. A number of these organizations operate food-distribution programs, clothing and blanket drives, and other programs. What a mess!

Along the Chūō Line: A Look at Suburbia

It is not possible in this brief review of 'epitome districts' to represent every type of neighborhood in Tokyo. The city is simply too big and too varied. However, as I look over what I have written, I see that there is at least one critically important aspect of Tokyo not yet adequately represented: that of the suburban areas such as the Tama region of *Tōkyō-to* and in neighboring prefectures. This in itself is a complicated topic because the area is so big, with a great variety of places to be found there. We saw in Chapter 4 that the suburban ring includes planned new towns, factory cities, *danchi* estates, college towns and at least one famous neatly laid-out garden city, as well as places that mix these and other characteristics. So what I plan to do here is to focus on what seems to be most typical. To do so, we can return to the Chūō Line, the super-crowded commuter train line, and look at some details about communities along its course through the western suburbs. It is appropriate to organize this discussion around the theme of commuting, because it is so much a part of being a Tokyoite. As Douglass expressed it so well: 'The new Tokyo family, in fact, does not really live in a place at all: it lives at a given distance from a daytime function' (Douglass, 1993, p. 106).

A good place to begin is the vicinity of Musashisakai, a moderate-sized train station in Musashino City, 23 minutes (eight stations) west of the giant commuter interchange at Shinjuku. This is an area in the Tama district of *Tōkyō-to*, a few minutes west of Tokyo's westernmost wards. It is a highly mixed suburban district that itself reflects the complexity of Tokyo; it includes a diverse population and a wide range of housing types, commercial centers, workplaces and recreation facilities. There are similar places along the Chūō and other lines, so it seems representative. My practical reason for choosing this place in particular is that it is where I moved after leaving the neighborhood near Shinjuku. What I observed during one year of living at Musashisakai is that (1) there is a different, but complementary, set of daily routines from those in closer-in neighborhoods and business districts; and (2) that except for an awful morning train commute and some minor annoyances, suburban Tokyo can be extremely pleasant and comfortable. I make the latter point especially because it differs from the impression one gets with a first look at the suburbs, when one notices mostly the displeasing aspects of endless urban sprawl and look-alike developments.

The focus of activity in the Musashisakai area is, like the focus of so much else in urban Japan, the train station and its adjacent blocks. In the mornings on workdays we can see the large extent to which the neighborhood is a bedroom appendage to inner Tokyo, as thousands of commuters zero in on one or the other of the station's two entrances to board the Chūō Line's *nobori densha*, or in-bound train. The march to the station starts before 6 a.m. and builds to a peak about two hours later when the downtown-bound platform becomes dangerously overcrowded and every car on every one of the trains that come by three minutes apart is hopelessly jammed. It is not until well after 9 a.m. that the rush period slows and crowds thin out enough to make room on trains and in-bound loading platforms. The commuters converge on the station on foot, by bicycle, by motorcycle and by bus, as well as by another train, a short line that is part of the Seibu Railway empire's reach into the suburbs (see Chapter 4), that uses one of the tracks at

Musashisakai as a terminus. On average, more than 57 000 people board Chūō Line trains at Musashisakai each day (calculated from *Tokyo Statistical Yearbook, 1994*, p. 216).[11] As we can imagine from such a total and the various ways that commuters travel to the station, the catchment area of Musashisakai Station is quite large. I do not have an exact measure, but from the routes of feeder buses it is clear that it includes, at a minimum, all the western part of Musashino City as well as big sections of neighboring towns such as Mitaka, Fuchū and Koganei, and that the population is in the range of 300 000 or so.[12]

The commute from Musashisakai to the city is worth describing: it is what legends are made of. A train pulls up to the platform, already so full that faces are pressed against the inside glass of the sliding doors, and the ends of coats and book bags that didn't quite make it in protrude through the door openings. Several hundred or more of your neighbors are waiting to board. They crowd the platform, itself very long to correspond to the length of a nine- or ten-car train, and have arranged themselves in separate groups of twenty or more every few feet where a door will open. The train stops, the doors slide apart, and virtually no one gets off! Almost everyone is going to the same place as you are, to the center of Tokyo. In the few seconds during which the train stops, you and a score or more other new riders at your door press inside, backs first so as to not confront anyone directly, and force the doorway standers further in. To do this, you gain leverage for arms from the walls inside the train just above the door and for legs from the edge of the platform. White-gloved platform attendants push in the last passengers just as the doors come together. Two or three minutes later the scene is repeated at the next station, and it is you who are pressed by a score or more additional riders with leverage from the doorway and the force of a new set of platform attendants. At the same time, another crowd of riders has already gathered at your home station, and is hearing the loudspeaker announcement of the arrival of the next *nobori densha*, barely three minutes after your train departed. By the time one of these trains reaches the interchange at Shinjuku, it is filled to nearly three times capacity, and has a total of 4000–5000 passengers.

The experience on the train itself is almost intolerable: it is hot, you can hardly move a muscle, even if you are being jabbed by an umbrella or a briefcase, and the pressure on your body is sometimes so great that it is hard to breathe. It is even worse if the person pressed next you happens to smell. You close your eyes, concentrate on private thoughts or on the Walkman, and suffer. Once I saw a man who had been lifted out of one shoe by the press of the crowd, and who had the most awful time trying to retrieve it during the frantic moment that the door was open at the next station. On another occasion, when the train lurched unexpectedly as it switched tracks, I saw a woman bump face first against the man in front of her, a total stranger, and leave a lipstick mark on his white shirt that reproduced remarkably faithfully the shape of her lips.

The morning exodus through the station substantially differs from the sex and age structure of the population of Musashisakai. As is typical of bedtown suburbs, the majority of people who leave Musashisakai for the city during the morning rush period, perhaps as many as two-thirds of the total, are men aged between their 20s and 60s on their way to work. Most of them wear conservative suits, ties and white shirts, and fit the stereotype of the Japanese salaryman (*sarariman*). They are white-collar employees who put in long hours of dedicated work in exchange for the security of lifetime employment with a trusted company, and spend comparatively little time at home. Other commuters are women, especially young women without children who work as 'office ladies' ('OL') and in the retailing sector until they start families of their own, and students of all ages and both sexes. Mothers stay behind, as do younger children and elderly people. The neighborhood belongs to them (and to shopkeepers) all day, and it is these categories of people almost exclusively whom one sees around the neighborhood until the evening rush home. Because the Musashisakai area is a mature neighborhood, having been built up as a suburb some decades ago (much of it even before the Second World War), it has a substantial fraction of older people. Many of them are 'empty-nesters' who have already raised their children and now live alone as older couples or widows or widowers. They are especially visible during the day in the neighborhood's shops and supermarkets, and in street-side conversations between neighbors in the residential precincts.

The area that is closest to the station is a commercial district. This is also the case for just about every other busy rail station in the metropolitan area. At Musashisakai, the commercial center is on the scale of a small downtown. It is marked by a cluster of taller buildings – six and seven stories – and a variety of retail stores, restaurants and drinking places, banks and other offices, entertainment facilities and other commercial land uses. It is divided neatly into two halves, one on either side of the rail tracks, reflecting at one train station the two principal styles of shopping center design at suburban commuter centers. The north side has the older fashion, similar to the commercial landscape described in Chapter 1: an extended shopping street that is lined on both sides with a great variety of stores, most of them family-run operations that have been in the area for a long time, as well as some shopping on the side streets that intersect with the main shopping street. The other side of the tracks is a newer-style shopping center (Figure 5.21). It is actually one big building, five stories plus a basement and a rooftop level, that is a huge department store, a large supermarket (the basement), an assortment of restaurants and some other businesses (mostly the top floor), and a sports club with tennis courts (the roof). The building is one of a chain of similar developments that some giant retailing corporations (in this case, Itō Yokado) have opened at preferred sites in the residential rings around Tokyo and other large cities.

In a pattern that is a microcosm of the city as a whole, the blocks nearest the commercial core are themselves becoming commercial and high density. In just the one year that I kept track, five or six new mid-rise office buildings opened within a two-minute walking radius of the station. Tenants include branch banks, real-estate companies, professional offices such as doctor's offices, and the ubiquitous private cram schools called *juku*.[13] So, too, there are several new mid-rise (seven stories on average) apartment and condominium (*manshon*) buildings in this area. This reflects the much higher values of land in the vicinity of busy train stations, and the premium that commercial users and residents alike pay for being located within a short walk of station exits. A negative consequence of this is that, just as in the city, there are long-time residents who find their preserves outside the city are no longer quiet, and that urbanization engulfs them. Thus, the sight of an older house that is completely surrounded by stores and tall buildings is quite common at places like Musashisakai. Likewise, there is a beautiful temple garden where I like to sit that is

Figure 5.21 *A station-front shopping center in the suburbs. The example is from Musashisakai Station in Musashino City on the Chūō Line*

walled in on three sides by tall buildings. It reminds me of my previous hideaway in the old neighborhood, where the giant City Hall towers have pierced the sightline and loom over the peaceful enclosure.

The rest of suburbia lies beyond this nucleus. It is mostly residential, but not homogeneously so, and also contains a variety of other land uses. In the area around Musashisakai, which is largely a middle-class district with lots of families, the typical street is a short, quiet residential lane with newer single-family houses hidden behind walls and barriers of greenery (Figure 5.22). It is similar to the quiet residential streets in the better neighborhoods of the central city, except that the houses tend to be somewhat more substantial in size and farther apart, and their gardens are bigger. Other aspects of the residential landscape are apartments, including some stands of *danchi* erected by companies to house their employees and their families, and condominiums. As in the city as a whole, the latter are ever more prevalent, and are continually being built in the vacant spaces between existing developments and on redevelopment sites. There are also some aging wooden farmhouses that stand amidst small orchards and remaining patches of farmland. In some sections, generally on larger land parcels further away from the station, there are sizable tract developments of similar single houses aligned close together in straight rows. These are some of the newest suburbs, and reflect in their higher densities and quick construction the high cost of land in the Tokyo area and the great demand for housing.

There is also considerable non-residential land. The most important examples include large tracts given to industry and to institutions such as college and university campuses. This has been the case since the early part of the century, as the initial growth of the Musashisakai area (together with several other Tama district suburbs) is attributed more to the presence of large factories and other

Figure 5.22 *A typical single home in suburban Tokyo, showing the required off-street parking space, privacy wall, and greenery in the private garden*

sizable employment centers than to service as a bedroom community for the central city. Their inducement was ample land and good freight-rail connections to Tokyo and the port of Yokohama, as well as the added advantage for some firms of plentiful water supplies (Allinson, 1979, p. 55). The most famous company in the area in the past was the Nakajima Aircraft Corporation. It opened two large plants in Musashino on the north side of the Chūō Line tracks in 1937 and 1938, and then became one of the largest manufacturers of military planes and engines during the Second World War. The entire complex was destroyed by US planes in 1945 and the site is now housing, a park, some commercial blocks, and other community facilities.

One of the biggest firms close to Musashisakai today is the Subaru automotive company, which operates a large engineering and testing facility in Mitaka a few minutes south of the station. Other companies in the general area, although not necessarily closest to Musashisakai Station, are manufacturing plants of Yokogawa Electric, the Citizen Watch Company, Nissan Motors, and Fuji Heavy Industries. The campus of the International Christian University is also close to Musashisakai, as is Asia University, Musashino Women's University, and Seikei University. The presence of these factories and most of the education institutions reflects long-standing policies by Tokyo government to encourage decentralization of large employers. The result is a stronger local tax base for Musashino and other cities in the Tama district and less reliance on long-distance commuting to work in central Tokyo. Many residents of the Musashisakai area and places like it work locally, travelling there by bus, by bicycle, or by car. There is also noticeable reverse commuting, as workers and students take outbound trains (or private automobiles) from central Tokyo to their companies or schools in the Tama area.

The commercial center at Musashisakai Station is a local center only. There are also larger, regional shopping centers that are distributed further apart. One is the

Figure 5.23 *Families and couples enjoying an outing in one of Tokyo's many attractive suburban parks. This example is from Shōwa Memorial Park in Tachikawa City*

center of Tachikawa City, a larger industrial and bedroom suburb six stations further out on the Chūō Line, while another is Kichijōji, in Musashino, two stations closer to central Tokyo than Musashisakai. Both have several competing department stores within a short walk of their respective stations, as well as dozens of other stores, restaurants, coffee shops and movie theaters. In Kichijōji, much of this is arranged along streets that have been closed to vehicular traffic and made into pleasant pedestrian arcades (Spivak, 1987). There is always a lot of activity during the times that stores are open, but the busiest time is weekends. This is when families have time together, and take care of shopping needs or use the opportunity to stroll and browse. The fact that there are large public parks within walking distance of both stations adds to the appeal of these centers for such outings (Figure 5.23). There are also great throngs of teenagers who frequent these shopping centers, particularly on weekends and during after-school hours. Kichijōji is especially popular, and is fast developing a reputation as not just a suburban shopping center but also an outlying version of Shibuya. It has many of the same stores and fashions, and is a favorite date-night hangout.

The automobile has a strong and visible role in the suburbs of Tokyo, although not to the extent that characterizes suburban areas in the United States and some other countries. Rates of car ownership now exceed 60 percent of all households in the suburbs and are rising, and most houses and apartments have off-street parking. The increasing car culture is seen, among other ways, in the weekend traffic jams and long lines to enter parking lots at Tachikawa, Kichijōji, and other shopping centers, in the big parking lots that surround suburban factories and some college campuses, and in car-oriented commercial ribbon developments along the busy streets and highways criss-crossing suburbia. The landscape is one of big, new supermarkets, brightly lit discount appliance stores, spacious family restaurants (more Denny's), all-night convenience stores and video rental shops with plenty of parking. The *pachinko* parlors, so bedizened with flashing neon and tasteless statuary that they resemble the Las Vegas strip, are most noticeable. There are also plenty of bright and clean multi-pump gas stations, rows of automobile dealerships and used-car lots, and learn-to-drive schools with their own enclosed practice courses. Even the love hotels are designed with the car in mind, and offer secluded interior parking to enhance privacy. Young people seem to be especially car-conscious. In a reflection of the affluence Japan now enjoys, many older teenagers, college students, and others of that generation drive fancy sports cars or 4×4 vehicles, and show them off in cruising, California style, around the shopping malls and past favorite drive-in hangouts. The car's presence is also seen in the large numbers of small animals being killed along roads, particularly in areas of new residential and commercial development. I have a dot map of where road-kill raccoons have been recorded in Machida, a fast-developing municipality at the western edge of *Tōkyō-to*, but decided not to reprint it.

As people move from the city to the urban fringe, they seek not just to escape Tokyo's high prices and crowding but also to enjoy rural surroundings. They often strive for connections with a nostalgic agrarian past, and like to think of themselves as 'new pioneers' beyond the city, even as their surroundings urbanize and become choked with buildings, people and cars. This is the subject of a fascinating ethnography by anthropologist Jennifer Robertson of Kodaira, a suburban municipality north of the Chūō Line a little further from the city than Musashisakai (Robertson, 1991). The book focuses on *furusato-zukuri*, literally 'the making of hometowns or old villages', a politically driven process taking place in many Japanese urban communities that seeks to reshape the town's self-image by promoting an idealized version of its past. In Kodaira, as in Musashino (Musashisakai's municipality) and elsewhere, there are many local festivals, parades and other events that are staged to build community identity and strengthen ties between new residents and their neighborhoods. Likewise, newly created green spaces and historical markers are designed to connect suburban residents with the past and feel pride about where they live.

The point of all this is to emphasize that just outside the limits of central Tokyo there exists a physical environment and style of life that is quite different from what was described for the 23 wards. It is hard to generalize, because the suburban ring is so big and varied, but on the whole we see a pleasant and comfortable existence in an environment of lower density, less crowded housing, and more use of private automobiles. Where I lived is convenient to the center of the city, to a choice of local and regional shopping centers, and to many other facilities. It is also incredibly quiet, clean, safe, and well serviced. Instead of the light from a restaurant that intruded into my old house and ear-splitting all-night motorcycle races on Yamate-dōri, the night at Musashisakai was dark and quiet, the only outside sounds coming from crickets and the rustling of bamboo. There were also some welcome reminders from time to time that one was not alone. On cold winter nights, usually shortly after 10 p.m., the itinerant baked sweet potato salesman made his rounds down our small street, calling out again and again in a deep singsong: *Ishiyakiimo, oishii desyoo* ('baked potatoes, they're delicious'). It is one of the traditional foods to help you stay warm and sleep better, and is distributed in a time-honored way that was one of the sounds of the night of feudal Edo. However, instead of walking behind a pushcart, today's *ishiyakiimosan* drives a Toyota pick-up with a charcoal stove on the back, and his voice is on cassette tape and comes through a speaker system.

CHAPTER 6
TOKYO DIRECTIONS

Tokyo keeps building. As the century during which the city was rebuilt three times, twice out of necessity and the third for a combination of both profit and urban improvement, winds down, Tokyo makes plans for even more construction, setting directions for itself in the twenty-first century. The goals are to enhance the quality of urban living and, at the same time, to better position the city for competition with fast-building rivals in the Pacific Rim and elsewhere: Hong Kong, Shanghai, Singapore, Jakarta, Los Angeles, New York, London, and others, including Osaka in its own backyard. The construction will expand Tokyo in all possible directions: (1) up to new heights of skyscrapers; (2) out to more distant edges of the Kantō Plain and ever further into Tokyo Bay; and (3) down below ground where more of the urban infrastructure is being located.

In this chapter we turn our attention to how Tokyo will look in the near future. We begin with a review of city planning in Tokyo, including its history and present objectives, and then focus on a series of key places that represent urban development trends in the metropolis. Thus, we continue with an 'epitome districts' approach to Tokyo, focusing on the newest developments and future plans.

CITY PLANNING IN TOKYO

Perhaps more so than in most cities of the world, city planning has come to be a topic of lively interest among the citizenry of Tokyo. This is especially true about large redevelopment and new other construction projects that relate to the planning of land use. We see this interest in the bookshops where paperbacks about grand schemes for the waterfront or urban design for the twenty-first century compete on front shelves with popular novels and top magazines; in daily newspapers which devote prominent space to details of government policy for controlling the price of land, the building of new residential estates, commercial centers, industrial districts, or the planning of new highways to ease a chronic traffic problem; and in the popularity of occasional television specials on public as well as commercial networks that discuss urban problems and necessary action. Much of the population seems informed, at least in a general way, about how Tokyo is expected to change in the future, and up to date about the principal characteristics of many current redevelopment proposals and other large constructions.

However, all this is not to say that Tokyo has been a model of how city planning should work. In fact, perhaps the opposite is true. As Tange Kenzō has observed in a call for radical redesign of the city: 'Tokyo has formed as a result of totally planless spontaneous growth on the basis of self-assertion of the inhabitants. [There has been an] irritating ... lack of leadership on the part of governments in enforcing a rational plan for Tokyo' (Tange, 1987, p. 8). In this city, as indeed in many places across the world, urban development has been propelled largely by the interests of private capital. Those who stand to profit most are generally closest to decisions about land use; while they often use their influence to promote what they see as the public good, they also exploit the planning process, such as it exists, to increase the value of their own businesses. For the most part, there is fairly little significant citizen input, despite such established mechanisms for participation as needs assessments, attitude surveys about city services, and public hearings. Instead, the public in Tokyo is mostly a passive albeit interested body, and accepts the new urban development projects that are announced in newspapers and on television as necessary or inevitable, and most probably in its own best interests.

HISTORY OF CITY PLANNING

Despite the fact that city planning has been generally poorly developed in Tokyo, it has a long and interesting history.[1] We can trace it at least as far back as 1590, when Tokugawa Ieyasu arrived in Edo, saw a town in great disrepair, and initiated a series of remarkable public works projects that changed the place forever. This included the reclamation of marshland at Nihombashi and other low-lying shore areas to enlarge the city; the construction of a canal to bring fresh water about 20 kilometers from Lake Inokashira; and major reconstruction of the previous castle, moats, and surrounding fortifications. Social space was manipulated to emphasize the hierarchy of classes and to protect the shogun and his closest retainers. Thus, we recall that the overall form of Edo as determined by Ieyasu's plan was an irregular clockwise spiral, reminiscent of the *hiragana* symbol for the syllable *no*, that unwound outward from the castle to the edge of the city through districts of ever-lower social classes.

Other notable examples of early planning are seen in various efforts during Edo to check the spread of the periodic fires that swept the city. For example, after the huge Meireki inferno of 1657 there was a coordinated effort to plaster the straw and shingle roofs of the city with mud. After 1720, following still other conflagrations, the preferred roofing material was changed by another civic improvement project to tiles. So, too, efforts were made during Edo times to enhance the effectiveness of streets and watercourses as firebreaks and to reduce the density of the built-up area by opening new districts for urban expansion. The results, however, were only partly successful at best. Even the rebuilt districts were mostly congested tinder-box, and the so-called 'flowers of Edo' continued to storm across the city every few years to destroy buildings and lives.

The beginning of modern city planning in Tokyo, like so many other things in Japan to which the adjective 'modern' is applied, is traced to the Meiji period (1862–1912). The great Ginza fire of 1872, only four years after the start of the new era, was occasion for yet another rebuilding of a key part of the city. This time, however, the modernization of Tokyo in the Western image was a prime objective. Thus, the entire Ginza district was refashioned in red brick, not just to better protect against fire but also to plan Tokyo as a showpiece for foreigners by giving it a more European flavor (Smith, 1978, p. 54). Other examples of planning for a Western-style city during Meiji included the construction of government buildings at Kasumigaseki, and the famed Mitsubishi Londontown development of the 1890s. The latter was a brick-faced commercial center designed by Josiah Conder for the Mitsubishi trust and patterned after architecture in the British capital.

Another product of Meiji modernization was the first legislation in Tokyo to facilitate city planning. This was the 'Tokyo Urban Improvement Ordinance' of 1888, a 16-point initiative that created a city planning board with responsibilities for policy formulation and execution, and that set in motion various improvements to infrastructure, especially in the downtown area. The greatest attention was given to road building projects. This is seen in the priorities of Tokyo governor Yoshikawa Akimasa as expressed in his written appeal in 1884 to Central Government calling for planning in the city:

> The primary need is for roads, bridges and canals. Water, housing and sewers come afterwards. Thus, if plans are determined for roads, bridges and canals, which are the fundamental needs, it will facilitate the attainment of the other objectives (Tokyo Metropolitan Government, 1972b, p. 8).

Accordingly, in the first three years after funds were made available, some 80–90 percent of the total outlay went for the paving and straightening of the 'confused maze-like spaces' that comprised the center of the city (Ishizuka and Ishida, 1988, p. 13). However, because of outbreaks of cholera, increased attention was given in subsequent years (the mid-1890s) to supplying water and removing sewerage. The principal objective of focusing so much on infrastructure was to solidify Tokyo's hold on its role as national capital, as well as to surpass Osaka as a center of commerce (Tokyo Metropolitan Government, 1972b, p. 8).

The next city planning law in Tokyo, called the 'Town Planning Act', was adopted in 1919 during the rule of the Taishō emperor. It followed a time of unusually rapid urbanization and expansion of industry, and was one of the first uses in Japanese of the term 'city planning' (*toshi keikaku*). Again, the emphasis was on infrastructure to establish a modern, competitive economic base. This included construction of roads, railways, port facilities, and similar projects, as well as provisions to identify districts within the city for special planning, to delineate fire-prevention zones, and for modifications to the city's river system. It also provided for land adjustment such as the straightening of roads and property lines in suburban areas that were soon expected to change from farms to houses. Companion legislation in the same year, the Municipal Area Building Law, established the first zoning provisions in Tokyo. In large part this was to separate industry that was a fire hazard or a source of pollution from other sections of the city.

The first true test for these advances came with the Great Kantō Earthquake of 1923. In reducing some 60 percent of Tokyo to ashes, this disaster provided planners with an enormous opportunity to restructure the city according to the most modern standards. Gōtō Shimpei, a national figure who had proposed grand plans for the city while he was mayor just before the emergency, was put in charge of reconstruction and once again drew up impressive plans: laying out new street lines and wider streets; reorganization of the rail network; improvements to water and sewer systems; and creation of open spaces. However, because the cost was to have been considerable, and because of angry opposition by powerful landowners who felt threatened by the new design, only a few elements of the total scheme were actually completed.

Something of the same can be said about what happened to entirely new sets of rebuilding plans that were put forward after destruction of the city by American bombing in 1945. For example, Ishikawa Eiyo, Tokyo government's chief planner, prepared a 'War Damage Rehabilitation Plan' that included a symmetrical radial and ring-road network for Tokyo, strategically spaced green belts and separation of land uses through zoning. Once again the costs proved to be prohibitive, especially in the light of the nation's ruined economy after the hostilities. Moreover, there was such a rush of population to Tokyo after the war – citizens who had previously evacuated the city, military personnel from fighting zones, and Japanese from lost colonies abroad – and the press for housing and other space so great that schemes on paper for urban reorganization were simply impractical. Thus, more effective planning for the city would be deferred until later when new problems in a worsening urban environment would make ameliorative measures absolutely unavoidable, and rising incomes would make planning goals more attainable.

Improvements in planning began in the mid-1950s in response to extraordinarily rapid population growth and economic expansion. One of the first steps was the creation of the national cabinet-level Capital Region Development Commission in 1956. This facilitated cooperation between numerous political jurisdictions, including Tokyo Metropolitan Government, the governments of neighboring prefectures, and government in such localities as urban wards and smaller towns and villages. The Commission provided a framework, albeit one that was weak and inexperienced, for dealing with the many competing development initiatives that were being put forward by private sector interests such as land-development companies and private railway corporations. One of its first achievements was publication in 1958 of the National Capital Region Development Plan. This was a comprehensive, general plan that addressed all major categories of land use and various types of social needs, that encompassed a huge territory with a radius of some 100 kilometers centered on the 23-ward nucleus. In many respects it was based on Sir Patrick Abercrombie's concept for London in 1944 (Hall, 1984, pp. 33–4 and 39–44). The main feature was a greenbelt zone about 16–27 kilometers from the center of Tokyo.[2] Development of all types would be greatly restricted within this belt, while housing and other building projects would be directed to a more distant zone located between 27 and 72 kilometers from central Tokyo. This outer zone would include a number of new satellite towns to house much of the region's population growth and to provide centers for economic expansion. The plan also called for the construction of an integrated network of expressways and arterial highways connecting newly urbanized areas of the Kantō Plain, as well as linking them to the center.

In addition, there was considerable attention in the 1958 plan on the need to direct growth within Tokyo itself. Thus, provisions were made for various redevelopment projects in the central city to reduce crowding and encourage more efficient use of land, as well as to alleviate the extremely vexing problem of over-development and excessive land costs at the city's principal business district. A specific step in these directions was to encourage growth in the station-front districts of Shinjuku, Ikebukuro, Shibuya, Ōtsuka, Gotanda, and Kinshichō, as strategically sited alternatives to the CBD. Furthermore, there was a law passed in

1959 that prohibited construction of factories and universities within the 23-ward area. Both uses were understood to be among the major attractions for migrants to Tokyo, and therefore were steered by this regulation to designated areas in the outlying zone. However, because other places in the Tokyo area besides the 23 wards were also suffering from too much growth, the establishment and enlargement of industries and universities was also restricted in the 1958 plan for Musashino, Mitaka, and parts of Yokohama, Kawasaki and Kawaguchi. These were previously existing central cities in the Tokyo orbit, and were referred to by protective planners as 'mother towns' (*haha toshi*) (Ishizuka and Ishida, 1988, p. 28).

The 1958 plan was revised substantially in the 1960s. Development pressure from an overcrowded Tokyo was simply too great to maintain a greenbelt so close to the city. Moreover, the plan itself had almost no powers to enforce any compliance with ideals. A good example of this was the Japan Housing Corporation, a public agency established in 1955 to ameliorate housing shortages in urban areas, which was using the greenbelt zone for many of its housing development sites. Consequently, in recognition of what real estate developers were doing anyway on their own, a revised document issued in 1965 erased the greenbelt altogether and marked its zone for suburban growth. A year later the outer boundaries of the Capital Region planning district were extended substantially beyond the 72-kilometer limit. This too was in recognition of on-going development patterns. The new boundaries encompassed some 36 500 square kilometers within an area with a radius of approximately 150 kilometers from Tokyo's center. The large, open spaces that had been the objective of the greenbelt were reduced to vestigial units often well beyond the built-up area and along floodplains of rivers. Another change from the 1958 plan was the abolition in 1963 of building-height restrictions in the 23 wards. This too reflected the intense pressure on space that existed in Tokyo, and launched the city into an era of skyscraper construction. The first of these was the Kasumigaseki Building, completed in 1968.

The 1964 Summer Olympics provided a special stimulus for detailed planning in Tokyo. The Japanese viewed the Games as their world debut after the war, and made certain to present their capital city in the best possible light. Consequently, there was considerable public support for ideas contained in another planning document, this one called 'Tokyo Plan 1960' and released in 1961, that simultaneously proposed to ready the city for the Olympics and solve numerous long-standing urban needs. Its main author was the city's budding superstar of urban design, Tange Kenzō. Thus, following an energetic redevelopment campaign, Tokyo received a much-expanded road system within the 23-ward area, new parks and recreation facilities, an augmented system for water supply, a major national rail line (the 'bullet train' Tokaidō Line), the famous monorail to Haneda Airport, major expansions in its subway system, several new Western-style hotels, and, of course, the Olympics facilities themselves. The most striking landmark, often presented as a symbol of modern Tokyo, was Tange's own magnificent National Gymnasium complex in Yoyogi Park.

As impressive as many of the results of Olympics construction were, most of Tokyo remained rather backward. The needs of residential neighborhoods had been given short shrift during every point in planning since the landmark laws of 1888 and 1919 that favored infrastructure projects and the downtown. So, too, the neighborhoods were lower priority during reconstruction following the 1923 earthquake and the wartime bombing. For the most part, basic needs of citizens such as improved housing, sanitary sewers, and spaces for recreation were deferred, while emphasis was given to the larger goal of putting the city's economy back into shape. In the words of the then prime minister Ikeda Hayato, as he explained about the persistence of residential crowding, poor public services and chronic air pollution: 'We must first make the pie bigger' (Tokyo Metropolitan Government, 1972b, p. 10). So little was being done at that time to build a better living environment that it should have been no surprise that citizens had to suffer a severe water shortage during the Olympics summer (Tokyo Metropolitan Government, 1972b, p. 10).

It was in this context that planning in Tokyo began to move in new directions after the mid-1960s. The immediate reason was that citizens had become fed up with the poor condition of the city and the slow pace of improvements to their neighborhoods, and voted out of office the conservative municipal government that had long held sway. The principal victim of their wrath was the governor of Tokyo, Azuma Ryutarō, the Olympics governor who had the good sense not to even try for re-election. He was in trouble anyway because of scandals involving voter fraud and financial misdealings, but then received an even greater setback in the summer of 1965 when a noisome plague of black flies descended on the blue-collar wards east of the Sumida River from late June and into July. They had come from the city's garbage dump in Kōtō Ward, a landfill site with the ironic name Yumenoshima, 'Dream Island', and came to symbolize his administration's failure to take care of basic needs for the public (Seidensticker, 1990, pp. 259–60).

Thus, the next gubernatorial election of 1967 was carried by Minobe Ryōkichi, a university professor and longtime critic of the government, and leader of a successful Socialist–Communist coalition. He was a skilled lecturer and experienced TV personality, and was blessed with an infectious smile, the 'Minobe *sumairu*' as it was called, that couldn't help but get him votes. In his campaign, he captivated the public with nostalgic stories about what the city was like during his boyhood, and promises about an alternative image for Tokyo. He talked about clean rivers and blue skies, about charming urban districts not yet covered over with concrete, and, as an alternative to garbage flies, butterflies, dragonflies and fireflies (Lockheimer, 1967, p. 13). He promised to work toward a more healthful Tokyo, and became an extremely popular two-term governor (until 1979) who reoriented much about planning in the city and priorities in government spending. Unfortunately, he is also remembered as the person who so favored expensive urban programs that he almost brought the city to bankruptcy.

The goals of Minobe-era planning are spelled out in the aptly titled *Tokyo for the People*, a booklet produced in English to inform a wider public about the city's new order. It promised to 'guarantee all citizens . . . the minimum standards necessary to live a decent life' (Tokyo Metropolitan Government, 1972b, p. 7), setting out an ambitious program to improve housing, promote social programs and to clean the environment. The plan sought to construct some 200 000 high-rise apartment units within the city, to develop attractive, new multi-function residential community centers at other sites, and to eliminate the tens of thousands of unsound, fire-prone wooden houses still standing in Tokyo. In doing so, the plan promised to increase floor space in the new units, extend sewer systems to all districts, and to provide for such community needs as schools and kindergartens, libraries, sports facilities, parks and playgrounds. Other parts of the housing plan addressed location problems, stressing the need to reduce the time Tokyoites spent commuting on crowded trains. There were also programs to separate residential environments from industrial pollution and other noxious sites. Still other parts of the plan considered improvements to roads and other transportation, open space, waste disposal and the return to Japan of US military bases within Tokyo. For all these aspects, there were noteworthy provisions that instituted mechanisms for citizen participation. This was a new component to planning in Tokyo, directly reflecting the social activism that brought Minobe to power and characterized the times.

'MY TOWN TOKYO' AND BEYOND

Suzuki Shunichi, a long-time civil servant and former vice-governor, was elected governor of Tokyo Metropolis after Minobe, returning the office to the powerful Liberal Democratic Party (LDP). He served four terms, April 1979 to April 1995, accumulating considerable power and having an enormous influence on Tokyo's planning and development. He called his vision for the city 'My Town Tokyo', referring to his goal that the city should be both humane and intimate.[3] His administration put together a series of three comprehensive plans: 1982, 1986 and 1990. Concern for citizen participation in the planning process was continued in each of them, as was attention to 'Tokyo for the People' issues such as improved housing, more open space and a cleaner environment. The biggest difference from the previous administration was an important one: a return of emphasis on the CBD and other major commercial districts, where construction of large, showy projects was intended to advance Tokyo as a business center and international metropolis.

Thus, there are two essential features of Tokyo as envisioned in Suzuki-era planning: (1) the city as workplace, focusing on a thriving business center with all the necessary improvements to keep it competitive with other urban centers; and (2) the city as a place to live, represented as a broad, healthful residential ring with plenty of green spaces. This dual image is encapsulated in an illustration that graced the front cover of the 1986 *2nd Long-Term Plan for the Tokyo Metropolis*, the most widely distributed of the three Suzuki-era planning documents (Figure 6.1).[4] In the background it shows Tokyo as a giant business city with super high-rises packed close together and fast communications (by futuristic plane) with the rest of the world. By contrast, the foreground and the center box portrays a bucolic 'My Town Tokyo': a fine place for families and older people to live and enjoy blue skies (on the color cover), ample greenery, clean water, and nice homes spaced far apart. A horizontal line and the edges of the box mark clear separations between these two worlds. They do not mix and are some distance apart – long commuting distance. We also see corresponding social roles. According to the illustration, 'My Town' is for stay-at-home wives, active children and their pets, and old people. Middle-aged men are not pictured; presumably they are at work in the distant tall buildings or jetting off for business elsewhere. Students of both sexes, as well as workers who are not middle-aged men, are also missing from the scene. Presumably they too are in the distant city.[5]

2ND LONG-TERM PLAN
for the
TOKYO METROPOLIS

Figure 6.1 *The cover of the* 2nd Long-Term Plan for the Tokyo Metropolis. (Courtesy of Tokyo Metropolitan Government.) © Tokyo Metropolitan Government

The details of 'My Town Tokyo' are spelled out in the contents of this and the other planning documents. Objectives include improvements to residential districts and construction of new housing; redevelopment in the center of the city; expansion and improvement of other commercial districts; modernization of industrial zones; major improvements to transportation such as roads, subways, and train lines; enlarging harbor and airport facilities; redevelopment of waterfront areas for residence and recreation; cleaning up environmental pollution; improving disaster-prevention measures; and development of new parks and recreation facilities. The planning documents also give considerable attention to social services of all kinds, especially those for an aging population. These are all noble goals that everyone would support. During the 15 years he was in office, most of them prosperous ones for Tokyo's economy, impressive gains were made in achieving these goals. There was construction everywhere, as the city undertook its third rebuilding of the twentieth century (see Chapter 4), and many improvements were made to where people live, work, shop, or go for recreation, and to the commuter rail lines and highways that connect these places. Most cities would be envious of what was accomplished in Tokyo.

Criticisms of Suzuki-era planning focused on its affinity for large, flashy construction projects said to be too expensive and maybe even unnecessary. One target was the new City Hall constructed in Shinjuku (Chapter 5). For many people, particularly those residing in the Sumida River wards and other parts of eastern Tokyo, the project was unpopular to begin with because of inconvenient location on the far side of the CBD. They also complained that the administration was favoring the trendier, *yamanote* side of Tokyo. Criticisms mounted as the gargantuan scale of the project came to be apparent, as well as details about its architectural pretensions and high costs (157 billion yen). By 1991, when the new facility was opened, some were calling it 'Tax Tower', the 'Tower of Bubble', the new Edo Castle, and a self-serving monument to both Suzuki and Tange Kenzō, the architect (*The Japan Times*, 10 April 1991, p. 18). Similar criticisms were aimed later at the Tokyo International Forum, a luxurious convention and exposition center that was put on the site of the old City Hall at a cost of approximately 165 billion yen (Chapter 4).

However, the primary target of Suzuki's critics was at the waterfront. This was the site of Tokyo Teleport Town, an enormous new urban center being constructed on land reclaimed from Tokyo Bay (Figure 6.2). Plans called for housing for 63 000 inhabitants and a working population of 106 000, and a great variety of new commercial, residential, industrial and recreation districts. The estimated cost was to be 8–10 trillion yen. Private developers were to pay for the construction, but as the economic bubble of the 1980s deflated and demand for office and other commercial space in Tokyo plummeted, developers backed out and Tokyo government began to lose huge sums on its initial investments. By April 1996 it was reported that the project had drained 2 trillion yen from municipal accounts and that *Tōkyō-to* was struggling with a debt of 1 trillion yen (*The Japan Times*, 27 April 1996, p. 3). Even so, the new islands that had been fashioned in Tokyo Bay were largely empty, as the few clusters of completed commercial buildings and residential complexes were separated by vast empty spaces, and new roads and the fancy monorail line ran past open fields and stalled construction sites.

The waterfront became a principal issue in the gubernatorial election of 1995. Governor Suzuki decided not to run for a fifth term, citing his age of 84 and desire to retire, but doubtlessly also feeling the sting of criticisms. He repeated his 'My Town Tokyo' theme:

> With love from the bottom of my heart, I have devoted my years to creating a Tokyo where people can live feeling at home. Now I feel as if Tokyo is one of my children (*The Japan Times*, 27 December 1994, p. 3).

The LDP chose Ishihara Nobuo, a long-time political insider and Deputy Chief Cabinet Secretary, a major national post, to run for the position. The major

Figure 6.2 *Model of Tokyo Teleport Town in the future, before scaling-down of the project in the recession of the 1990s. Access from central Tokyo via Rainbow Bridge and the new beach at Daiba are shown on the left.* © Tokyo Metropolitan Government

opponent turned out to be Aoshima Yukio, a member of Tokyo's House of Councilors, but much better known throughout Japan as a television comedian. His most famous role was on a TV show called *Ijiwaru bāsan* ('Nasty Granny') performing slapstick antics in an old woman's wig and kimono. He ran as an independent, and spent almost no money on the campaign. His principal promise to voters was to cut back on waterfront construction, citing specifically a plan to cancel the world's fair that Suzuki had scheduled for summer, 1996. Called 'World City Exposition Tokyo '96 – Urban Frontier', the fair was to be a showcase of Tokyo's most recent rebuilding, as the 1964 Olympics showcased the city's post-Second World War construction, and a forum on solving urban problems around the world. The main venue was to be a giant new building nicknamed Tokyo Big Sight – a 189 billion yen exhibition center totaling 80 000 square meters.[6] At a time when the fair's planners were still optimistic, they thought that as many as 20 million people would attend the event.

Aoshima won the election by a huge margin. Newspapers called his victory a major upset and a revolt by voters against the established politicians (*The Japan Times*, 10 April 1995, p. 1).[7] For weeks afterwards, there was turmoil about the fair's future, including a resolution passed by a 100–23 vote in the Tokyo Assembly urging Aoshima to continue with the event. The financial stakes were high and thousands of jobs hung in the balance. Nevertheless, near the end of May 1995 the governor kept his campaign promise and formally shut down the event. He said that for the time being the 448-hectare site should be a green space, and cautioned that 'Tokyo needs sufficient time and wisdom to find the best way to develop the area' (*The Japan Times*, 1 June 1995, pp. 1–2). He then traveled abroad to apologize to foreign governments for the inconvenience and reimburse them for their expenses in constructing pavilions. It was a signal that the long-time sway of big developers in Tokyo was being challenged, and that the era of Suzuki's 'My Town' concept had ended. However, Tokyo Big Sight was an exception to the closing; it was allowed to be completed because construction was considered to be too far advanced to stop.

It is too early to assess what new directions, if any, other than retrenchment at the waterfront the Aoshima administration will take Tokyo. In fact, it could well be that the administration will be short-lived and the LDP will assume control again (Robinson, 1995). What we will do instead to look into Tokyo's future is visit several of the newest construction projects in the city and neighboring prefectures to see what urban development trends are evident. For the most part, these are projects built during the Suzuki years, especially the last ones, or at least conceived then. Because it is no longer appropriate to think of just *Tōkyō-to* as the urban unit, the discussion includes examples from throughout the metropolitan area, including Chiba Prefecture, Yokohama and other jurisdictions. I have organized the presentation as follows: (1) new commercial centers in and near Tokyo, particularly the so-called 'multi-nodal metropolis' plan; (2) developments at the Tokyo Bay waterfront, including details about Tokyo Teleport Town; (3) new residential developments in Tokyo, both near the center of the city and in the Tama district; (4) expansion of parks and greenery in the Tokyo area; (5) major new towns and other large developments in neighboring prefectures; and (6) below-ground development, the so-called 'geofrontier'. It will also be necessary to introduce (7) the widening discussions taking place in Japan about limiting Tokyo's growth and moving the nation's capital to a new location.

MULTI-NODAL METROPOLIS

As the term suggests, this is an idea to reorient the spatial organization of Tokyo so that the city focuses less on the CBD and more on alternative commercial nodes elsewhere. This is because of overcrowding in the center, excessive land costs, and the chronic problem of long-distance commuting. It is an expansion of an idea that was developed first during the Minobe administration to make Tokyo into a 'bi-polar metropolis' focused on the CBD and a cluster of expanded urban centers in the Tama district. The new scheme identifies as many as 22 subcenters (*fukutoshin*), twelve of them within the limits of *Tōkyō-to* and ten in the neighboring prefectures (Figure 6.3). Most of the subcenters are established commercial nodes that have been in existence for some time, such as the CBD of Yokohama, the centers of Tachikawa, Chiba, and Ōmiya, and the station-front districts of Shinjuku, Shibuya, and other close-in Tokyo districts, and have been singled out as places that should grow to become even more important in the future. Some others, however, notably Tama New Town in *Tōkyō-to* and Tsukuba Science City in Ibaraki Prefecture, are newer developments that were designed from the start to be growth centers.

The greatest attention in the multi-nodal plan is given to a group of subcenters that is closest to the CBD and arranged in a ring around the inner wards as stations on the Yamanote Rail Line. This is the all-important loop line that encircles the core of the city and intersects with all the train and subway lines that run in and

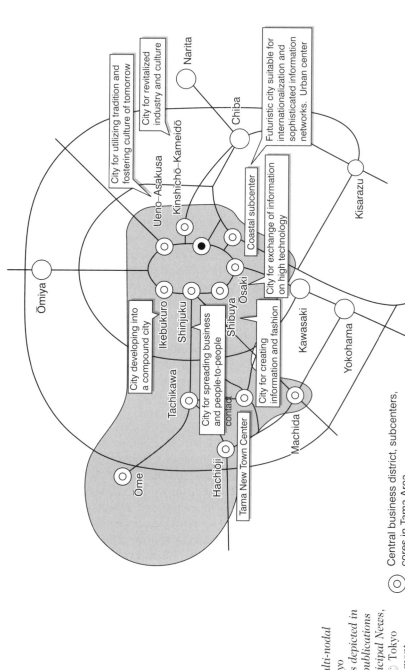

Figure 6.3 *The multi-nodal structure of the Tokyo metropolitan area as depicted in Tokyo government publications* (Source: *Tokyo Municipal News*, **37**, 3, 1987, p. 2). © Tokyo Metropolitan Government

out of its heart (see Chapter 2). Each of the biggest stations, Shinjuku, Shibuya, and Ikebukuro on the west side of the loop and the Ueno–Asakusa complex to the north and east, are designated as new nodes for Tokyo, as is a place called Ōsaki, a newly developed commercial center on the southwest side of the loop. New subcenters for Tokyo are promised at Kinshichō-Kameidō, a mixed industrial–residential area in Sumida Ward, and at the Tokyo Bay waterfront (Tokyo Teleport Town). All seven of these places are close enough to the CBD (always well within 10 kilometers) to make it possible to envision their eventual coalescence into one super-giant business core. We have seen in the earlier discussion about expansion of the CBD (Chapter 4) that the CBD and both Shinjuku and Shibuya are all growing together, and that the CBD is rapidly expanding in the directions of the waterfront and Ueno.

According to publicity about the plan, each of the new subcenters of Tokyo is to be distinctive based on its history and characteristic economic functions. For example, Shinjuku, which we have already discussed as becoming the principal 'new center' of Tokyo because of the new City Hall, is to emphasize its role as an office and hotel concentration, and as a preeminent center for the all-important eating, drinking, and entertainment functions that characterize Tokyo's after-work and after-school life. The latter assignment was determined presumably because of the presence in Shinjuku of the Kabukichō district (Chapter 5). Shibuya, on the other hand, which we discussed as being especially popular among high-school and college students, is given the general charge of being 'a town that generates information and fashions'. Some of the other designations seem less specific: Ueno–Asakusa is to be promoted as 'a traditional town that creates tomorrow's culture'; Kinshichō–Kameidō is to be 'an activated industrial and cultural town'; and Ikebukuro, which seems to be a little bit of everything, is 'a town expected to grow into a composite city' (Tokyo Metropolitan Government, 1987b, pp. 206–7). Unfortunately, none of these distinctions is defined very well, even though they have been repeated everywhere and often in publicity by Tokyo government (Figure 6.4). Perhaps only time will tell what the results will be in practice.

It is especially interesting to look more closely at the subcenter being developed at Ōsaki (Figure 6.5). This is an entirely new project, being built from the ground up at Ōsaki Station on the JR Yamanote Line, historically the least used of all 29 Yamanote stations. Developers include the Japan Railways Corporation (JR), local landowners, Shinagawa Ward, and several outside investors, all acting in partnership. They named their project 'Ōsaki New City' (also written *Ohsaki New City*). Tokyo government has touted it as 'a town for high-tech information exchanges'. A popular television drama *Sora ni hoshi ga aru yōni* ('As if There Were Stars in the Sky') was set there, I am sure, in part, to publicize the existence of the place and promote its development.

If we go to Ōsaki New City we see very little yet that is actually 'high-tech information exchange'. Moreover, we see nothing else that would seem to make this subcenter distinctive from the others. Instead, the place looks pretty much like any of a number of other developments in Tokyo and, indeed, other Japanese cities. There is a certain style of building design and project layout that seems to be spreading so widely in the country that it is now a cliché for its modern urban environment. Thus, at Ōsaki New City we see four high-rises (the tallest is 21

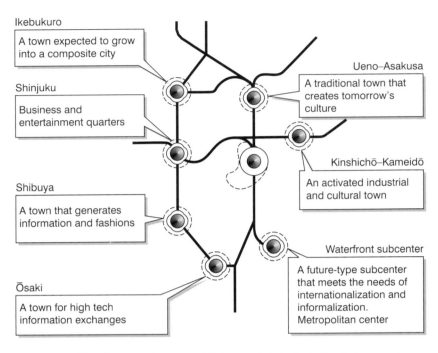

Ikebukuro
A town expected to grow into a composite city

Shinjuku
Business and entertainment quarters

Shibuya
A town that generates information and fashions

Ōsaki
A town for high tech information exchanges

Ueno–Asakusa
A traditional town that creates tomorrow's culture

Kinshichō–Kameidō
An activated industrial and cultural town

Waterfront subcenter
A future-type subcenter that meets the needs of internationalization and informalization. Metropolitan center

Figure 6.4 *The close-in subcenters of Tokyo and their 'individual character' as illustrated by Tokyo Metropolitan Government* (Tokyo Metropolitan Government, 1990a, p. 55). © Tokyo Metropolitan Government

Figure 6.5 *Ōsaki New City and Ōsaki Station on the Yamanote Line*

stories) that look not only like each other but also pretty much like the new commercial buildings at the Sunshine 60 complex in the Ikebukuro subcenter, at Ark Hills (see Chapter 4), at Tama New Town (Chapter 4), and all over the CBD. As seen from a distance, they are big light-colored blocks that stand on end. Three of the Ōsaki buildings are office buildings and one is an hotel, one of a major chain. A fifth building, one that is low in profile, is a rather standard indoor shopping mall. Although some tenants have been in Ōsaki for many years, the mall is mostly given over to chain stores. There is a Humpty Dumpty Crepe House at one of the entrances, and a squeaky-clean McDonald's in the center of the mall. Between the buildings is a plaza. It is paved with square tiles in a white and gray checkerboard pattern, with some stands of potted trees and other landscaping, two bubbling fountains, and a modern-art sculpture of a shapely young woman, the most common theme for public art in Japan's newest redevelopment projects.[8] Perhaps to give the development more of an international flavor, there is also a plaque telling distances and directions to various capital cities in the world. The only 'high-tech' in evidence is a futuristic-looking pedestrian bridge from the train station and chrome-plated mechanical sculptures along its length. It is all very nice, very clean and comfortable – and very predictable. It is also not impressive.

WATERFRONT DEVELOPMENT

Tokyo has always turned to its bayfront when it needed to expand or change image (Chapter 3). Thus, it is appropriate that the largest of all subcenters in the multi-nodal scheme is to be developed in Tokyo Bay. This is Tokyo Teleport Town, a totally new development on freshly reclaimed islands. The bay area is also the site of considerable redevelopment on existing islands and shoreline extensions. In comparison to many other cities in industrialized societies, Tokyo has lagged in conversion of old industrial and harbor precincts to amenity uses such as waterfront parks, upscale residential developments and marinas. There has also been little in the way of restaurants, waterfront hotels, or Rouse-type malls. Indeed, public access to much of the waterfront has been blocked; instead, it is a landscape mostly of industry and warehouses, docks, rail sidings, and cement walls that protect against floods and tidal surges.

Tokyo Teleport Town is the biggest development. With its goal of 6300 residents and 106 000 workers, it is more than just another of the commercial subcenters; it is a major extension of Tokyo – a new town in the bay. Called 'Teleport' for short, its name is meant to convey its character: a highly futuristic city with advanced telecommunications technology. According to the publicity, this is where Tokyo will concentrate its greatest efforts to become *the* international business center for the twenty-first century. The details are yet to be worked out, but plans call for being in instant touch with other global cities through fiber-optics technology and satellites, and for having state-of-the-art technology for information processing and office automation. Teleport is also to be highly advanced in the design of its buildings, as is the case with the already-completed 'intelligent' office building called Telecom Center, and in technology for providing utilities, removing wastes, traffic control, and many other aspects of urban development. In fact, official

Figure 6.6 *Newly reclaimed land from Tokyo Bay. This is an area of industry and warehouses. Most of the trucks seen on the highway are carrying trash for disposal on the island at the far side of the tunnel to build up new land*

publicity has spoken grandly about this being an 'ideal' urban environment and the 'frontier for developing the cities of the 21st century' (*Tokyo Municipal News*, **40**, 1, 1990, pp. 1 and 2). It is for these reasons that Teleport was to have been the site of 'Expo '96 – Urban Frontier', the ill-fated international fair about solving urban problems.

The specific location of Teleport is a 440-hectare island in Tokyo Bay about 6 kilometers from the center of the CBD. It was made from municipal waste and landfill brought in from construction sites all over the metropolitan area, and was originally referred to unceremoniously as No. 13 Reclaimed Land. It is now divided into four named districts, each having a different focus: (1) Aomi, a business center with intelligent office buildings; (2) Ariake Minami, where conventions and exhibitions are held and where the world's fair would have been; (3) Ariake Kita, a mid- and high-rise housing area and the site of Ariake Tennis Park; and (4) Daiba, an attractive area of luxury high-rises, hotels, shopping centers and recreation. The Daiba area is especially impressive. It focuses on a new, L-shaped beach, and is where Tokyo resembles the easy life of Waikiki or beachfront Santa Monica. Now, thousands of young Tokyoites gather there on hot summer days for sunbathing, shops and restaurants in a trendy air-conditioned mall named Decks, and evening concerts on the beach. I was skeptical when I saw illustrations in a 1988 Tokyo planning document showing that beach-goers and windsurfers would soon be using this area, thinking that this would not be possible in polluted, industrial Tokyo Bay. However, the Daiba development, among others, has shown me to be wrong. By summer 1996, when I was lucky enough to have an apartment only a few minutes from the beach, there were plenty of windsurfers and swimmers, as well as boaters and people fishing from rocky jetties extended from the shore (Figure 6.7).

Figure 6.7 *The new beach at Daiba in Tokyo's waterfront. The background has apartment and office buildings and a popular shopping mall*

Development of Tokyo Teleport Town was slow at first because of poor transportation linkages with Tokyo proper. However, the situation has now improved, as one of the city's principal subway lines has been extended to the area, and a new monorail, the Yurikamome Line, has been built. There have also been major improvements to highway connections. Rainbow Bridge, now one of the city's principal landmarks, carries both a new expressway and the monorail line between Teleport and Tokyo's center (Figure 6.8). Good connections with Tokyo's two airports, Haneda and Narita, is also supposed to stimulate development. It is easy to imagine that when the economy improves, developers might flock to Teleport's most attractive areas, such as Daiba, to expand the neighborhood. However, there are so many empty tracts in Tokyo Teleport Town, and the distances are so great, that it is also possible to envision a flat wasteland in the bay inhabited principally by seagulls and flies feeding off garbage from landfill sites.

As big and important as the Teleport project is, it is but one of several major developments taking shape at the waterfront. Some of the other landfill islands have also been targeted for construction of offices, hotels, and high-rise residences, as have large stretches of the shoreline (itself made of landfill) and several areas immediately behind the shoreline. The biggest projects have been proposed for three large rectangular islands that lie between the Teleport site and the core of the city: Tsukishima, Harumi and Toyosu. Most of the land uses there now are related to the port, but the future would reorient this area to be an extension of the CBD. At Toyosu, for example, which is now 105 hectares of petroleum storage tanks and other industrial facilities, the plan would create a giant cluster of sleek office and commercial buildings and high-rise residences not unlike those in Tokyo Teleport Town. More high-rise cities are planned for the Hinode and Takeshiba Pier areas and at Tennosu Isle. The latter project, also written Tennoz Isle, covering 20 hectares, is

Figure 6.8 *Rainbow Bridge connecting the main part of Tokyo in the background with new islands in Tokyo Bay. The bridge carries vehicular traffic as well as a monorail line. The photograph is taken from the Daiba beach*

being developed by a consortium of 22 corporate investors, including Citibank, Ube Industries, Fujitsu, Peat Marwick and Japan Airlines, into what promoters call a 'futuristic new business area'. The first phase, called Sea Fort Square, opened in June 1992. It centers on three high-rise office buildings and a luxury hotel, and features a theater, condominiums, shops, restaurants and a waterfront park with boardwalk. The nearby Shibaura factory and warehouse district is also being transformed into a CBD extension. The area's electronics industries are relocating factories outside the city and erecting office towers in their places. Two highly visible examples near Shibaura are distinctive new headquarters buildings for the giant Tōshiba Corporation near Hinode Pier and NEC a few blocks inland near an old shoreline.

A general description of what is to be at these various sites is the quotation below. It is taken from a publication (in English) by the Tange architects' group, and was written specifically to describe what Toyosu, the landfill island mentioned above, might look like in the future. What strikes me most about it is that in a few words this one paragraph incorporates all of the buzzwords that characterize contemporary planning in the center city of Tokyo, and thus encapsulates the image that planners have for the area as a whole in years to come. That is, we can substitute the word 'Toyosu' with 'Teleport', 'Harumi', 'Tsukishima', 'Hinode', 'Tennosu' or any of several other waterfront place names, and still be fairly accurate about the plans.

In terms of the great demand for office space in Tokyo, Toyosu [or whatever place] can be a central, dense, internationalized, and information-oriented business district. In addition, it will include good-quality urban-style housing, international business and convention facilities, a commercial zone making good use of the waterfront, and recreational functions. With all of these amenities the Toyosu district [or other place] will occupy an important position in the waterfront region and the entire city of Tokyo in the twenty-first century (Tange, 1987, p. 26).

I can name more than 40 different projects under way now in or along Tokyo Bay. Not all of them are in Tokyo itself, as the waterfront extends in one direction and the other into Kanagawa and Chiba Prefectures, and not all represent the Tange vision described above. Other kinds of examples include improvements to piers and other port facilities at Ōi and Shinagawa Wharves, on Tsukishima (the innermost landfill island) and other places in the inner waterfront; a huge new wholesale market for produce and marine foods near the waterfront in Ōta Ward; development of an impressive Wild Bird Park in the marshes nearby; a new beach, park and aquarium at Kasai in Edogawa Ward; expansion and eventual relocation of Haneda Airport further into the bay; and the construction of an attractive residential complex called River City 21 at one of the edges of Tsukishima (Chūō Ward). Projects in neighboring prefectures include improvements to harbor facilities in Yokohama, Kawasaki, and the industrial areas of Chiba; construction of large blocks of apartments in Urayasu City near the Tokyo Disneyland complex (Chiba Prefecture); a 70-hectare 'Sea Park' in Yokohama; a new conference center ('Shonan International Village') in the Yokosuka area in Kanagawa Prefecture; and the construction of a new city center with a high-tech, international focus in Makuhari City, Chiba Prefecture.

YOKOHAMA'S MINATO MIRAI 21

Perhaps the most highly publicized project of all, one exemplifying the scope and spirit of most of the planning at the Tokyo Bay waterfront, is a project called Minato Mirai 21 ('MM21'). This is a giant new urban center being built on a 186-hectare site on the waterfront near the Yokohama CBD. Its goal is to promote Yokohama as a major international metropolis. The project's name, unusual for development projects in Japan because it is in Japanese, means 'port of the future for the twenty-first century'. Until the mid-1980s, much of the area was a railroad marshalling yard, a dock and a Mitsubishi Heavy Industries shipyard. The industries were relocated to the Kanazawa Reclamation District further south in Yokohama, clearing about 60 percent of the area needed for the planned new construction. The remainder of the site is freshly reclaimed land. Redevelopment was spurred initially by an international exhibition commemorating various specific landmark events in the city's history, the Yokohama International Showcase '89 (YES '89). The fair called public attention to the site, allowing developers to promote their plans, and provided a basic infrastructure for the construction that followed.

MM21 is a coastal 'city within a city' with a broad range of commercial, cultural, residential and recreation facilities neatly arranged around a choice waterfront setting. When finished, it is expected to have a daytime population of 190 000 employees and some 10 000 permanent residents. The project could well have been described in the all-purpose quotation above, except that MM21 is, in fact, much more attractive than parallel developments in Tokyo and has a more distinctive look. Its centerpiece is Landmark Tower (back to English!), an appropriately named 70-story, 296-meter high-rise that is Japan's tallest building (compare with Table 2.10). Tenants include the 660-room Yokohama Royal Park Hotel Nikko, 48 floors of offices, and Landmark Plaza, a seven-level shopping mall with nearly 200 shops and boutiques. The mall has come to be quite crowded on Sundays and other holidays. Other MM21 attractions are a 30-story hotel and conference center ('Pacifico Yokohama'), the Yokohama Museum of Art (designed by Tange), a maritime museum aboard a restored historic schooner, and a spacious amusement park complete with a giant roller coaster called Cosmo Clock 21.

About one-quarter of the total area is given to recreation and open space. There is a new highway that serves MM21 and plenty of parking. Visitors also arrive by water taxi from other parts of Yokohama, getting a dramatic view of the development from offshore. However, most arrivals to MM21 come by train, getting off at Sakuragichō Station and using the long moving walkway that takes them directly to Landmark Tower. Because of its large scale and strategic importance, the MM21 project has been designated a 'national project' by the Japanese government and a 'shining example' for showcase development projects in other cities (Edgington, 1991, p. 74).

HOUSING DIRECTIONS

A good place to begin a discussion of Tokyo's new directions in housing is a recently opened residential complex in Chūō Ward named River City 21. It illustrates the on-going high-rising of the city, as well as construction of planned, mixed-use developments that stand apart from surrounding neighborhoods, and greater attention in design to amenities, aesthetics, and improved housing quality. It also illustrates what planners hope will be a growing trend to locate new housing in Tokyo's inner wards, in contrast to the suburbs, stemming the area's tide of long-term population decline. The fact that River City 21 is a waterfront development adds to the previous section and allows for a smooth transition.

River City 21 is near Tokyo Bay at the mouth of the Sumida River. It is on a tip of Tsukudajima, one of the inner landfill islands, precisely where the river enters the bay and splits into two equal distributaries. The site was previously industrial: the location of a giant shipyard. It is close to the CBD and was identified for redevelopment in the 1960s as part of a campaign to relocate industry from the center of the city. Its developers include the old shipbuilding concern and other private interests, as well as the Tokyo government, Chūō Ward and the national Housing and Urban Development Public Corporation. What makes River City 21 stand out is that it is primarily a housing development instead of an expansion of the CBD, i.e. one of the few places in central Tokyo where a serious effort is being made to increase, rather than decrease, the residential population. Furthermore, because residents will be able to walk or bicycle to work, or take a short bus or subway ride to the CBD or one of the new waterfront commercial developments, the project is intended to cut down on long-distance commuting. Hence, the '21' in its name: River City 21 is an idea for the twenty-first century.

The total population of River City 21 is expected to reach 7000 inhabitants in approximately 2500 units, all of them in high-rise structures. About half the housing is built by government for low- and moderate-income residents chosen by lottery. The rest of the units, in a more pleasant part of the complex facing a busy river channel and the CBD skyline, are expensive apartments and condominiums. The latter buildings are especially attractive and nicely set. Because the site is the tip of a peninsula and surrounded on three sides by water, the development is breezier and sunnier than most parts of the city, and relatively free of traffic noise and exhausts. Most units, except those in the more crowded core of the subsidized housing section, have views of the river or the bay. The views from upper stories in the prime buildings are superb: the whole center of Tokyo is visible, as are the Sumida River with its series of historic bridges, the islands and bridges of Tokyo Bay, and the comings and goings of ships in the inner harbor and planes at Haneda Airport. Realtors who sell the expensive River City 21 units like to point out that in the evening one can see the Electric Parade at Tokyo Disneyland from the balconies.

The site plan is well thought out. Although only a little more than one-half of the project is finished, there is already a lot of open space and greenery between buildings, several pleasant winding paths, nice playgrounds and small parks, and a superb waterfront promenade. There is also local shopping, a new elementary and middle school, and other community facilities. These are shared with an historic neighborhood, Tsukishima, that is immediately adjacent: an area of older houses, many of them wooden, that are squeezed between factories and what is left of a fishing fleet harbor (Chapter 5). All these features, plus the quiet and feeling of spaciousness that one gets from being surrounded on three sides by water, convey a sense of relaxed living. Therefore, it is not surprising that there have been long waiting lists for units in this project, and that prices for the market housing are high, even by Tokyo standards. In fact, there has been so much demand for River City 21 that extraordinary measures have been needed to keep out the kind of speculators who would buy there just to make a profit from fast resale (Yada, 1989a, p. 28).

Some distance away in the Tama section of *Tōkyō-to* are at least two excellent examples of another major direction in Tokyo's housing, planned residential new towns on previously undeveloped land. The first example is Tama New Town; its Development Plan is shown in Figure 6.9. With more than 160 000 residents today and a total expected of over 300 000 when construction is completed by 2010, this is the biggest and most publicized of several new bedroom communities in the metropolitan area. Others in the same vein are Kohoku New Town in Kanagawa Prefecture, and Chiba New Town and Ryugasaki New Town in Chiba Prefecture. They illustrate continued decentralization of the metropolitan population, in numbers much larger than any recentralization that River City 21 and inner-city developments like it (e.g. Gotenyama Hills in Shinagawa Ward) might represent. They also illustrate a trend for the mid-rising of suburbia, and even some high-rising, as the majority of new dwellings are in multi-level structures.

Tama New Town is on approximately 2340 mostly wooded hectares in the Tama Hills section of south-central *Tōkyō-to*, west of most of Tokyo's population. It was developed by Tokyo Metropolitan Government and two public development

Figure 6.9 *Tama New Town development plan. (Source: Tokyo Metropolitan Government, 1994a, p. 61)*

Keio–Sagamihara line

Odakyu–Tama line

Nagayama

Tama Center

Karakida

Fuchu country club

Keio Horinouchi

Minami Osawa

N

2000 meters

Residential

Business district

Parks, greenery etc.

Development not started

Land readjustment projects

Tama New Town boundary

Rivers

Major roads

Railways and stations

Table 6.1 Land-use Plan: *Tama New Town (land area in hectares)*

Land-use classification	Area	Percentage
Residential	853.0	36.5
Commercial, business facilities	76.2	3.2
Specified business facilities	43.8	1.9
Education	246.4	10.5
Parks and green spaces	430.2	18.4
Roads	446.4	19.1
Public utilities	243.6	10.4
Total	2339.6	100.0

Source: Tokyo Metropolitan Government (1994a, p. 61).

corporations, the Tokyo Metropolitan Housing Supply Public Corporation and the Urban Development Public Corporation. Construction started in 1965 after enactment of the 1958 Law for Town Development for the National Capital Region. The purpose was to provide housing and community services for overflow population from the central city, as well as local places of employment. Less of the latter was actually built than planned, and the area evolved more as a bedroom town for commuters than a full blend of land uses (Table 6.1). Nevertheless, there is a budding commercial center with a growing concentration of company offices and other employers, as plans continue to have Tama New Town develop into one of metropolitan Tokyo's planned subcenters (see Figure 6.3).

The principal node of Tama New Town is Tama Center. It is built around two adjacent train stations, those of the competing Keiō and Odakyū Lines, connecting the development directly with Shinjuku. There is also a new monorail line to Tachikawa and other outlying commercial centers. Near the station are several department stores, large supermarkets and other shops to serve the local population. The main street, a broad pedestrian mall named *Parutenon-dōri* (Parthenon Street), ascends a low hill atop which is a community center capped by a post-modern rendition of Athens' Parthenon. Many of the area's banks and other office buildings are on either side of this street.

Housing in Tama New Town consists of distinctive clusters of townhouses, mid-rise multi-family buildings (up to about 10 stories), and attractive suburban-style single-family structures not unlike those on display at the model home park in Shinjuku. It is arranged in neat neighborhood groupings separated by greenery and recreation spaces. There are parking lots at the edges of the housing clusters, as this part of Tokyo is increasingly automobile-oriented and many residents depend on cars to get to jobs or run household errands (Figure 6.10). The area also has lots of parks, playgrounds, bike paths, streams and ponds, and public fountains and sculptures for residents to enjoy. While one could fault the design for being too conspicuously clean and orderly (and therefore not especially stimulating for true cityphiles), the place succeeds well as an escape from urban crowding for growing families and a chance for comfortable, reasonably affordable housing. A survey of residents' opinions shows rather high scores on most 'quality of life' indicators (Table 6.2) (Hovinen, 1988).

Figure 6.10 *Apartment buildings in the Minami Osawa area of Tama New Town. Almost all commuters to Tokyo ride the trains, but automobiles are indispensable for most local needs*

Table 6.2 *Evaluation of the Quality of Life in Tama New Town by Residents, 1987*

Quality of life indicator	Score
Abundant green space	1.32
Clean air	1.39
Sunny and breezy	1.40
Drainage and sewer system	1.50
Parks	1.52
Garbage disposal	1.53
Assembly facilities	1.71
Appearance of buildings	1.76
Friendliness	1.86
Safety of transportation	1.89
Community activities	1.97
Crime prevention, public morals	2.04
Housing	2.08
Noise, vibration	2.08
Convenience of shopping areas	2.22
Convenience of transportation	2.35
Medical facilities	2.37
Retail prices	2.81

Scores are based on a questionnaire designed so that 1.00 was 'good', 2.00 was 'rather good', 3.00 was 'rather bad' and 4.00 was 'bad'.

Source: Hovinen (1988, p. 55), after a report in Japanese of a survey conducted by local government in Tama New Town.

The second example is in Hachiōji, one of Tama New Town's neighbors. This is a large, fast-growing suburban jurisdiction within which a planned new town is being developed. The area has more success at becoming an important employment nucleus, partly because of Hachiōji's long history as a factory center specializing in textiles, but also because of the establishment of numerous colleges and universities after 1959. This is the year when a Tokyo growth-control ordinance was enacted to prohibit new campuses from opening within the boundaries of the 23 wards, and when tight controls were put on the expansion of existing campuses. Hachiōji became a preferred location for higher education because of its pleasant surroundings, and because it was thought to be far enough away from the center of Tokyo to help reduce the crowding problems caused by overconcentration of education functions, but near enough so that students and educators could enjoy the capital's benefits and attractions. There are now more than a score of colleges and universities in and near this city, employing several thousand individuals and having thousands and thousands of students, both residents and commuters. In addition, because of the higher education base, Hachiōji has emerged recently as a significant center for high-technology research and development.

Hachiōji New Town is the newest phase of this development. Located on 390 hectares in the southern ward of Hachiōji City, it is a plan by Tokyo government for a carefully designed, self-contained community that will have some 28 000 residents, a full range of attractive community facilities, and numerous new workplaces in various high-technology fields. The goal is to strengthen the role of Hachiōji, and indeed the central Tama region in general, as a major concentration of growth industries, and in doing so to lessen the need for residents in the western outlying zones of Tokyo to commute long distances to work. The ground plan for Hachiōji New Town promises a more pleasant environment than most urban land around Tokyo, and features a balanced mix of residential neighborhoods next to landscaped office and industrial parks and school campuses. The fact that Hachiōji has achieved a reputation as a rather fashionable suburb of Tokyo, as well as the shortage of housing in the Tokyo metropolis as a whole, will doubtlessly help make this development a commercial success.

WATER AND GREENERY

Closely related to improvements in housing and neighborhoods are improvements to residents' access to open space and outdoor recreation opportunities. This has long been one of Tokyo's major weaknesses, as crowding and over-development have consumed almost all available land, leaving little room for parks and other public spaces. However, this began to change with rising national wealth in the 1960s, and the planning objectives of 'Tokyo for the People' and 'My Town Tokyo'. Since then, the amount of park area in both the 23 wards and the Tama section of Tokyo has expanded greatly (Figure 6.11).

There is also considerable variety in the kinds of new parks that have been developed. A number of these places have already been mentioned: the new beach

Figure 6.11 *Photographing the wildflower stand in Shōwa Memorial Park, Tachikawa City*

at Daiba in Tokyo Teleport Town; the tennis park nearby in Ariake; the beach, waterfront park and aquarium complex in Edogawa Ward's Kasai area (Kasairinkan-kōen); the open spaces and playgrounds at River City 21, and in both Tama New Town and Hachiōji New Town; the wild bird park (Yachō-kōen) near the warehouses and industrial plants along Ōta Ward's waterfront; Shinjuku Central Park; Meiji Park and Washington Heights-turned-Yoyogi Park nearby. In the distant reaches of the Tama area, new parks include hiking areas through the mountains and fishing in rocky streams. One of Tokyo's biggest new parks is Shōwa Park in Tachikawa. Developed on what had been a US military base, the park offers something for everyone: swimming, boating, bicycling, picnic grounds, ball fields, nature photography and many other activities (see Figure 5.24 again). The banks of the Tama River is also a popular recreation area offering everything from ball fields to places set aside for racing dirt bikes. I found the jogging paths along the river in Fuchū and Chōfu cities to be especially pleasant. Finally, in neighborhoods all over Tokyo and its suburbs, there are dozens of tiny new parks designed for play by small children or simply for sitting. Ironically, there is now more room for these little islands of urban greenery because more of the rest of the city is concentrated in high-rises.

My reason for making this inventory is to stress that although Tokyo continues to be primarily a huge and hopelessly overcrowded city, it has moved significantly in recent years in the direction of providing space and greenery for its inhabitants, and can now boast of many impressive achievements. I have seen the changes myself in the years I have studied the city, as many of the parks I know are quite new. Thus, my overall impression of Tokyo has changed: one of my many images of it now is of a city that provides plentiful opportunities for outdoors life and family fun.

NEIGHBORING PREFECTURES

Each of the prefectures that border *Tōkyō-to* have variations on the planned urban development that is taking place in central Tama. For some of the best examples, we can go to the opposite side of Tokyo to Chiba Prefecture where what is called the Chiba New Industry Triangle Concept is taking shape amidst suburban satellite towns, paddy fields, and wooded hills. This is another emerging high-tech zone to be built around a grouping of designated, close-together towns. As the proper name suggests, three towns in particular are most important: Makuhari, a rather ambitious new town on Tokyo Bay between Tokyo and Chiba City (Ōtani, 1990); Narita, the historic temple-town-in-the-farmlands turned in the 1970s amid considerable turmoil into the site of Tokyo's giant new international airport (located a famously inconvenient 60 kilometers from the center of the city); and Kazusa, a 1000-hectare site in the broken terrain of Chiba Peninsula that is supposed to become a model research and development town with numerous private laboratories, especially in medicine. The similarity of this concept to the Research Triangle area in North Carolina in the United States is intended. In fact, the official guidebook to these developments gives a photograph of a university scene in North Carolina in the absence of completed buildings in Kazusa (Chiba Nippōsha, 1989, p. 177). So, too, the Silicon Valley of California has been a model for this development. We see this in the new nickname that promoters hope will catch on for the prefecture: 'Chibafornia' (Ōtani, 1990, p. 458).

The plan for Makuhari New Town is especially well publicized. An article about it in the usually reserved *Japan Quarterly* opens with the proclamation that it is 'the hottest location in the Tokyo Bay area' and 'will be the attraction of the future, beckoning local and international populations' (Ōtani, 1990, p. 451). The town is being built as a 'ground-up' new town on 522 hectares of reclaimed land in industrial Chiba City, and is expected to house 26 000 residents and have some 150 000 full-time employees (Table 6.3). The focus is a huge international-scale convention facility, formally named the Nippon Convention Center but more commonly called Makuhari Messe,[9] near the waterfront. Its main features are three gigantic structures for meetings and exhibitions that, in profile, are meant to suggest a traditional Japanese village set in front of a backdrop of misty mountains. When the facility opened in 1989 it was, in the words of a publicity brochure produced in 1994 by Chiba government, 'the largest convention complex in the East'. According to the 1994 brochure, more than 8 million visitors from within Japan and abroad had come to the complex, using the password 'Meet Messe'. The waterfront near Messe is given to recreation: Makuhari Seaside Park, Makuhari Beach (for which sand was brought in), and a baseball stadium seating 30 000, the home field for the professional Chiba Marines.

There is also a sizable 'Business Research Zone' where prestigious companies, both Japanese and foreign, have constructed showy office towers and other facilities. Prominent examples include NTT, IBM-Japan, Tokyo Gas Company, BMW Japan, Canon and Fujitsu. The buildings are set amid blocks of greenery, artificial waterfalls, statues and other public art, and are connected by pedestrian walkways a level above street traffic. During my tour I was surprised to encounter an obelisk of Wisconsin dolomite, a gift to Chiba Prefecture from my home state. What was

Table 6.3 Land-use Plan: Makuhari New Town (land area in hectares)

Land-use classification	Makuhari New City	Reserve area	Total
Industrial and R&D	52.8	31.0	83.8
Town Center	24.6	8.4	33.0
Residential	38.9	–	38.9
Education	88.2	–	88.2
Parks and Green Spaces	103.7	3.8	107.5
Public Utilities	11.8	16.8	28.6
Roads and others	117.7	24.5	142.2
Total	437.7	84.5	522.2

Source: Makuhari New City, Development Division.

missing on the day I went there was people: even though it was an ordinary business day, there was hardly anyone outdoors in the office zone, and certainly no one was taking the time to enjoy the landscaping. Like so many other new developments in and around Tokyo (e.g. Tama Center, Ōsaki New City and Tokyo Teleport Town's office zone), outdoors Makuhari is strangely empty despite planners' best efforts to provide an interesting environment for crowds to enjoy. The residential area of Makuhari, much of which is also near the waterfront, is to have 8100 housing units in buildings ranging in height from 5 to 40 stories. There is not much shopping available yet, but Funabashi, a busy Chiba Prefecture commercial center identified as one of the favored subcenters in the decentralization plan for Tokyo metropolis, is only a few minutes away by car or train. A shopping mall there called Lala Port (because 'Lala literally means "lively or active mind"' according to the English-language brochure) is especially popular. Furthermore, Makuhari is convenient to central Tokyo by new train line and by expressway, and is within minutes of such attractions as Tokyo Disneyland, the Maihama resort hotel strip on the water at Urayasu City, and a huge year-round indoor skiing facility beside the tracks in Funabashi. All this adds to the appeal of the setting, if not Makuhari itself, and is expected to contribute to the development's growth.

The future of the Tokyo metropolitan area is also seen in Kanagawa Prefecture, located on the opposite side of the city from Chiba Prefecture. With more than 8 million people, the third largest total among Japan's prefectures, it is an extraordinarily complex place with urban development patterns worthy of a detailed study of their own. Yokohama's Minato Mirai 21 is but one of the stories. There are quite a few other waterfront developments in Kanagawa, both within Yokohama and elsewhere along the coast, as well as big inland projects in Yokohama, Kawasaki, and other cities and towns of all sizes. Because of proximity to central Tokyo and central Yokohama, as well as to the Keihin industrial zone (Chapter 3), the prefecture's verdant hills have recently seen considerable suburban expansion, including development of at least one planned new town, Kohoku New Town, similar in concept if not scale to Tama New Town.

What is perhaps most significant about new directions in Kanagawa is the prefecture's extraordinarily important role as Japan's leading industrial research and development center. Many of its industries are cutting edge in terms of technology, and emphasize what are called *nayedoko* functions: literally 'seedbed' functions for new industrial products. This aspect of the local economy is traced to 1978 when a governor of the prefecture, Nagasu Kazuji, first proposed that Kanagawa be made into Japan's 'brain center' (Obayashi, 1993, p. 121). The area has since received considerable investment for this purpose from the national government, local governments, and private industries. One of the key elements is construction of Kanagawa Science Park, a research complex in Kawasaki city not unlike the functions of California's Silicon Valley or the Route 128 corridor near Boston. Much of its research is geared to pilot production of new products being manufactured by small, highly specialized firms concentrated in the fast-growing boundary area between Kanagawa Prefecture and Tokyo. Market testing takes place nearby, in various districts of Tokyo and Yokohama. Successful products are also assembled in this area for export (Obayashi, 1993, p. 129). Thus, for us Kanagawa Prefecture is a reminder that the Tokyo area, as well as Japan more generally, is a vital manufacturing zone, and that continued progress in manufacturing for export will remain a key 'direction' for Tokyo.

TSUKUBA SCIENCE CITY

There is one other new town project that I want to introduce, even if it is further from central Tokyo than all the other projects described. This is Tsukuba, one of the most famous and largest of Japan's new towns, and a leading center for basic research in fields ranging from high-energy physics to biology, medicine, computer technology, building materials, earthquake prediction and social policy. It is sometimes referred to in Japan as 'the City of Brains' (in comparison to Kanagawa's claim to being Japan's 'Brain Center'). Its daytime population is now over 150 000, of whom some 30 000 are researchers, students, administrative staff, and their families (Tatsuno, 1986, p. 100), and nearly 6000 are foreigners. Located a little more than 60 kilometers from central Tokyo in a foothills area of Ibaraki Prefecture close to Mount Tsukuba, the city is separated from the nearest edges of the Tokyo built-up area by long stretches of farmland and other non-urban terrain. It was conceived in the early 1960s to be a vital national research center that would feed the high-growth economy of Japan with competitive advantages and new ideas. The reason for putting it so far from the city was to avoid the high cost of urban land and the increasing congestion and pollution of 'business-first' Tokyo. The goal was also to provide researchers with a pleasant environment for their work and living. Lessons for this are said to have come from site visits in March 1966 by Japanese government officials to renowned science cities and research parks around the world such as Stanford Industrial Park, Research Triangle in North Carolina, Sophia Antipolis and South Ile in France, and Louvain Science City in Belgium (Tastuno, 1989, p. 97).

I want to make two particular points about Tsukuba. First, it seems clear that despite the fast growth of this city and the huge sums that have been spent on construction (central government alone has spent over $1 billion on the project), it is not generally regarded as a popular place to be. There is greenery, streams, vistas of hills, and other natural beauty, but the project is thought by many residents and visitors to be contrived and somewhat sterile, and a poor alternative to the excitement and cultural stimulation of Tokyo. In fact, there were some rather well-publicized protests by university faculty and other skilled professionals in the 1970s against plans by their employers to relocate there from the capital. While this situation has improved considerably in recent years, especially because Tsukuba has matured somewhat as a city and because of increased services and public facilities, there are still many workers who choose to not live there, but prefer the long commute (about two hours each way) from Tokyo. My point is that Tsukuba, as large and famous as it is, and as expensively planned as it has been, is still at many levels below that of overgrown, congested, and unplanned Tokyo in desirability. This is precisely the criticism of Makuhari described above.

Second, Tsukuba illustrates something about the tremendous reach of the Tokyo metropolis. Even though many miles of farmland still separate Tsukuba from the outer edges of what are clearly bedroom suburbs of Tokyo, the new town is less and less the isolated think tank in the mountains that designers wanted it to be, and more an outer outpost of Tokyo. Not only is rail and highway access to the central city quicker, but the built-up area around Tokyo, and particularly around its out-lying growth nodes such as Narita, is spreading beyond the inner ring of suburban prefectures (Chiba, Kanagawa, and Saitama) to an outer ring that includes, as in this case, Ibaraki Prefecture. Thus, Tsukuba indicates that 'far' is another direction of Tokyo's growth.

THE GEOFRONT DIRECTION

We have already seen the expansion of Tokyo in various directions: up to new heights of ever-taller skyscrapers; out to new islands in Tokyo Bay; and far into the distant reaches of the Kantō Plain. We now turn to the newest direction of growth, down below ground to what is being called in Japan the 'geofront' or 'geofrontier'.

There are many expressions of subsurface development in Tokyo already, particularly within the 23 wards. First, there is the city's celebrated subway system. With more than a dozen different lines and over 200 kilometers of track, this is the world's most extensive underground transportation network. So, too, the subsurface has elaborate networks of water lines, sewer lines, electrical cables, gas pipes, and many other elements of urban infrastructure. Other below-surface examples include underground shopping promenades beneath busy commercial centers (most notably at Shinjuku and the Yaesu exit of Tokyo Station), and the growing numbers of high-rise buildings with extensive basement-level commercial space. Especially in high-rent shopping and entertainment areas such as Shibuya, Harajuku, and Shinjuku, there are many new buildings with two or three (and sometimes more) distinct basement levels (called 'B1', 'B2', 'B3', etc.), full of the kinds of shops and eating and drinking places that abound at street level and on the upper floors of multi-story commercial arcades.

What 'geofront' means is that Tokyo will continue to grow down to new depths below the surface, and will include there various new facilities and other new uses. To make this possible, the national Diet has passed legislation that limits ownership of land to a depth of 50 meters. The effect of this is to enable construction of subway lines, subterranean highways, and other underground projects without having to compensate the landowners above. This avoids one of the most expensive components of any construction project in Tokyo, and opens the way for numerous capital improvements at reduced cost. Already, a new subway line, the No. 12 Shinjuku–Nerima Metropolitan Subway Line, and a new highway, a ten-kilometer stretch of the Chūō Kanjō Highway in the vicinity of Shinjuku, are under construction with benefits derived from this legislation. Other ideas for the deep subsurface include 'underground rivers' to bring in fresh water, other rivers to take away wastes, high-speed inter-city rail systems, and earthquake-safe storage facilities for valuable documents, records, and computing equipment under conditions of constant humidity and temperature. There are also more distant possibilities for underground residential complexes, shopping centers, offices, factories, and other urban activities. There are some rather impressive drawings of what this might look like by city planners in Tokyo, and by artists in the employ of the same giant construction companies that have previously expanded Tokyo upward and outward (Golany and Ojima, 1996; Ojima, 1991; National Land Policy Institute, 1997).

MOVING THE CAPITAL?

There is one more direction for Tokyo for us to discuss – the possibility that the national capital might be taken from the city and moved to a new location.[10] Such a possibility is being hotly debated in Japan and could happen as early as 2010. A high-level government commission charged with studying the topic, the Investigation Committee for Relocation of the Capital, headed by Uno Osamu, a prominent business leader, has recommended this, stating in its December 1995 report that construction of the new capital should start as soon as the year 2000. At present, the debate in Japan concerns whether the capital should or should not be moved, and if so, where it should be. Public opinion about the first of these questions seems equally divided, although surveys show that support for relocation is growing and that well over half of the people are at least 'interested' in the possibility (*Asahi Evening News*, 19–20 March 1996, p. 5).

One of the main reasons given for moving the capital is Tokyo's earthquake danger. Advocates of relocation often cite the city's historic 70-year pattern of devastating quakes (Chapter 2), arguing that the next disaster is already 'overdue' from 1923. For many Japanese, the terrible Great Hanshin Earthquake of 17 January 1995, which destroyed Kobe in full view of television cameras, drove home the need to relocate the capital to a safer site, no matter what the cost. The sense of urgency in the relocation commission report is based largely on this event. Other important reasons for moving the capital are that Tokyo is too big and crowded, and needs to control growth; and that its high land costs result in excessive costs for maintaining government. Supporters of relocation also argue that Japan needs to separate the headquarters of government from the headquarters of big business, because the two are much too cozy and there is too much corruption. A different kind of argument, put forward most often by representatives of smaller cities and rural prefectures, is that moving the capital will reduce regional inequality in Japan and promote economic development in regions where growth has been lagging. Finally, it is worth noting that construction companies and other business interests have cited job creation and other economic benefits as reasons for relocating government.

Opinions in Tokyo oppose moving the capital. While many citizens would welcome a strategy to draw in the reins on growth, and see removal of government functions as an opportunity for creative land-use planning to improve the city, most oppose the change, citing negative economic impact on Tokyo and excessive costs for the nation as a whole of building a new capital. Governor Aoshima and the governors of adjacent Chiba, Kanagawa and Saitama Prefectures have been especially vocal against relocation. In their opinions, Japan can safeguard against the chaos that would be caused by a massive earthquake by investing more in earthquake-proof construction, disaster preparedness, and earthquake forecasting, and by promoting decentralization of power and deregulation instead of moving the capital. They have also argued that Tokyo's plan for a multi-centered metropolis, focused on the two dozen-odd commercial subcenters in their respective prefectures, is the best way to reduce crowding in the central city and lower the price of land. Tokyo's politicians are most strongly opposed: shortly after release of the investigative commission's recommendation to move the capital, the Tokyo Metropolitan Assembly voted unanimously to oppose relocation.

There is also the question of where to put a new capital. This too is not yet resolved and is being hotly debated. A number of local governments in various parts of Japan have volunteered their own areas for the distinction, doubtlessly looking forward to the prestige and economic gains that would come with being selected. As early as the 1980s, several prefectural assemblies, including Fukushima, Shiga and Tochigi, adopted resolutions that the capital should be located within their jurisdictions. There has also been support for a site in Yamanashi Prefecture at the foot of Mount Fuji, first proposed in 1960 by Tokyo Metropolitan University professor Isomura Eiichi as a way of easing Tokyo's congestion. Other possible sites are Sendai and Nagoya, two cities that have lobbied to become the capital; somewhere in Shizuoka Prefecture, close to the geographic center of Japan's population; northeastern Honshū, which is said to need an economic boost; and Kyoto, which would be a return to the capital's historic location. A different kind of idea is that capital functions should be shared among various sites along a proposed 'maglev megalopolis' extending along a high-speed rail corridor between Tokyo and Osaka. Another proposal, by celebrated architect Kurokawa Kishō, would relocate government offices to a huge new island to be built in the middle of Tokyo Bay. Figure 6.12 summarizes the main proposals that have been introduced.

The report of the investigative commission did not identify a favored site: its main recommendation was to find a location that is easily accessible from all parts of Japan and within a 60–300-kilometer radius of central Tokyo – i.e. within about two hours by train from the present capital but far enough away to avoid its shortcomings. The commission's nine criteria for location of the proposed new capital are listed below (*Asahi Evening News*, 19–20 March 1996, p. 5):

- The location should be accessible from all parts of the country
- It should be within a 60–300-kilometer radius of Tokyo

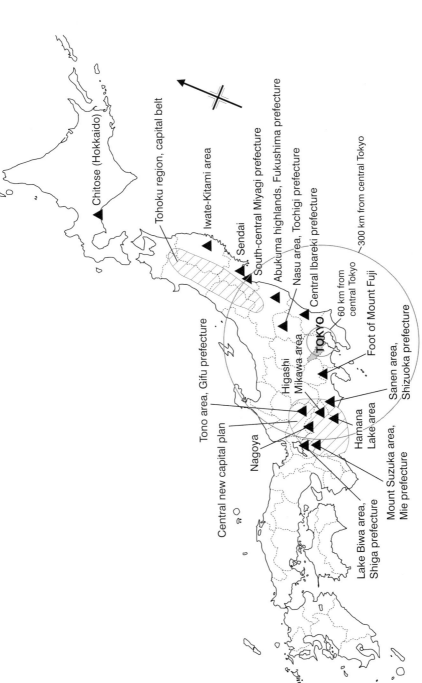

Figure 6.12 *Proposed locations for Japan's new capital. (Sources: Nomura Research Institute, Asahi Evening News, other newspaper sources)*

- It should be within 40 minutes by train of an international airport
- There should be at least 9000 hectares of land that can be easily acquired and developed for a population of 600 000
- It should be relatively safe from earthquakes
- It should be relatively safe from other natural disasters, such as flooding
- The land should be relatively flat and avoid steep mountain terrain
- There should be an ample water supply
- The site should be far enough from existing cities to avoid their expansion into the new city

Anything can still happen with respect to Japan's capital. It might be that a site will be selected soon and that the commission's target of a new capital constructed by 2010 will be reached. There are already quite a few proposals for its design, most of them calling for a neatly organized city with lots of greenery, imposing open spaces, and the latest technology for traffic flow and the operation of its buildings. On the other hand, it could well be that nothing will happen and that government functions will stay in Tokyo, at least until the next round of debate and plans. And if the capital does move, it would remain to be seen what impact on Tokyo would follow. Would the city slow its growth and bring development under control? Or would it make no difference, as Tokyo seems to have growth momentum of its own, rebounding from whatever setback to become bigger than before?

CHAPTER 7

TOKYO 21

As Tokyo prepares to enter the twenty-first century, it is a much better city than ever before. People are more comfortably housed, have more time and facilities for recreation, the air and water are cleaner, and there are more protections from environmental disasters. The 'pie' that reconstruction-era prime minister Ikeda had said must first become bigger before 'quality of life' issues could be addressed is now quite large indeed (see the beginning of Chapter 6), and the citizenry as a whole shares in its rather generous slices. Not only are there the successful 'glamor projects' such as the Daiba beachfront and River City 21, there are also hundreds of other smaller, more local capital improvements in *Tōkyō-to* and surrounding prefectures. Depending on which part of the metropolis you visit, there are new community centers and neighborhood parks, improved roadways, extensions to subway lines and new stations; pedestrian bridges over rail tracks and busy roads; enlarged facilities for sewage treatment and garbage disposal; better flood control; landscaping for streets, sidewalks, and station-front plazas; new neighborhood shopping arcades; public swimming pools, safe bicycle paths and other welcome changes. It is easy to be impressed.

On the other hand, it is also easy to be alarmed about Tokyo's directions. The city may be better on the whole, but it is bigger than ever before, distressingly so. As the population continues to grow in the metropolitan area, the last farmlands and forests recede from the Kantō Plain and Tokyo Bay diminishes in favor of space for crowded housing, jammed roadways and busy shopping centers. Every place, it seems, is being high-rised. It was not long ago that much of Tokyo from the air was a sea of end-to-end tile roofs of low single homes. However, now the vista is of taller buildings; the sea's surface, especially in the 23 wards, is of flat roofs several stories above the ground, and a clutter of rooftop air-conditioner units, elevator shafts, neon advertisements, and lines for airing household laundry. Many old neighborhoods have made their last stand and have fallen to developers, being replaced by a rising tide of *manshon*, tall apartment blocks, and look-alike office buildings. Despite all the planning of alternative commercial subcenters and comprehensive new towns in the suburbs, most commuters still ride enormous distances on sardine-can trains to Tokyo's center, which itself is rising upward and spreading outward without much plan. Moreover, the downtown has more people than ever during the day, risking catastrophe from the inevitable next giant quake. If Godzilla were to return to the city, there would be so much more to destroy.

Thus, Tokyo's great paradoxes continue. It is simultaneously a great city and one that is frightening for its size and potential for disaster. While planning programs have improved the quality of urban life in countless ways, they have failed to deal in a productive way with the city's biggest problem: that Tokyo is too big and getting bigger. One looks in vain through Tokyo's planning documents for strategies to control growth and finds instead rosy descriptions of 'new frontiers' for still more development. There is not even an acknowledgment in the city's latest comprehensive plans that with over 11.8 million people on just over 2000 square kilometers of land, Tokyo is overpopulated. On the contrary, the tone of the documents reveals that the goal of planning in Tokyo is to help the city become bigger by providing the necessary infrastructure and facilities. We are not surprised, then, that Tokyo's leaders bristle at suggestions that the national capital should be moved elsewhere to make the city smaller.

The bottom line is that Tokyo is, first and foremost, a place of business and that its development emphasizes business needs above others. Despite all the rhetoric about 'My Town Tokyo' and how the city is to be primarily a place for healthful community life, it is the power of business leaders that determines the growth of the city, much like the power of the shogun once determined the shape of Edo. Instead of a giant castle surrounded by moats to signify authority, the new rulers have constructed soaring office towers and showpiece development projects at the waterfront and elsewhere in the city, and shape Tokyo to be the capital of the global economy. The aim of today's *daimyō* is to vanquish rival cities in economic competition and make Tokyo the undisputed leader of international business, particularly in Asia. In a candid magazine interview about the need to have large waterfront development projects, Ishikawa Rokurō, chairman of Kajima Corporation, a giant construction firm whose business includes many of Tokyo's largest building projects, explained it as follows:

> Unless something is done to redevelop Tokyo and make it more attractive to foreign businessmen as Asia's center of commerce, nothing will prevent them from going off to Hong Kong or Singapore (*Business Tokyo*, May 1987, p. 20).

In what sounds like the same voice, Tange Kenzō, the noted architect to whom I have referred often, has written:

> Tokyo is burdened with the fatal flaws of congested automotive traffic and lack of personal communication caused by excessively great commuting distance. Moreover, from the viewpoint of foreign enterprises contemplating the idea of opening outlets and offices there, the unprecedented and unparalleled high cost of land in Tokyo puts Japan in what looks like a state of hopeless isolation. If nothing is done to remedy this situation in the next four or five years, Tokyo will no longer be qualified to bear the responsibility of one of the world's urban poles. Indeed, some Western information-oriented and finance related business are already seriously contemplating Hong Kong, Singapore, or Shanghai as possible alternative locations (Tange, 1987, p. 11).

Therefore, we can expect that Tokyo's principal direction in the coming years will be to continue rising.[1] As we have discussed, the city will build upward to new heights, outward beyond its present limits, and downward to the 'geofront' below the surface. Ever true to Tokyo tradition, the next generation of showpiece buildings, being proposed now by architects and construction companies will put earlier ones to shame. One intriguing proposal, announced in January 1988 by the powerful Mitsubishi Estate Company, seeks to completely redevelop the Marunouchi district. This is the strategically located subdistrict of the CBD that sits between the main gates to the Imperial Palace and the principal entrance of Tokyo Station; it has come to be one of the most important office districts in the city (see Chapters 3 and 4). It was first established about 100 years ago by the forerunners of the famous Mitsubishi *zaibatsu*, and is still largely controlled by

Mitsubishi companies. The buildings are not so old – most of them were built after the 1945 disaster – but they are not particularly tall and have not commanded the kind of rents per land parcel that owners believe are possible. Consequently, the plan is of true Tokyo scale: it would more than double the floor space-to-land ratio to about 20:1 and consist of 60 (yes, 60!) high-rise office buildings, all between 40 and 50 stories. They would be aligned neatly in rows and columns over a 113-hectare site (Matsuda, 1988). Not surprisingly, the proposal has sometimes been called the 'Manhattan Plan'. Because the Tokyo Station building would be dwarfed by it all, one version of the plan, a short-lived idea that pretended to support the preservation of that historic landmark, suggested that the whole structure be lifted to the roofline of the high-rise towers that would be built on its site so that the old building could be seen from a wider area!

It is not certain what will become of the Mitsubishi proposal. It was widely criticized when it was announced, and even ridiculed for similarities to a graveyard scene (*The Japan Times*, 24 January 1988, p. 16). The weak economy of the 1990s and the glut of office space in central Tokyo has also quieted the idea. In its place have come other ideas, equally grandiose. The best known is Millennium Tower, a monstrous high-rise being favored by the Obayashi Corporation, a construction company that wants the construction contract, and British architect Sir Norman Foster. It would be some 840 meters high, almost twice the height of Chicago's Sears Tower, and house as many as 50 000 residents (Obayashi Corporation, 1991–3, p. 120). The same company has also proposed a 2000-meter, 500-story sky-scraper for Tokyo. Residents of the upper floors would require oxygen supplements to avoid altitude sickness (Crowell, 1994, p. 35). Other proposals include 'Sky City 1000', a 1000-meter-tall artificial city covering 800 hectares that Takenaka/Esco wants to build; 'Tokyo Bay City', a complex chain of new islands in the bay proposed by Tange to house between 1.5 and 2.3 million inhabitants; the 'New Tokyo Plan 2025', an even bigger Tokyo Bay project by architect Kurokawa Kishō; Shimizu Corporation's TRY2004, an office and residential pyramid 2004 meters high made of 204 stacked pyramids; and Geotrapolis, a gigantic 'inverse high-rise' office building that Tōkyū Construction Company wants to extend below ground (Crowell, 1994). Presumably, the people who work there would press the 'down' button on the elevator when they arrive in the morning.[2]

I thought I had found a place in Tokyo that would never be touched by all the building and rebuilding. It is a relatively inaccessible little neighborhood in Arakawa Ward named Shioiri, tucked into a bend of the Sumida River and isolated from the rest of the city by unattractive industrial land and freight railyards. It is hard to get to because it is not served by train or subway lines, and requires either a long walk from the nearest station or knowing just which bus to catch. Two friends, experts on Tokyo, took me there when I was just learning my way around the city, with advice that I should get to know this place where, as much as is possible in Tokyo, time had stood still. Here was a compact maze of narrow, winding streets; old wooden houses with tile roofs; small private gardens, thousands of potted plants; folksy 'ma-and-pa' shops along the narrow central street; a quaint old *sentō* (public bathhouse); a small but beautiful old temple; and many other charms. Neighbors, many of them elderly, were in conversation seemingly

Figure 7.1 *A sign of quiet protest on a wooden fence in Shioiri. It reads: 'The approval of residents should come before decisions about development planning'*

everywhere; all of them always noticed the foreigner–stranger who kept returning periodically to walk the streets and take pictures. I found it to be like a tiny village within the giant metropolis, a nice little community. I came to think of it as one of my 'secret places' in Tokyo, where I proudly took some of my students and foreign visitors to show a hidden face of the great city.

Tange Kenzō has found Shioiri too. This man who has done so much to build Tokyo up over these past decades of great growth has determined that it too shall be high-rises. His plan, which I first saw detailed in an issue of *Japan Architect*, calls for the whole neighborhood to be made over into what so much of the rest of Tokyo is becoming (Tange, 1987, pp. 36–7; see also Yada, 1989a, pp. 200–2). Called 'Kawanote New City Center' ('*kawanote*' being a play on the name of the historic district '*yamanote*', and meaning 'in the direction of the river'), the proposal is for a sizable (175-hectares) mixed-use development of commercial and residential high-rises set among planned green spaces, institutions, and recreation facilities. Therefore, according to 'objective' measures, it would improve the area. Several large buildings are already completed on land that was vacant at the edge of the old neighborhood; their total number of residents is probably larger already than the maximum number of 'villagers' in Shioiri. Soon construction will commence in Shioiri itself. The majority of houses and old shops have already been acquired by the developers and torn down, leaving gaping holes in what was once a compact settlement and an unfamiliar stillness where neighbors once gathered. Before the demolitions began, one of my students, Shimizu Aoi, wrote a very thoughtful paper that effectively conveyed the sadness of residents that it will soon be their turn, as it was the turn of people in other neighborhoods before them, to make way for the progress of Tokyo. Their lament is reflected in Figure 7.1. When I last visited Shioiri I felt as if I was attending a funeral.

Figure 7.2 *Two schoolgirls painting pictures of a pagoda in the Asakusa temple district as part of a lesson in class about the history of Tokyo and traditional architecture*

It is natural to be critical of all the high-rising that is going on, and to lament the loss of historical urban fabric. This is an understandable and correct reaction. However, as I hope that I have successfully explained in the preceding pages, the very essence of Tokyo is change: not staying still. Certainly more than any large urban center that I know, this city is process and not artifact, and needs to be evaluated as such. There are ways, sometimes distinctively 'Tokyo ways', in which the past is retained in the city and held deeply inside, even as the surface changes completely in profile. I think that the good student of Tokyo recognizes this, and admires Tokyo both for its unsurpassed dynamism and for its ever-present traditions (Figure 7.2).

NOTES

CHAPTER 1

1. Japanese names are given in this book with the family name first.
2. A very enjoyable account of the American scene in Tokyo that readers might not otherwise come across is the article 'Transplanted landscapes' by Robert Mason (Mason, 1996).
3. A short slip-over jacket with an employer's crest on the back that is often worn by workmen, and that has become popular among youths during festivals in which a portable shrine is carried.
4. This place is not off the beaten path at all, but is instead a popular attraction for worshipers and tourists alike.
5. There is now a post-modernist rendition of a traditional Japanese waterfall on this rooftop.

CHAPTER 2

1. The fact that these islands are technically within the same entity of local government that is Tokyo gives the city a distinction that is probably unique among urban areas in the world: its territory extends for the greatest distance from end to end (approximately 1300 kilometers); and it covers the greatest range of geographical environments, from tiny tropical isles rimmed with palms, white sands and coral reefs, on the one hand, to heavily forested mid-latitude mountain slopes with four well-defined seasons, on the other.
2. This is based on numbers of corporations with annual 1982 sales in excess of US$1 billion. Tokyo had 81 such companies, London was second with 67, and New York third with 44. However, New York ranked first in total sales by these companies, London second, and Tokyo third. Tokyo has doubtlessly improved its position in this regard since 1982.
3. See also: 'When the great quake comes to Tokyo', *Tokyo Business*, **3**, No. 7 (Summer), 1989, pp. 5–10.
4. Use of the term primate city ignores the fact that in correct English the adjective 'primate' refers to a zoological category. It is never a synonym for 'first-ranking' or 'primary.'
5. The small house described in Chapter 1 rented for the equivalent of about $4000 per month, more than five times the largest amount I ever paid for housing in the United States. Of course, my salary and benefits in Tokyo were also higher.
6. The suffix 'gawa' or 'kawa' means river. Thus, an alternative is Edo River, Ara River, and Sumida River.
7. The number of visitors cited is as of December 1995.
8. Daytime and nighttime panoramas of Tokyo from Tokyo Tower are available on the internet at http://www.ntv.co.jp/tko.rockin/HBJ/002/ALI/Panorama.html
9. *The Economist* (3 October 1987, p. 25) once reported that a piece of land in the center of Tokyo that is about the size of this page would cost over $12 000 to buy.
10. The Kasumigaseki Building was a great novelty in low-rise Tokyo. There were long lines of curious visitors to ride the elevator to the observation area at the top for several months after the official opening. Moreover, because of its size the building became such

a prominent local landmark that it came to be used in the city, only half-jokingly, as a measure of volume: i.e. so many Kasumigaseki Buildings of beer were drunk in Japan last year, etc.

11. Almost all these employees, by the way, as well as all ticket sellers and attendants at the wickets where tickets are checked, are males. The rail system is so set in its ways that it stands out even in ultra-sexist Japan for refusal to admit women employees. This criticism applies equally to the government of Tokyo which operates most of the subway lines, to Japan Railways (JR), a newly privatized institution that runs most of the national rail network, and to the many private enterprises that make a business of providing commuter train services. It is only in the last few years (since about 1990) that any females could be seen working at these jobs; their numbers are still very small.

12. I witnessed such a suicide once. It stopped the trains on this particular line for about 15 minutes and slowed them for about two hours while an army of railway employees and city police cleaned up the area. In an amazing example of the versatility of tools that are part of a nation's material culture, I was astounded to see that the smallest pieces of human tissue were collected with chopsticks.

13. It is important to add that there are many accusations against police and prison officials in Japan with respect to serious human rights violations.

14. Largely because of the exceptional brutality of the crime, police suspect that the supermarket murders mentioned above may have been committed by non-Japanese (*Daily Yomiuri*, 30 July 1996, p. 2).

15. There is also a postal code for each address. This is used to assign mail to the correct post office.

CHAPTER 3

1. An excellent source for details about the construction of Edo Castle, especially its *tenshu* or central tower, is the new book by William Coaldrake, *Architecture and Authority in Japan* (Coaldrake, 1996, pp. 129–37).

2. This style of *sushi* has since spread widely to be the most popular type of *sushi* in Japanese restaurants around the world.

3. It is not known exactly how the Long-Sleeves Fire started. While some versions have it that the kimono was being worn when it ignited, another story says that the kimono was deliberately set afire in a religious ceremony because it had brought unusually bad luck to all previous owners. In either event, a great wind is said to have come along and spread the flames (Nouèt, 1990, p. 105).

4. The present Naniwachō district.

5. A financial combine or group of closely related companies.

6. There is still a clock in a two-story tower at the same intersection. However, the building that it graces is a newer (1932) structure, now the Wako department store, and the clock is actually a Seiko quartz model (Waley, 1988b, p. 7).

7. This building was also called the *Jūnikai*, 'the twelve-story'.

8. Since this paragraph was originally written a large museum dedicated to Tokyo's history was opened in Sumida Ward near Cenotaph Hall. It is called the Edo–Tokyo Museum and is operated by Tokyo Metropolitan Government. It is a wonderful resource for the study of the city's history, as well as a marvelous piece of post-modern architecture. On the point being made here, it is interesting to note that this museum's exhibit about the air raids is also low-key. At the time I am writing this (early 1997), construction is underway in Chiyoda Ward on a memorial hall honoring Japan's war dead from the Second World War. It was supposed to have opened in 1995 to coincide with the 50th anniversary of the war's end, but disputes about the design of the building itself and its contents have caused a delay.

9. The 'yokochō' part of 'Ameyayokochō' means alley.

10. The Eiffel Tower was 300 meters high until 1959, when the addition of a radio antenna increased the height to 320 meters.

CHAPTER 4

1. Life expectancy for males born in Tokyo in 1990 is 76.04 years. For females the figure is 81.94 years. The comparable figures for Japan as a whole are 75.92 and 81.90 years, respectively (*Tokyo Statistical Yearbook, 1994*, Table 19, pp. 48–9).
2. However, during the economic recession of the 1990s, vacancy rates have been somewhat higher.
3. There is an excellent new book on this topic that appeared just as this book was entering final production (Clammer, 1997).
4. Important exceptions are noted several paragraphs below.
5. The current official plan, *The 3rd Long-Term Plan for the Tokyo Metropolis*, contains similar language, as well as the added objective that Tokyo should 'give full scope to its experience and expertise in contributing to the solution of urban problems facing the world and to the conservation of the global environment' (Tokyo Metropolitan Government, 1991, p. 36).
6. Another prominent model home park temporarily occupied the large redevelopment site at Shiodome in the CBD, mentioned earlier.
7. The source is *Tokyo Municipal News*, **38**, No. 2, 1988, p. 8. The poll was conducted in November 1987 of 3000 men and women aged 20 and over, but was not broken down according to where in Tokyo respondents lived.
8. There is more detail about the Imperial Palace compound in the next chapter.

CHAPTER 5

1. Tokyo Tower, located further south from the palace than the Kasumigaseki Building, offers a partial view only, because the Kasumigaseki Building blocks all but a small part of the imperial residence.
2. Other aspects of this scheme, in addition to those that concern Shinjuku specifically, are discussed in Chapter 6.
3. This is a complicated topic. It is not just New York that is copied in Shinjuku; even my home city of Philadelphia is in evidence there. There is a replica of the Liberty Bell affixed high near the top of one of the Shinjuku high-rises, and a reproduction of Philadelphia's bright-red landmark LOVE sculpture by Robert Indiana in the plaza in front of another new building.
4. This is done also in Ginza and many other of the biggest shopping districts in Tokyo and other Japanese cities.
5. A number of restaurants, including a McDonald's I know, take fax orders from workers who can't leave their offices for a meal.
6. The massage parlors used to be called *toruko-buro* ('Turkish baths') until complaints from a Turkish student in Tokyo and the Turkish embassy led to the new name.
7. The unusual name for a store, 109 and its various derivations, comes from a play on the word Tōkyū: one meaning in Japanese for the sound *to* is 'ten' and for *kyu* is 'nine.'
8. This is a new word and means 'casually dressed in Shibuya' ('Police Target "Shibukajizoku" Youths', *Japan Times*, 5 March 1990, p. 2).
9. There is a gate like this as well at a main entrance to Shinjuku's Kabukichō.
10. See the discussion of homelessness below.
11. This is an average based on 20 904 000 riders getting on at Musashisakai each year, and includes both in- and out-bound traffic.

12. Although this is a number that is big enough to constitute a substantial city or town, the station itself, with its 57 000-plus daily riders, is only moderate in size on the scale of Tokyo.

13. Once I looked through the door of a small school that teaches English and saw the teacher explaining the sentence 'I help pigs' that she had written on the board.

CHAPTER 6

1. There is a new, very nicely illustrated book on this topic in English by Tokyo Metropolitan Government that I highly recommend: *A Hundred Years of Tokyo City Planning* (Tokyo Metropolitan Government, 1994d).

2. The provision for greenbelts was actually a revival of a 1939 plan for Tokyo called the Tokyo Green Space Plan. Like the 1958 idea, it too was based on an English model, but was interrupted by the war and was never put into effect.

3. The slogan was expressed in English, much like commercial advertising slogans in Japan often are.

4. This is the English-language edition. The Japanese edition has the same illustration. My analysis of this and other illustrations in Tokyo planning documents is patterned after the methodology developed by anthropologist Constance Perin in her book about the planning profession in the United States (Perin, 1977).

5. The cover of the *3rd Long-Term Plan for the Tokyo Metropolis* published in 1991 illustrates the same pattern. The main difference is that the family has been reunited: mom, pop, their two children, grandma and grandpa, and the dog are shown standing together in a leafy-green setting, with the skyscrapers of the city (and a Shintō shrine) in the distant background.

6. Its formal name is Tokyo International Exhibition Center.

7. The political issues in the election were more complex than just those dealing with government spending at the waterfront. Voter dissatisfaction with the LDP and with the nation's uncustomarily weak economy were also important. On the same day as the election was held in Tokyo, voters in Osaka also elected a new governor, 'Knock' Yokoyama, another independent candidate and television comedian-turned-politician.

8. See the excellent analysis of public art at Tokyo's new redevelopment projects, emphasizing its sexist aspects, by Shimizu (1994).

9. The nickname Makuhari Messe is eagerly promoted by Chiba government and other developers of the project because, according to them, the words 'messe' and 'convention' 'are used much in the same way in the international community,' and both 'mean a place for comprehensive communication, integrating people, objects and information' (Chiba Nippōsha, 1989, p. 103).

10. An excellent summary of this topic is Natori (1997).

CHAPTER 7

1. My choice of wording here refers to the excellent history of Tokyo's recent growth by Edward Seidensticker (1990) and the terrific title that he chose for his book, *Tokyo Rising*.

2. I have the urge to write its name as 'GeoTRAPolis'.

LIST OF FIGURES

LIST OF TABLES

BIBLIOGRAPHY

Alden, J. 1984: 'Metropolitan Planning in Japan', *Town Planning Review*, **55**, 1, pp. 55–74.

Alden, J. 1986: 'Some Strengths and Weaknesses of Japanese Urban Planning', *Town Planning Review*, **57**, 2, pp. 127–34.

Alford, R. T. 1996: 'Shinjuku's Homeless', *Asahi Evening News*, 28 January, p. 6 and 11–12 February, p. 6.

Allinson, G. D. 1975: *Japanese Urbanism: Industry and Politics in Kariya, 1872–1972*. Berkeley: University of California Press.

Allinson, G. D. 1978: 'Japanese Cities in the Industrial Era', *Journal of Urban History*, **4**, 4, pp. 443–76.

Allinson, G. D. 1979: *Suburban Tokyo: A Comparative Study in Politics and Social Change*. Berkeley and Los Angeles: University of California Press.

Allinson, G. D. 1984: 'Japanese Urban Society and Its Cultural Context', in *The City in Cultural Context*, J. A. Agnew, J. Mercer, and D. E. Sopher (eds), pp. 163–85. Boston: Allen & Unwin.

Arisue, T. and Aoki, E. 1970: 'The Development of Railway Network in the Tokyo Region from the Viewpoint of the Metropolitan Growth,' In *Japanese Cities: A Geographical Approach*. S. Kiuchi *et al.* (eds), pp. 191–200. Tokyo: The Association of Japanese Geographers.

Ashihara, Y. 1987: 'Chaos and Order in the Japanese City,' *Japan Echo*, **XIV**, Special Issue, pp. 64–8.

Ashihara, Y. 1989: *The Hidden Order: Tokyo through the Twentieth Century*. Tokyo and New York: Kodansha.

Awata, F. 1988: 'Disneyland's Dreamlike Success', *Japan Quarterly*, **35**, 1, pp. 58–62.

Awata, F. 1989: 'Making Magic Pay', *Look Japan*, **35**, 401, August, pp. 4–7.

Barr, C. W. 1997a: 'Rocks Set by Crows Rattle JR East', *The Japan Times*, 5 February, p. 6.

Barr C. W. 1997b: 'Tokyo's Survivors: Islands of Old in Oceans of New', *Christian Science Monitor*, 5 February, pp. 10–11.

Barr, P. 1968: *The Deer Cry Pavilion: A Story of Westerners in Japan, 1868–1905*. New York: Harcourt, Brace & World, Inc.

Barthes, R. 1982: *Empire of Signs*. London: Jonathan Cape.

Bayley, D. H. 1991: *Forces of Order: Policing Modern Japan*. Berkeley: University of California Press.

Bennett, J. W. and Levine, S. B. 1977: 'Industrialization and Urbanization in Japan: The Emergence of Public Discontent', *Habitat*, **2**, No. 1/2, pp. 205–18.

Bestor, T. C. 1989a: *Neighborhood Tokyo*. Stanford, California: Stanford University Press.

Bestor, T. C. 1989b: '*Tōkyō no Daidokoro:* Research on the Tsukiji Wholesale Fish Market,' *Japan Foundation Newsletter*, **XVII**, No. 4, pp. 17–21.

Bestor, T. C. 1990: 'Tokyo Mom-and-Pop,' *Wilson Quarterly*, **XIV**, 4, Autumn, pp. 27–33.

Betros, C. 1985a: 'Down and Out in Tokyo', *Japananlysis*, 1–2, February, pp. 20–1.

Betros, C. 1985b: 'The Shepherds of Sanya', *Asahi Evening News*, 25 January, p. 3.

Betros, C. 1988: 'Tsukiji: *Afish*ionados', *Look Japan*, **34**, 391, pp. 54–5.

Blake, S. L. 1995: *Spatial and Social Structures of Tokyo's Ethnic Communities*. Unpublished PhD Dissertation, University of Tokyo.

Booth, A. 1985: *The Roads to Sata: A 2000-Mile Journey through Japan*. New York: Weatherhill.

Bureau of Reconstruction and the Tokyo Institute for Municipal Research, 1929: *The Outline of the Reconstruction Work in Tokyo and Yokohama*. Tokyo: Sugitaya Press.

Burks, A. W. 1984: *Japan: A Postindustrial Power*. Boulder and London: Westview Press.

Busch, N. F. 1962: *Two Minutes to Noon*. New York: Simon and Schuster.

Caldarola, C. 1968–9: 'The *Doya-Gai*: A Japanese Version of Skid Row', *Pacific Affairs*, **XLI**, 4, pp. 511–25.

Center for Urban Studies (ed.) 1988: *Tokyo: Urban Growth and Planning, 1868–1988*. Tokyo: Tokyo Metropolitan University Center for Urban Studies.

Chapman, C. 1987: 'Denenchōfu: An Oasis of Spacious Living', *Look Japan*, 33, 377, pp. 38–9.

Chen, N. Y. and Heligman, L. 1994: 'Growth of the World's Megalopolises', in *Mega-city Growth and the Future*. Fuchs, R. J., Brennan, E., Chamie, J., Lo, F., and Uitto, J. I. (eds). Tokyo: United Nations University Press.

Christopher, R. C. 1983: *The Japanese Mind*. New York: Fawcett.

City Planning Association of Japan (ed.) 1969: *City Planning in Japan*. Tokyo: Sugitaya Printing Co.

Clammer, J. 1997: *Contemporary Urban Japan: A Sociology of Consumption*. Oxford: Blackwell.

Clay, G. 1973: *Close-Up: How to Read the American City*. Chicago: The University of Chicago Press.

Coaldrake, W. H. 1986: 'Order and Anarchy: Tokyo from 1868 to the Present,' in *Tokyo: Form and Spirit*, M. Friedman (ed.), pp. 63–75. Minneapolis: Walker Art Center/New York: Harry N. Abrams, Inc.

Coaldrake, W. H., 1996: *Architecture and Authority in Japan*. London: Routledge.

Collcutt, M., Jansen, M. and Kumakura, I. 1988: *Cultural Atlas of Japan*. New York: Facts on File Publications.

Connor, J. and Yoshida, M. 1984: *Tokyo City Guide*. Tokyo: Ryuko Tsushin, Co.

Crowell, T. 1994: 'Tokyo of the Future: Dazzling Ideas that Will Reshape City Life', *Asia Week*, 1 May, 34–5, 38, 40–4, cover.

'Crows Caught in the Act', *The Japan Times*, 26 June 1991, p. 2.

Cybriwsky, R. 1988a: 'Shibuya Center, Tokyo', *Geographical Review*, **78**, 1, January, pp. 48–61.

Cybriwsky, R. 1988b: 'Takadanobaba: The Shogun and the Show Girl', *Look Japan*, **34**, 392, pp. 38–9.

Cybriwsky, R. 1993: 'Tokyo', *Cities: The International Journal of Urban Policy and Planning*, **10**, 1, pp. 2–11.

Cybriwsky, R. 1997: 'From Castle Town to Manhattan Town with Suburbs: A Geographical Account of Tokyo's Changing Landscapes', in *The Japanese City*, P. P. Karan and K. Stapleton (eds), pp. 56–78. Lexington: University of Kentucky Press.

Daniels, G. 1977: 'The Great Tokyo Air Raid, 9–10 March 1945', in *Modern Japan: Aspects of History, Literature and Society*, W. G. Beasley (ed.), pp. 113–31 and 278–9. Berkeley and Los Angeles: University of California Press.

Davies, B. *et al*. 1990: 'Upon a Property Seesaw', *South*, No. 112, February, pp. 13–16.

de Bary, B. 1988: 'Sanya: Japan's Internal Colony', in *The Other Japan: Postwar Realities*. E. P. Tsurumi (ed.), pp. 112–18. Armonk, New York and London: M. E. Sharpe.

Dogan, M. and Kasarda, J. D., 1988: 'Introduction: How Giant Cities Will Multiply and Grow', in *The Metropolis Era, Vol. 1: A World of Giant Cities*. M. Dogan and J. D. Kasarda (eds), pp. 12–29. Newbury Park, CA: Sage.

Doi, T. 1968: 'Japan Megalopolis: Another Approach', *Ekistics*, **26**, 152, July, pp. 96–9.

Dore, R. P. 1958: *City Life in Japan: A Study of a Tokyo Ward*. Berkeley and Los Angeles: University of California Press.

Douglass, M. 1988: 'The Transnationalization of Urbanization in Japan', *International Journal of Urban and Regional Research*, **12**, 3, pp. 425–54.

Douglass, M. 1993: 'The "New" Tokyo Story: Restructuring Space and the Struggle for Place in a World City', in *Japanese Cities in the World Economy*, K. Fujita and R. C. Hill (eds), pp. 83–119. Philadelphia: Temple University Press.

Downer, L. 1994: *The Brothers: The Hidden World of Japan's Richest Family*. New York: Random House.

Drennan, M. R. 1996: 'The Dominance of Finance by London, New York and Tokyo', in *The*

Global Economy in Transition. P. W. Daniels and W. F. Lever (eds), pp. 352–71. Harlow: Addison-Wesley Longman.

Eastham, K. 1995: 'Requiem for a Neighborhood', *Tokyo Journal*, October, pp. 33–6.

Edgington, D. 1991: 'Economic Restructuring in Yokohama: From Gateway Port to International Core City', *Asian Geographer*, **10**, 1, pp. 62–78.

Enbutsu, S. 1984: *Discover Shitamachi: A Walking Guide to the Other Tokyo*. Tokyo: The Shitamachi Times, Inc.

Enbutsu, S. 1993: *Old Tokyo: Walks in the City of the Shogun*. Rutland, VT and Tokyo: Charles E. Tuttle.

Fallows, J. 1986: 'The Japanese are Different from You and Me', *The Atlantic*, **258**, 3, September, pp. 35–41.

Fallows, J. 1988: 'The Other Japan', *The Atlantic*, **261**, 4, April, pp. 16–18 and 20.

Fallows, J. 1989: 'Tokyo: The Hard Life', *The Atlantic*, **263**, 3, March, pp. 16–26.

Fawcett, C. 1986: 'Tokyo's Silent Space', in *Tokyo: Form and Spirit*, Mildred Friedman (ed.), pp. 179–91. Minneapolis: Walker Art Center/ New York: Harry N. Abrams, Inc.

Forbis, W. H. 1975: *Japan Today: People, Places, Power*. Tokyo: Charles E. Tuttle.

Fowler, E. 1996: *San'ya Blues: Laboring Life in Contemporary Tokyo*. Ithaca and London: Cornell University Press.

Friedman, M. (ed.) 1986: *Tokyo: Form and Spirit*. Minneapolis: Walker Art Center/New York: Harry N. Abrams, Inc.

Fujii, N. 1987: 'Directions for Growth', *Japan Echo*, **XIV**, Special Issue, pp. 12–19.

Fujimori, S. 1984: 'Kanto's Main Problem is Growing Urbanization', *Asahi Evening News*, 29 September.

Fujimori, T. 1987a: 'Shitamachi, In Tokyo's Left Hand', *Japan Quarterly*, **34**, 4, October/ December, pp. 410–17.

Fujimori, T. 1987b: 'Urban Planning in the Meiji Era', *Japan Echo*, **XIV**, Special Issue, pp. 45–9.

Fujimoto, K. 1987: 'Trying to Save Tokyo Station', *The Japan Times*, 15 November, p. 8.

Fujioka, W, 1989: 'Learning to Live the Good Life', *Japan Echo*, **XVI**, 2, Summer, pp. 30–4.

Fujita, K. and Hill, R. C. 1993: *Japanese Cities in the World Economy*. Philadelphia: Temple University Press.

Gill, T. 1990: 'Sanbanchō's Last Stand', *Tokyo Journal*, **9**, No. 11, February, pp. 82–6.

Gill, T. 1994: 'Sanya Street Life under the Heisei Recession', *Japan Quarterly*, **41**, July– September, pp. 270–86.

Gluck, P. 1977: 'Shinjuku', *Architectural Record*, **162**, September, pp. 101–4.

Golany, G. S. and Ojima, T. 1996: *Geo-Space Urban Design*. New York: John Wiley.

Greenbie, B. B. 1988: *Space and Spirit in Modern Japan*. New Haven and London: Yale University Press.

Guillain, R. 1981: *I Saw Tokyo Burning: An Eyewitness Narrative from Pearl Harbor to Hiroshima*, W. Byron (trans.) Garden City, New York: Doubleday & Company, Inc.

Guzewicz, T. D., 1996a: 'A New Generation of Homeless', *Japan Quarterly*, **43**, 3, 43–53.

Guzewicz, T. D., 1996b: 'Out of Sight, Out of Mind, Out of Reach', *Asahi Evening News*, 4 February, p. 6.

Haberman, C. 1987: 'Tokyo Aims to Reshape Itself as a "World Class City"', *The New York Times*, 8 February, p. 14.

Hadfield, P. 1992: *Sixty Seconds That Will Change the World: The Coming Tokyo Earthquake*. London: Pan Books.

'Hachiōji Market Killings Remain Unsolved', *Daily Yomiuri*, 30 July 1996, p. 2.

Hall, P. 1984: *The World Cities*. London: Weidenfeld and Nicolson.

Hane, M. 1982: *Peasants, Rebels and Outcastes: The Underside of Modern Japan*. New York: Pantheon Books.

Hattori, K., Sugimura, N. and Higuchi, S. 1980: 'Urbanization and Commercial Zones', in *Geography of Japan*. Association of Japanese Geographers (ed.), pp. 320–46. Tokyo: Teikoku-Shōin.

Hayase, Y. 1974: *The Career of Gōtō Shinpei: Japan's Statesman of Research, 1857–1929*. PhD Dissertation, Florida State University.

244

Hebbert, M. 1986: 'Urban Sprawl and Urban Planning in Japan', *Town Planning Review*, **57**, 2, pp. 141–58.

Holloway, N. 1988: 'Tokyo: Time to Tame the Monster of the Capital', *Far Eastern Economic Review*, **16**, June, pp. 53–5.

Honjō, M. 1975: 'Tokyo: Giant Metropolis of the Orient', in *World Capitals: Toward Guided Urbanization*. H. W. Eldredge (ed.), pp. 340–87. Garden City, New York: Anchor Press/ Doubleday.

Hovinen, G. R. 1988: 'The Search for Quality of Life in Japanese Planned Communities', *Proceedings of the Middle States Division of the Association of American Geographers*, 21, pp. 47–56.

Imaoka, K. 1988: 'Regional Tribute-Bearers in the Capital', *Japan Echo*, **XV**, 3, pp. 55–8.

Inouchi, N. 1987: *Tokyo*. Tokyo: International Society for Educational Information.

Ishida, Y. 1988a: 'Chronology on Urban Planning in Tokyo, 1868–1988', in *Tokyo: Urban Growth and Planning, 1868–1988*. Center for Urban Studies (ed.), pp. 37–68. Tokyo: Tokyo Metropolitan University Center for Urban Studies.

Ishida, Y. 1988b: 'Ougai Mori and Tokyo's Building Ordinance', in *Tokyo: Urban Growth and Planning, 1868–1988*. Center for Urban Studies (ed.), pp. 83–6. Tokyo: Tokyo Metropolitan University Center for Urban Studies.

Ishimizu, T. and Ishihara, H. 1980: 'The Distribution and Movement of Population in Japan's Three Major Metropolitan Areas', in *Geography of Japan*. Association of Japanese Geographers (ed.), pp. 347–78. Tokyo: Teikoku-Shōin.

Ishizuka, H. and Ishida, Y. 1988: 'Tokyo, the Metropolis of Japan and Its Urban Development', in *Tokyo: Urban Growth and Planning, 1868–1988*. Center for Urban Studies (ed.), pp. 3–35. Tokyo: Tokyo Metropolitan University Center for Urban Studies.

Isoda, K. 1987: 'Tokyo and the Mythology of Modernity', *Japan Echo*, **XIV**, Special Issue, pp. 59–63.

Isomura, E. 1960: 'Tokyo: An International City', *New Japan*, **12**, pp. 26–8.

Itakura, K. and Takeuchi, A. 1980: 'Keihin Region', in *An Industrial Geography of Japan*. K. Murata and I. Ota (eds), pp. 47–65. New York: St Martin's Press.

Ito, M. 1988: 'Coming to Terms with the Tokyo Problem', *Japan Echo*, **XV**, 3, pp. 50–4.

'Japanese Property: A Glittering Sprawl', *The Economist*, 3 October, pp. 25–8.

Japan Almanac 1996, 1995: Tokyo: Asahi Shimbun.

Jefferson, M. 1939: 'The Law of the Primate Cities', *Geographical Review*, **29**, pp. 226–32.

Jinnai, H. 1987: 'Tokyo Then and Now: Keys to Japanese Urban Design', *Japan Echo*, **XIV**, Special Issue, pp. 20–9.

Jinnai, H. 1988: *Ethnic Tokyo*. Tokyo: Process Architecture, No. 72.

Jinnai, H. 1990a: 'Can the Tokyo Waterfront be Revitalized?' *International Social Science Journal*, **42**, 3, 379–86.

Jinnai, H. 1990b: 'The Spatial Structure of Edo', in *Tokugawa Japan: Social and Economic Antecedents of Modern Japan*, C. Nakane and S. Ōisi (eds), C. Totman (trans.). Tokyo: University of Tokyo Press.

Jinnai, H. 1993: 'Parks and Squares in the Scheme of Tokyo's Urban Spaces', Paper presented at the annual meeting of the Association for Asian Studies, Los Angeles, 25–28 March.

Jinnai, H. 1995: *Tokyo: A Spatial Anthropology*. K. Nishimura (trans.). Berkeley and Los Angeles: University of California Press.

Jones, H. J. 1980: *Live Machines: Hired Foreigners and Meiji Japan*. Tenterden: Paul Norbury Publications.

Karan, P. P. and Stapleton, K. 1997: *The Japanese City*. Lexington: University of Kentucky Press.

Katayama, O. 1989: 'The Spice of Life', *Look Japan*, **34**, 394, January, pp. 4–7.

Katō, H. 1979: 'Comparative Study of Street Life: Tokyo, Manila, New York', Tokyo: Gakushuin University for Oriental Cultures. Occasional Paper No. 5.

Katō, H. 1987: 'Tokyo Comes of Age', *Japan Echo*, **XIV**, Special Issue, pp. 8–11.

Katō, Y. 1990: *Yokohama Past and Present*. Yokohama: Yokohama City University.

Kauffman, R. 1988: 'Tokyo's Housing Dilemma: Who's Paying the Price?' *Tokyo Journal*, **8**, 1, pp. 78–83 and 104.

Kawai, K. 1960: *Japan's American Interlude*. Chicago: University of Chicago Press.

Kawamoto, S. 1987: 'Okubo: Ethnic Melting Pot', *Japan Echo*, **XIV**, Special Issue, pp. 73–6.

Kawazoe, N. 1987: 'The Flower Culture of Edo', *Japan Echo*, **XIV**, Special Issue, pp. 53–8.

Kelley, W. W. 1994: 'Incendiary Actions: Fires and Firefighting in the Shogun's Capital and the People's City', in *Edo and Paris: Urban Life and the State in the Early Modern Era*. J. L. McClain, J. M. Merriman and K. Ugawa (eds), pp. 310–31. Ithaca and London: Cornell University Press.

Kennedy, R. 1988: *Home, Sweet Tokyo: Life in a Weird and Wonderful City*. Tokyo and New York: Kodansha International.

Kennerdell, J. 1988: 'Golden-Gai', *Tokyo Journal*, **8**, 4 (supplement), p. 13.

Kenzo Tange Associates 1991–3: 'The New Tokyo City Hall Complex', *The Japan Architect*, **3**, Summer, pp. 16–43.

Kim, M. 1993: *The State, Housing Producers, and Housing Consumers in Tokyo and Seoul*. Unpublished PhD dissertation, Brown University.

Kingston, J. 1988: 'Artist Captures the Charm of Old Tokyo', *The Japan Times*, 18 December, p. 5.

Kiritani, E. 1995: *Vanishing Japan: Traditions, Crafts and Culture*. Rutland, VT: Charles E. Tuttle.

Kirwan, R. M. 1987: 'Fiscal Policy and the Price of Land and Housing in Japan', *Urban Studies*, **24**, pp. 345–60.

Kishi, N. 1987: 'On the Waterfront', *Business Tokyo*, May, pp. 18–21 and 25.

Knox, P. 1982: *Urban Social Geography: An Introduction*. London and New York: Longman.

Kojiro, Y. 1986: 'Edo: The City on the Plain', in *Tokyo: Form and Spirit*. Mildred Friedman, (ed.), pp. 37–53. Minneapolis: Walker Art Center/New York: Harry N. Abrams, Inc.

Kosai, Y. 1986: *The Era of High-Speed Growth: Notes on the Postwar Japanese Economy*. Tokyo: University of Tokyo Press.

Kornhauser, D. 1982: *Japan: Geographical Background to Urban–Industrial Development*. London and New York: Longman.

Kurasawa, S. 1986: *Social Atlas of Tokyo*. Tokyo: University of Tokyo Press.

Kurokawa, K. 1987: 'New Tokyo Plan, 2025', *The Japan Architect*, 367/378, pp. 46–63.

Kurokawa, N. 1990: 'Getting Serious About Land Prices', *Japan Quarterly*, **37**, 4, pp. 392–401.

Lane, R. 1978: *Images from the Floating World: The Japanese Print*. Secaucus, New Jersey: Chartwell Books.

Lee, C. and DeVos, G. 1981: *Koreans in Japan: Ethnic Conflict and Accommodation*. Berkeley and Los Angeles: University of California Press.

Levin, M. 1986: 'Staunching the Flow of Pornography: Band-aid on a Bullet Wound', *Tokyo Journal*, **6**, 8, pp. 46–8.

Levy, D., Sneider, L. and Gibney, F. B. 1983: *Kanban: Shop Signs of Japan*. New York and Tokyo: Weatherhill.

Lewis, M. 1989: 'How a Tokyo Earthquake Could Devastate Wall Street and the World Economy', *Manhattan, Inc.*, June, pp. 69–79.

Lewis, P. F. 1976: *New Orleans: The Making of an Urban Landscape*. Cambridge: Ballinger Publishing Co.

Littleton, S. 1986: 'The Organization and Management of a Tokyo Shrine Festival', *Ethnology*, **25**, 195–202.

Lockheimer, F. R. 1967: 'The People's Choice: Ryōkichi Minobe', *East Asia Series* (American University Field Staff), **XIV**, 4 (Japan), pp. 1–18.

Longstreet, S. and Longstreet, E. 1988: *Yoshiwara: The Pleasure Quarters of Old Tokyo*. Rutland, VT and Tokyo: Yenbooks.

Ma, K. 1989: 'Parking Lot or Pond', *The Daily Yomiuri*. 11 September.

McClain, J. L., Merriman, J. M. and Ugawa, K. (eds) 1994: *Edo and Paris: Urban Life and the State in the Early Modern Era*. Ithaca and London: Cornell University Press.

Machimura, T. 1992: 'The Urban Restructuring Process in Tokyo in the 1980s: Transforming Tokyo into a World City', *International Journal of Urban and Regional Research*, **16**, 1, pp. 114–28.

Machimura, T. 1994: *The Structural Change of a Global City*. Tokyo: University of Tokyo Press.

Maekawa, M. and Takezawa, K. 1988: 'Two Cities Bid for the Capital', *Japan Echo*, **XV**, 2, pp. 22–7.

Mammen, D. 1990: 'Toward an Urban Policy for Central Tokyo', *Japan Quarterly*, **37**, 4, pp. 402–14.

Marlin, J. T., Ness, I. and S. T. Collins 1986: *Book of World City Rankings*. New York: The Free Press.

Martin, J. H. and Martin, P. G. 1996: *Tokyo: A Cultural Guide to Japan's Capital City*. Rutland, VT and Tokyo: Charles E. Tuttle.

Masai, Y. 1986: *Atlas Tokyo: Edo/Tokyo through Maps*. Tokyo: Heibonsha.

Masai, Y. 1990: 'Tokyo: From a Feudal Million City to a Global Supercity', *Geographical Review of Japan*, **63** (Ser. B), No. 1, pp. 1–16.

Masai, Y. 1994: 'Urban Development of Edo, Tokyo, and the Tokyo Region', Rissho University offprint, No. 10.

Masler, D. 1987: 'Tsukudajima: An Island in Time', *Look Japan*, **33**, 237, pp. 38–9.

Mason, R. J. 1996: 'Transplanted Landscapes: The American Scene in Tokyo', *Society for Commercial Archaeology Journal*, **14**, 2, pp. 10–14.

Matsuda, K. 1988: 'A Bold Plan to Remodel Tokyo's Business Center', *Japan Echo*, **XV**, 2, pp. 28–30.

Matsushita, M. and Lo, J. 1988: 'Selling Culture: Department Stores – Cross-Cultural Comparisons', *Look Japan*, **34**, 393, December, pp. 7–9.

Meech-Pekarik, J. 1986: *The World of the Meiji Print: Impressions of a New Civilization*. New York and Tokyo: Weatherhill.

Miyamoto, K. 1993: 'Japan's World Cities: Osaka and Tokyo Compared', in *Japanese Cities in the World Economy*, K. Fujita and R. C. Hill (eds), pp. 53–83. Philadelphia: Temple University Press.

Miyazawa, S. 1992: *Policing in Japan: A Study on Making Crime*. Albany: State University of New York Press.

Morris-Suzuki, T. 1985: *Showa: An Inside History of Hirohito's Japan*. New York: Schocken Books.

Munsterberg, H. 1982: *The Japanese Print: A Historical Guide*. Tokyo: Weatherhill.

Murata, K. and Ōta, I. (eds) 1980: *An Industrial Geography of Japan*. New York: St Martin's Press.

Nagaharu, H. 1988: 'The Tsutsumi Brothers, Feuding Magnates', *Japan Quarterly*, **35**, 2, pp. 192–5.

Nagai, K. 1972: *A Strange Tale from East of the River and Other Stories*. E. Seidensticker (trans.). Rutland, VT and Tokyo: Charles E. Tuttle.

Nagashima, C. 1967: 'Megalopolis in Japan', *Ekistics*, **24**, 140, pp. 6–14.

Nagashima, C. 1968: 'Japan Megalopolis: Part 2, Analysis', *Ekistics*, **26**, 152, p. 95.

Naitō, A. 1987: 'Planning and Development of Early Edo', *Japan Echo*, **XIV**, Special Issue, pp. 30–8.

Naitō, Y. 1996: 'Rocks Set by Crows Rattle JR East', *The Japan Times*, 9 July.

Nakamura, H. and White, J. 1988: 'Tokyo' in *The Metropolis Era: Mega-Cities, Volume 2*. M. Dogan and J. D. Kasarda (eds), pp. 123–56. Newbury Park, CA: Sage Publications.

Nakazawa, M. 1993: 'Tattered Lives', *Tokyo Journal*, 03/93, pp. 34–9.

National Land Policy Institute 1997. *Underground Space Use in Japan*. Tokyo: National Land Policy Institute.

Natori, M. 1997: 'Relocating Japan's Capital Functions: Current Thinking and Issues', *Nomura Research Institute Quarterly (NRI Quarterly)*, Spring.

Nishida, K. 1963: *Storied Cities of Japan*. Tokyo: Weatherhill.

Nishibe, S. 1989: 'Defending the Dignity of the Symbolic Emperor', *Japan Echo*, **XVI**, 2, pp. 22–7.

Noguchi, K. 1988: 'Construction of Ginza Brick Street and Conditions of Landowners and House Owners', in *Tokyo: Urban Growth and Planning, 1868–1988*. Center for Urban Studies (ed.), pp. 76–86. Tokyo: Tokyo Metropolitan University Center for Urban Studies.

Nouët, N. 1990: *The Shogun's City: A History of Tokyo* (translated from the French edition by J. and M. Mills). Sandgate, Folkestone: Paul Norbury Publications.

Nussbaum, S. P. 1985: *The Residential Community in Modern Japan: An Analysis of a Tokyo Suburban Development*. Unpublished PhD dissertation, Cornell University.

Obayashi, M. 1993: 'Kanagawa: Japan's Brain Center', in *Japanese Cities in the World Economy*. K. Fujita and R. C. Hill (eds), pp. 120–40. Philadelphia: Temple University Press.

Ojima, T. 1991: *Imageable Tokyo: Projects by Toshio Ojima*. Tokyo: Process Architecture.

Ōtani, K. 1990: 'Makuhari New Town', *Japan Quarterly*, **37**, 4, pp. 451–8.

Perin, C. 1977: *Everything in Its Place: Social Order and Land Use in America*. Princeton: Princeton University Press.

Phalon, R. 1988: 'Land Poor', *Forbes*, 14 November, pp. 56–62.

Pons, P. 1984: 'Shinjuku, Le Kaleidoscope Babylonien', *Autrement*, No. 8, pp. 32–9.

Pons, P. 1988: *D'Edo à Tokyo: Memoires et Modernités*. Paris: Gallimard.

Poole, O. M. 1968: *The Death of Old Yokohama in the Great Japanese Earthquake of September 1, 1923*. London: George Allen and Unwin.

Popham, P. 1985: *Tokyo: The City at the End of the World*. Tokyo: Kodansha International.

Rauch, J. 1992: *The Outnation: A Search for the Soul of Japan*. Boston: Harvard Business School Press.

Reischauer, E. O. 1981: *The Japanese*. Cambridge and London: The Belknap Press of Harvard University Press.

Relph, E. 1987: *The Modern Urban Landscape*. Baltimore: The Johns Hopkins University Press.

Richie, D. 1991: *A Lateral View: Essays on Contemporary Japan*. Tokyo: The Japan Times.

Rivas-Micoud, M., Zanghi, J. and Hirokawa, M. (eds) 1991: *Tokyo*. Singapore: APA Publications.

Robertson, J. 1987: 'Affective City Planning in Kodaira City (Tokyo)', Unpublished paper prepared for the annual meeting of the Association of American Geographers, Portland, Oregon, 22–26 April.

Robertson, J. 1991: *Native and Newcomer: Making and Remaking a Japanese City*. Berkeley and Los Angeles: University of California Press.

Robertson, J. 1987: 'A Dialectic of Native and Newcomer: The Kodaira Citizens' Festival in Modern Tokyo', *Asian Folklore Studies*, **60**, 3, 124–36.

Robinson, M. 1995: 'Trial by Fire: The Political Education of Yukio Aoshima', *Tokyo Journal*, November, pp. 32–7.

Rozman, G. 1973: *Urban Networks in Ch'ing China and Tokugawa Japan*. Princeton: Princeton University Press.

Sabouret, J.-F. 1984: 'Tokyo, Boulot, Ghetto', *Autrement*, **8**, pp. 310–11 and 314–17.

Saitō, I. 1996: 'Triple Deckers', *Asahi Evening News*, 11 July, p. 5.

Sassen, S. 1991: *The Global City: New York, London, Tokyo*. Princeton: Princeton University Press.

Satō, M. 1988: 'Shinkawa: A City Center is Born', *Japan Echo*, **XV**, 2, pp. 31–3.

Scoggins, G. 1989: 'Yokohama: The City Across the Bay', in *Yokohama: City of Firsts*, pp. 8–11. Tokyo: Cross Cultural Communications.

'The Secrets of Japan's Safe Streets', *The Economist*, 16 April 1994, pp. 90–6.

Seidensticker, E. 1983: *Low City, High City: Tokyo from Edo to the Earthquake*. Rutland, VT and Tokyo: Charles E. Tuttle.

Seidensticker, E. 1990: *Tokyo Rising: The City Since the Great Earthquake*. New York: Alfred A. Knopf.

Seigle-Segawa, C. 1993: *Yoshiwara: The Glittering World of the Japanese Courtesan*. Honolulu: University of Hawaii Press.

Seymour, C., 1991: 'A Look at the Other Japan: Sanya's Dying Mavericks', *The New Leader*, **74**, 12, 8–10.

Shapira, P., Masser, I. and Edgington, D. (eds) 1994: *Planning for Cities and Regions in Japan*. Liverpool: Liverpool University Press.

248

Shibusawa, K. 1958: *Japanese Life and Culture in the Meiji Era*. C. S. Terry (trans.). Tokyo: Ōbunsha.

Shimizu, A. 1994: *Sexism in Tokyo's New Public Art: Results from Field Research and Opinion Surveys*. Unpublished MA Thesis, Temple University.

Short, K. 1988: 'Tokyo Bay: An Ecosystem in the Clutches of Development', *The Japan Times*, 24 February, p. 16.

Simmons, D. 1988: 'Asakusa: Into the Twilight Zone', *Look Japan*, **33**, 386, pp. 38–9.

Smith, C. 1988a: 'Paying for Past Neglect', *Far Eastern Economic Review*, **16**, June, pp. 49–51.

Smith, C. 1988b: 'Tokyo: Retain the City, but Shift the Functions', *Far Eastern Economic Review*, **16**, June, pp. 55–6.

Smith, C. 1988c: 'Japan's Regions: Solving the Development Imbalance', *Far Eastern Economic Review*, **16**, June, p. 56.

Smith, H. D. II 1973: 'The Tyranny of Tokyo in Modern Japanese Culture', *Studies on Japanese Culture*, **2**, pp. 367–71.

Smith, H. D. II 1978: 'Tokyo as an Idea: An Exploration of Japanese Urban Thought Until 1945', *The Journal of Japanese Studies*, **4**, 1, pp. 45–80.

Smith, H. D. II 1979: 'Tokyo and London: Comparative Conceptions of the City', in *Japan: A Comparative View*. A. M. Craig (ed.), pp. 49–99. Princeton: Princeton University Press.

Smith, H. D. II 1986a: 'Sky and Water: The Deep Structures of Tokyo', in *Tokyo: Form and Spirit*. M. Friedman (ed.), pp. 21–35. Minneapolis: Walker Art Center/New York: Harry N. Abrams, Inc.

Smith, H. D. II 1986b: 'Edo-Toyko Transition: Search of Common Ground', in *Japan in Transition: From Tokugawa to Meiji*. M. B. Jansen and G. Rozman (eds), pp. 347–74. Princeton: Princeton University Press.

Smith, T. C. 1973: 'Pre-Modern Economic Growth: Japan and the West', *Past and Present*, **60**, pp. 127–60.

Sorkin, M. 1992: *Variations on a Theme Park: The New American City and the End of Public Space*. New York: Hill and Wang.

Spivak, M. 1987: 'Kichijōji: What More Could You Want?', *Look Japan*, **33**, 378, pp. 38–9.

Stanley, T. A. 1983: 'Tokyo Earthquake of 1923', in *Kodansha Encyclopedia of Japan, Vol. 8*, p. 66. Tokyo: Kodansha.

Steiner, K. 1965: *Local Government in Japan*. Stanford: Stanford University Press.

Sternberg, R. 1985: 'Shibuya Town Playguide', *Tokyo Journal*, **5**, May, pp. 56–8.

Storry, R. 1960: *A History of Modern Japan*. New York: Penguin Books.

Stroh, M. 1996: '"Compensated Dates" Lead to an Outcry in Japan', *Philadelphia Inquirer*, 2 October, p. A8.

Suginohara, J. 1982: *The Status Discrimination in Japan: Introduction to Buraku Problem*. Kobe: The Hyogo Institute of Buraku Problem.

Sugiura, N. 1987: 'The Urbanization of Nostalgia: The Changing Nature of Nostalgic Landscape in Postwar Japan', Unpublished paper prepared for the annual meeting of the Association of American Geographers, Portland, Oregon, 22–26 April.

Suzuki, E. 1988: 'Makichō Avenue Project and Excess Condemnation', in *Tokyo: Urban Growth and Planning, 1868–1988*. Center for Urban Studies (ed.), pp. 87–91. Tokyo: Tokyo Metropolitan University Center for Urban Studies.

Swinbanks, D. 1988a: 'Conflicting Views on Extent of Earthquake Threat to Tokyo', *Nature*, **336**, 15 December, p. 609.

Swinbanks, D. 1988b: 'Builders Look to "Anti-Quake" Device', *Nature*, **336**, 15 December, p. 609.

Symposium Executive Committee (ed.) 1990: *Symposium on Proposed Construction of Shinobazu Pond Underground Parking Lot*, 3 March, (proceedings). Tokyo: Symposium Executive Committee.

Tabata, M. 1991: 'Symbol of the Capital City', *The Japan Times*, 10 April, p. 18.

Taira, K. 1969: 'Urban Poverty, Ragpickers, and the "Ants' Villa" in Tokyo', *Economic Development and Cultural Change*, **17**, No. 2, pp. 155–77.

Takami, M. 1988: 'A Myriad of Projects in the Offing', *The Japan Times*, 4 February, p. 16.

Takashima, S. 1987: 'Tokyo: Creative Chaos', *Japan Echo*, **XIV**, Special Issue, pp. 2–6.

Takatani, T. 1987: 'Tokyo Street Patterns: A Historical Analysis', *Japan Echo*, **XIV**, Special Issue, pp. 39–44.

Takeuchi, H. 1987: 'The Two Faces of Shinjuku', *Japan Echo*, **XIV**, Special Issue, pp. 69–72.

Takeuchi, M. 1987: 'Edo Style and the Aesthetic of *Iki*', *Japan Echo*, **XIV**, Special Issue, pp. 50–2.

Tamura, A. 1987: 'Deconcentrating Tokyo, Reconfiguring Japan', *Japan Quarterly*, **34**, 4, pp. 378–83.

Tanaka, A. 1994: *Tokyo as a City of Consumption: Space, Media and Self-Identity in Contemporary Japan*. Unpublished MA thesis, University of British Columbia.

Tanaka, K. 1972: *Building a New Japan: Remodeling the Japanese Archipelago*. Tokyo: Simul Press.

Tange, K. 1987: 'A Plan for Tokyo, 1986–', *The Japan Architect*, 367/368, pp. 8–45.

Tasker, P. 1987: *Inside Japan: Wealth, Work and Power in the New Japanese Empire*. London: Penguin Books.

Tatsuno, S. 1986: *The Technopolis Strategy: Japan, High Technology, and the Control of the Twenty-first Century*. New York: Prentice Hall.

'Tokyo Frontier', *Tokyo Municipal News*, **40**, 1, 1990, pp. 1–3.

'Tokyo in Torment: The Disoriented City', *The Economist*, 9 April, pp. 21–4.

Tokyo Metropolitan Government 1969: *Sizing Up Tokyo*. Tokyo: TMG Municipal Library No. 3.

Tokyo Metropolitan Government 1970: *An Administrative Perspective of Tokyo, 1970*. Tokyo: Tokyo Metropolitan Government.

Tokyo Metropolitan Government 1972a: *Tokyo's Housing Problem*. Tokyo: TMG Library No. 5.

Tokyo Metropolitan Government 1972b: *Tokyo for the People: Concepts for Urban Renewal*. Tokyo: TMG Municipal Library No. 6.

Tokyo Metropolitan Government 1984: *Plain Talk About Tokyo*. Tokyo: Tokyo Metropolitan Government.

Tokyo Metropolitan Government 1985: *Planning of Tokyo, 1985*. Tokyo: Tokyo Metropolitan Government.

Tokyo Metropolitan Government 1986: *The Fiscal Outlook for the Metropolis of Tokyo*. Tokyo: Tokyo Metropolitan Government.

Tokyo Metropolitan Government 1987a: *Plain Talk About Tokyo*. Tokyo: Tokyo Metropolitan Government.

Tokyo Metropolitan Government 1987b: *2nd Long-Term Plan for the Tokyo Metropolis*. Tokyo: Tokyo Metropolitan Government.

Tokyo Metropolitan Government 1988: *Planning of Tokyo, 1988*. Tokyo: Tokyo Metropolitan Government.

Tokyo Metropolitan Government 1989a: *The Fiscal Outlook for the Metropolis of Tokyo*. Tokyo: Tokyo Metropolitan Government.

Tokyo Metropolitan Government 1989b: *Tokyo: Yesterday, Today and Tomorrow*. Tokyo: Tokyo Metropolitan Government.

Tokyo Metropolitan Government 1990a: *Planning of Tokyo, 1990*. Tokyo: Tokyo Metropolitan Government.

Tokyo Metropolitan Government 1990b: *Tokyo Industry, 1990: A Graphic Overview*. Tokyo: Tokyo Metropolitan Government.

Tokyo Metropolitan Government 1991: *3rd Long-term Plan for the Tokyo Metropolis*. Tokyo: Tokyo Metropolitan Government.

Tokyo Metropolitan Government 1993: *Tokyo: The Making of a Metropolis*. Tokyo: Tokyo Metropolitan Government.

Tokyo Metropolitan Government 1994a: *Planning of Tokyo, 1994*. Tokyo: Tokyo Metropolitan Government.

Tokyo Metropolitan Government 1994b: *Tokyo Teleport Town: Metropolitan Waterfront Subcenter*. Tokyo: Tokyo Metropolitan Government.

Tokyo Metropolitan Government 1994c: *Urban White Paper on Tokyo Metropolis, 1994*. Tokyo: Tokyo Metropolitan Government.

250

Tokyo Metropolitan Government 1994d: *A Hundred Years of Tokyo City Planning*. Tokyo: Tokyo Metropolitan Government.

Tokyo Metropolitan Government 1995: *Tokyo and Earthquakes*. Tokyo: Tokyo Metropolitan Government.

Tokyo Metropolitan Government, Bureau of Labor and Economic Affairs 1996: *Industry and Labor in Tokyo 1996*. Tokyo: Tokyo Metropolitan Government.

Tokyo Statistical Yearbook, 1982: Tokyo: Tokyo Statistical Association.

Tokyo Statistical Yearbook, 1987: Tokyo: Tokyo Statistical Association.

Tokyo Statistical Yearbook, 1994: Tokyo: Tokyo Statistical Association.

Tracey, D. 1985: 'Zushi's Green Revolt', *Japanalysis*, **2–1**, February, pp. 16–19.

Trewartha, G. T. 1965: *Japan: A Geography*. Madison: University of Wisconsin Press.

Uchino, T. 1978: *Japan's Postwar Economy: An Insider's View of Its History and Its Future*. Tokyo, New York, and San Francisco: Kodansha International.

Udagawa, H. 1988: 'Tokyo Reaches the Outer Limits', *Tokyo Business Today*, April, pp. 34–7.

Ueda, T. 1990: 'Be Prepared!' *Look Japan*, **35**, 407, pp. 26–7.

Van Hook, H. 1989: 'Prime Time in Kabuki-Cho', *Tokyo Journal*, **9**, 3, pp. 4–9 and 12–17.

Vogel, E. F. 1971: *Japan's New Middle Class: The Salary Man and His Family in a Tokyo Suburb* (second edn). Berkeley, Los Angeles, London: University of California Press.

Wade, D. 1988: 'Shibuya: Old Dog, New Sticks', *Look Japan*, **34**, 393, pp. 38–9.

Wagatsuma, H. and DeVos, G. A. 1980: 'Arakawa Ward: Urban Growth and Modernization', *Rice University Studies*, **66**, 1, pp. 201–224.

Wagatsuma, H. and DeVos, G. A. 1984: *Heritage of Endurance: Family Patterns and Delinquency Formation in Urban Japan*. Berkeley and Los Angeles: University of California Press.

Waldichuk, T. 1997: 'The Changing Demand for and Provision of Leisure Facilities and Social Services for Retirement-Aged People in Bedroom Communities in Japan: A Case Study of Ushiku City', Paper presented at the 42nd International Conference of Eastern Studies, 30–31 May, Tokyo.

Waldichuk, T. and H. Whitney 1997: 'Inhabitants' Attitudes Toward Agricultural Activities and Urban Development in an Urbanizing *Konjuku* Area in the Rural–Urban Fringe of Tokyo', forthcoming paper to be published in *Geographical Review of Japan, Series B*.

Waley, P. 1984: *Tokyo Now and Then: An Explorer's Guide*. New York and Tokyo: Weatherhill.

Waley, P. 1987: 'Fukagawa: Memories of Edo', *Look Japan*, **33**, 373, pp. 38–9.

Waley, P. 1988a: 'The Shinjuku Story', *Tokyo Journal*, **8**, 4 (supplement), pp. 14–15.

Waley, P. 1988b: 'The Ginza Story', *Tokyo Journal*, **8**, 9 (supplement), pp. 5–7.

Waley, P. 1989a: 'Twelve Stories – Asakusa's Towering Cultural Achievement', *The Japan Times*, 24 January.

Waley, P. 1989b: 'Remaining *Nagaya* Serve as Reminders of a Poorer Life', *The Japan Times*, 3 September, p. 12.

Waley, P. 1991: *Tokyo: City of Stories*. New York and Tokyo: Weatherhill.

Waley, P. 1992: *Fragments of a City: A Tokyo Anthology*. Tokyo: The Japan Times.

Watanabe, H. 1992: 'Continuity and Change in Harajuku', *Japan Quarterly*, **39**, 2, pp. 238–50.

Wegener, M. 1994: 'Tokyo's Land Market and Its Impact on Housing and Urban Life', in *Planning for Cities and Regions in Japan*, P. Shapira, I. Masser and D. Edgington (eds), pp. 92–112. Liverpool: Liverpool University Press.

Wildes, H. E. 1954: *Typhoon in Tokyo: The Occupation and Its Aftermath*. New York: Macmillan.

Wilkinson, J. 1996: 'Fighting Back Against the Metropolis: Shinjuku's Homeless Speak Out', *Tokyo Observer: Radical Takes on the Metropolis*, 14, February, pp. 1 and 5.

Witherick, M. E. 1981: 'Tokyo', in *Urban Problems and Planning in the Developed World*. M. Pacione (ed.), pp. 120–56. New York: St Martin's Press.

'When the Great Quake Comes to Tokyo', *Business Tokyo*, **3**, 7, 1989, pp. 5–10.

Whitin Kiritani, E. 1987: 'Nezu: A Quiet Haven', *Look Japan*, **33**, 380, pp. 38–9.

The World Almanac and Book of Facts 1996. New York: World Almanac Books.

Woronoff, J. 1991: *Japan as – anything but – Number One*. Armonk, New York: M. E. Sharpe.

Wurman, R. S. 1984: *TokyoAccess*. New York: Access Press.

Yamaga, S. 1970: 'Urbanization in the Northern Suburbs of Tokyo', in *Japanese Cities: A Geographical Approach*. S. Kiuchi *et al.* (eds), pp. 73–8. Tokyo: Association of Japanese Geographers.

Yawata, K. 1988: 'Why and Where to Relocate the Capital', *Japan Quarterly*, **35**, pp. 127–32.

Yazaki, T. 1963: *The Japanese City: A Sociological Analysis*. San Francisco and Tokyo: Japan Publications Trading Company.

Yazaki, T. 1966: *The Socioeconomic Structure of the Tokyo Metropolitan Complex*. M. Matsuda (trans.). Honolulu: Social Science Research Institute, University of Hawaii.

Yazaki, T. 1968: *Social Change and the City in Japan: From Earliest Times Through the Industrial Revolution*. Tokyo: Japan Publications.

Yoshino, I. R. and Murakoshi, S. 1977: *The Invisible Visible Minority: Japan's Burakumin*. Osaka: Buraku Kaihō Kenkyūsho.

Zetter, J. 1986: 'Challenges for Japanese Urban Policy', *Town Planning Review*, **57**, 2, pp. 135–40.

Sources in Japanese

Chiba, M. 1990: '*Nishi Shinjuku o tsukuru kage no shuyaku tachi*' ('The Behind-the-Scenes Leaders of Nishi Shinjuku'). *Tōkyō Jin*, **31**, April, pp. 76–9.

Chiba Nippōsha. 1989: *Makuhari 2001: Official Guide Book*. Chiba: Chiba Nippōsha (in Japanese with some English text).

Eguchi, E., Nishioka Y. and Katō Y. 1985: *Sanya: Shitsuygō no gendaiteki imi* (Sanya: Today's Meaning of Unemployment). Tokyo: Miraisha.

Fukuda, J. 1990: '*Shinjuku maketo no shōrai o uranau*' ('Predicting the Future of the Shinjuku Market') *Tōkyō Jin*, **31**, April, pp. 68–73.

Gallery-Ma (ed.) 1994: *The Architectural Map of Tokyo*. Tokyo: Toto Shuppen (in Japanese with some English text).

Gekkan Akurosu (ed.) 1987: *Tōkyō no shinryaku* (The Encroachment of Tokyo). Tokyo: Parco.

Hakuhodo Institute of Life and Living, 1985: *Town Watching*. Tokyo: PHP Institute.

Ishizuka, H. and Narita, R. 1986: *Tōkyō-to no hyakunen* (One Hundred Years of Tokyo). Tokyo: Yamakawa.

Jinnai, H. 1985: *Tōkyō no kukan jinruigaku* (The Anthropology of Tokyo Space). Tokyo: Tsukumashobō.

Katō, A. 1986: *Harajuku monogatari* (The Harajuku Story). Tokyo: Sōshisha.

Mitsuoka, K. 1989: *Za-Shibuya kenkyū* (Research about Shibuya). Tokyo: Tōkyū Agency.

Nakawa, M. *et al.* 1989: *Shinjuku: Tōkyō no atarashii kao* (Shinjuku: Tokyo's New Face). *Weeks*, October, pp. 8–21, 23–39 and 41–2.

Ogawa, I. 1989: *Tōkyō daitoshi ken no chiiki henyō* (Tokyo Metropolitan Area Changes). Tokyo: Daimeidō.

Ojima, T. 1989: '*Tōkyō saiseikeikaku to shitemo geofuronto kaihatsu*' ('Revitalizing Tokyo by Geofront Development'). *Newton*, 14 February, pp. 116–24.

Sode, E. 1987: *Tōkyō machi bisunesu* (Tokyo Business Towns). Tokyo: Nippon Keizai Shinbunsha.

Tōkyō-to (Tokyo Metropolitan Government) 1989: *Tōkyō no toshi keikaku hyakunen* (One Hundred Years of Planning in Tokyo Metropolis). Tokyo: Tokyo Metropolitan Government.

Tsutsui, M. 1988: *Tōkyō daitenkan* (Major Change of Tokyo). Tokyo: Jyutaku Shinpōsha.

Tsutsui, M. 1989: *Tokyo Bay Network*. Tokyo: Jyutaku Shinpōsha.

Yada, A. 1987: *Tōkyō wa ko kawaru* (How Tokyo is Changing). Tokyo: Asahi Sonorama.

Yada, A. 1989a: *90 nendai no shin Tōkyō ken* (New Tokyo Region in the '90s). Tokyo: Nippon Keizai Shinbunsha.

Yada, A. 1989b: *Shin Tōkyō ken* (New Tokyo Region). Tokyo: Tokumashoten.

INDEX